The Creativity of Action

For Christian

The Creativity of Action

Hans Joas

Translated by Jeremy Gaines and Paul Keast

The University of Chicago Press

HANS JOAS is Professor of Sociology at the Free University, Berlin. His
published titles in English are *G. H. Mead: A Contemporary-Reexamination of
His Thought* (1985); *Social Action and Human Nature* (with Axel Honneth,
1989); and *Pragmatism and Social Theory* (published by the University of
Chicago Press, 1993).

The University of Chicago Press, Chicago 60637

Polity Press, Cambridge CB2 1UR in association with
Blackwell Publishers Ltd, Oxford OX4 1JF

Printed in Great Britain

05 04 03 02 01 00 99 98 97 96   1 2 3 4 5
ISBN: 0-226-40043-3 (cloth)
ISBN: 0-226-40044-1 (paper)

Published with the financial support of Inter Nationes, Bonn

Originally published as *Die Kreativität des Handelns* © Suhrkamp Verlag 1992.

Library of Congress Cataloging-in-Publication Data

Joas, Hans, 1948–
    [Kreativität des Handelns. English]
    The creativity of action / Hans Joas : translated by Jeremy Gaines
and Paul Keast.
        p.   cm.
    Includes bibliographical references and index.
    ISBN 0-226-40043-3 (cloth : alk. paper). – ISBN 0-226-40044-1
(pbk. : alk. paper)
    1. Social interaction.   2. Social psychology.   3. Interaction
(Philosophy)   I. Title.
HM291.J56213   1996
302 – dc20
                                                            96–21992
                                                            CIP

This book is printed on acid-free paper.

Contents

Creativity is our great need, but criticism,
self-criticism, is the way to its release.

John Dewey

Preface

I have wanted to write this book for quite a long time. Shortly after completing my books on George Herbert Mead and on the anthropological foundations of the social sciences I contemplated setting forth the ideas of American pragmatism in terms of their consequences for a present-day theory of action and of society. Only by taking such an approach could I adequately explain and justify to myself the deep fascination these ideas have exerted on me. However, working out the details of the plan took a lot longer than I had anticipated. Not only did other work come between me and it – sometimes on subjects like educational research and the sociology of war and peace, topics that had little or nothing in common with the project – but it also proved necessary to acquire a deeper knowledge of pragmatism, to study its relation to other philosophical traditions and to examine my own nascent conception by contrasting it with important contemporary theories. Some of the work I undertook in this context has been published in my volume on *Pragmatism and Social Theory*, which appeared almost simultaneously with the German edition of the present book.

My thanks go to all who helped me in various ways to construct this book. I would like to thank those friends and colleagues who read either part or the whole of the manuscript and gave me invaluable hints, specifically Frank Ettrich, Axel Honneth, Wolfgang Knöbl, Hans Peter Krüger, Claus Offe, Hans-Joachim Schubert, Peter Wagner and Harald Wenzel. My thanks go to Karin Goihl for her swift typing and last but not least to Jeremy Gaines and Paul Keast for their translation. I would also like to thank all the participants in those of my university seminars that covered subjects dealt with here, especially my students at the universities of Erlangen-Nuremberg and Oslo, where I had the opportunity to present the full outline of the book. My wife Heidrun also contributed to the writing of this book by providing me with honest support and warm encouragement throughout. And there are good reasons for my having dedicated it to my son Christian. I would like to thank Friedhelm Herborth of Suhrkamp, the German publishers, for his ongoing trust in my work and, finally, Marianne and Horst Wriecz, who made it possible for me to work peacefully in the Brandenburg countryside.

Introduction

'Action' is a key concept in philosophy and almost all the social and cultural sciences today; efforts to construct a 'theory of action' meet with especial interest in all these fields. For outsiders it must be difficult, to say the least, to understand why this should be the case. Indeed, it may be regarded as proof of a suspicion they have long since had, namely that the academic world prefers to tackle unnecessarily abstract problems of its own choosing instead of dedicating its efforts to solving the truly pressing problems of the day. The apparent absence of any link between the various debates on action theory in the different branches of the social sciences is additionally confusing and gives cause for mistrust. As once again becomes evident in this connection, each field constitutes a discourse of its own that more or less isolates itself from those in the other disciplines. This is, of course, not to say that chains of influence are non-existent – individual philosophical schools, in particular, tend to impact on specific fields in the social sciences. Yet, on the whole, little notice is taken in psychology, economics and sociology respectively of arguments put forward in debates in each of the other fields.

In economic theory, certainly since the second half of the nineteenth century if not earlier, the abstract notion of a '*homo oeconomicus*' and thus of a type of rational choice and rational action has become the fundamental point of departure of all further discussions. Admittedly, controversies on whether this point of departure is justified, in particular with regard to the precise logical status of such an abstraction, have never quite died down, but a theory of rational action nevertheless undisputedly forms the paradigmatic core of the discipline.

Things are less clear in the case of psychology. Originally, introspective research into the facts of the individual's consciousness existed alongside a more or less reductionist physiologically based psychology. From the twenties onwards behaviourism became the order of the day, although, and to a greater extent than was the case in economics, the dominance of this school of thought was always disputed. The central concept of 'behaviour' which gave the school its name may have been well able to replace the earlier guiding notions of 'consciousness' or 'organism', yet because of the behaviourists' radical claim that behaviour was entirely determined by the particular situation, the concept clearly did anything but emphasize freedom of choice or decision. This distinguished it clearly from the '*homo oeconomicus*' model. It was not until the 'cognitive' turn in psychology that behaviourism was changed sufficiently or even superseded so as to allow the conceptions of action held by the persons studied to become an object of inquiry. Increasingly, the idea is gaining currency that psychology's overall conceptual edifice must be changed: instead of centring on a notion of behaviour it must concentrate on that of action.

In sociology, the classical thinkers of the discipline in this century who have shaped mainstream theory formation – be they Max Weber or Talcott Parsons – attempted to ground not only their own studies but also the discipline as a whole in a theory of action. The same is also true of important side-currents, such as the schools of thought based on the ideas of George Herbert Mead or Alfred Schütz. Here, the specifics of each attempt to provide a foundation in a theory of action may have been open to dispute, but not the necessity of the attempt as such. Almost all of the most important contemporary theories can be characterized in terms of a specific theory of action. They range from the various theories that borrow from and adopt to a great extent the economic model of rational action, via neo-Weberian and neo-Parsonian projects, to major new theories that go beyond earlier models. The best-known and most significant of these are Habermas' theory of communicative action, Giddens' theory of (activistic) structuration and Castoriadis' new version of Aristotelian practical philosophy with its emphasis on creativity and novelty, as well as that presented by Touraine, who was influenced by Castoriadis. There are also important attempts, influenced by structuralism or systems theory, to question these conventional foundations in a theory of action in principle and to free sociological theory of any such basis.

Things are similar in philosophy. At the beginning of the seventies, the American philosopher Richard Bernstein[1] boldly tried to reduce the most important schools of modern thought to a common denominator, namely their effort to define and emphasize the active character of human nature. He uncovered this trend in Marxism – at least in all those forms of Marxism which did not conceive of it as a teleological philosophy of history – as well as in existentialism. Pragmatism, the main philosophical current in the United States, also already contained the notion of the practical in its name. Finally, he demonstrated that the tradition of analytical philosophy increasingly conceptualizes human speech as action, and that authors concerned with an analytical understanding of language were focusing on microscopic attempts to clarify concepts that somehow referred opaquely to the notion of action. In the present day, when, for example, 'post-structuralist' authors and many philosophers influenced by a renaissance of the thought of Nietzsche and the later Heidegger are sceptical of and ambivalent towards the human ability to act, it has become more difficult to view the theme of action as a point of convergence of various philosophical efforts. Yet Bernstein's proposition continues to hold true for the currents he studied. Moreover, the other trends mentioned can clearly also be understood in terms of their relationship to the topic of human action in that they specifically set themselves off from some activistic exaggeration of the idea of subjectivity.

Such a cursory overview as that given here of the numerous different attempts to address the topic of 'action' in the various academic fields serves perhaps to show how often the theme crops up. Yet it will also probably increase confusion on the reasons for this preoccupation. What also becomes clear is not only that the different disciplines rest in different ways on a foundation in action theory, but also that each of them even contains different versions of such foundations. The problem is complicated still further by the fact that debates on action theory not only represent one of many possible subjects of scholarly controversy but also comprise arguments about the direction each discipline should take and how it should mark itself off from other fields. Therefore, it is hardly to be recommended that a discussion of issues in action theory focuses on the full complexity of all these different versions of said theory. Nor, for that matter, can the sides to the problem concealed in the multiplicity of discourses and positions simply be prejudged by definitional prescriptions. I have elected to take a different tack, as this book is meant not to provide an encyclopedic overview, but instead to advance a particular approach to a theory of action. The theory proposed here will be developed primarily via a discussion of only one field and the form of action theory that predominates there. In the process, however, I shall frequently be referring to insights and arguments arising from other disciplines. It is my perhaps overly ambitious expectation that the thoughts I am thus presenting will also be of interest outside this particular discipline.

The following discussion will, for the main, be concerned with *sociological* action theory. The reason for this is not only that I am best acquainted with this field, but also that the original wealth of problems have persisted in this discipline to a greater extent than in others, where they have been lost from the outset owing to a greater degree of abstraction. Commentators often bemoan sociology's lack of a firm paradigm. Yet the positive side to this absence is that it allows certain losses of abstraction to remain visible which, for example, are simply ignored by the model of a rational economic subject adopted in economic theory or by psychology's notion that the organism merely reacts to outside stimuli. Those economists and psychologists who are willing to reflect on the initial abstractions on which their disciplines are based will therefore find the sociological deliberations of interest. The same is also true of philosophical debates. But many of them exhibit a high degree of intrinsic differentiation as well as a proximity to empirical phenomena only when synthetically combined with sociology or psychology. By contrast analytical philosophy, which has taken a fruitful methodological path of its own, is at a disadvantage compared with sociology, for it has contributed little to defining the social character of action and the orientation of actors to one another; the reason here is that analytical philosophy takes the individual actions of an individual actor as its starting point. My choice of sociology as the main terrain for the following deliberations on a theory of action is not absolutely compelling on the basis of the above remarks, but should at least be comprehensible for those whose thought is shaped by other disciplines.

The central thesis in this book is the claim that a third model of action should be added to the two predominant models of action, namely *rational* action and *normatively oriented* action. What I have in mind is a model that emphasizes the *creative* character of human action. Beyond that, I hope to show that this third model overarches both the others. I do not wish simply to draw attention to an additional type of action relatively neglected to date, but instead to assert that there is a creative dimension to all human action, a dimension which is only inadequately expressed in the models of rational and normatively oriented action. Both these models ineluctably generate a residual category to which they then allocate the largest part of human action. Defining human action as creative action avoids this problem. It does not engender a residual category of non-creative action, but rather is able to pinpoint the parameters for the meaningful application of the other models of action by illuminating the tacit assumptions the latter contain. I claim that only by introducing a concept of action which consistently takes account of this creative dimension can the other models of action be assigned their proper logical place. As a consequence, only in such a manner can the wealth of concepts involved in the concept of action, such as intention, norm, identity, role, definition of the situation, institution, routine, etc., be defined consistently and in a manner that does justice to what they are meant to express. Intellectual history already provides us with the essential basis for such a comprehensive model. However, throughout the history of action theory this model has been marginalized, for reasons that must be explained. I shall thus start in chapter 1 by ascertaining the reasons why sociological action theory has taken the shape it has and will trace the marginalization of the creative dimension to action in that theory. I shall then, in chapter 2, examine the approaches in which the creativity of action was indeed situated at the heart of a theory but where this again entailed specific distortions or false generalizations. Whereas the first chapter is aimed in particular at readers who are sociologists or economists, the second chapter is geared more towards readers with an interest in philosophy. Following these two investigations of the history of action theory, chapter 3 will focus on reconstructing three tacit assumptions that remain latent in the models of rational action and normatively oriented action: namely the teleological character of human action, corporeal control by the actor, and the autonomous individuality of the actor. The intention is then to introduce them explicitly into action theory. The overall goal of the chapter is to show how we can avoid generating residual categories in the way mentioned above. The claim that precisely these tacit assumptions are characteristic not only of action theory but of the discourse of modernity as such has ramifications that in fact go much further. In chapters 4.1 and 4.2 I shall therefore explore what consequences a theory of action revised in the manner I have suggested would have for an understanding of processes of collective action and whether it enables us to sidestep functionalist theories as a means of solving the problems involved in developing a social theory that takes adequate account of present-day phenomena. I shall bring the study to a close by drawing two possible conclusions for a diagnosis of present-day society from the restructured foundations of a theory of action. In chapter 4.3 I shall, on the one hand, address the proposition that conflicts within the developed western and eastern societies can be interpreted in terms of conflicts about 'a democratization of the differentiation issue', whereas in chapter 4.4 I shall investigate what fate awaits creativity under present-day conditions. Both studies go at least some way towards showing that 'theories of the constitution of society' based on a theory of action can hold their own both against functionalist theories of differentiation and against postmodernist diagnoses. Notwithstanding these attempts to demonstrate the possible consequences of a revised theory of action, the main focus of my presentation will be on the competing assumptions of different theories of action. The sections dealing with intellectual history, the reconstruction of concepts and possible applications are all intended to serve one common goal: to show both the meaning and the necessity of taking the creative character of human action into consideration.

1

The Emergence of the Theory of Action

1.1   The Beginnings: Parsons' Attempt at Synthesis

No one has linked the different dimensions of the issues entailed in
action theory as daringly as Talcott Parsons in *The Structure of Social
Action*, which first appeared in 1937. One could term the book the
little-known classic of a little-known discipline.[1] Sociology is, of
course, not unknown as such and – needless to say – Parsons is well
known within the bounds of the subject. However, in other subjects
and among the public as a whole sociology is frequently regarded
merely as a source of empirical information relating to social problems
and social developments. The theories sociology itself puts forward
are often treated as though they were merely statements of cultural
critique and are not accepted by philosophers as interpretations equal
in status to those which they themselves come up with. Characteristically, for example, despite the exceptionally broad interest in Jürgen
Habermas' social philosophy outside the world of sociology, no one
has seen fit to investigate the undisguised fact – and Habermas readily
admits this himself – that his study of *The Theory of Communicative
Action* is directly structured along the lines of Parsons' book. And
even within sociology, the fate of *The Structure of Social Action* has
certainly been remarkable. On publication, it is true, the work was
discussed at length and duly applauded by important reviewers, but
very few colleagues in the field actually read it. It took until the fifties
for the work to acquire the reputation of a decisive theoretical
achievement. And even then, it was Parsons' later works, which
earned him a commanding position in post-war sociology, that led to
an interest in his early work. There are also good grounds for doubting
whether the book was widely read even at this time. The protest

against the hegemony of Parsons' theory essentially engendered by the social movements in the sixties curbed any serious reception. No one asked at the time whether the criticism of Parsons' position on, for example, social change, the nature of American society or the family could equally be applied to his early book on action theory. Nevertheless, in the half a century since the book first appeared there have been a wealth of serious discussions of it, albeit scattered far and wide. There is no better way of introducing the discourse on the theory of action than to study Parsons' arguments and the possible objections to them.

Parsons' work was an unprecedented attempt to bundle together in concentrated form historical, epistemological–methodological and substantive aspects of a theory of action. His reconstruction of the history of social theory attained fame under the label *'convergence thesis'*. The essential leitmotif of this thesis is a definitive *critique of utilitarianism*, in which Parsons demonstrates that utilitarian thought is indelibly flawed. In order to overcome utilitarianism, Parsons has to engage in epistemological deliberations: he terms his position here *'analytical realism'*. Based on these assumptions Parsons puts forward his own solution to the problems he has discussed in the form of a *voluntaristic theory of action* and, closely bound up with this, a *normativist theory of social order*. It is Parsons' ambition to use this multi-tiered approach to present a conceptual frame which contains all the valuable insights of the classical heritage of European sociology. He believes that this heritage provides the foundations on which to base our further acquisition of knowledge, and which ensure that such knowledge rests on duly professional principles and will continue to be acquired as a cumulative process. What is the exact nature of these propositions and how well do they stand up to the objections that have been raised against them?

First of all, Parsons' so-called convergence thesis is both spectacular and provoking. Parsons' book consists in large part of monography-like discussions of the thought of Alfred Marshall, the British economist, and the classics of German, French and Italian sociology, namely Max Weber, Émile Durkheim and Vilfredo Pareto. The link binding together these exhaustive interpretations of authors who at the time the book was written were by no means world-famous – indeed, some of them were largely unknown in the United States – was Parsons' assertion that their respective works converged *with regard to a theory of action*. Parsons claimed that a common conception of action theory could be detected in the work of four representative authors from four different countries whose thought had emerged in quite different national theoretical environments and had had almost no impact on one another. The theoretical points of departure taken by the four were also very different. Parsons attributed the course taken by Marshall and Pareto to utilitarianism, Durkheim's thought to positivism and that of Weber to German idealism. To Parsons' mind the convergence he traced amounted, as it were, to empirical proof of the approach he was developing, or at least confirmed its plausibility. For he maintained that such convergence could not simply be construed as the expression of a common ideological ground that was typical of the epoch, but rather could only be regarded as a 'multiple discovery', as the solution, often reached simultaneously by several researchers working independently of one another, to research problems that had finally matured, that is, as the solution at long last found to a traditional theoretical problem. Parsons went on to argue that the authors he dealt with remained unaware both of the convergence of their work with that of others and of the precise nature of the solution they had found in the course of their substantive research. What was therefore needed was an additional act of reflection in order to present this solution in due clarity and thus point out the hitherto merely latent fixed core that constituted sociology as a discipline in its own right alongside others.

Yet, what was the problem that had purportedly been solved in this convergent manner? Parsons mentions the solution of the Hobbesian problem and the common attempt to overcome the false manner in which utilitarianism construed the problem. Parsons terms as 'Hobbesian problem' the question Thomas Hobbes put with such unsurpassed clarity at the beginning of modern social philosophy: How could subjects whose tendency in the condition of nature was to act egoistically develop a peaceful social order? As is well known, Hobbes himself tackled this problem by recommending that these subjects collectively submit to the will of a Leviathan, that is, to the strong institutions of a state over which the citizens had no say. Parsons by no means shares the premisses of Hobbes' anthropology nor does he concur with the fiction of a presocial condition of nature. Rather, he uses the way Hobbes formulates the problem for the purposes of a thought experiment. In this context, beyond the domain of the tradition which gives itself that name, Parsons also terms as 'utilitarian' all those assumptions in which human action is conceived of as *a priori* individual, independent and oriented towards clear individual goals. Such action, he maintains, necessarily leads to competition between the actors, as either several actors need the same scarce goods to achieve their goals or indeed other actors have to serve as a means to reach such goals. There are thus, he continues, two conceivable ways in which the actors relate to one another. Either an actor can use force to turn others into the means of achieving his goals or to prevent these others from using the scarce goods. Or an actor can use deception and misinformation to trick other actors into abandoning their own goals and becoming instruments of the former or to distract their attention away from the scarce goods. Hobbes called this state of affairs 'force and fraud'.

To continue the thought experiment, force and fraud cannot just be imputed to one actor resorting to these strategies in order to achieve his goals at the cost of those of the other actors, but must, needless to say, also be imputed to all the others. Every actor therefore not only resorts to force and fraud in order to achieve his goals, but must also realize that he is always on the receiving end of the force exerted by others and the fraudulent attempts of others. Thus, a free-for-all prevails, a battle which no one wanted and which no one can withstand. All are a long way from achieving their respective goals and even if they do reach them there is no safety in which to enjoy them. Parsons perceives with great clarity that this problem, originally formulated by Hobbes, does not simply apply to the historical conditions prevailing in Hobbes' day, but is also of immense importance for a cultural diagnosis of the present. There is more at stake here than the problems of England at the time of the religious and civil wars; Parsons saw that Hobbes' ideas were directly relevant to questions of the social viability of unrestrained competition in economic markets or in the political arena. Because Parsons precisely does not start out from the fiction of a condition of nature in order to search for a solution to what makes social order possible, Hobbes' question gets turned on its head. Parsons believes that a certain measure of social order and trust between humans always exists. As Kant based his thought on the incontrovertible existence of Newtonian physics and of a human ability to take moral decisions and then went on to ask under what conditions knowledge and morality were possible, Parsons, in like manner, commences by noting the fact of social order and subsequently asks what were the problematic assumptions that must lie at the root of a theory which cannot explain precisely this incontrovertible existence. Parsons' thought experiment in Hobbes' wake is therefore intended not in the least to justify a strong state, but rather on the contrary, to highlight the inherent limitations to a moral and social philosophy that was called utilitarian.

Parsons locates this limitation – and it is one that *must* exist by dint of the fundamental inability of this philosophical tradition to solve the problem of order – in the fact that the concept of action on which the thought experiment is based is unable to explain the origin of the goals of the individual actors. It may initially appear not to matter too much if a theory is only able to make statements about the linkages between means and ends and simply assumes that these ends or goals can be taken for granted. This can in fact be an advantage, since, by presuming rational action to exist in the first place, an element of free will and indeterminacy is introduced into the conception of the world. For the same reason, however, silence on the origin of goals is a provocation for a 'positivistic' understanding of science geared to making statements akin to laws. Parsons realizes that the abstinence in offering an explanation for the origin of the goals of actions does not simply involve a pragmatic assumption that can then be revoked in another context, but rather rests on the theoretical assumption that the wishes on which such goals are based are thoroughly subjective in nature. Explicitly or implicitly, so he asserts, wishes are considered to be subjective in two ways.[2] Wishes, he maintains, are thought to be generated subjectively by each individual and are unique to that individual, bearing no necessary relation to the wishes of others. The others only constitute the means or condition for the fulfilment of one's own wishes but are not constitutive of the wishes themselves. In a positivist view of the world, regarding wishes as the purely subjective product of each individual can only mean that they are statistically subject to random variation. Given such premises, any possible statement akin to a law on the distribution of wishes would call into question the free will of each individual. To Parsons' mind the dilemma utilitarianism faces thus consists of it having either to assume that free will exists and therefore to assert that goals vary at random, or conversely to assume that goals do not vary at random, at the cost of no longer being able to find a place for free choice and individual decisions in its conceptual framework. Parsons considers the first assumption to be untenable, as there is no sense in human choice from among random goals. In a manner reminiscent of the criticism made of Sartre's notion of a human liberty that is not 'grounded in reasons', Parsons insists that choice already presumes intrinsically unique structures in the sphere of alternative choices, as otherwise choice itself would resemble chance.[3] If the first assumption can be ruled out, then all the more attention must be paid to the second. Indeed, Parsons believes that, once they have overcome their ignorance of the problem as to the origins of the goals of action, all utilitarian thinkers are compelled to treat in a reductionist manner the role played by such goals as an independent factor in explaining actions. This reductionist treatment can take one of two basic forms. The problem of the origin of the individual goals of action no longer breaches the positivistic explanatory framework if either the goals themselves are treated as if they were the conditions of action or if the relations between goals and action situations are considered to be optimally adjusted. Once goals themselves are understood not as subjective products but as the result of deterministic processes such as those within the personality of the actor, the tension between utilitarian model of action and proposed positivist explanation is eased. Typical examples of this are theories which construe human wishes as the result of hereditary processes or determinant influences such as environment or 'milieu'. If, on the other hand, the goals of action are not believed to force their way into the action situations as if they were part of a foreign world, but instead a choice between goals is seen to arise in the situation itself, then, viewed positivistically, this choice between goals would rest on an optimal knowledge of the empirically given conditions and means of action. Admittedly, it is impossible to assume that the actor always possesses such an optimal knowledge. However, the only possible explanations for action goals that deviate from the ideal of optimal adjustment to a situation would then be ignorance and error. If an actor ignores certain conditions or erroneously assumes a particular means to be suited to the end he has in mind, the action will have a suboptimal effect. Parsons claims, in other words, that of logical necessity this utilitarian dilemma culminates in an 'anti-intellectualist' or a 'rationalist positivism', in a reduction to determinism by heredity or the environment or in an understanding of action as adjustment to the given situation. He therefore judges utilitarian theory to be intrinsically unstable, as it is only able to uphold its model of rational action by deliberately suppressing a series of problems. However, what it suppresses does not thereby disappear, leading to a reduction of the model and the collapse of a prototypical action theory.

At no point in this does Parsons claim that theories which actually existed in history are identical to the different logical positions he has outlined. Most of them are in fact opaque versions or combinations of several of these logical alternatives. In a major overview of intellectual history, or at least primarily that of the English-speaking world, he uses his logical model to interpret Hobbes and Locke, the classics of political economy and the Marxist critique of them, Darwinism and nineteenth-century hedonist utilitarianism. This history is thus given a logical consistency and ceases to appear to be a random sequence of contingent positions. Such an approach is typical of Parsons' method, which links the history of theory with systematic theoretical reflection. It also gives us a greater awareness of the meaning behind Parsons' term for his own epistemological approach, namely 'analytical realism'. Indeed, this book begins and ends with fundamental deliberations on the relation in the social sciences between theory construction and the gathering of empirical facts.

If utilitarianism, and reductionist, positivist forms of it, served as both the point of departure and the main adversary in Parsons' thought on action theory, then empiricism can be seen as his main antagonist when it came to his methodology and epistemology. Parsons doggedly opposes any view that regards scientific progress as an accumulation of known facts, and defends instead the significance of conceptual frames of reference. He attempts to show that these referential frameworks constitute the basis of all attempts to formulate an empirical observation and therefore that the real question is not whether a conceptual frame of reference is necessary but rather to what extent this frame is reflected on. After decades in which this level of Parsons' argument was simply ignored by his supporters and critics alike, scholars gradually began to pay it increasing attention, prompted, above all, by Harold Bershady.[4] Based on the critical distance he placed between himself and an empiricist position – which, although short-lived in terms of the philosophy of science, continued to dominate the way researchers saw themselves – attempts have since been made to portray Parsons as a pioneer of the contemporary post-empiricist philosophy of science (Jeffrey Alexander) and as a consistent adherent to Kantian basic philosophical principles (Richard Münch).[5] Biographically speaking, it is probably more accurate to detect here the influence on Parsons of Alfred Whitehead, the philosopher of science who also taught at Harvard.[6] We cannot pursue this question here. For the purposes of a theory of action it is solely of importance that because Parsons based his approach on such a philosophy of science, he gave himself the scope to relativize the model of rational action. Parsons by no means intended his critique of utilitarianism to prove the impossibility of systematic general theory. On the contrary, when describing the methodological writings of Max Weber, he defends, as does Weber, the necessity of forming abstract concepts, and criticizes the latter for having stopped short at historical and interpretative ideal types and not really pressing forward to the level of a universal theory of society. Thus, in order to uphold the ideal of theory construction promulgated by utilitarianism while at the same time countering that system's model of rational action, which was demonstrably unstable in itself, Parsons resorts to Whitehead's notion of 'misplaced concreteness'. This term sums up Whitehead's argument that elements of a whole which could be isolated through analysis should not be equated with concrete occurrences. In the case of action this meant that, although the model of rational action correctly pinpointed certain elements of human action (such as ends, means and conditions) and successfully dealt with certain facts, it was wrong to conclude that the model is a reflection of concrete reality and should therefore serve as a guide for all attempts to explain action.[7] Under empiricist conditions, a logically self-contained system then becomes transformed into an empirically self-contained system. In other words, Parsons criticizes not the applicability of the model of rational action as such but rather a false understanding of its applicability. The concept of analytical realism is meant to show that although the goal is still to provide an explanation of reality, this can be achieved only by isolating specific analytical elements; instead of 'reifying' them, that is, falsely equating them with traits of reality, the task – as Parsons saw it – was to arrive at a systematic appraisal of these analytical elements.

The above detour into methodology was necessary in order to present Parsons' alternative to the model of rational action. To understand this alternative it should also be remembered that Parsons saw a link between utilitarianism's inability to explain the existence and genesis of social order, on the one hand, and its inability to explain the origin of action goals, on the other. His alternative consists in assuming that social order is guaranteed by mutually formed values and in maintaining that the model of rational action can be overcome by considering those normative orientations which are involved in the constitution of goals and the choice of means. If social order is to signify more than the mere factual order of an aggregation of actions and more than the temporary stabilization of competition for resources and power, then this presumes that all actors share *common* orientations that are not subject to the individual actor's subjective calculations of utility, but, on the contrary, are what make individual calculations of utility possible in the first place. For Parsons, the individual goals of action are the result neither of chance subjective whim nor of adaptation to past or present conditions, but rather they come about in the context of the individual goals of the other actors. Only this view, he believes, can lead to an improved theory of action and an understanding of the existence of social order. Parsons wishes to bring the notions of 'value' and 'norm' to bear on action theory in order to be in a position to defend a *normative* concept of social order.

This solution to the problem, no matter how plausible, may appear arbitrary and give the impression that a *deus ex machina* has been introduced. Indeed, Parsons was accused of not explaining the existence of social order but merely defining it differently. This accusation is based at several levels on a failure to understand his approach and his conception of action theory. Firstly, Parsons never set out to explain the existence of social order: rather, he wanted to make its existence, as a fact confirmed by experience, the starting point for reflection. Secondly, he claims that the instability of utilitarianism must be proven by logical rather than empirical means. He wishes to uncover conceptual alternatives under certain premises and, by referring to the factual history of theory, examine whether his schema of possible alternatives is appropriate. For this reason, Parsons is compelled to present exhaustive interpretations of the development of the theories of particular thinkers because his approach combines reference to reality with a conceptual reflection. If Parsons claims that the factual convergence he pinpoints shows that his approach offers an empirical proof, then he is adding a hermeneutically unnecessary claim to his approach.[8] Finally, these interpretations go beyond the different possible solutions to the utilitarian dilemma; they focus their attention on a quite different school of thought, namely that of idealism, and it is precisely here that Parsons finds clues to elaborating the significance of values and norms for human action.

We shall focus only on the logical core of these interpretations here. In the study on Alfred Marshall, the British economist, Parsons predominantly wants to show that although he was one of the founders of modern (neo-classical) economic theory and thus a consistent champion of a model of rational action, within his theory he at the same time developed strands that pointed beyond that model. For Marshall devised, albeit with no great clarity, a concept of 'activity' and intended this to apply to actions that do not serve the fulfilment of wishes but rather are intrinsically valuable and thus desirable in themselves. He radically rejects the notion that actions serve to satisfy the actor in the sense of some hedonistic psychology. Particularly the prototype of rational action in the area of economics, he asserts, results more from an ascetic work morality than from an indulgence in one's own needs. Marshall is interested in the psychological preconditions and effects of economic action and therefore discovers, or so Parsons maintains, the existence of value systems. However, Marshall immediately fudges the issue because he is only able to conceive of an evolution towards a value system based on economic virtues and does not presume that there can be a true plurality of value systems.

It was Vilfredo Pareto, another of the most important representatives of modern economic theory, who took this latter step. Parsons shows in his interpretation that Pareto is much more consistent in recognizing the plurality of human value systems, even if he has no theoretical means with which to analyse them and is merely able to list them. Pareto simply contrasts logical action with the vast realm of the non-logical, which embraces both ultimate value orientations and unreflected emotions. He thus opens out the domain of norms and values to a far greater extent than does Marshall, yet he lacks the conceptual means to map out this area effectively. Parsons judges Durkheim to have found these means and it is the interpretation of the latter's thought that is perhaps the key section of the whole book.

Quite unlike that taken by Marshall and Pareto, Durkheim's point of departure was not rooted in utilitarianism; what was decisive for his development, so Parsons claims, was his discovery that the compulsions affecting actors are not all of *one and the same* type, but rather that social compulsion is quite different from natural causation. Durkheim, Parsons continues, uncovered the specific character of normative rules backed by sanctions. He thus had to change his initial equation of the 'social' with the 'external' and the 'compulsory–restrictive' decisively; social norms can be internalized and trigger actions. Social relations may admittedly be beyond the individual's influence, but this does not mean to say that they are therefore naturally permanent. 'The social milieu constitutes a set of conditions beyond the control of a given concrete individual, but not beyond the control of human agency in general.'[9] In the further development of his thought Durkheim was to expand this insight into the unique character of norms to yield a theory of education and, above all, of institutions. This, Parsons proposes, reached its climax in Durkheim's epoch-making attempt to create a theory of religion, in which a theory of the sacred, the symbolic and the ritual served to analyse the existence of ultimate values, values that cannot be subsumed under the model of rational action. Whereas Pareto came to assume there were ultimate values only indirectly, that is, via a thought experiment in which he traced chains of means–ends causation, Durkheim, so Parsons argues, focused directly on these ultimate values and the forms in which they are manifested. Yet, in so doing he neglected purposive rationality and ended up adopting a one-sided, idealist position.

It was this idealism which, according to Parsons, formed Max Weber's point of departure; not in a biographical sense, admittedly, but in the sense of idealism's decisive impact on the intellectual milieu from which Weber tried to extricate himself. Unlike utilitarianism, idealism always believed values and norms had a great bearing on human action. However, it did not succeed in shedding light on the relation of the actor to these norms and values. To an idealist's mind, an individual's actions are merely the expression of a suprapersonal spiritual entity. Parsons goes on to suggest that a wide range of different positions in the philosophy of history and in historicism, above all in nineteenth-century German thought, all shared his view of action as expression.

The sole difference between the various currents was whether, like Hegel, they construed this suprapersonal spiritual entity in terms of a philosophy of history, namely as some world spirit that recognized itself or realized itself in the course of world history, or whether they conceived of it in historicist and relativistic terms as the individual spirit of a nation or a particular age. Weber's methodological battle was directed at all versions of such an idealist construction of action as emanation, without him thereby becoming a utilitarian or positivist. Parsons cites the example of Weber's attack on historical materialism, in which he emphasized precisely the importance of 'religious interests' and thus of norms and values. All his studies on the economic ethics of world religions were devoted to the task of explaining history in terms of the complex interplay of values and other elements of action. Despite this exemplary substantive research, Weber nevertheless failed to generate a truly universal analytic theory.

Parsons claims that, whereas each of the traditions he discusses had granted absolute status to particular elements, his own theory of action is able to accommodate the key elements from all of them. He takes from radical positivist thought the notions of heredity and environment as ultimate conditions and means of action; from utilitarianism he adopts the linkage of means and ends; and from idealistic thought he takes aboard the notion of ultimate values that are the basis of all individual goals and choices of means. In other words, formulating a theory of the normative orientation of action involves integrating all the separate achievements of the different schools of thought. Quite in passing, Parsons mentions a further element of his theory of action which does not simply follow on from one of the strands he focuses on, namely the force which relates normative and conditional elements to each other in the course of action. He terms this 'effort' and likens its analytical status to that of energy in physics. Parsons followed up his early book on action theory by attempting to fill the gap he thus pinpointed, and in order to generate the dynamic concept of action that was still missing he turned his attention to the psychoanalytical theory of Sigmund Freud.

We shall not pursue this strand any further. We are interested here neither in a presentation of Parsons' further development and the ongoing modifications of his theory nor in discussing whether his objections apply to later work undertaken in the traditions he analyses, for example the ongoing attempts by advocates of the rational action model to 'solve' the problem of social order.[10] The task at hand here is solely to provide an introduction to the problems underlying action theory by referring to one of its key texts. The question that now arises is therefore what objections can be raised to Parsons' impressive theoretical edifice and to what extent do they show that a theory of action must be shaped differently?

1.2   The Debate with Parsons: Rehistoricizing the Convergence Thesis

A large number of the objections raised by commentators are levelled at Parsons' convergence thesis, which many find particularly provocative. Sometimes, however, they lose sight of the fact that Parsons never claimed to provide an exhaustive intellectual history of the eighteenth and nineteenth centuries, nor did he ever speak of there being a convergence between the authors he addressed in any other area than that of a 'voluntaristic' theory of action. Thus, all references to traditions and thinkers omitted from Parsons' scheme and all corrections of his faulty interpretations of classic writings miss the mark and do not weaken Parsons' conception, as long as they fail to shed light on what theoretical consequences the additional inclusion of particular thinkers or a more correct interpretation would have for his overall scheme. All the same, however, such pointers, even if not intended directly to formulate theoretical consequences, provide an indication of where one would need to look in order to improve on Parsons' conception.

In various retrospective judgements on his own work Parsons himself conceded that there were gaps in his edifice. What most strikes the eye is undoubtedly the fact that Parsons perceives a convergence towards a positive solution among European thinkers only and completely ignores contemporary thought in the United States, his home country. In *The Structure of Social Action* he gives the reader the impression that American thought has been completely dominated by utilitarian individualism and the naive evolutionism of Herbert Spencer. Having initially only treated it cursorily, in his later work Parsons fully developed the notion of the internalization of values and norms.

This enabled him to concede that, in particular, American thinkers such as Cooley, Thomas and, above all, Mead had developed the notion to a stage far beyond that attained by the European classics.[11] Even this admission was problematical, however, as Parsons treated this socio-psychological achievement in isolation from its conditions and further elaboration. While it is true that the majority of the efforts of the more important American thinkers in the decades prior to *The Structure of Social Action* were devoted to a theoretical modification of Spencer's assertions, here Spencer was 'more whipping boy than master'.[12] As early as 1939 Louis Wirth pointed out in a review[13] that in the persons of Dewey and Mead two Americans had long since been advocating a possible voluntaristic concept of action; in the early sixties Roscoe Hinkle demonstrated just how broad a spectrum of action theories existed in the United States prior to Parsons.[14] Of importance in our context is that Parsons, for whatever reasons, did not expressly refer to the philosophy underlying these trends, namely the philosophy of pragmatism, and ignored the profundity of pragmatism's critique of the very model of rational action that he, too, was attacking.

Parsons himself conceded that his convergence thesis made two other major omissions. Most of all, he bemoaned the neglect of French intellectual history, both of what he called its 'liberal' (Rousseau, Saint-Simon and Comte) and its 'conservative' (Bonald, de Maistre, Tocqueville) wings. Only in passing does he mention the neglect of the single most important individual figure whom he should have taken into consideration, namely Georg Simmel.[15] In both cases he himself does not state what impact the inclusion of these strands of thought would have had on his theoretical edifice. The French thinkers would merely have left the book more balanced, for its main emphasis lies lop-sidedly on American and German thought. And Simmel's work is not accorded a true theoretical status; rather Parsons treats it as merely a collection of essays on microsociological topics. Later critics, above all Donald Levine,[16] have, however, attempted to stop Parsons getting away so easily. They point out that French thought, largely shaped by Catholicism, was more characterized by a tendency to treat morality in social terms and to link rationality and morality, something that was foreign to Protestant intellectual currents, and therefore call into question Parsons' portrayal of Durkheim as a thinker who had *broken* with French traditions. And the case of Simmel is quite spectacular: towards the end of his life the unflagging persistence of his critics caused Parsons to shed some light on the fate of a chapter on Simmel he had written for *The Structure of Social Action* but then omitted.[17] In 1979, Parsons conceded in a letter that he omitted Simmel because the latter's theoretical agenda did not fit in with the convergence thesis. Levine draws a far-reaching conclusion from this, namely that Simmel's starting point, the *relations* between actors, was at odds not only with Parsons' concentration on action but also with the latter's move towards functionalism. These admissions, therefore, seriously undermine the convergence thesis.

And the problems mount as soon as one casts a further glance at the history of theoretical development. Commentators agree that Parsons' treatment of Marx is not merely insufficient but self-contradictory. Marx appears in Parsons' reconstruction, on the one hand as a proponent of German idealism and, on the other, as a utilitarian. For these two assertions not to appear mutually contradictory, it would have been necessary to interpret Marx's thought as the complex attempt to synthesize these two traditions, yet precisely such an interpretation was not forthcoming in Parsons' work. Indeed, his overall presentation of German idealism is impaired by the fact that he deals only with the later figures of a historically informed political science [*Staatswissenschaft*], but not with the representative German philosophers. In so doing, he portrays Werner Sombart as fully believing in cultural determinism, an almost untenable position. What is more important is that Parsons, for all his justified criticism of the notion that action lends expression to some suprapersonal spirit, blocks his own access to a model of action as the self-expression of the actor for he has too rudimentary a knowledge of the origins of the anthropology of expression in the thought of Johann Gottfried Herder. We shall return to this point below.

The debates on the accuracy of Parsons' interpretations of the two classical theorists of sociology most discussed today, namely Émile Durkheim and Max Weber, attracted most public attention. Given that Marshall and Pareto have played only a marginal role in debates on action theory since Parsons, there have been few critical investigations of Parsons' presentation of their thought. The few comments that have been made were generally sceptical of Parsons' purported exaggeration of the part played by consensus and order, pointing out that Pareto in particular, but also Marshall, both regarded conflict and inequality as important themes of their work. In the decades following publication of Parsons' first book, and particularly in recent times, Durkheim and Weber have, by contrast, increasingly become key figures in discussions of social theory as a whole. Theoretical controversies in the humanities and social sciences often culminate in arguments as to how particular canonic texts should be properly understood. In the case of Weber, there is a clear division between, on the one hand, those who regard Weber as a realist when it comes to conflicts and interest-based action, and on the other, Parsons, who stresses Weber's emphasis on normative agreement in his theory of legitimacy and religion. Parsons was thus often rebuked for having weighted things too heavily in favour of Weber's sociology of religion and having neglected his political sociology. Jeffrey Alexander has attempted to prevent an overemphasis on the opposite interpretation and has explained Weber's classic work in terms of a permanent tension between different trends inherent to it which cause the different parts of the overall oeuvre partially to contradict one another.[18] Alexander believes Weber concerned himself with trying to integrate 'ideas' and 'interests'. He achieved such an integration in exemplary fashion in parts of his overall oeuvre, such as his class theory and his urban sociology. Other parts, such as the comparative studies of the economic ethics of the major religions are, by contrast, extremely uneven. Alexander thus contrasts the unsuccessful study on China to the successful investigation of ancient Judaism. What is decisive here, however, is that this is not merely an insignificant consequence of Weber having not fully elaborated parts of his work; rather, he consistently adopts a reductionist method in an essential part of his work, namely in his analysis of modernity. Alexander observes that, even if the analysis of the genesis of modernity is 'multidimensional', when it comes to actually portraying modernity, at the level of Weber's theoretical programme this multidimensionality gets lost. Be it the sociology of law or of stratification, the sociology of bureaucracy or of democracy: everywhere, the one-sided emphasis on the utilitarian traits of modernity, Alexander argues, asserts itself and leads to empirical weaknesses in the analysis. Alexander rightly states that this cannot be justified by regarding such an emphasis as purportedly the true expression of the essence of modern society, for Weber's approach conceptually predetermines what needs to be ascertained empirically. Thus, the question of whether Parsons' interpretation of Weber is correct leads to the substantive issues of any theory of modernity.[19]

By comparison, there is no clear overall strategy behind those commentators who have called Parsons' interpretation of Durkheim into question and their claims have no clear theoretical ramifications. In fact, his individual interpretations of almost all of Durkheim's works have been treated with suspicion.[20] This ranges from the question whether Durkheim was ever interested in a theory of action and a critique of utilitarianism in the first place, via a questioning of

Parsons' reading of Durkheim's book on the division of labour and his incorrect dating of Durkheim's work on education, to Parsons' complete ignorance of the work Durkheim undertook after his mature theory of religion. Often, the alternatives put forward are no less problematic and inadequate than Parsons' original interpretation. The discussion as a whole is a long way from having consistently superseded the picture Parsons painted of Durkheim. Whereas some critics have vociferously argued that the convergence thesis should be dropped altogether and even replaced by a divergence thesis,[21] or that Durkheim and Weber should be regarded as having provided two fundamentally different types of theoretical edifices, others, for all their indebtedness to Parsons' work, tacitly drop the convergence thesis. They submit that it can only be understood in terms of the corrections which Parsons covertly made to the weaknesses he intuitively recognized to exist in the works of the classics of sociology.

If the convergence thesis is called into question, this also casts doubt on what it originally intended to set itself off from, namely the critique of utilitarianism. Parsons used the concept of utilitarianism in both a philosophical and a historical sense at one and the same time. Philosophically speaking, the concept is intended to refer to a model of action which presumes that separate individuals rationally pursue given goals of action; historically speaking, Parsons wished to pinpoint a motif which he claims Hobbes first introduced and which supposedly shaped all Anglo-American thinking. It comes as no surprise that commentators have questioned the validity of this equation and attacked Parsons by pointing to the true complexity of the thought, for example, of David Hume, Adam Smith, John Stuart Mill and Herbert Spencer. These critics undoubtedly succeed in proving[22] that all these authors by no means asserted that human wishes were exclusively presocial or egoistic in nature but had in fact, using a variety of different approaches, elaborated altruistic motives, sociable instincts and the ability to show sympathy as well as the social character and indispensability of norms. Without this it would be hard to imagine why we can even talk of this tradition having come up with a *moral* or *social* philosophy. These approaches mean not only that the thinkers in question do not fit into Parsons' picture of them, but also that their thought is not caught on the horns of the utilitarian dilemma. In an endeavour to defend Parsons against this criticism, some reviewers have pointed out that it is all very well believing that classical utilitarianism may have included insights into the affective and communal roots of social order, but that these insights took the form of residual categories which were progressively eliminated from utilitarianism as it matured and were not integrated into a more comprehensive theoretical model.[23] An even stronger claim is that first put forward by Albert Hirschman,[24] namely that the moral philosophy of utilitarianism can be understood as a contribution towards disciplining the human being who simply has wishes and is driven by his or her passions, transforming him or her into a rational actor with clearly defined interests. In this case, Parsons might have been unclear when it came to the difference between wishes and interests, but the core equation of the model of rational action with the 'utilitarian' tradition would have been right. However, merely reverting to a philosophical definition of utilitarianism is certainly not a tenable position. Even Parsons' defenders have to account for how the original multiplicity of this school of thought could have been reduced to the model of rational action, that most slender of cores. And if they cannot, then the objection stands that Parsons vastly exaggerated the significance of a theoretical dilemma only applicable to the work of Hobbes (and perhaps Mandeville) and thus projected a difficulty onto the whole of European intellectual history that actually applied only to a far more specific context.

Thus far I have only presented those arguments that arose from reflections on the history of sociological theory. Not all of the critical commentaries have, however, focused on Parsons' theoretical position so indirectly. Debates on Parsons' 'analytical realism' are dominated by the question whether, in view of the historical character of the objects of sociological inquiry, the pursuit of a theoretical goal that consists in constructing a systematic edifice composed of transhistorical and analytical theoretical components, which merely need to be varied in order to fit actual historical phenomena, holds out any prospect of success. Scepticism has also been voiced over the fact that although the analytical character of the abstractions undertaken by Parsons is frequently stressed when trying to parry criticisms of his position, Parsons himself says nothing about the form argumentation should take at this analytical level. He should have been able to provide rational reasons for the direction to be taken when developing a conceptual framework construed in analytical terms. Parsons, however, provides neither a pragmatic methodology with which to make abstractions in suitable analytical form nor an anthropology of action. 'Analytical realism' is thus certainly not the pinnacle of epistemological reflection on action theory.

The scattered criticisms made of the substance of Parsons' theory of action focus on a wide variety of issues: from the subjective perspective of the actor (Alfred Schütz) to the general role of cognition in action (Stephen Warner), from the limitations of the means–ends schema of action (Niklas Luhmann), to the question as to the genesis of common norms and values (Alain Touraine). We cannot go into them at this stage of the discussion.[25] They will be addressed as part of the systematic elaboration of a theory of the creativity of action. Quite irrespective of whether we pass judgement on these issues or not, the assessment of the convergence thesis has brought us to a very decisive point in this introduction to the discourse on the theory of action. For the reader will inevitably have gained the impression that the attempt to present a substantively adequate theory of action that takes the history of the theory into account has foundered on the rocks before having really set sail in the first place.

There can be no doubt that Parsons' system must be corrected in important ways. Irrefutable flaws have been highlighted: his inability to generate any critique of the model of rational action other than to assert that the representatives of this model are unable to solve the problem of how a social order comes about; the difficulties of taking into account the nature of social relations or social interaction or spontaneous altruistic orientations without subsuming them under a concept of normative consensus; Parsons' ignorance of the model of action as self-expression; ambiguities in the weighting given to the social significance of normative factors; a lack of clarity in distinguishing between egoistic wishes and rational interest. All these points, which are of significance for action theory as a system, have come to light in our assessment of the convergence thesis. Are these faults simply the consequence of an exaggerated attempt to force all evidence into a systematic account of intellectual history? Certainly, Parsons took aboard a wealth of problems by regarding his theory of action and the classical writings in the development of sociological theory a solution to a problem that had existed for centuries but had hitherto been tackled in vain. Despite the strengths of his historical assertion, namely that it is possible to locate the emergence of a suitable theory of action in the period between 1890 and 1920 and in Europe, he tends to leave the more specific social and epistemological preconditions for this purported convergence unexamined. Parsons clearly *dehistoricized* the convergence on an emergent theory of action because he was interested precisely in demonstrating that the theory arrived at was relatively independent of its actual genesis; this would then clear the way for the steady future advance of the social sciences and put an end to the ebb and flow of ideological currents. Despite the exhaustiveness of his interpretations, they reveal few self-reflective pointers to the conditions under which convergence was possible or the conditions for Parsons himself being able to grasp this convergence. Parsons' oeuvre does not, in other words, provide us with fruitful objections to alternative interpretations, for example to an account of sociological theory as the result either of a latent dialogue with Marxism and the labour movement or of attempts to overcome problems that were perceived as the consequences of a moral crisis. Nevertheless, it would be wrong to conclude that after decades of debate all that is left of Parsons' conception is rubble and ruins, and a sense of wonder at how such an idiosyncratic and faulty system could have attracted so much interest in the first place. For two constructive reactions to the faults are possible. On the one hand, the convergence thesis can be dropped in order to salvage Parsons' theory of action. And, on the other, an attempt can be made to *rehistoricize* the convergence thesis and thus to create the basis for taking his theory of action further in a manner that also takes account of the less historical and more systematical objections raised against it.

Jeffrey Alexander opted for the first path in his four-volume *Theoretical Logic*. Although *The Structure of Social Action* was the model on which he based that study, he explicitly discards the convergence thesis and does not concern himself with the works of such theorists as Marshall and Pareto, both of whom Parsons had treated as examples of utilitarianism's inherent tendencies to attempt to overcome its own limitations. The problem with this approach was that it left the interpretations given without the original systematic framework. Alexander replaces this lost framework with a new one; the underlying principle he adopts is to assume both that there is an eternal conflict between sociological idealism and sociological materialism and that a programme can be founded to overcome this conflict by pursuing a 'multidimensional' 'synthetic' approach that is no longer one-sided. To Alexander's mind, Marx and Durkheim present mutually exclusive one-sided theories. The counterpart to the sociological materialism of the one, which systematically prevents it from achieving an adequate grasp of norms and the cultural sphere, is the sociological idealism of the other, which, although having provided decisive contributions to a theory of normativity, was not able to incorporate this convincingly in the real world of conditions and means. Alexander situates both thinkers between the two opposing poles of this conflict and he believes their disciples, the Marxists and the Durkheimians, are caught in the dilemma of surviving with the consequences of the one-sidedness of their respective strategies. He judges both Weber and Parsons to have attempted to find a synthesis of the two extremes. This edifice, with which he intends to replace the convergence thesis, is however, only convincing if the concepts of 'sociological idealism' and 'materialism' indeed stand for central problems in sociological theory and in the oeuvre of the two classic thinkers and if the writings of Weber and Parsons can indeed meaningfully be construed as attempts to synthesize the thought of Marx and Durkheim. This is by no means self-evident. I shall mention only one of the various objections to this interpretative framework. Alexander means the terms 'sociological materialism' and 'idealism' not to denote two equally obsolete epistemological approaches, but rather quite clearly to describe the conflict between a 'utilitarian' and a 'Kantian' conception of morality and social life. If he had used these latter terms to describe what he was doing it would have immediately been evident that such a characterization does not apply without qualification to the sociological classics and certainly does not exhaustively account for their work. Thus, although Alexander's study seamlessly replaces the convergence thesis with another hypothesis, the latter is just as bereft of historical content as was the former in Parsons' work.

Donald Levine and Charles Camic have taken the alternative approach, namely to rehistoricize Parsons' thesis. They refer his assertions back to a contemporary controversy within economics and to the institutional problems sociology had in finding a position for itself relative to economics and other scholarly disciplines. This first step itself already shifts the focus of interest to the context in which the convergence thesis initially figured. It immediately becomes clear why for Parsons the definition of action theory was from the outset subject to the proviso that economics be upheld unscathed as an abstract, analytical discipline, that is, that the theoretical core of the model of rational action be retained. Neither Levine nor Camic, however, put this important idea to fruitful use for an interpretation of the classical sociological texts themselves. Yet only by doing precisely that can the redeemable core of the convergence thesis be extracted. Furthermore, they fail to take the discussion beyond its roots in the struggle between the academic disciplines and to ask what consequences their new view of the origins of Parsons' thought would have for a substantive assessment of his theory of action. Thus, they fail to achieve that linkage of the levels of intellectual history and systematic theory that Parsons himself achieved in such impressive manner. I intend to go further than Levine and Camic in both these respects and shall be using their chosen approach, namely the rehistoricization of Parsons' conception, not as an alternative to theoretical systematization, but rather as a point of departure for the further elaboration of sociological action theory.

This 'rehistoricization' begins by considering Parsons' development up to the first pinnacle of his efforts to synthesize previous positions, namely *The Structure of Social Action*. Parsons himself indicated what route could be taken when expressing his surprise that his path from economics to sociology had gone unremarked in the heated debates that surrounded his work.[26] As a matter of fact, Parsons was by training an economist and initially he published only in this area. The key problem in his first major book was the relation between economic and sociological theory, or so he commented retrospectively. And the original problem confronting Parsons can thus only be understood if we know what debates were raging within economics in the United States during the twenties and thirties. At that time, the discipline was divided into two camps: the marginal utility theorists on the one hand, and the institutionalists on the other. The former regarded the further development of rational action models as the major task facing theorists; these models were expected also to yield greater empirical insights, as the assumptions on which they rested provided at least a reasonable approximation of the real behaviour of economic actors. The institutionalists, who drew their main inspiration from Thorstein Veblen, believed this promise could not be fulfilled, as there was no reason to suppose that the historical and cultural multiplicity of economic behaviour could ever be adequately grasped by as brittle a conceptual framework as that of 'homo oeconomicus'. According to them, what was important was not deductions about reality made on the basis of assumptions given by theoretical models, but rather an open, inductive study of cultures and historical developments. Openness here did not mean that the study be devoid of theory, because, so the argument ran, this cultural and historical multiplicity was itself based on the laws of evolution.

If one consults Parsons' early works, then there can be no doubting that this controversy occupied his mind for years. He was attracted to the one side by the pristine theoretical structure and the theoretically informed and systematic treatment of empirical evidence. At the same time, he was repulsed by the 'economic imperialism', that is, the tendency among many economists to regard their models as exemplary solutions to all matters in the social sciences. The other side appealed inevitably to anyone who took the unique character of cultural values and institutions of economic behaviour seriously; what was less attractive about the institutionalist school was the unclear and naive character of its fundamental evolutionist assumptions and the impression that to forgo these compelled one to abandon all theory and instead simply collect data in an encyclopedic manner. Parsons was predestined to oscillate back and forth in this controversy. Despite all the prevailing trends to succumb to a biological or behaviouristic reductionism he had, influenced by British anthropology, learned during his time studying in London to emphasize the cultural and activistic traits of the human being, the human ability to make conscious choices. Intuitively and morally the approach taken by the institutionalists appealed to him more, whereas in theoretical terms he approved of the orthodox neo-classical economists. His doctoral thesis, written in Germany, dealt with the theories of capitalism put forward by Werner Sombart and Max Weber, and shows clear traces of the controversy.[27] Turning on Sombart, he expressly states that he does not share the latter's unfavourable appraisal of orthodox economic theory. Even Sombart and especially Weber were, however, of particular importance for him, he continued, because although they address similar themes to those taken up by the American institutionalists, they had overcome the naive belief in progress that characterized the latter's theories of capitalism. In that context, Weber had simultaneously upheld the core assumptions of orthodox economic theory. This can only mean that rather than seeing a need to drop the model of rational action in the interests of arriving at a realistic conception of the meaning of capitalism for human freedom, Parsons believed that precisely by correctly locating this model it would become possible to avoid the institutionalists' evolutionistic errors and their positivistic understanding of theory.

The works Parsons subsequently produced intervened directly in the debates on economic theory, thus preparing the way for *The Structure of Social Action*. What becomes clear is to how great an extent the concept of utilitarianism constitutes a generalization of the model of rational action put forward in modern economic theory. The tension in Parsons' thought was, moreover, intensified by the fact that the questions he was interested in were at the same time the questions involved in marking the academic disciplines off from one another. In the neo-classical understanding, economics was the only discipline among the social sciences which could seriously lay claim to approximating to the scholarly level of the natural sciences. In the view of the institutionalists, by contrast, economics as a separate discipline was neither necessary nor desirable, as its tasks could be accomplished only in association with anthropology, history, psychology and sociology. For the proponents of neo-classical economics and the universities that were their strongholds, all other disciplines in the social sciences were still bogged down in a pre-scientific stage and they were accordingly treated with contempt; indeed, at times they were even prevented from gaining any institutionalized footing at all. This was particularly the case at Harvard University, where Parsons worked as a young man. The situation at such a traditional Ivy League school was unlike that in Chicago, which had introduced all the various social science disciplines simultaneously at the time of its foundation at the end of the nineteenth century. To be sure, intellectual controversies were not foreign to Chicago either, but there they did not take the form of a struggle over the delimitation of the disciplines or involve the legitimacy of one or the other being cast into question. In other words, by dint of the approach he was taking, Parsons realized he was being forced out of the prestigious discipline he had started his career in. His university offered no alternative to the economics faculty and at other universities his admiration for the achievements of orthodox economists would not have met with the same understanding among members of the economics departments or any of the other social science departments. It would therefore appear to be no coincidence that this great theorist should encounter difficulties and obstacles in the early part of his career.

Sociology offered Parsons a way out of this personal and theoretical crisis as well as a solution to the problem of defining economics' proper field of inquiry. The proof that the model of rational action should be understood *analytically* in economic theory, that is, not as a reproduction of reality but as an abstract representation of some individual elements of action, and the substantive demonstration that values and norms were indispensable to the existence of a social order together created the foundations for an additional discipline. This was to be conceived of as a discipline specializing in those value elements of action which also had to be understood in an analytical sense. Parsons defines sociology as 'the science which attempts to develop an analytical theory of social action systems in so far as these systems can be understood in terms of the property of common value integration'.[28] This definition was meant to give sociology a clearly delineated object of inquiry, thus ensuring that it was no longer an encyclopedic social science. However, the object of inquiry was defined not as an empirical object but as a specific analytical perspective. This definition was modelled decisively on economics, but only on an economics that had at long last arrived at a suitable, that is, analytical, understanding of what it was meant to be. Such an understanding had been articulated at an early date by John Stuart Mill, but even today there is still controversy over a whole list of questions: Do the assumptions underlying the rational action model constitute empirical assumptions about human action? Should they be understood psychologically, anthropologically or historically? Have they or have they not been disproved as empirical assumptions, and should we alternatively interpret them in normative terms, that is to say, such that everyone who wishes to act rationally has to follow such insights? Or do they merely offer clarification on the options the actor has which enable him to avoid his action having undesired consequences without at the same time being compelled to adopt some goal or form of action? Parsons makes such a point of expressly advocating an analytical understanding of economic theory because only this enables us to accord that theory a cognitive value specific to the discipline alone, while at the same time providing the definition for other social scientific fields. He is concerned not only with sociology in this context, but also with political science, psychology and other disciplines. Certain disciplines, he claims, should focus on the conditions of action (biology and psychology), others on various aspects of the relation between means and ends (technology, economics, and political science), and finally sociology should concern itself with 'ultimate values' and their bearing on action. One by-product of this endeavour to systematize the structural elements of human action would thus be a schema for the organization of the humanities.

By defining sociology as a specific science of human action, Parsons thus sets out to solve a multiplicity of problems, and it would be an inadmissible oversimplification to concentrate on the single aspect of the conflict between the disciplines in the institutional context of the American university scene, and even more myopic to reduce this context to the relationship between economics and sociology. In particular, another ever-present theme underlying Parsons' work is the need to distance himself from the biologistic and behaviouristic errors of action theory. The task facing us here is not, however, to reconstruct this context perfectly.[29] Only one further line of demarcation between the disciplines is of essential importance here, namely the relationship of sociology to philosophy. I have already pointed out that Parsons did not mention or address the philosophical tradition of pragmatism, whose main advocate, namely John Dewey, was regarded during Parsons' early years as the representative American philosopher par excellence. This is a strange blind spot for Parsons to have had, not only with regard to the genesis of his conception, but also, and in particular, with regard to its systematic elaboration.[30] With his work on action theory Parsons enters the epistemological arena, and it was precisely in this arena that pragmatism had already broadly developed a category of action. In view of this it should be clear that Parsons' 'analytical realism' could only define in a negative way what a theory of action could not be and could not serve to develop the epistemological aspects to action theory. A theory of action cannot avoid the self-reflexive question whether it has suc-ceeded in construing itself in terms of the categories it deploys, that is, it must be possible to understand the drafting of a theory of action itself as an action and it must be possible to correlate the ideal explanation it seeks to provide and the conceptions of human action which it contains.

Viewed thus, Parsons' position is to sit on the fence in a strangely inconclusive way. On the one hand, he is perfectly clear that the theory of action he develops should not be understood to be an explanatory theory according to the yardstick used in the natural sciences. On the other hand, he does not then apply this insight in order to cast even the slightest doubt on the appropriateness of this ideal explanation for a science of human action. Parsons believes that the framework for action theory that he devises enables us to describe facts in terms of clear concepts; this description, in turn, purportedly enables variables to be related to one another in a controlled manner and thus generates causal explanations based on hypotheses regarding universal laws. Without the framework of action theory, he claims, the social sciences would run the risk of reducing their object to some positivistic account of it. Yet, without proceeding to the level of causal explanations of the type described above, the social sciences would be reduced to historical relativism. This view of things corresponds to the observation that Parsons' theory of action was not linked in any way with a consideration of either the empirical methodology of understanding [*Verstehen*] or the interpretation of actions. Further confirmation is to be found in Parsons' reaction to Harold Bershady's attempt, only a few years before the former's death, to shed light on the type of explanation involved in action theory by following more recent attempts in analytical philosophy. Bershady had stated that actors explained the actions of others not by subsuming these under universal laws but rather by assuming certain intentions and action goals to exist. This type of explanation – a 'practical syllogism' – might, Bershady argued, usually only be possible after the event and thus does not enable the person to forecast actions, but precisely this accords with the indeterminate, that is, creative, character of human action. In his response to this attempt, Parsons admitted that since writing his early masterpiece he had increasingly been beset by doubts regarding the model of explanation derived from physics, but stated that the area in which he was now searching for an alternative was the 'teleonomic' type of explanation afforded by biology. He went on to indicate that an explanation of human action based solely on intentions involves a mere reduction in logical rigour and not a true epistemological alternative. Final proof of Parsons' continued adherence to an explanatory model not tailored specifically to scientific studies of human action is to be found in his express endorsement of Pareto's methodological conceptions, and his rejection of Max Weber in this respect.

Precisely the growing belief that Parsons failed to develop the epistemological side to the concept of action adequately has led contemporary thinkers to go back in time to a point before Parsons and examine again the work of Max Weber. Whereas Parsons believed general theories should be concerned solely with universal analytical laws, Weber never lost sight of the fact that unique historical phenomena had to be accounted for. While Parsons compiled a catalogue of possible value orientations, Weber was thinking of an inexhaustible plurality of conflicting values. While Parsons endeavoured to form a scientific conceptual framework that was independent of the historical context in which it was born, for Weber all knowledge was a unique statement and thus remained contingent and selective. Ultimately it was Parsons' failure to strike a balance between the formation of a general theory and the corresponding diagnoses of situations based on practical judgements that has caused interest in his work – unlike that of Max Weber – to be confined mainly to the academic world.

Parsons' lack of clarity also sheds light on an aspect of the substantive thrust of his theory of action. In *The Structure of Social Action* the underlying action-theoretical framework consists precisely of the elements of action itself, the ends, the situation (formed by conditions and the means available), and the norms which serve to regulate the choice of means and constitute ends. Parsons presents this scheme as the ineluctable logical framework for the theory, analogous to the space–time framework presupposed by classical physics.

> Every physical phenomenon *must* involve processes in time, which happen to particles which can be located in space. It is *impossible* to talk about physical processes in any other terms, at least so long as the conceptual scheme of classical physics is employed. Similarly, it is *impossible* even to talk about action in terms that do not involve a means–end relationship. It is not a phenomenon in the empirical sense. It is the indispensable logical framework in which we describe and think about the phenomena of action.[31]

Here, the means–ends relationship is thus made the definition of all action. It is striking that something identical does not occur in Parsons' work before or after *The Structure of Social Action*. For, in an early essay on the place of ultimate values in sociological theory,[32] Parsons mentioned realms of phenomena that could not be explained with an action theory based on the means–ends schema. He referred there to art and to 'communal' relations, for example in marriage, in order to show that it was difficult, if not impossible, to classify them in terms of the means–ends schema. Art was, he claimed, not some goal being reached but rather the expression of evaluative attitudes. In marriage and in any 'community' there were, he continued, also no specified common goals, but rather common attitudes and unspecific interests; thus the partners' actions should be construed not as the pursuit of their own interests, but rather as the expression of an attitude of love or affection.

In *The Structure of Social Action* there is little mention of forms of action that cannot be subsumed under the means–ends schema. In the context of his interpretations of Pareto and Durkheim, Parsons does, admittedly, mention ritual as the diametrical opposite of strictly instrumental actions, distinguishing here between an intrinsic means–ends relationship and a relationship between symbol and meaning. Yet only in a small footnote does he mention that art and play will be discussed later,[33] a promise which he does not keep. More than a decade later, in *The Social System*, his second major book to synthesize the different strands of his thinking, Parsons consistently elaborated the contrast between instrumental and expressive orientations towards action.[34] We can at this juncture treat as a moot point whether Parsons does indeed do justice to the phenomena he has in his sights when defining such actions as the expression of ultimate evaluative attitudes. The intention here has been merely to show that, as was the case with his construction of the epistemological side to the concept of action, Parsons again incurs problems with regard to his substantive theory of action for which alternative philosophical solutions existed at the time. Yet, because *The Structure of Social Action* doggedly adhered to economic theory as the methodological model it wished to emulate, Parsons in the final instance stripped his theory of action of all those elements which did not fit in with the theoretical edifice he had in mind.

My attempt to render the character of Parsons' work more readily understandable by referring it back to the historical and biographical conditions under which it was produced should at least have dispelled the impression that Parsons' theoretical edifice was one gigantic idiosyncratic white elephant. Rather, the achievements and limitations of his work become comprehensible if one considers that he regarded the economic theory of rational action as the exemplary model to be followed. Parsons never claimed to have 'invented' an exhaustive theory of action; to his mind, such a theory had arisen a generation earlier in the thought of the writers he dealt with. His interpretations of their thought and his global hypothesis on them can only be given the benefit of our doubt if we can uncover a similar relation to economic theory in these sociological classics. It is therefore of crucial importance for a concluding assessment of Parsons' blueprint for a theory of action whether these thinkers were indeed caught up in a struggle between opposing camps in a manner similar to the situation in which Parsons found himself. The next step in my argument will therefore be to investigate whether this was in fact the case. If it proves possible to provide a differentiated affirmative answer to this question, it still remains unclear whether these classical thinkers addressed those aspects Parsons elided from his theory of action, and which critics have subsequently insisted were necessary. I shall claim that compared with these thinkers Parsons paid a high price for the greater integrity of his normatively oriented theory of action, since he had to forgo quite radically any consideration of the creative dimension of action. I shall therefore pay close attention to establishing in what way this creative dimension exists in the writings of the sociological classics. Only thus can we derive from the historical genesis of sociological action theory an adequate picture of the marginal position in that theory of the creative dimension of action.

1.3   Economic and Social Action

The proposition that the economic theory of rational action served as a model to be followed by sociology was not only promulgated with respect to Parsons, but in fact cited for the emergence of sociology as a discipline at the end of the nineteenth century. In particular, Göran Therborn and Simon Clarke[35] have claimed that the work of the first-generation classic sociological theorists can only be understood in terms of a tacit acceptance of the model of rational action which had otherwise asserted itself in virtually every aspect of economics following the revolutionary impact of the theory of marginal utility in the second half of the nineteenth century. Yet Therborn and Clarke wished to emphasize the degree to which economists as well as sociologists departed from the ideal of Marxist theory, namely a theory of society based on a critique of political economy. In so doing they simply assume that an economic theory which is informed by the rational model is purely ideological in character. One need not subscribe to this view. The historical substance of the argument remains important even if we assume that any modern theory of society must naturally take account of individual decisions on actions, purchases and choices and can therefore not dispense with the model of rational action. If the historical proposition is true, this would give us the following picture: sociology was not constructed on the model of rational action in the way that economics was, yet it accepted the validity of this theory for the purposes of economics. At the same time, it claimed that precisely those tasks and objects of inquiry now fell within the scope of sociology which the above form of economics had not wished to take on board from earlier economic theory and political philosophy. The intention was thus for sociology to be responsible for analysing those dimensions of social life which could not be grasped by economics; and for them to be analysed by means of a theory of action which precisely included non-rational forms of action. Sociology therefore required a fundamental theory of action which was able to define various types of action according to how they differed specifically from rational action. It required a theory of society as an interconnection of actions that was more than merely the unintended linking of actions motivated by self-interest. And that was why sociology attached such great importance to the normative agreement of the members of the society. Just as fixating on an enemy affects an individual as profoundly as does emulation of a role model, so, too, sociological action theory is permeated with the theory of rational action precisely because it sees types of action only as gradations of deviation from rationality in the full sense of the concept and not as unique phenomena in their own right.

The question is whether this picture actually agrees with the facts. To begin with, there can be no doubt that classical political economy, from Adam Smith onwards, had a powerful impact on all avenues of intellectual life. Even those who disputed the accuracy of the concrete contents of the theory nevertheless took it as a yardstick for the theoretical and empirical level at which the question as to the causes of a nation's wealth had to be put. This is not to say that there was any lack of critiques of political economy. Marx and Engels were not the only writers who understood their thought as a critique of political economy. The currents of historicism and early attempts to devise a sociology were also, to a greater or lesser extent, a polemic against political economy. They were often interested not in improving the

latter but in refuting it, as the approach taken by political economy
was often equated with an effort to legitimate a society in which no
intervention was allowed in the effects unleashed by market activity.
Some of Adam Smith's followers were indeed interested in such a
legitimation. Both the German historical school of economics and, in
France, Auguste Comte's sociological programme constituted prag-
matic-reformist attempts to limit the legitimation of the principle of
'laissez-faire' in the vulgarized forms in which classical economics
had permeated European thought. Comte's main objection was to the
absence of a moral dimension, while the German school criticized the
lack of a political dimension based on the nation-state. Indeed,
classical economic theory looked set to fail owing to its inability to
generate any further insights into either the inescapable social problems thrown up by a market economy or the national framework of
countries which had somehow to come to terms with England's
domination of the world market. The weak link in these counter-
currents, however, was that they were unable to derive the limits of
the principle of 'laissez-faire' from an economic theory of the market
economy itself and thus were also unable to calculate in economic
terms the benefits of the social reforms and forms of state intervention
that they themselves favoured. In the middle of the nineteenth
century, at least in continental Europe, one could get the impression
that classical economic theory was on the retreat again, so far as it had
ever been able to impose itself.[36]

In other words, a theory was in jeopardy which, for all its flaws,
had consistently maintained that human institutions had to be related
to the actions and needs of individuals, and which refused to recognize
the sacrosanct aura of either the state or abstract morality. The critique
of political economy put forward by Marx and Engels preserved this
driving force in classical economics more clearly than do the other
variants. But their project came up against similar limits to those
which classical economic theory had confronted, albeit limits that
were located elsewhere. All the various proponents of a theory of
objective value since John Locke, and in particular David Ricardo, had
primarily been concerned with solving what was essentially a question
of social theory, namely to uncover the laws by which class-specific
revenues were generated, and were less interested in applying their
own value-theoretical assumptions to solving the more narrowly
economic question of the dynamics of price formation. As the various
forms of a market economy asserted themselves, so this omission
increasingly came to appear as an intrinsic deficit of economic theory.

In this situation, other theorists (who indeed lived in different countries and worked independently of one another) launched an offensive to limit and more closely specify classical economic theory. I am referring here to the revolution caused by the theory of marginal utility. The marginal utility theorists advocated a reappraisal of value theory, thereby altering the epistemological status of economics in the hope that this would enable them to answer the question of price formation and the exact nature of the possibilities and limits of state intervention in the economy. Value theory was henceforth not to proceed from the question of who created *objective* values in the production process and how, but rather to start from individuals with existing preferences and resources and thus from the issue of how the value of a particular product was constituted *subjectively*. This point of departure could then lead to the development of a new understanding of private property and the division of labour, as well as of the market and money as means of optimally allocating resources. Needless to say, this involved adopting many of the methods of classical economic theory. But what had often only been implicit in the latter, and inconsistently applied, was now made explicit in the theory and used consistently. Economic theory was to be regarded no longer as a comprehensive theory of society that remained close to political science and moral philosophy, but purely as a theory of the actions of individuals with random goals and limited resources that could be applied in different ways. Such a pure theory had inevitably to rest on idealized assumptions and thus had to presume a measure of rational action, of competition and a knowledge of conditions such as was not actually to be encountered in reality. Yet these idealizations were seen not as an empirical objection to the theory, but merely as a methodological detour which the theory had to take.

The classical sociologists reacted in various ways to this crisis in classical economic theory and to the 'neo-classical' route out of the crisis. The conceptual framework that is best suited to demonstrating the exemplary role played by economic theory and the conception of sociology as a supplement to economics that could grasp non-rational action is to be found in Vilfredo Pareto's work. Pareto termed all rational action in all domains 'logical action', and this included even such domains as those that were not directly economic such as the military domain and the political and the legal spheres. All other action he lumped together under the heading 'non-logical' action. In other words, he assigned all those forms of action – and in his opinion they constituted the vast empirical majority of all actions – to a negatively defined residual category. This is not to say that he did not comment on them further. Quite the opposite: what elevates Pareto above all the other economic theorists was the fact that he did not merely treat the issue of a theory of non-economic spheres of society and 'non-logical' action summarily. One of the most important motives behind his work was the wish to proceed inductively in this area in order to be able to describe these actions adequately and thus to ensure that they did not merely resemble pathological deviations from a normal type. Via this inductive method, however, he arrived at a differentiation of types of action according to the role played by rational considerations in constituting them. 'Logical actions are at least for the main the result of a consideration, non-logical actions arise mainly from a particular emotional state, feelings, sub-conscious, etc.'[37] Pareto wished to show that individuals portray most of their actions, both to themselves and to others, as pseudo-rational, despite the widely different causes of such actions. Based on this assumption he developed an extensive systematic framework for classifying motives and forms of rationalization, which commentators have regarded as a form of demystifying ideology critique in the fashion of Nietzsche.[38] Even if what Parsons wrote about Pareto may not be true, namely that the latter defected from economics to sociology, it is most certainly correct that Pareto conceived of sociology as a supplement to an economics that was based on the theory of marginal utility and devised his theory of action to serve this purpose, a theory that has been widely forgotten today.

The position of Max Weber's action theory vis-à-vis economic theory is much more complex in terms of its genesis but quite similar in its effect. Weber's definitions are certainly the most influential text in the whole of sociological action theory. Weber came up with the well-known definition of sociology as 'a science concerning itself with the interpretative understanding of social action'.

> We shall speak of 'action' insofar as the acting individual attaches a subjective meaning to his behavior – be it overt or covert, omission or acquiescence. Action is 'social' insofar as its subjective meaning takes account of the behavior of others and is thereby oriented in its course.[39]

With this distinction Weber already sets sociology off from economic theory, which is permitted to focus only on rational action as such. There can be no doubt that Weber developed his sociological theory of economic action, which takes up so much of *Economy and Society*,[40] *alongside* pure economic theory and based upon it. The thrust of this assertion cannot be dulled by proving how strongly Weber's thought was influenced by the historical school of economics and in general

by German historicism.[41] Although he took on many of the issues
raised and the solutions found by these schools, he never came out
unequivocally in their favour in the controversy between this camp
and the theorists of marginal utility. The necessity of distinguishing
clearly between value and factual judgements and the defence of a
purely theoretical core matched the thought of Menger much more
closely than it did Schmoller. Where Weber expressly criticized the
theory of marginal utility and did not merely express his disinterest
in the details of that theory – given that any preoccupation with the
theory of marginal utility was also subject to the law of declining
marginal utility – he challenged both the false understanding Menger
and others had of their theory as well as the possibility of grounding the model of rational action in psychology and anthropology.
Weber attempted to create a synthesis of the competing schools of
economic theory by conceiving of the model of rational action as a
historical ideal type. This meant, on the one hand, accepting the
model of classical economic theory and, on the other, subordinating
it to the more comprehensive task of overall historical cognition. To
Weber's mind, sociology was to be a form of researching history and
the present which was based on a better and more systematic
clarification of its conceptual assumptions than was usual in
historiography.

What became known as Weber's theory of action was his typology
of the ways of defining social action, and it is this aspect that has had
the greatest influence:

> Social action, like all action, may be oriented in four ways. It may be:
> (1) *instrumentally rational (zweckrational)*, that is, determined by expec-
>   tations as to the behavior of objects in the environment and of other
>   human beings; these expectations are used as 'conditions' or 'means'
>   for the attainment of the actor's own rationally pursued and calcu-
>   lated ends;
> (2) *value-rational (wertrational)*, that is, determined by a conscious belief
>   in the value for its own sake of some ethical, aesthetic, religious, or
>   other forms of behavior, independently of its prospects of success;
> (3) *affectual* (especially emotional), that is, determined by the actor's
>   specific affects and feeling states;
> (4) *traditional*, that is, determined by ingrained habituation.[42]

The interpretations of this proposed typology and the controversial
discussions it triggered have shown that the principle underlying
Weber's definitions is far from transparent. Wolfgang Schluchter has
undertaken the clearest attempt to distil what that principle is.[43] He

maintains that Weber arranged his types of action along a scale of
rationality, whereby rational control could be directed towards any or
all of the four components of action, namely means, purpose, value
and consequences. That type of action in which the actor rationally
weighed up all these components individually and against one another
would thus be highest on the scale and by extension the type of action
that was fully rational. Purposive-rational action, which was in this
manner charged with a certain ethic of responsibility, would then be
able to make the strongest claim to being considered an action. Action
oriented towards an absolute value, by contrast, does not include any
reflection on the consequences, affectual action jettisons any consideration of values, and traditional action even abandons any thought of
purposes. If this interpretation is accurate, then Weber's typology of
action, like that of Pareto, is shaped by the fact that types of action
which deviate from the norm of rational action are classified predominantly in terms of this deviation, that is, as deficient modes of rational
action. Given the multifaceted nature of Weber's concept of rationality,
this statement can certainly not be the last word on his contribution to
action theory, but it could present the final judgement on both the
typology he put forward and the effect of the model of rational action
on his deliberations on action theory.

In other words, from the point of view of action theory, there are
distinct similarities between Pareto's and Weber's reactions to the
change which the theory of marginal utility brought about in economics. Alfred Schütz, although writing a generation later, could also
be considered as belonging to the same group, insofar as his early
work was intended not just as an abstract synthesis of the thought of
Weber and Husserl but also as the basis for a theory which presented
the interaction of the abstract types of action Weber had distinguished
in concrete non-economic actions and was thus meant as a sociological
extension of orthodox economic theory.[44]

It was, however, possible to react quite differently to the change, as
can be seen in the work of all those thinkers who claim that the model
of rational action is of no use even for economic theory. This was a
widespread reaction among American theorists at the time. Veblen's
critique of the theory of marginal utility and his championing of an
evolutionist theory of economics is a particularly famous case. It is a
less well-known fact that Charles Cooley's work stems directly from
early versions of the institutionalist strand in American economics. He
quite clearly believed that his social psychology refuted the individualistic assumptions of the model of rational action.[45]

Of the classical sociologists, it is, above all, Durkheim who belongs in this second group. He had from an early date – since a visit to Germany in 1885–6 – been fascinated by the historical school in German economics and jurisprudence. However, he indicated that he distanced himself from the way that school's theories centred on a notion of the state and that he was searching instead for 'communitarian' solutions, such as were to be found in the writings of Albert Schäffle.[46] Durkheim differed from Weber in that he did not reject the possibility of grounding the theory of marginal utility in psychology in order to be able to uphold that economic theory in a limited context by changing the epistemological interpretation of the model of rational action. This explains why Durkheim had to concentrate on refuting any hedonist psychology. The sharpness of the distinction he makes between sociology and psychology and between the social domain and the individual can be understood only if we bear in mind both that he, at least for a time, identified psychology with these hedonist assumptions and that to his mind the individual was a label for inclinations which were not subject to normative regulation. If, moreover, economic theory was not granted validity in a particular sphere, then it was only logical to claim that its subject matter constituted an area best addressed by a sub-sector of sociology, namely economic sociology. Durkheim admittedly had little chance of actually integrating economics into sociology or subjugating the former to the latter, as economics was a discipline strongly entrenched in French universities. Nevertheless, the school of sociology he founded took the stage with an imperial flourish. Durkheim's crass severing of any link between sociology and individual action is clearly the reason for the fact that initially his work does not appear to contain any basis for putting sociology on an action-theoretical footing. This changed in the course of his life to the extent that Durkheim increasingly turned his attention to the question as to the processes of action constitutive for those values which were used as a means of orientation and a yardstick in action, explicitly including economic action. Durkheim devised an action-theoretical explanation for the genesis of values, but never quite relinquished the idea that economic action and in particular production and labour were per se presocial or antisocial. Even in his later theory of religion we still encounter the dualism of individual utilitarian everyday action and collective, symbolic–expressive extraordinary action. Durkheim's conception of human nature rests on a notion of anarchic–egocentric instincts. Owing to the dualism underlying his work, Durkheim cannot posit sociality as a dimension in which everyday interpersonal action conflicts are solved. We therefore find that a *reconstruction* of the tacit assumptions behind the model of rational action is absent from his writings too. The fact that he rejects this model out of hand leads him initially to counterpose it with a purely mentalist conception; later he opts instead for a quite different type of action, namely the ecstasy of collective ritual, which he does not, however, link back to the structure of rational, 'utilitarian' action. In other words, just as there can be no talk of economic theory playing an exemplary role in Durkheim's thought, neither can it be claimed that he succeeded in developing a comprehensive theory of action. His writings that point in this direction are instead characterized by polemical attacks on the model of rational action and to this extent are still fixated on the latter.

The only form of thought that could lead beyond Durkheim in this respect was one which applied the idea that values were constituted in action to everyday action, and in particular one which addressed the question as to how the value of rationality itself was constituted. Cooley, Mead and Dewey all made progress pursuing the first step here.[47] The formulation that values should be considered a social phenomenon and the programme put forward for providing 'social psychological' foundations for value theory both stress that values acquired objective validity in social action – thus countering both the old objective doctrine of value per se and the new 'subjective' doctrine. This new emphasis demonstrated a wish to invert the relationship between economics and sociology. It was now not economics but rather the newly declared programme of social psychology that was to form the point of departure. From this starting point, however, economics could still be accorded a place befitting it.

Georg Simmel's *The Philosophy of Money* was alone in clearly making decisive progress in respect of the second step.[48] Simmel also attempts to provide a psychological foundation for the objective validity of values – and he succeeds, because he construes the value of a good not in terms of how it corresponds to a person's impulsive needs but rather as the result of reflective acts of valuation. A conscious act of valuation requires precisely, he claims, that 'the naive–practical unity of subject and object'[49] first be overcome. 'It may be said, therefore, that the value of an object does indeed depend upon the demand for it, but upon a demand that is no longer purely instinctive.'[50] This change in the psychological presuppositions about value judgements also shifts the general focus of attention. Simmel is interested not in economic theory in the narrow sense, but instead in reconstructing those processes which gave rise to the distance between individuals and the objects they desire. The reconstructive picture he paints traces both the emergence of a modern money-based economy and the manner in which this goes hand in hand with social processes whereby non-economic spheres become progressively fragmented and subordinated to 'rationalization' processes based on the rationale of money or analogous structures. The suggestive appeal of Simmel's analysis of the style of modern life is based on his contention that money, law and intellectuality exhibit parallel structures. Thus, the very economic system that is characterized by its unleashing rational forms of action also rests on principles of valuation which cannot simply be derived from it. It is a well-known fact that Simmel's diagnosis of his time had a strong impact on Weber's own endeavours to analyse the genesis of modern capitalism. Weber, like Simmel, was also intent on showing that all economic action, and therefore in particular rational action as well, was based on cultural values. Whereas, as we have seen above, Weber's action theory itself remained dependent on the model of rational action, Simmel dispensed with trying to provide a more exact, action-theoretical account of the assumptions on which his theory of valuation rested. This deficiency led to a profound ambivalence in both men's notions of the way the model of rational action was progressively imposing itself on the reality of the modern age. It remained a moot point whether modernity should be interpreted as a culture based on the value of rationality or as a culture which, while admittedly exhibiting certain trends towards rationalization, also always contains counter-currents. In the one case, non-rational forms of action are either relics of pre-modernity or examples of anti-modern deviance; in the other, they can lay equal claim to being modern and to being valid in contemporary society. A theory of action which, by virtue of its conceptual structure, considers non-rational action to be a deficient form of rational action provides a hermetic interpretation of modernity that rests on the principles of rationality. In order to generate an alternative diagnosis of contemporary society that does not think of everything in terms of an optimistic or pessimistic account of a linear process of rationalization we must therefore reconstruct and reintroduce those assumptions on which the model of rational action is based.

If we survey the varying ways these early sociologists reacted to economic theory and thus their respective stances on the model of rational action, then we can certainly state that, for all the distinctions we must make between them, the basic problem facing Parsons was the same as that which faced the generation of classical sociological thinkers. The convergence Parsons claims to find is therefore not without some basis in fact. At the same time, it becomes clear how little this concept captures of the overall setting that led to the genesis of action theory. Although we must agree with Parsons in distancing ourselves from the model of rational action, it does not follow that we must agree that his solution, namely the development of a normativist conception of action, is really the best way to lay the foundations for an approach that goes beyond the rational model. For a start, it hardly bolsters one's confidence to know that Parsons completely ignored the philosophical schools, be they pragmatism or the philosophy of life, which were emerging contemporaneously with classical sociological thought and which doubtless had a major impact on the thinkers he discusses. However, this need not concern us here, as I intend to keep my argument within the bounds of his theory. A substantial part of the convergence thesis rested on the fact that Parsons pointed to the astonishing similarities between Weber's theory of charisma and Durkheim's theory of the sacred. Even Alexander is prepared to accept the convergence thesis if it is limited to this one aspect. It is therefore quite in order to ask whether these two fragments of the respective theories really do point towards a normativist theory of action or whether instead they contain the seeds of a model that goes further, namely that of the creativity of action.

1.4   Weber's Theory of Charisma and the Problem of Creativity

Let us start with Weber. The suggestion that Weber's theory of action is derived from the model provided by economic theory rested on an examination of his 'Basic Sociological Categories' and thus on his express contribution to the conceptual arsenal of the social sciences. However, that text certainly did not form the basis of his substantive work, but was rather a retrospective reflection on his work and an attempt to propose a consistent terminology. The self-interpretations of their method provided by even the greatest thinkers frequently do not correspond to the approach they actually take in their substantive work. In order to take account of the substance of Weber's work when examining his action theory, we shall investigate the relationship between that action theory and his theory of charisma, which was emphasized by Parsons and which is undoubtedly of major significance for Weber's sociology of domination and his oeuvre as a whole. To do so we shall attempt to answer the question: Is Weber's own typology of action adequate to the task of apprehending the phenomena he bundles together under the notion of 'charisma'? If not, what implications does this have for Weber's 'official' theory of action?

As a first step towards answering this question it is worth looking at how Weber himself relates his concept of charisma to his action theory. At the beginning of the chapter in *Economy and Society* devoted to the sociology of religion Weber introduces the term 'charisma' as an umbrella covering all those 'extra-ordinary' powers for which ethnology, drawing on the languages of the peoples researched, has a large number of stock labels. Such powers are said to have 'effects in meteorology, healing, divination and telepathy'.[51] Within the space of a few pages, Weber provides two different and partly contradictory definitions of action motivated by magic or religion. He at first concludes from the absence of a notion of 'the other world' in archaic religions that such action is 'oriented to this world'. 'That it may go well with thee . . . and that thou mayest prolong thy days upon the earth,' he writes, 'expresses the reason for the performance of actions enjoined by religion or magic.' Weber expressly does not wish to separate religious or magical action from 'the range of everyday purposive conduct, particularly since even the ends of the religious and magical actions are predominantly economic'. He terms such action 'relatively rational behavior. It follows rules of experience, though it is not necessarily action in accordance with a means–end-schema.' Although this initially seems to imply that Weber is inter-preting magic and religion hyper-rationalistically as underdeveloped forms of technological control over nature, shortly thereafter he introduces an element into the analysis which would appear to contradict this. For Weber differentiates between the 'magician', who uses his charismatic qualities as a profession and has built his enterprise on this, and the layman. The layman is not simply the passive object or the admirer of the magician's charismatic qualities, but rather he occasionally participates in that state which the magician is able to induce at will: ecstasy.

> For the layman, this psychological state is accessible only in occasional actions. Unlike the merely rational practice of wizardry, ecstasy occurs in a social form, the *orgy*, which is the primordial form of religious association. . . . Because of the routine demands of living, the layman can experience ecstasy only occasionally, as intoxication. To induce ecstasy he may employ any type of alcoholic beverage, tobacco, or similar narcotics – and especially music – all of which originally served orgiastic purposes.

Weber even goes so far as to derive the notion of a soul from the experiences made in orgiastic states. In other words, there is no longer any mention of religious action having quasi-rational structures. In his 'Basic Sociological Categories' charisma is categorized in terms of action theory in a third way. Here, Weber points to the exceptional importance of instinct-based behavioural control in the early days of humankind and assumes that in the further course of human history other decisively important aspects of human behaviour were also controlled not through meaning and understanding but in a mechanical, instinctual manner. He adds:

> This is particularly true of all 'traditional' action and of many aspects of charisma, which contain the seeds of certain types of psychic 'contagion' and thus give rise to new social developments. These types of action are very closely related to phenomena which are understandable either only in biological terms or can be interpreted in terms of subjective motives only in fragments.[52]

The first attempt to interpret Weber's notion of charisma in terms of his action theory thus leaves us confused. On the one hand, we encounter a rationalist interpretation of it as a 'primitive technique': this enabled Weber to categorize charisma in terms of his typology, but only by considerably pruning the actual phenomenon. On the other, we come across deliberations on religious experience in states of group ecstasy and yet there is no discernibly obvious place for this description in Weber's typology of action. And then again, we find charisma apparently subsumed under affective action and almost relegated to the animal kingdom. Moreover, this is based on an anthropology that hardly meets current standards and also leads to intrinsic theoretical difficulties, for precisely this instinctive behaviour then becomes the cause of the concept of the soul.

In this situation it would be in order to draw on Weber's broader discussion of charisma in the context of the sociology of domination.[53] This is much more fruitful for a study of the routinization of charisma than it is for an analysis of how charisma evolves in the first place. We are faced, above all, with the difficulty that Weber now uses the concept of 'charisma', which was originally part of a theory of religion, exclusively to discuss a type of domination and therefore does not do justice to the breadth of phenomena which it could have been used to address. Essentially, Weber presupposes that extra-ordinary qualities are ascribed to persons who consequently acquire the status of 'leaders'. In this context, he is not interested in issues that would be characteristic for action theory: neither the nature of these persons nor a more careful analysis of the situations in which such qualities are attributed to them, nor the interactions between charismatic persons and their disciples, nor the needs of collectives that are driven forward by being 'charisma-hungry'[54] are of importance for him. Instead he focuses on the internal structure of domination based on charisma, while conceding that such forms of domination are dependent on the qualities thus attributed to the ruler continuing to be upheld. I need not go into the specifics of charismatic administrative apparatuses and legislation, nor the degree to which such a form of domination ignores rules and economic imperatives. Wolfgang Mommsen and Shmuel Eisenstadt have covered all the important issues in their respective interpretations.[55] Mommsen, in particular, has shed a great deal of light on the background of intellectual history and political theory against which Weber's conception of charisma must be seen. It becomes clear that Weber painted the charismatic leader in colours which he had taken from Nietzsche's theory of personality. Such a figure is an elitist individual who is capable of blithely breaking with all traditional or rational norms and of initiating a revolutionary upheaval of all values. Seen thus, the charismatic leader is the vanishing point of Weber's ethical claim that the individual must himself choose the ideals that determine his life and must be able to seek a following for those ideals. Eisenstadt, in turn, uses the conception of charisma to bring a functionalist theory of differentiation closer to real history, with its dramatic crises and contingent events. In Eisenstadt's work, unlike that of Shils, the 'Dionysian' character of charismatic innovation does not dissolve into some general concept of the sacred. Yet a whole series of questions on charisma cannot be answered on the basis of Weber's writings, or, for that matter, within the framework of action theory as such. They do not enable us to assess either the socio-structural conditions for such charismatic attempts at innovation as described above, or the empirical chances of these innovations actually asserting themselves, nor do they help us to answer the more general question as to whether charisma can avoid being sidelined into the domains of art, eroticism and institutionalized religion.

Mommsen, Eisenstadt and, most recently, Arnason all regard the concept of charisma as a form of counterbalance to Weber's theory of rationalization. This interpretation reinforces the impression that charismatic forms of action do not fit in with Weber's typology of action, with its orientation towards the model of rational action. Naturally, any typology which, like Weber's, contains a more or less clandestine residual category is able to classify all phenomena, although the quality of the classification then leaves much to be desired. What is decisive, however, is that the principle underlying this typology does not do justice to that dimension of action which is revealed in exemplary fashion in charismatic action, namely the creative dimension. Weber's typology of action is only suited to categorizing the normative and purposive-rational dimensions of action. Only in the context of a sociology of domination, if at all, is his conception of charisma able to compensate for this limitation.

In the secondary literature there have been various attempts to overcome this limitation by going one step further in drawing on Weber's writings. The majority of these attempts take one of two directions. Firstly, there are those who have suggested that an interpretation of Weber's study of the Protestant ethic and especially his essay on sects, as well as his other studies on the sociology of religion and, above all, his study of ancient Judaism may show us that Weber did indeed consider historical change resulting from the intervention of innovative minorities that were not to be construed as the followers of a charismatic leader. Secondly, his two lectures on science and politics as vocations have been interpreted as revealing that Weber took precisely the emotional attachment to an issue, to the inner logic of cultural domains, and played it off against an arbitrary claim to innovation. However, these two arguments prompt the question whether they do not in fact unintentionally make clear how little Weber's theory as a whole does justice to the elements these writings contain. A comparison with a different intellectual tradition may make things clearer here. Classical American thought in the republican tradition sidesteps the conflict between construing individuals either as mere executors of an already given process of world history or, conversely, as the sole agents capable of altering history. Major figures are instead seen as innovators who creatively articulate a collectively preformed meaning. According to this way of thinking, the innovative individual thus deviates cognitively or normatively from the collective's received notions but uses arguments in an attempt to win support for his new view of the world. The collective can either reject these arguments or embrace them. What is decisive is that here a discursive relation is posited between innovator and collective. For such a relation to exist, not only must the innovator rise above the old norms, but the collective must also be able to create some sort of hypothetical distance between itself and its own norms. This propensity for hypothetical distance is most frequently demonstrated using the example of the logic of scientific progress, yet it is also claimed to be what characterizes democratic culture. Only in an ultra-stable order can change exclusively occur through the medium of charismatic individuals and their followers. In democracy as an 'institutionalized revolution', by contrast, innovation is an everyday occurrence. Even the existing institutions that are meant to embody democracy are creatively transformed by public learning processes and social movements.

If one refers this back to Weber, then two things become clear. First of all, Weber's theory of charisma retains a model of change that is not compatible with democratic conditions. It focuses not on the powers of persuasion of a leader but solely on the latter's personal charisma. In no sense whatsoever is Weber's outlook of a 'democracy of leadership based on plebiscite' capable of unleashing the potential for democratic culture and a democratic public sphere that can satisfy the needs of our current age. It is precisely for this reason that the task of action theory must consist in overcoming these contradictions in Weber's oeuvre. Parsons' formulation that norms and values must be taken into consideration when studying human action is at any rate quite inadequate for such a task. Secondly, while the scale of values that Weber applies in his diagnosis of the age he lived in, and in particular in his critique of the comprehensive bureaucratization of all areas of life, is indisputably based on an idea of creative *and* responsible individuals, this idea is not developed in his action theory as such. Indeed, Weber's action theory fails to give adequate space to the possibility of creative everyday action.

1.5   The Problem of the Emergence of a New Morality as the Underlying Theme in Durkheim's Work

In his reception of Émile Durkheim's work, Parsons particularly emphasized a sudden shift whereby Durkheim switched from being a positivist to being a normativist. Many other commentators also perceive a stark contrast between his early programmatic and substantive works, which were the basis for his reputation as an arch-positivist, and his later work on the theory of religion. According to Parsons, what was decisive for the change in Durkheim's thought was his insight into the fact that social controls were effected via the internalization of norms; this, said Parsons, revolutionized Durkheim's entire theoretical framework, yet it also prompted him to take an utterly normative deterministic approach. However, there are philological and systematic flaws in this hypothesis. At the philological level,

Parsons completely ignored Durkheim's early oeuvre, that is, the writings pre-dating his magnum opus on the division of labour, and misinterpreted his theory of education as a specific stage in his development, whereas in fact it played an important role throughout his life's work. Jeffrey Alexander's modification of Parsons' interpretation is no less problematical.[56] This may indicate that only by overcoming the schema of 'utilitarianism versus normativity' that both Parsons and Alexander use to explain Durkheim's thought can we arrive at an appropriate reconstruction of the latter's work. Yet all those researchers who endeavour to understand Durkheim solely in terms of a desire for community do little to overcome that schema, irrespective of whether, like Nisbet, they label Durkheim a conservative, or whether, like Giddens, they classify him more correctly as a progressive republican.[57]

Whereas in the case of Max Weber all we had to do was to contrast his conception of charisma with his theory of action, in the case of Durkheim we have to focus on the inner logic of his oeuvre as a whole. We shall therefore add yet another hypothesis to the wealth of theories on Durkheim's work, namely that it can best be understood if we consider it as an ongoing attempt *to answer the question as to how a new morality can emerge.* I am referring primarily not to the concrete question as to the contents of such a new morality, but instead to the more abstract question as to what form a theory of action and of society must take if their conceptual backbone is to allow a systematic conception of the genesis of a new morality. The strongest pointers in this direction are to be found in the thought of René König, the Grand Old Man of German Durkheim scholars, and in particular in his *Kritik der historisch-existenzialistischen Soziologie* written as early as 1937, but not published until decades later.[58]

To my knowledge, no one devoted more effort than König to interpreting Durkheim as being not simply a moralist within sociology, nor merely a sociologist for whom the subject was essentially a science of morality, but rather as a thinker in the historical ambience of the *fin de siècle* who was concerned above all with the conditions for the formation of a new morality. König was able to achieve this not only because he had a better overview of the philosophical and cultural environment in France than many historians of sociology – who paid more attention to the *sociologists* who were Durkheim's predecessors than to his *philosophical contemporaries* – but above all because he drew on Durkheim in the conviction that the latter provided a way out of German philosophy of life [*Lebensphilosophie*] and its political and moral consequences. In so doing, he precisely did not juxtapose Durkheim to the philosophy of life as a representative of scientism, but rather as a thinker who pursued the project of reconstructing rationalism so that he could take up the justified elements of a critique of rationality embedded in the philosophy of life and at the same time overcome them. In this respect, the thought of Bergson and Durkheim as well as that of Sorel and Durkheim can be placed more closely alongside one another in a manner completely different than if one merely presumes that French philosophy of life and positivistic sociology are antipodes. To my mind, König does not provide enough theoretical depth for this promising approach and also does not always mark the theories off from one another in the right places. However, his work can inspire a theoretical attempt to view Durkheim not as a theorist of order and of normativity per se, and certainly not of anomie, functionalism, the progressive division of labour or ongoing differentiation, but rather as a theorist of the constitution of a new order, of new norms. The theoretical bearing of this altered interpretation lies in expanding the model of utilitarianism and normativity to include a third position, namely creativity. Only an inquiry into the conditions for the creativity of collective and individual action as well as into the linking of creativity and responsibility (normativity) can result in a frame of reference which is appropriate to an understanding of Durkheim.

I wish to devote but scant space to buttressing this image of Durkheim at the biographical level as well. No one disputes the great degree to which Durkheim's interest in sociology derived from a profound sense of crisis on his part and the equally great degree to which sociology was a part of an endeavour to overcome this crisis. Regardless of whether this crisis is viewed as particularly French or as holding for modern societies in general, most interpreters agree that Durkheim did not want to offset the destructive impact technical and economic progress had on community, bonds and norms by restoring pre-industrial conditions or trusting in the benevolent effects of evolution. His profound insight into the linkages between morality and social structure made him immune to any such idea of restoration; his polemics criticizing utilitarianism were aimed at shattering confidence in evolution. Recent biographical portraits by French scholars have provided solid confirmation of König's description of the hidden passion of Durkheim's apparently compulsively over-disciplined personality; Durkheim seemed to possess more the traits of a charismatic prophet than of a cold positivist or scholastic rationalist.[59] However, until now too little attention has been devoted to the fact that, for all his sense of crisis, Durkheim by no means saw rationality as a remedy for the problems, but rather from an early date proceeded from the assumption that there was precisely a crisis of rationality as well. The importance of the young Durkheim's enthusiasm for Schopenhauer has only very recently[60] been considered seriously: although the literature[61] has reported for some time now that Durkheim owed his nickname 'Schopen' to his enthusiasm. Schopenhauer and not Hobbes – the assumption made by Parsons, who had a rather limited background in nineteenth-century continental philosophy – must be seen not only as the source of specific assumptions in, for example, the study on suicide, on the dangers of the anarchy of the individual's instinctual life, but also for the presuppositions of Durkheim's 'rationalism', which from the outset was never a simple rationalism. The frequent description of Durkheim as being a Kantian is therefore not very helpful because it would make sense only if we imagined a Kant who would have been able to take up Schopenhauer's challenge. My biographical thesis thus reads that Durkheim was not a staunch rationalist who only fought against irrationalism in his writings for reasons connected with his cultural politics, but rather a 'reconstructed' rationalist deeply fascinated, even, by irrationalism just as he was a lifelong atheist fascinated by religion. Durkheim's personal profile cannot be described in terms of the character of Settembrini as opposed to Naphta, but is rather characterized by the passionate endeavour to achieve a synthesis of these antipodes, as in the case of Thomas Mann himself or, better still, of Robert Musil.

Durkheim's early writings, in particular his inaugural lecture in Bordeaux and its programme for an empirical science of morality, have been understood in the sense of a radical positivism, which is intended here to mean the reduction of moral questions to empirical matters. This understanding has been contested by reference to Durkheim's alleged Kantianism. Both views are to my mind wrong – proving the point shall now form *the first step* of my proposed interpretation. This part will be the most extensive one because Durkheim's early writings are less well known.

If we interpret Durkheim's early programme by drawing on his early reviews and above all the major piece on 'La science positive de la morale en Allemagne', then it quickly becomes clear that Durkheim was concerned with overcoming the contradiction between Kantianism and utilitarianism by means of this programme. In addition to a number of reviews, Durkheim's early writings consist primarily of his two comprehensive reports on his one-year stay in Germany. The reviews dealt mainly with contemporary publications which sought to define the object of study of the new discipline of 'sociology' and to anchor this discipline among the established fields of academic inquiry. Durkheim's commentary on the works of the early German sociologist Albert Schäffle tended to have a political slant. He defended Schäffle not only against the allegation that Schäffle blindly transposed a model of society as an organism onto social issues, but rose especially to Schäffles defence in his political differences with the 'lecture-theatre socialists' [*Kathedersozialisten*]. Schäffle's antagonists relied on authoritarian means of state intervention as the way of eliminating social inequalities, and thus overestimated the potential of legislative action. Durkheim, by contrast, portrayed Schäffle as searching for a path between the 'laissez-faire' of political economy and the 'lecture-theatre socialists' faith in the state. Durkheim's sympathies evidently lay with this search.

A further aspect of Durkheim's early writings involved his attention to religion and his participation in the contemporary debate on its future. Not only in his late work on the theory of religion but already in his earliest published pieces, Durkheim is to be found expressing his conviction that, contrary to the expectations of a vulgarized Enlightenment, if religion vanished, then something else had to take its place. To be sure, the Durkheim of this period – as evidenced in a review of Alfred Fouillée and in contrast to the late works – regarded religion only as a different form of moral rule ('une discipline sociale') alongside morality in the stricter sense and law. This rather narrow understanding of religion was, at the same time, the basis for the criticism Durkheim levelled against Jean-Marie Guyau, the French philosopher whose work was brought to a premature end by his early death. As is well known, Guyau's concept of an ethics which transcended duty was one of the ideas from which Nietzsche drew his inspiration. Guyau understood modern morality to be a form which does justice to the degree to which modern man is individuated; as a consequence, such a morality could no longer be composed of fixed rules, but had to be shaped by each individual. Guyau used the term 'anomie' positively to describe this situation: moral anomie was the morality of this highly developed state and religious anomie characterized an individuated religiosity without ties to institutions of the church or fixed dogmas. For the Durkheim of this period, who believed morality and religion were characterized by their obligatory character, this concept was a contradiction in terms. Thus he failed to see that Guyau's philosophy of morality and religion was as much as his own an attempt to overcome the antithesis between Kant and utilitarianism.

All of these early works were, however, limited in scope, and they command our attention in retrospect only because we may regard them as preliminary stages en route to Durkheim's later masterpieces. It was not these works, however, which made Durkheim well known at the time, but rather the two reports from Germany. The first, entitled 'La philosophie dans les universités allemandes', served more to describe the structures and curricula of German universities and ventured only marginal commentary on German philosophy itself. The study 'La science positive de la morale en Allemagne' was, by contrast, devoted exclusively to the nature of the humanities and political sciences in Germany. The essay is marked throughout by Durkheim's fascination with the high standards and the breadth of German scholarship. Durkheim has no doubt that these disciplines are more highly developed in Germany than in France; at the same time, however, he hopes that the more pronounced French public sphere will help these disciplines to obtain a greater practical effect than is possible in Germany.

As Durkheim grew older, the French public put him under increasing pressure on account of this favourable assessment of the state of the sciences in Germany; the tides of nationalism rose in the years leading up to the First World War and cast increasing suspicions on the free exchange of ideas between the two countries. This trend climaxed at the outbreak of the war, which prompted each of the warring nations to produce uninhibitedly one-sided interpretations of the intellectual history of its enemies.[62] Durkheim was thus forced repeatedly to proclaim his strong allegiance to the French tradition in a wide variety of contexts, as well as to convey the fact that he attached the greatest importance not only to the German political economists and legal historians, but also to the English and American ethnologists and religious historians. He was compelled to claim that the idea of sociology, however, derived from neither the one nor the other, but had rather to be traced back to French origins in Comte and Saint-Simon. Modern readers of Durkheim should keep their distance from the overly nationalist aspects of this question of influences on his work; it is of far greater importance to identify which substantive achievements of German scholarship were admired by Durkheim and what position he took on them.

The overriding issue in this essay by Durkheim is whether the contradiction between Kantianism and utilitarianism can potentially be overcome by means of an empirical study of moral phenomena. His first sentence laments the fact that the French debate had to move exclusively within this spectrum.[63] Later in the essay he makes clear why this option is a poor alternative:

The Kantians make morality into a specific but transcendent fact which escapes scientific observation; the Utilitarians make it into a fact of experience, but one which is not specific. They reduce it to this confused notion of utility and see nothing in it but an applied psychology or sociology. Only the German theorists understand moral phenomena as facts which are both empirical and 'sui generis'. Ethics is not an applied or derived science, but an autonomous one.[64]

The simultaneous opposition to both the Kantians and the utilitarians, in the form in which it is proclaimed here, runs like a red thread through Durkheim's works. It is visible not only in this early piece, but also in the introduction to the first edition in 1893 of the work on the division of labour and in the 1898 commentary on the Dreyfus scandal; even the 1906 essay on the definition of the moral fact is marked by the fervid conviction that Durkheim's own theory had achieved the synthesis which he had called for in his early writings. For that reason, and despite the fact that Durkheim makes use of Kantian motifs, I see no sense in labelling Durkheim a 'sociological Kantian'. For Durkheim, the similarities of the two feuding schools outweigh the differences, and he sees himself positioned at equal distance from each of them. He accuses both schools of taking not an inductive approach to morality – that is, by exploring moral phenomena – but a deductive one, for they decree moral laws. Both sides

> begin by reasoning as if the moral law was to be entirely invented, as if they were before a clear table on which they could erect their system to suit their taste; as if it were a question of finding, not a law summarizing and explaining a system of facts actually realized, but the principle of a moral law which would settle everything. From this point of view the schools cannot be distinguished. The argument of the empiricists is no less premature nor summary than that of the rationalists.[65]

This would suggest that the only difference between Kantians and utilitarians lies in the type of principle on which they base their deductions. Durkheim believes that the utilitarians take the principle of self-interest as their starting point whereas the Kantians start from the principle that a moral position is completely detached from any motives of selfishness. The utilitarians work from the experience of the agent, though defining the concept of experience in extremely narrow terms, while the Kantian concept of practical reason has room only for a pure morality, but not for the concrete features of social communities. In contrast to both the Kantians *and* the utilitarians, Durkheim and the German scholarly disciplines he admired wished to overcome the deductive method and to provide an exhaustive analysis of concrete moral phenomena. 'One cannot construct an ethic in its entirety and impose it on reality later; one must rather observe reality to infer morality from it.'[66] Durkheim maintained that the works of the German historical political economists constituted an initial step in this direction.

The German school of historical law had gone even further. To be sure, in his criticism of Ihering's *Der Zweck im Recht* Durkheim objected to the underlying rationalistic concept of action, which he claimed overemphasized the purposiveness of action. In contrast, Durkheim's repeated emphasis on how often we act without pursuing a clear objective virtually sounds like German philosophy of life.[67] 'To live is not to think, but to act, and the consequence of our ideas is nothing but a reflection of the stream of events which perpetually unravel in us.'[68]

Especially with regard to the theory of action, Durkheim finds a superior approach in the works of Wilhelm Wundt, whose synthetic thrust and comprehensive empirical orientation towards 'folk psychology' [*Völkerpsychologie*] Durkheim applauded as the basis for ethics. Durkheim stresses the 'law of the heterogeneity of purposes' formulated by Wundt; all actions produce more consequences than can have been entailed in the motives for action. The consequences of action never coincide with its motive. But as soon as we notice the consequences of our actions, we begin to formulate new objectives. These new motives for action are just as distinct from the previous motives as from the consequences of the new actions. 'The results of our actions always spread beyond their motives and, to the extent that motives approximate them, they move further away.'[69] Both Wundt and Durkheim regard this action-theoretical conclusion to be a further reason for adopting an empirical-experimental approach in the field of moral theory. It does not suffice to treat motives alone; not through introspection, but only in the world of the facts themselves can we determine what consequences actions truly have. We do not know all the consequences of our actions, nor do we always act with clear purposes, nor are the reasons for which we think we act necessarily the true reasons.[70] Hence we must rely on more than mere *raisonnement* in order to achieve progress in moral theory.

Although Durkheim regarded Wundt's work as the crowning glory of German scholarly endeavours in the field of morality, he by no means believed that his goal had thus been reached. Durkheim demands an even more radically empirical approach than Wundt. In his eyes, Wundt, too, held onto the notion of a *unitary* morality or religion and refrained from relativism in the field of moral theory (which is not identical with relativism in morality itself). The only approach which Durkheim recognized as an exception to this rule was that taken by the legal historian Albert Hermann Post, whom he judged to be truly prepared to apply a historical-comparative method without reservation to the study of moral phenomena. Such a method, Durkheim thought, led to the realization that each type of society has its own corresponding type of morality. However, such a typology was absent from Post's work; yet without it, Durkheim argued, even the comparative method would be difficult to put into practice. It was only after Durkheim had concluded his comprehensive survey of the literature that he encountered an attempt to establish precisely such a typology. I am referring to Tönnies' pioneering study *Community and Society* published in Germany in the same year as Durkheim's survey appeared in France. Durkheim's review of this book is characterized mainly by his admiration for and agreement with Tönnies, not only regarding the necessity of distinguishing two primary types of sociality and for a more precise definition of the type of 'community', as Tönnies termed it, but also in particular regarding the strategy of treating '"community" as the primary fact and "society" as the derived end'.[71] Durkheim's suspicion of German state-centredness, however, leads him to read into Tönnies' concept of 'society' traits which were far from the latter's mind.[72]

In terms of method, therefore, Durkheim is concerned to resist utilitarian reductionism as well as Kantian transcendentalism; he wants an empirical science which neither misses the specific character of 'ought' as opposed to 'is' nor remains lodged in mere philosophical speculation about that 'ought'. In Germany, of course, this programme ends in the snares of historicism.

Let us summarize Durkheim's vision of the empirical study of moral phenomena contributing to the solution of moral questions. He presupposes that philosophical moral theories respectively contain certain empirical assumptions about moral experience, moral reflection, moral deliberation or moral action. These assumptions, however, can be false or at least falsely generalized, as in the case of Kantian *and* utilitarian conceptions. The initial effect of the study of the historical and cultural variety of morality is to undermine our inner attachment to false ideas of morality. We acquire a more adequate image of what it is that actors actually do and experience in situations where morals are concerned. This has two contradictory consequences. It expands our own possibilities for action, and it raises our respect for given forms of morality. On the one hand, we become freer, namely freer of religious or philosophical ethics, and come closer in our self-reflection to the intrinsic character of moral decision-making; on the other, we reject the illusion of the arbitrary feasibility of moral phenomena. Durkheim stresses both that the science of morality helps us to exercise morality as an art in everyday behaviour more effectively and that every superficial modification of morality – for example, by political decree – rules itself out after a study of the internal systematics or morality and especially of the relationships between 'rules' and 'conditions'. One can find further proof for this interpretation in the fact that Durkheim actually practised this programme in subsequent writings. In this context, the penultimate chapter of *Suicide*, 'Relations of Suicide with Other Social Phenomena', and the 1911 essay on 'Value Judgements and Judgements of Reality' are revealing. In both cases it is taken as self-evident that 'ought'-questions cannot be solved by 'is'-judgements. However, it would not be true to say that – since no amount of empirical knowledge can relieve us of the burden of making normative decisions – we feel just as uncertain about the normative issues after reading Durkheim's discussion as we were before reading it. To be better informed on factual matters does not resolve moral questions, but alters them nevertheless.

Durkheim's approach on this point strongly resembles the pragmatism in ethics championed by John Dewey and George Herbert Mead, who also both presuppose a uniform act of reflection in which empirical knowledge becomes an element of moral consideration. This notion is elaborated in pragmatism via the idea of the experiment; Durkheim speaks of the historically and culturally comparative method as the counterpart in the social sciences to experimentation in the natural sciences. However, the pragmatists speak of the experiment because they are thinking of the actor's situation which is in principle uncertain and risky and whose future is unclear. Durkheim's plea for historical comparison is also oriented not towards a history which is of no use or even detrimental to life, but rather towards an improved means of coping with morally problematic situations by means of reflection on traditions, a reflection which is the prerequisite for developing them further through modification. Science, for Durkheim, does not purport to invent a new morality, nor does it presume to take the place of the members of society in solving moral problems; but by clarifying the conditions which enable a new morality to arise, science promotes the spontaneous formation of a new morality. It is in this sense that a 'science of morality' serves a new morality.

We must bear in mind this specific understanding of empirical research in terms of the science of morality if we wish to understand correctly Durkheim's major work, *Division of Labour in Society*. This is my *second step*. This study is without doubt an empirical investigation of the connection between the structures of the division of labour and the structures of morality and especially of the genesis of a new form of morality. If we think of Durkheim as a positivist, however, then this book contains an empirical theory as to how increasing 'volume' and increasing 'density' compel a division of labour to arise which leads via interdependence to organic solidarity. Now while this theory may well be empirically false, the fact that Durkheim also personally wanted this new morality to assert itself would then be but a secondary private concern. If, conversely, we think of Durkheim as merely a moral philosopher, then his preferences manifest themselves quite clearly; yet in this light, it would appear that they were without any relationship to the course of history observed or that he had simply transformed them by means of categorical self-deception into the automatic result of history. However, if this were the case, it would mean that he had had to resort to a position he had himself previously criticized: the belief in the benevolent moral consequences of the modern economy, which he regarded as an illusion of political economy. Both the 'positivist' and the 'moralist' interpretations are surely equally far removed from Durkheim's own understanding of his method. Both exclude from their considerations the moral self-reflection of the actors – the sole means by which the comparative method can become morally influential.

The interconnection of the division of labour and morality is conceived of in both interpretations as actions becoming habitualized as rules of action. It would seem to me, however, that Durkheim was thinking here of the reflexive insight into the requirements for co-operation. The morality of cooperation he seeks is neither a compulsory morality imposed by rulers nor a voluntary agreement between subjects as to the conditions which appear acceptable to them for dealing with each other, but rather the product of an insight to be gained reflectively into the functional requirements for egalitarian cooperation.

Weight is lent to this interpretation if we take into account the fact that Durkheim considered the enforced division of labour to be one of the pathological forms. If such rules were merely the habitualization of actions, then it would be impossible to understand what is pathological about this form. If, however, only just rules fulfil Durkheim's concept of organic solidarity, then it must mean that this concept is of value in itself. Durkheim's concept of the division of labour is intrinsically bound to his notions of justice, and Durkheim argued not for the necessity of social order as such, but for the necessity of a just order. Organic solidarity would then be a type of morality which arises in the participants by means of an act of reflection on the universal conditions of their cooperation. The more widespread cooperation is, the greater the likelihood of this reflective insight occurring. The modern division of labour can therefore lead to this new morality.

Now, there can be no doubt that Durkheim himself was far from clear as to how this programme should be implemented and consequently his efforts were fraught with internal contradictions. For one thing, Durkheim lacked the means in terms of a developmental psychology and a theory of socialization that would have actually enabled him to describe the genesis of a morality of cooperation. This deficiency comes into sharpest relief when compared with the empirical study Jean Piaget published in 1923 on moral judgement in children. Piaget was also the most vociferous critic of this deficiency in Durkheim's work. In the meantime, this criticism has often concealed the extent to which Piaget based his moral theory on Durkheim and to which Piaget's theory must be seen as a correction of deficiencies inherent in Durkheim's attempt to implement his own programme. Piaget expressly bases his argumentation on Durkheim's distinction of two types of 'solidarity' and also accepts their ties to two forms of moral consciousness. Piaget holds Durkheim's typology to distinguish between a heteronomous and an autonomous morality. In his theory of education, however, Durkheim's attention was riveted on the relationship between the child and the educating authority and did not account for the relationship of children with each other. Durkheim continues to see each type of morality as imposed on the child, even under the conditions of organic solidarity. 'As a consequence,' Piaget writes,

> where we would look upon the 'active school', self-government and autonomy of the child as the only educational methods which lead to a morality based on reason, Durkheim, by contrast, defends a pedagogy which is a paragon of traditionalistic education and, despite all the restrictions, assumes methods that are at heart authoritarian in order to arrive at the inner freedom of consciousness.[73]

Durkheim is, hence, unable to reconstruct the stages in the development of a child's ability to cooperate. It is therefore by no means a contradiction that Durkheim also construes the division of labour in a profoundly ambiguous manner. He does not distinguish between the antagonistic division of labour by the marketplace and the non-antagonistic division of labour by organized cooperation.[74] Yet the notion of the morality of cooperation refers exclusively to the non-antagonistic division of labour. Modern society based on capitalist industrialization, which Durkheim wants to analyse, is, however, characterized not simply by the extension of cooperative relationships, but rather by the generation of market-like processes and, as Marx would have stated, the contradictory unity these form with the expanded hierarchical cooperation within the factory. Durkheim's thought therefore necessarily itself becomes contradictory if he expects a new morality to emerge from this modern society. In fact, his observations confirm the dominance of anomie, and his attempt to interpret the anomic character of the actual division of labour as a transitional phenomenon is clearly an evasion. Durkheim's honesty as a scientist nevertheless clearly reveals this discrepancy between pro-gnosis and facts. As Hans-Peter Müller[75] in particular has shown, he shifts the weight of unresolved problems onto the level of politics and expects organic solidarity to be produced by the 'smooth coordination between professional groups, the democratic State and the individu-alistic ideal'. The study on suicide demonstrates anew the dramatic proportions of the crisis of the day and the sole possibility of resolving it – by means of a new morality.[76]

My *third step* is to attempt to explain the emergence of Durkheim's mature theory of religion in terms of this problem. My thesis here is that the theory of religion is intended to conceptualize the possibility of a stabilization and institutionalization of a morality of cooperation. Since Durkheim does not recognize the internal conceptual weak-nesses of *Division of Labour in Society*, he hunts for ways of additionally promoting and supporting the desired collective insight into the need for a morality of cooperation, which has not been forthcoming of itself. The theory of education had always served this end, and the theory of religion now increasingly comes to do the same. These two areas are linked by the question as to how an equivalent for the religious reinforcement of morality is to be found in education.

In particular it has been Ernest Wallwork[77] who has pointed out in his excellent works on the subject that Durkheim's famous shift to a theory of religion, which Durkheim himself attributed to his reading of Robertson Smith in 1895, should not simply be viewed as a shift to a discussion of religion, since Durkheim's earliest works already stress the role of religion as a social phenomenon. Moreover, this accords with the theory promulgated by his teacher, Fustel de Coulanges. In Durkheim's early works, the strength of common convictions is already linked to an experience of transcendentality and this is in turn derived from social phenomena. The early critique of utilitarianism already refers to moral and legal obligations legitimated by religion. In other words, the precise nature of this shift still needs to be pinpointed. It cannot consist simply of Durkheim's adoption of the theory of ritual, as Steven Lukes has assumed, since the latter theory did not appear in his works until many years later. Still less can it consist in the idea of collective effervescence. Although one repeatedly finds references by Durkheim to emotionalized collective states, it is not until later that they start to play a systematic part in his theory. This may be demonstrated by comparing the study on primitive classification systems with the major work on the elementary forms of religious life.

Wallwork maintains that the change is of a different nature. It consists in Durkheim's recognizing that religion is more than morality, value ideals more than obligation and sociality more than normativity. Durkheim was in a position to refer to this aspect as early as the chapter on altruism in *Suicide*. At this point it already becomes clear that solidarity cannot consist solely in subjecting oneself to common obligations, but also requires one to be tied to common values. This distinction is also at the root of that interpretation of the intrinsic logic of Durkheim's typology of suicide which enjoys the greatest acceptance among scholars today. With regard to educational theory, the case he submits is very clear. He wants not to retain 'under the name of rational morality ... an impoverished and colorless morality' by secularizing moral education, but instead to 'discover the rational substitutes for those religious notions that for a long time have served as the vehicle for the most essential moral ideas'.[78] Thus Durkheim accepted, with all the radical consequences this has, the problematic situation expressed in Nietzsche's dictum that 'God is dead' or in Dostoevsky's fear that all morality would collapse once the transcendental pillars of morality had crumbled away. However, he believes that he can show that there can be an intra-mundane substitute for this transcendental pillar. By this he does not mean the artificial stabilization of an outdated and decrepit religiosity or a bureaucratically prescribed substitute for religion.

The whole purpose of Durkheim's theory of religion is to provide an empirically founded theory of religious experience and religious action in order to be able to preserve precisely these modes of experience and action under non-religious conditions. The science of morality is thus transformed into a science of religion which, however, has the same status: neither science is dogmatic in moral or religious terms or indifferent towards morals or religion. In the theory of religion, however, Durkheim elucidates not the ways in which the actors relate moral obligations to situations, but rather the manner in which actors are attracted by ideals and are lifted beyond themselves, and how these ideals in turn have resulted from action. Here the question of the emergence of a new morality becomes the question of the emergence of new institutions. This latter question is more comprehensive in the sense that Durkheim does not mean it to address only obligatory rules, but rather principles constitutive for one's world. The theory of religion is intended in its most developed form to demonstrate how such structures emerge from the collective, expressive and extra-ordinary action to categorize the world, create social structures and forge interpersonal ties. It thus represents the step towards a theory of the creative character of sociality, a theory of society as the originating foundation of its own ideals. Morals and institutions are no longer viewed only as fixed forms, but rather are related to the process of their formation.

Just as many interpretations of Durkheim's further development have left the earliest writings aside, so, too, the late works which appeared after his magnum opus on the theory of religion are often ignored. Of these, the lectures on 'Pragmatism and Sociology' are worthy of mention. Regardless of precisely what motivated Durkheim to choose this theme – whether, as Robert Bellah thought, he wanted to avoid his work being confused with pragmatism, or whether, as is my contention, he recognized that pragmatism was the only serious competitor in the race to provide a theory of the social constitution of categories – these lectures fit superbly into the outline proposed here, whereas they cannot be grasped in terms of concepts such as idealism and positivism.[79]

My *fourth step* is to show precisely this. The more Durkheim focused on the world-constitutive role played by religion, the more important the cognitive processes involved in world-projection that also under-lay the moral regulations had to become for him. The debate with pragmatism offered him the chance to clarify his own theory on this point and at the same time to proceed with the old strategy of conceding that the criticism that specific 'vulnerable points' were purportedly irrationalist was justified, while at the same time making use of this criticism in order to reformulate the rationalist-Enlighten-ment heritage. A careful examination of his argument, however, also shows that, in a few specifics, his theory of institutionalization diverges from the assumptions of pragmatism. Durkheim believes that institutions emerge only in extra-ordinary, collective, expressive action. Yet none of these three forms of determination are at all self-evident. For one thing, such a theory focuses exclusively on major dramatic innovations and not on the gradual accumulation of consequences of action. Furthermore, unlike the pragmatists, Durkheim's exclusive emphasis on the creativity of *expressive* action ignores the link between this and the creativity of *instrumental* action, which is, after all, central to the development of science, technology and the economy. In the theory of religion, the exclusive emphasis on the creative collective also becomes problematic to the extent that the interplay of innovator and collective which characterizes Weber's charisma theory and Mead's conception of science receives short shrift. However, this appears to reflect the subject matter – totemism – since Durkheim shows in other works that he is clearly familiar with the innovating individual.

Durkheim weighs his programme down with paradoxes and flaws by concentrating exclusively on extra-ordinary experience and attempting to arrive at a social theory of the constitution of categories without a conception of everyday social interaction. However, even if, together with Simmel or Mead and in opposition to the late Durkheim, we continue to regard categories and rules as being constituted in partially anthropological and universal, partially historical and culture-specific structures of social interaction, we can nevertheless agree with Durkheim in maintaining that *comprehensive systems of interpretation* only become viable through situations of collective effervescence. If we are interested in the emergence of a culture's fundamental institutions and its world view, then Durkheim's emphasis may well be justified.

The arguments Durkheim fields against pragmatism, however, consist for the most part in stressing that action and consciousness are distinct and can be separated from one another. These arguments enable us to show that it is wrong to view Durkheim as being on the road to symbolic interactionism[80] or to interpret him as representative of the paradigm shift 'from purposive action to communicative action'.[81] In so doing, Habermas subsumes Durkheim's theory of action under his own in a manner just as rash as is his use of the idea of the 'linguistification of the sacred' to graft his own theory of evolution onto Durkheim's. Although there can be no doubt that in the field of law, for example, Durkheim really presupposes that the sacred core will pass over into political structures of legitimation, this by no means implies, as Habermas assumes, that a justified consensus can take on the socially integrative and expressive functions of ritual praxis. For Durkheim it is much more a question of the interplay of ideals and institutions. Not the ideal of consensus as such, but rather only its institutional forms can replace ritual praxis. In view of the particularity of each form of life, however, each of these institutional forms is permanently subject to the risk of diverging from the ideal which legitimates it. Yet such divergences raise anew the question of new institutions or new versions of the moral ideal. Durkheim is thus thinking not of a linear process of linguistification of the sacred, but rather of the emergence of a new morality and new institutions which express the new quasi-sacred contents. No ideal can elude this interplay of institution and institutionalizing process.[82]

In the months prior to his death, Durkheim worked on his last, never completed book on morality. A few sentences taken from the introduction, which was the last piece Durkheim was to write, demonstrate emphatically how central the question of creativity was to Durkheim's theory of morality and sociology as a whole:

> Every moral system . . . has an ideal. . . . But, beyond this ideal there are always others which are in the process of formation. For the moral ideal is not unchangeable; it lives, evolves, and is transformed ceaselessly, despite the aura of respect which surrounds it. Tomorrow's will differ from today's. New ideas and aspirations spring forth and lead to modifications and even profound revolutions in the existing moral code. The role of the moralist is to prepare these necessary transformations. Since he does not allow himself to be hindered by established morality but claims the right to make a *tabula rasa* of them if his principles demand, he can do original work and move into new areas. The various currents which flow through society, attracting adherents, achieve self-awareness and deliberate expression through him. It is these very currents which give rise to moral doctrines, for it is in order to satisfy them that moral doctrines arise. Only those eras which are morally divided are inventive in the sphere of ethics. When traditional morality is uncontested and no need for renewing it is felt, reflection on matters of ethics languishes.[83]

1.6   Elements of the Philosophy of Life in the Work of Ferdinand Tönnies and Georg Simmel

As we now know, in an early version of *The Structure of Social Action* Talcott Parsons devoted a whole chapter to a discussion of the work of Simmel and Tönnies. The references to Simmel were more or less completely omitted from the final version that went to press. The discussion on Tönnies was reduced to an excursus on his main book

Community and Society which was printed in a smaller typeface.[84] Even if the original text had been published, the discussion of these two early German sociologists would still not have been nearly as rigorous and as thorough as Parsons' analysis of Pareto, Durkheim and Weber. In his consideration of the latter three thinkers, Parsons paid equal attention to methodological and substantive issues, whereas his interest in Simmel and Tönnies was clearly limited. He was interested specifically in Simmel's attempt to define the object of sociology. And with regard to Tönnies' typology of community and society Parsons was intrigued by the question whether 'community' as a type could be adequately grasped using the means offered by a voluntaristic theory of action. When considering this problem, Parsons again touches on the question of how best to conceptualize a form of action that is not characterized by a clear distinction between means and ends. In Parsons' later work, Tönnies' definitions played an important role in identifying distinct 'pattern variables' of action. Initially, however, Parsons had only a relatively superficial knowledge of the writings of these authors.

This fact bears mentioning because it highlights the fact that Parsons isolated these thinkers from their philosophical and cultural background, an omission that was to have a profound impact on the subsequent reception of their work. What was true of Weber and Durkheim is true to an even greater extent of Simmel and Tönnies: it is predominantly their directly sociological works that have been studied, although these could hardly be adequately understood if read in isolation from their other works. We must therefore shed some light on the background involved if we are to prove that the issue of creativity also played a major role in the thought of these two classical sociologists.[85]

On various occasions, Ferdinand Tönnies himself indicated the significance of both Schopenhauer's and Nietzsche's thought for his own development.[86] As a young man, Tönnies positively enthused over Nietzsche's early essays and they, in turn, inspired him to study Schopenhauer. Nietzsche appealed to a whole generation because – in Tönnies' words – his writings presented young readers with a 'gospel of creative power, an appeal to the genius, pouring delightful scorn on narrow-minded authorities and conventional opinions'.[87] This sentence is admittedly to be found in Tönnies' critical reflections on the Nietzsche cult he himself had once been quite close to – he devoted an entire book to studying this phenomenon. It is easy to forget that Tönnies had once been an admirer of Nietzsche, knowing as we do that his most important ambitions were pro-scientific, pro-

Enlightenment and in favour of social reform. Yet this did not mean, any more than it did in Durkheim's case, that Tönnies was utterly ignorant of, or totally opposed to, the strands of cultural critique and a critique of rationality that were present in *fin de siècle* thought. Tönnies hoped that the nascent social sciences would provide a synthesis for all this, something that could not be expected of the fashionable irrationalist 'philosophies of life'.

This also gave him the confidence to launch a polemic against Schopenhauer, whom he attacked for having ignored one of the most important scholarly innovations of the nineteenth century, namely the theory of evolution, and to attack Nietzsche for 'the most profound ignorance of the social sciences'[88] which the latter's critique of morality displayed. However, all this was not the result of a vulgar positivist having failed to understand philosophy. The whole thrust of Tönnies' main work remained influenced by Schopenhauer. After all, the simple idea of deriving the basic forms of sociality from the basic forms of the will can be grasped only within the framework of such an influence. Tönnies did not, of course, wish to be identified with Schopenhauer's metaphysical concept of the will; but even Nietzsche had already started to read Schopenhauer less as a metaphysician and more as a psychologist. Although it is certainly true that Tönnies' biography was influenced by the early forms of a philosophy of life,[89] and the conceptual framework of his main work was indebted to it, what is even more important, to my mind, is the fact that such a nascent philosophy of life was also the source of allusions to a third entity that transcended the dualism of community versus society, of the essential will [*Wesenwille*] versus freely chosen will [*Kürwille*]. Paragraph 34 in the section on the theory of the will, for example, not only contrasts the two types of will with reference to gender-specific roles, but also envisions a type of personality that overcomes this dualism. This type is promptly labelled 'genius': 'Genius, as mental will, has an equal part in both characters; based on feminine nature but perfected in the man, it is as much inner, dark, and passive, as outer, bright, and active life and thinking.'[90] However 'patriarchal' Tönnies' language may be, the theoretical conception is highly modern. With regard to the two types of sociality he construes, we again find that Tönnies occasionally indicates that new communities could indeed emerge and thus that the historical trend towards the loss of community can indeed be halted, for example, by fostering the cooperative elements in modern 'society'. Here too, with regard to the emergence of new communities, Tönnies draws on the body of thought associated with the tradition of creativity. In a letter to Harald

Höffding he emphasized that 'at the present time, as at any time, a free association *could* establish a true and perfect community, indeed even the highest form of community, given the right attitude among its members and provided that all efforts are directed towards this goal. It is a kind of progenitive act – like artistic creation.'[91]

In the case of Georg Simmel, Parsons' exclusive focus on the former's specifically sociological writings is even harder to justify than it was in the case of Tönnies. German sociology in Simmel's day was presumably more strongly influenced by his philosophical essays and his cultural criticism than by his explicitly sociological writings. As early as the mid-1890s, Simmel started to turn his back on the academic currents which had initially shaped his thought and to turn instead to Nietzsche's philosophy.[92] At a later date he was also influenced by Henri Bergson's philosophy of life, the importance of which he even defended during the First World War, in other words at a time when such praise for an intellectual representative of the enemy was decidedly inopportune.[93] His book *Schopenhauer and Nietzsche*, published in 1907, is a brilliant example of his study of the philosophy of life.[94] In his examination of the culture of his day Simmel proceeds from an investigation of how the theory of differentiation and of a form of rationalization induced by a money-based economy collides with the individual's claim to creative development as championed by the philosophy of life. In the course of this development, the concept of form, which he had initially used as an abstract epistemological notion, increasingly becomes imbued with a meaning drawn from the philosophy of life. In some of his books, Simmel analyses great creative individuals such as Michelangelo and Rembrandt. The pathos of creativity and indeed even his favourite examples, Shakespeare and Strasburg Cathedral, are presented as if Simmel were taking up ideas of the *Sturm und Drang* movement where the young Goethe and the young Herder left off. Yet this should not be allowed to disguise the fact that Simmel took a predominantly tragic view of modernity. In modernity, the eternal conflict between pulsating life and ossifying form becomes intensified, so Simmel believed, to the point of a 'struggle of life against the form as such, against the *principle* of form'.

> This tension soon expresses itself in this sphere and in that; eventually it develops into a comprehensive cultural necessity. Thus life perceives 'the form as such' as something which has been forced upon it. It would like to puncture not only this or that form, but form *as such*, and to absorb the form in its immediacy, to let its own power and fullness

stream forth just as if it emanated from life's own source, until all cognition, values, and forms are reduced to direct manifestations of life.[95]

Simmel interprets a wealth of modern cultural phenomena, ranging from expressionist art to pragmatist philosophy, in terms of this struggle against the principle of form. What is decisive here is that the vantage point from which Simmel evaluates the trends towards rationalization and differentiation in modernity and is sensitized to their existence stems from intellectual endeavours to grasp the essence of creativity.

In other words, the thought of all of the writers on sociology whose works Parsons analyses (including Simmel, although he no longer featured in the final version of *The Structure of Social Action*) cannot be understood adequately if addressed solely in terms of 'utilitarianism versus normativity'. This schema may be useful when studying their relation to economic theory but not their links to philosophy. Parsons failed to recognize that the classical thinkers of sociology were not attempting to erect the new discipline on traditional philosophical foundations, but that sociology was itself a philosophical project. Notions of the creativity of human action played a clearly constitutive role in the work of these authors.[96] However, none of the thinkers Parsons studied succeeded in smoothly integrating their thoughts on a theory of creativity into the rest of their work. One of the reasons for this may have been the insufficient clarity of the theory of creativity itself. Our next step will therefore be to establish what fundamental types of theories of creativity have evolved in the course of intellectual history and elucidate what their achievements and shortcomings teach us with regard to a theory of action.

2

Metaphors of Creativity

The marginal role accorded creativity in sociology, especially among the ideas of human action that are so fundamental to that discipline, is by no means typical of the other currents of intellectual history over the past two centuries. On the contrary, since the mid-eighteenth century the idea of the creative possibilities of human action has itself become the point of departure for a number of major intellectual innovations. Each of these innovations has, admittedly, had its own inherent problems, unintended subsequent effects and insurmountable deficiencies. The aim of this chapter is not to construct a coherent history of the idea of creativity, but rather to proffer a typology that characterizes the most important forms in which the idea of creativity has surfaced and become influential. The terms used in such contexts were seldom introduced with clear and precise definitions; for the most part, the writers were tentatively groping for a theoretical articulation of phenomena known to them from personal experience. Their formulations consequently were not phrased in terms of the emotionless objectivity of pure thought, but frequently remained metaphorical and circumscriptive, and often conveyed a mood of enthusiasm. It is for this reason that I refer not to concepts or models of creativity, but to *metaphors*. When attempting to understand metaphors we have to apply skills different from those used in dealing with scientific concepts in the strict sense. We at least have to be willing to accept the tentatively circumscribed phenomenon as something which can actually be experienced.

From the period between 1750 and 1850, I would single out three such metaphors as being of particular importance. I shall examine each in turn by considering the work of an author whose ideas on action were fundamentally influenced by the metaphor in question. I am referring here to the idea of expression in the work of Johann Gottfried Herder, and the ideas of production and revolution in Karl Marx's writings. Although it is difficult to trace precisely how these three ideas were subsequently received, they appear to me to be more than merely a random selection from the pool of available ideas on creativity. Rather, each of them represents an attempt to anchor human creativity in at least one of the three ways of relating to the world.[1] The idea of *expression* circumscribes creativity primarily in relation to the subjective world of the actor. The idea of *production* relates creativity to the objective world, the world of material objects that are the conditions and means of action. And finally, the idea of *revolution* assumes that there is a potential of human creativity relative to the social world, namely that we can fundamentally reorganize the social institutions that govern human coexistence. However, none of these three ideas is able to define creativity in a manner broad enough to cover all three ways of relating to the world. There is therefore a danger with all of them that the type of human action which each idea serves to elaborate might be falsely generalized as an exhaustive definition of human action as such. Attempts to interpret all human action as either expressive, productive or revolutionary can thus never produce fully satisfactory theories. It was not until the latter half of the nineteenth century that attempts were made to define creativity in a more profound way than simply by reference to one single type of human action, which obviously could not encompass all action. As I see it, the two most important attempts in this direction are, in Europe, the philosophy of life – which was, admittedly, indebted to the early ideas of Schopenhauer – and, in America, pragmatism. The term 'life' in the philosophy of life and the concept of '*intelligence*' in pragmatism are different ways of trying to grasp creativity. The difference between these two attempts appears to me to be of crucial importance to the present-day intellectual situation. What is at stake here is whether the nexus between creativity and action is upheld. One possible consequence of the metaphor of 'life' is that creativity is, so to speak, given a position at too deep a level, that is, deeper than human action. In this case, we have to insist not only, in opposition to the reductionist outlook of utilitarian and normativist approaches, on the *creativity* of action, but also, in opposition to the philosophy of life, on the creativity of *action*.

It would, of course, be quite wrong to assume that the development of sociological theory took place in isolation from the currents of thought described here. We can hardly overestimate the impact the philosophy of life had on the classic figures of European sociology, and the significance of pragmatism for the founders of American sociology, the Chicago School. The thought of Karl Marx was of eminent significance, at least for the early German sociologists, no matter how critically they regarded it. And Herder's idea of expression not only influenced the German idealism of Goethe's time, but also became decisive for Dilthey's attempts to construct a hermeneutic theory of the humanities and for 'philosophical anthropology' in Germany, two further intellectual strands without which German sociology would be unthinkable. My claim is not, therefore, that sociology must be opened up to these currents of thought. Rather, I am saying that the conception of action which is so crucial to how sociology understands itself needs to be reconstructed in such a way that this conception is no longer confined to the alternative of a model of rational action versus normatively oriented action, but is able to incorporate the creative dimension of human action into its conceptual structure and thus also to take adequate account of the intellectual currents which hinge on this dimension.

There are problems with any attempt of this kind. The notion of creativity, which first entered the German language (as '*Kreativität*') after the Second World War as a borrowing from the scientific language of American psychology, is today regarded as an 'in-word'. In the language of advertising, and particularly in leisure culture, it has become a slogan for activities which help to relieve the stress of work or to compensate for the emptiness of life as a housewife. This reduces the concept to trivial aesthetic activities in the private sphere (a classic example being pottery). Neo-conservative writers, from Niklas Luhmann to Allan Bloom, pour scorn on the yearning of the masses for self-development and self-realization, and decry 'creativity' as a ridiculous democratization of the ideology of the genius.[2] A more obvious interpretation would be to consider the ideology of the genius as an undemocratic distortion of the idea of creativity. The fact that 'creativity' has become a fashionable word is, however, a relatively minor obstacle to a serious study of the phenomenon it denotes. A greater barrier is the fear, particularly widespread in Germany, that to stress creativity is to take up the thread of the worst sides of the German tradition, namely anti-Enlightenment and irrationalism, which – so it is argued – leads from the pseudo-geniuses of the *Sturm und Drang* generation via Nietzsche's arrogance towards the average human being down to the absolute nadir, namely the Führer cult during the Third Reich. The emphasis on human creativity in production or revolution, which originated in Marx's thought, appears to be no less compromised from a political and moral point of view, seeming as it does to be the source of a theoretical compulsion to attribute creative qualities to a macrosubject that pervades the whole of society, thus providing totalitarian one-party dictatorship with a clear conscience from the point of view of the philosophy of history. The general fear, then, is that any emphasis on creativity may open a Pandora's Box which, for the sake of rationalism and Enlightenment, would be best left closed. This aversion, which, given Germany's history, is not altogether unfounded, can be overcome by looking at the intellectual history of the English-speaking world. Here the antagonism between rationality and creativity has never been as stark as in Germany. The idea of 'creative imagination' evolved in the context of a network of Enlightenment concepts and an early empirical psychology.[3] Whereas in Germany the concept of creativity was later characteristically narrowed to the aesthetic sphere, in the English-speaking countries this change did not take place, or at least only to a much lesser extent. There, it was possible for Newton to stand on an equal footing alongside Shakespeare as a paradigm of the genius.[4] It is therefore small wonder that the rediscovery of Herder, whose thought had lost favour in Germany owing to the sympathy shown towards him by the Nazis, was mostly initiated by English-speaking philosophers (Isaiah Berlin, Charles Taylor).[5] Within Marxism, too, a number of attempts have been made, and are still being made, to salvage the pathos of human creativity evidenced in Marx's theory in the name of democracy, anti-Leninism and anti-Stalinism. These ideas were developed primarily by East European dissidents, but also within French and Italian Marxism. And finally, in the case of the philosophy of life, a glance at the undeniable parallels with American pragmatism is enough to preserve it from all too hasty dismissal. Therefore, despite the strong case for scepticism, the final verdict on the power of the idea of creativity has not yet been pronounced. It may still be the case that creativity contains a potential for understanding all human action that none of the alternative models of action can replace.

A comprehensive history of the idea of creativity should not begin as late as the eighteenth century. On the contrary, it should go back to well before the Renaissance, which saw the revival of the ancient idea of divine inspiration, thus lending a proud new means of expression to the self-esteem of those involved in creative activity.[6] If we are justified in understanding the oldest known myths of creation as articulations of the human experience of the development and creation of something new, then it is surely with these myths that a history of creativity should begin. Sexual procreation, peasant cultivation, craft

production and victorious combat provide the background of experience which is typically drawn upon to explain the origins of the
cosmos or individual beings. The myths of creation vary not only in
the types of action on which they are based, but also in the answer
they give to the number of creators and the starting point of creation.
The decisive answer as far as European and American intellectual
history is concerned has of course been the Christian creed of *creatio
ex nihilo*, a creation of the world out of nothing by the one and only
God of creation. However, this Christian tradition has throughout its
entire history been permeated by the very different tenets of the
ancient Greek tradition, which, on the one hand, includes the concept
of the 'demiurge', implying action oriented towards eternal ideas and
the remodelling of material which it did not create itself but found
there to use; on the other hand, it is a tradition in which a wealth of
experiences survive to show creation not as a well-ordered process
but as one that is fraught with conflict and danger. The intimidating
nature of these notions and the obvious threat posed to Christian
monotheism by the idea of secondary and minor deities invested with
creative powers presumably led to the suppression of any real
discussion of creativity during the Middle Ages. This discussion re-
emerged in the early Renaissance, when, for the first time, reference
was made to the creative abilities of human beings themselves. The
poet and the artist, but also the mathematician and the inventor,
became the prototypes of the human capacity to actively create
something new. Thus, the relationship between divine and human
creativity, between infinite and finite creativity, became the central
philosophical problem of the day, losing the apparent clarity it had
during the Middle Ages. It was, above all, in England that the ideas
generated by the Italian Renaissance – as has been claimed for the
tradition of republicanism in the realm of political philosophy[7] – were
then developed further. The great advances in the experimental
natural sciences and the indisputable expansion of the known world
by bold discoverers reinforced people's sense that their actions were
not taking place within the framework of a creation that was given for
all time, but that they were capable of altering creation itself by their
own deeds. Likewise, literature was no longer necessarily the somehow idealized imitation of nature, but the creation of new works by
human beings acting as a 'second God'. Even if said without atheist
or anti-Christian intentions, it was still possible for talk of the creative
nature of human writing and poetry to be considered blasphemous in
Germany as late as the eighteenth century – after all, here were
faculties that a Christian could only recognize in God now being

ascribed to human beings.[8] To think of the creature as himself a creator was therefore an idea of the utmost audacity. Yet to apply this idea not only to a few 'original geniuses', outstanding scientists and artists, but to interpret the very creatureliness of humankind – of all human beings and the whole human being – as a creative force in itself went beyond even that. However, this was precisely the step taken by Johann Gottfried Herder when he developed his theory of expression.

2.1 Expression

The term 'expression' is undoubtedly a part of everyday speech. Without need of any definition, we understand this word and use it. 'Expression' is itself an expression of our language; yet we are well aware that, in addition to verbal expression, there are many other kinds of expression – the expression contained in a face or a body posture, for example. An expression – so we think – is given when something that was 'inside' surfaces on the 'outside' and becomes noticeable; thus expression allows us to draw conclusions about that which is inside. Yet 'inside' and 'outside' in connection with human action are mere metaphors. When we talk of something inside us, we do not mean a real physical inside that could be reached directly through an orifice in the body as an alternative to the merely indirect access we have via a person's expression. Whatever it is that expression brings to light, the relationship between it and the expression seems to be of a special kind. For in everyday speech we do not use the word 'expression' to denote every indication of something invisible. As a rule, we speak of expression only in connection with animate beings and their deeds. Yet not everything about these beings and their deeds can be considered an expression, and we know intuitively whether a sentence or a gesture has expressed something well or less well. We often look for a better expression and we can even help others in their search.[9]

In today's discussion of action theory, the phenomenon of expression is often so narrowly defined from the outset that it can easily be ingested into the conceptuality of specific theories of action. In the theory of rational action no mention is made at all of action as expression; if action is described as an expression of interests, the concept loses its incisiveness as a distinction, for one might just as well talk of the pursuit of interests. Parsons' normatively oriented theory of action rightly recognizes that the expression model constitutes an alternative to the means–ends schema of action. Yet Parsons was always only marginally interested in investigating this alternative; in *The Structure of Social Action* the expression model puts in an appearance as the quintessence of classical German philosophy. However, here Parsons interpreted it in an emanationist sense as the expression of suprapersonal entities in individual actions and not in the way which had developed prior to Hegel. Habermas' theory of communicative action refers to expression as an aspect of language. Correct though this may be, it is hardly satisfactory, as we must not allow ourselves to prejudge the question of whether all action may be construed in terms of the model of language and whether we are therefore entitled to conceive of the expressive character of a face or of a home interior or of a product of handicraft as a prior form or a mere analogy of linguistic expression. If we wish to take the wealth of phenomena of human action seriously, it may after all be necessary to regard language as a form of expression and not simply reduce expression to an aspect of language.

Herder's thought attempts to grasp the expressive character of human action with regard to an unsurpassed variety of aspects of it. It is this attempt which ensured that his thought, which covered so many different questions, none the less forms an integral whole. There is good reason to regard Herder as the father of modern anthropology, historicism, Romanticism and a cultural (as opposed to political) nationalism, as a 'German Rousseau'; indeed, within the context of the German Enlightenment, he can thus be seen to have inspired others to examine topics in a manner critical of the Enlightenment. Without this insight into the unifying theme behind his thought, Herder's work would clearly appear to be a disorderly collection of immature ideas which cannot compete with the great systems constructed by German philosophy. Herder's theory of language affords the easiest access to this unifying core.

In 1769, the Berlin Academy of Sciences held a competition in an attempt to resolve a dispute which had broken out between the members over whether the origin of language was divine or human. In the paper which Herder submitted in response to this question[10] he did not side with any of the various positions in the controversy, and instead put forward his own solution which justly deserves to be called a pioneering new approach to the subject. Herder won the prize; his paper on the origins of language was published in 1772. It is hardly surprising, given the context of Enlightenment thought, that Herder rejected the notion that human speech may have divine origins. The proponents of this position based their arguments mainly on the logical structures present in the grammar of human languages, and even on the miraculous fact that the sounds in all languages can be reduced to a small number of constantly recurring characters. Herder, of course, had little difficulty in refuting these claims. He questioned the validity of the alleged facts, pointing out, for example, that the most ancient languages did not display a perfectly logical structure, as one would expect if these languages were truly closest to the divine origin. And finally, Herder turned the argument on its head that language could not be of human origin because the invention of language required the presence of reason, for which in turn the prerequisite was language. For he argued that God could not have granted humankind the gift of speech unless human beings had already been predisposed to use reason themselves and to discover language.

He had greater difficulty refuting the typical Enlightenment claim that language had human origins in the sense of being a deliberate invention as a tool or a consciously adopted convention on the part of human beings. Herder extended this position to include thinkers who, strictly speaking, claimed that language had animal origins but believed that the transition from a natural state to a state of human social relations coincided with a conscious agreement to use language. In particular, Herder's polemic is directed against the hypothesis contained in Condillac's thought experiment, namely that the development of language was comparable to the interaction of two children in the wilderness. These children, Condillac claimed, learned gradually to associate a certain thought with the cry stimulated by a certain feeling, and then continually to reproduce this cry as a sign. Herder, however, stated that this ostensible explanation merely shifted the terrain in which the problem was discussed in a meaningless manner. After all, every animal produced cries in response to feelings, yet none developed human speech. No degree of refinement by the animal could propel this cry over the threshold to human language. The conventionalist theory of the origins of language could at best explain how individual linguistic signs were learned, assuming that the subjects already possessed the capacity for speech, but contributed nothing to our understanding of how this capacity for speech, or language itself, originated. Herder was thus implicitly adopting a new kind of position, not only on the specific question of the origin of language, but also on the question of the origin of society which is of such central importance to modern social philosophy.

Herder's own answer assumes that language originates in animal noises, but does not reduce human language to such noises, nor does he introduce reason like some *deus ex machina* as the ability to agree o)(

on conventions. The opening sentence of his paper, 'Even as an animal, man has language,' makes unmistakably clear his intention of locating the roots of human language in the expression of feelings. Yet it becomes human language only because the way in which human beings feel and the relationship between expression and feeling in human beings are not to be confused with the same phenomena in animals. In order to explain the origins of human speech, it was therefore necessary to found a new anthropology. The inability of both pre-Enlightenment and Enlightenment theoreticians to solve precisely this problem was proof in itself of the untenability of their anthropological assumptions. According to Herder, the specific quality of human language cannot be conceived of as an isolated faculty. The capacity for linguistic expression presupposes a fundamental difference in humankind's relationship to the world which has consequences for all forms of human action.

Herder therefore feels obliged not only to propound an expressivist theory of *language*, but also to outline an expressivist *anthropology*. The expressivist theory of language consists in viewing language not primarily as a means of labelling objects in the world but rather as an expression of feelings. The expressivist anthropology then focuses on all the physical peculiarities of the human being that make it possible for the structure of human expression to differ fundamentally from that of animals. Although Herder's writings contain a formidable list of human peculiarities – from the upright gait and the ability of humans to use their hands freely to the greater capacity of the human brain – he does not let these individual characteristics deter him from his search for a uniform underlying principle. Herder's influential definitions are well known from the history of philosophical anthropology in Germany.[11] The human being is initially regarded as a deficient creature, in that he is inferior to the animals in terms of the strength and reliability of his instincts. The corollary of this inferiority, however, is that the sensuality and the basic drives of the human being are concentrated less exclusively on a particular segment of the world. The opportunity of being more open to the world is thus a consequence of the danger of being less specialized. Man 'undertakes no task in which he therefore acts in a manner not open to correction; but he has much scope to practise with many things, indeed to improve himself constantly. . . . No longer an infallible machine in the hands of Nature, he becomes the purpose and end of work.'[12] Herder's aim is to identify in human beings a disposition which differs fundamentally from that of animals and for which he suggests the term 'circumspection'. The terminology itself is unimportant to him, however; his only concern is to avoid using a term liable to create the impression that this faculty is some kind of isolatable quality or that it differs only in degree from the capacities of animals. On the contrary, for Herder 'circumspection' characterizes humans in their whole being and from the very first moment on; it is not something grafted onto an animal substratum at a certain point in a child's development or in the course of human history. Thus, a reflective distance from the given realities of the world and from himself, born out of deficiency, becomes the unifying principle which separates man off entirely from the animals. And this circumspection, this reflective distance, is at the same time the precondition that renders the evolution of language possible.

Herder's anthropology thus differs radically from a rationalist definition of man as a rational being. He conceives of human reason not as a separate faculty which exerts a commanding influence on human sensuality, but rather as a specific way human beings have of interacting with themselves and the world. Language arises out of this structure of the human being's relationship to the world and at the same time refines it. Herder was an uncompromising opponent of Cartesian dualisms; the rational core of his opposition to Kant, which often overshoots the mark, lay in his resistance to the dualistic dichotomies in Kant's philosophy. Human expressive action is beyond precisely such dichotomies. Herder did not view linguistic expression in terms of some dualistic internal/external model as the mere transportation of an 'internally' preformed content of expression into an 'externally' perceptible form of expression. Rather, the human being who expresses himself is often surprised by what he expresses, and gains access to his 'inner being' only by reflecting on his own expressive acts. This draws attention to two peculiarities of expression which the dualistic model fails to address. Firstly, we form a clear picture of the meaningful substance of what we vaguely have in mind only through our efforts to express it; and secondly, in our efforts to express something, we always present that which is expressed in such a way that other people can appreciate it. Our relationship to ourselves is therefore conveyed via a medium which we share with others. Here, Herder is formulating insights which were to become seminal to twentieth-century philosophies of language – be it that of George Herbert Mead or that of Ludwig Wittgenstein. Yet he is interested not only in demonstrating the mediated nature of the act of expression, but also in the novelty of each new-found expression. Because of this emphasis, it is legitimate to describe Herder's emphasis on expressivity as a metaphorical version of the idea of creativity.

However, it is not his famous treatise on the origin of language but rather his theory of art which is the richest source of Herder's ideas on the creative process of the development of new expression. That linguistic and aesthetic theory should be interlinked follows necessarily from the concept of expression itself. If the human being who expresses himself strives for successful expression, then it follows that the expression can be successful to a greater or lesser degree. The poet is thus the human being who has the gift of being able to express his feelings where others fall silent in their helplessness, or attempt to express themselves but fail. The poet finds the new expression or the new style of expression. In order to find this expression, more is needed than a superior capacity for combining already existing possibilities for expression. Instead, a new kind of relationship must be found to one's own feelings. Herder's expressivist anthropology therefore strongly furthered the spread of the idea that the poet was to be conceived of as a 'genius' and led to the rejection of a literary scholasticism which attempted to lay down hard-and-fast rules for poetry. Creative self-expression is not necessarily attained by following these rules; indeed it may require the poet to contravene them, adapt them or even completely redefine them. The true poet does not bow down to any socially traditional form of expressing feelings, but grapples with the rules in search of himself. This search absorbs his whole person. Yet at the same time this means that art is the sphere in which a human being, whether creating or appreciating, expresses himself as a whole person; in this respect the realm of artistic expression goes beyond all rule-bound or set purposive actions.[13]

For all his enthusiasm for poetic creativity, however, it is far from Herder's intention to lend authority to those who would elevate art to a quasi-religion. Even if the expressive nature of human action is particularly apparent in art, he is certainly not saying that this expressivity is restricted to figures of exceptional genius and to their inspired phases. From the point of view of a theory of the creativity of action it is particularly important to observe how Herder seeks to avoid restricting creative action to artistic expression. Herder's resistance to this narrowing of perspective shows up in three respects: in his application of expressivist anthropology to the conduct of human life as a whole, in his assumption that the expressivist theory can apply equally to collectives, and in his reactions to those discussions of his writings which propagated an ideology of the genius or took an aestheticist stance.

In order to understand Herder's interpretation of the conduct of human life in the spirit of his expressivist anthropology, it is necessary to look briefly at the metaphysical background to his thought, which Charles Taylor has admirably reconstructed. Herder's expressivism is not a left-over from or a return to pre-modern ideas which saw the cosmos as a meaningful expression of a single creator's will in which each individual creature had its place, so that self-knowledge consisted in gaining insight into this predetermination and taking up one's place. Herder is very much already a child of a demystified world, in which meanings are thought to be subjectively constituted rather than objectively given, and the goals of development are viewed as the ends of actions rather than as some guaranteed finalism. Yet he protests against the total objectivization of the subjective, and against all bonds between the objective and the subjective being severed. In this context, Herder takes up the ideas of Aristotle, ideas which his contemporaries had just declared outdated, and gives them a new turn. His model of human development is no longer that of the unfolding seed which has been 'programmed' to grow and is now merely pursuing its prescribed course; at the same time, neither does Herder banish any trace of teleological concepts such as growth and development outside the sphere of biology. Rather, he conceives of human life as taking on the 'telos' and actively, consciously pursuing it. Each human is capable, he felt, of reaching the individual being that lies within him, his own developmental goal, by his own effort. Here Herder is thinking not of unhindered growth and universally binding developmental goals, but of the individual's unique core having to be actively unfolded. However hollow and clichéd phrases like 'self-development' and 'self-fulfilment' may sound to us today, in Herder they still have all of their original freshness. Herder's ideas on the conduct of human life are a synthesis of Aristotelian concepts with his expressivist anthropology. Just as linguistic and artistic expression cannot be seen as the mere externalization of an internally formed structure to which nothing is added in the act of expression itself, neither can the wide array of actions undertaken in practical life be regarded as merely the automatic realization of a life-purpose. On the contrary, inherent in Herder's emphasis on the active and individual character of each person's self-realization is the idea that it is only in our utterances and actions that we recognize our own potentiality. We accept a greater or lesser part of what we generate spontaneously as an appropriate expression of our being and accord this expression a level of recognition which we deny to other parts. It is only in the same process in which we realize ourselves that we become aware of the self that we are realizing. This is true not only of a gifted few, but of every individual. 'Every man of noble and vivacious sentiments is a genius in his place, in his work, to his destiny, and truly the best geniuses are to be found outside the reading room.'[14] Superior though the poet might be to other humans in his capacity for artistic expression, when it comes to the question of whether a person has realized his self, each person must judge for himself. If the conduct of human life as a whole is regarded as the expression of a self, then it encompasses at least the possibility of *all* actions and is valid for *all* humans.

The extension of his expressivist anthropology to apply to collectives and cultures is another indication that Herder was concerned with neither an elitist nor an aestheticist limitation of the idea of creativity. Herder did not only see collectives and cultures as the preconditions that make individual self-development possible, but conceived of cultural forms in terms of collective self-realization. Language, literature, religion, all the institutions of a people are themselves either a successful or an inappropriate expression of the life of that people. This idea places Herder among the originators of historicism and the 'humanities' [*Geisteswissenschaften*] which evolved so impressively in Germany during the nineteenth century. Yet the same idea is also frequently misinterpreted as the forerunner of a nationalism based on racial superiority. Herder's intention was not to define culture in biological terms, nor to claim that some peoples had a higher capacity for culture than others. Rather, he was striving to understand the individuality of each different culture. Just as each individual can ultimately only judge for himself whether his attempt at self-realization has been successful, so Herder believed that each individual culture was incommensurable with any other in the final instance. For this reason he is sceptical about the adoption of cultural models. His polemics against the uncritical adoption of French models or the use of Latin as the language of scholarly life is not an expression of German nationalism, since it is accompanied by a similar defence of the separate cultural identity of the Baltic and Slavic peoples. The application of the expression model to the interpretation of cultures points both to a strength and to a weakness in Herder's thinking. His strength was undoubtedly the attempt to champion the role and the irreducibility of culture in its broadest sense, in opposition not only to the Enlightenment tendency towards interpreting culture as something determined by nature (by the 'climate'), but also to all forms of aestheticism. The problem, however, is that in so doing Herder seems to assume the existence of a creative collective subject, thus setting in motion a kind of cultural emanationism. This is a consequence not of the expressivist anthropology as such, but merely of its indiscriminate

application to collectives without due consideration of their intersubjective structure. If this structure were taken into account, the culture
of a people could never appear to be a uniform product, but itself only
a multifaceted, varied and contradictory complex in which the
medium of self-understanding and self-realization is never entirely
'home-grown' but always also includes foreign elements.

As Herder does not seem to have been aware of the problematic
consequences of this step in his thinking, it is not possible at this stage
to determine how he would have dealt with them. Not so with the
ideology of the genius. In the German *Sturm und Drang* movement,
influenced to a significant degree by the early Herder's writings on
literature and aesthetics, we saw the emergence of an irrationalist cult
centred on intoxicated, self-obsessed creativity which felt no longer
bound by the constraints of taste and which gloried in its own
exceptionality. Herder was appalled by these developments. Although
his thought had done much to serve the cause of this cult, he soon
mobilized his full rhetorical force to combat it. As an anthropologist
Herder had been aware from the outset that there could be no smooth
transplantation of creative pathos onto human beings: the limitations
of the human organism, its frailty and finitude, were for him a fact
that had to be accepted with humility. With each revision of his essay
'Vom Erkennen und Empfinden der menschlichen Seele' the tone of
his opposition to the ideology of the genius became harsher and
harsher, and he stressed more and more forcefully that it was modesty
which characterized true genius and that there was genius in each
human being.[15] Towards the end of his life, when Weimar Classicism
had succeeded the faddish ideology of the genius and reduced it to an
object of ridicule, Herder was able to relax his guard and take up
again the strands of the creativity idea that were worth defending. He
now complains that 'because a few brash young men misused the
term genius the Germans themselves poured scorn and disgust on the
term',[16] and attempts to defend the spirit of his thought against the
schematic clarification of concepts undertaken in Kant's *Critique of
Judgement*. He is particularly fervent in his rejection of Kant's distinction between artistic genius, on the one hand, and inventors and
discoverers, on the other, who, unlike the former, did not – Kant
claimed – create works by relying on their unconscious but proceeded
according to clear and reduplicable rules. 'Homer and Wieland are
not likely to accept this praise at the cost of Newton. In precisely the
same way that the poet creates, whosoever *invents* scientifically
precisely also brings forth something original, something new from
within which he did not learn – otherwise it would not have been an

invention.'[17] The idea that genius could also – and in particular – be attributed to scientists was so central to Herder's exposition because he was especially concerned to prevent creativity from being reduced to a quality of the domain of aesthetics. Herder's aim takes in all 'inventions, activities and productions' which human nature has brought forth in the course of its history:

> How unfortunate, if this were only to involve sculpture, poetry, rhetoric and painting, as if only these were worth calling works of *genius*. Whatever human nature has brought forth in genius manner, be it science or art, an institution or action, is the work of the *genius*, and *any* ability to awaken human gifts and encourage them to fulfil their purpose is precisely *genius*.[18]

In his subsequent elaborations, Herder assigns predicates to creativity which even go beyond both artistic and scientific innovation. The activities and effects to which Herder refers encompass preserving and helping, healing and peacemaking. 'Higher geniuses', he says, are those who *serve* humanity. It thus becomes abundantly clear that Herder wishes to reveal that creativity is innate to all human action. The main accent lies no longer on whether the result of an action has a newness to it, or the quality of an oeuvre, but rather on the vitality of the 'whole', the holistic character of an action, the way it is imbued with meaning. It is open to question, however, whether the conceptual tools of an expressivist anthropology sufficed to gain a clear grasp of this idea.[19]

Writing a history of Herder's idea of 'expression' as a metaphor of creativity would be almost tantamount to compiling a history of classical German philosophy and literature.[20] In the limited space available here, we cannot possibly trace the dense network of reciprocating influences, self-corrections and non-derivative new approaches which developed in the decades between 1770 and the mid-nineteenth century. There can be no doubt that essential features not only of Goethe's oeuvre, but also of Romanticism, would be unthinkable without Herder's expressivist theory. Of even greater importance than the direct manner in which motifs from his work were passed down, however, was the transformation of the expression motif into something new. What gave rise to this development was above all the inescapable tension between the expressivist anthropology and Kantian philosophy. A case can be made for saying that Kant's epistemological theory itself rests on the idea of creative imagination to the extent that it is this imagination that structures the appearances of the things in themselves in the first place. Yet there can be no overlooking the difference between Kant's ethics and the normative implications of the expressivist anthropology. Whereas Kant conceives of human freedom as the ability to control natural instincts morally, the anthropology of expression placed precisely the transformation of spontaneous urges into authentic self-expression, as opposed to laws and rules, at the centre of its idea of freedom. The tension between these two poles increased still further when Fichte gave the activistic interpretation of Kant's transcendental ego a radical twist. Wave upon wave of attempts to resolve this tension then ensued: Schiller's idea of play and aesthetic education, Kant's own attempts at a synthesis of reason and imagination in the *Critique of Judgement*, Schelling's, Hölderlin's and the early Romantics' combination of Fichte with a pantheistic philosophy of nature – a philosophy which had also inspired Herder and Goethe – and finally, the most far-reaching and systematic attempt of all, namely Hegel's oeuvre.[21] The wealth of ideas generated during that period is inexhaustible. Within the narrow context of an attempt to formulate an action theory, these lines of thought can be seen as first steps towards an interpretation of normativity by means of a conception of creativity. Despite their impressiveness, they are not, therefore, to be treated here as new metaphors of creativity. The only exception, perhaps, is Schelling's philosophy of art and nature, where his emphasis on the expression model leads to his developing a notion of 'production'. Yet this does not become a proper concept in its own right until combined with ideas about labour in the writings of Karl Marx.

2.2 Production

Although the idea of 'production', or of 'labour' defined as 'production', is not the only foundation upon which the action theory contained in Marx's work rests, it none the less constitutes an essential part of that theory. In Parsons' pioneering book on action theory, Marx was treated as having inherited two traditions at once, that of idealism and that of utilitarianism. Valid though each of these categorizations may be when taken in isolation, Parsons was unclear as to how Marx had resolved the contradiction between the idealistic and utilitarian conceptions of action, if indeed he had done so at all. However, the question how these two categorizations might be linked to each other remains useful for an understanding of today's debates on Marx's theory of action.

To many readers it may already seem an exaggeration to talk of 'today's debates' about Marx. Whereas for almost twenty years many intellectuals regarded interpretations of Marx as a medium for developing their own understanding of world and self, very few people seem to be talking about Marx any longer. The dominant problems of western societies, the relatively uninterrupted economic growth experienced by these countries and the collapse of the Soviet Union and the communist regimes of Eastern Europe seem to be cogent reasons for considering Marx's thought to be outdated. From this viewpoint, the only remaining question appears to be whether Marx's work is only irrelevant to the present day, or whether it has always been a false, and indeed a dangerous and harmful, ideology.

Bar a few sectarian groupings, very few people these days are trying to make productive use of Marx's thought. Among these few are the authors who are attempting in neo-utilitarian fashion to salvage historical materialism using the tools of an analytic philosophy of science and specifically of game theory.[22] The price of this attempt, however, is that they jettison virtually all of the philosophical aspects of Marx's work, thus eliminating the remnants of a Romantic or Feuerbachian anthropology in Marx, not to mention all vestiges of German idealism. On the other hand, game theory can indeed be useful if the aim is to fulfil the promise of historical materialism, namely to provide an explanation for the origins of collective action, and in particular of the actions of entire social classes. The motives of the Marxist game theorists appear to be threefold. Firstly, their method promises to satisfy the well-justified need to go beyond the confines of a theory which merely confirms itself by virtue of its intrinsic consistency, and to provide empirically verifiable models and hypotheses. Secondly, in the minds of these thinkers, the political intention of according greater recognition than was usual in the Marxist tradition to the achievements of the liberal tradition, with its emphasis on inalienable individual rights and liberties, coincides with a reformulation of Marxism in terms of methodological individualism. Thirdly – and this is presumably the chief reason – the turn to game theory marks a departure from the covertly functionalist explanations of political, legal and cultural phenomena in 'western Marxism'.[23] Anti-functionalist Marxists do not consider a phenomenon to have been explained simply because its function for the capitalist class or the state has been proven – or indeed merely conjured up – but only if it has been shown to arise from actions and the interwoven pattern of those actions. The bankruptcy of functionalist Marxist assumptions about the origins of class consciousness and social movements thus strengthens the belief in the explanatory power of a particular variation of action theory.

Thus, whereas these attempts, by deliberately syphoning off the 'idealistic' aspects of his work, distil assumptions from Marx which correspond to the theories of rational action and which can form the basis for contemporary empirical research and be tested in it, other authors claim that the 'utilitarian' core of Marx's work is precisely the reason why it is outdated. Prominent among them is Louis Dumont[24] who, in his book *From Mandeville to Marx*, interprets Marx as having merely extended classical political economy from a politically radical standpoint, rather than having overcome it in sociological terms. For Dumont, Marx is therefore just as guilty of the notorious failure of the economic tradition to solve the problem of relating economics to social and cultural factors as were the writers against whom his critique of political economy was levelled. Jeffrey Alexander has pursued this line of attack to the full.[25] He is well aware that Marx's philosophical and historico-political writings contain a wealth of elements which cannot be classified as utilitarian; yet he claims these are not theoretically consistent with the scientific core of Marx's work, which is to be seen exclusively in the critique of political economy. For Alexander, Marx's work is a one-sidely anti-normativistic attempt to create a social theory. A very similar line is taken by those who argue from within Marxism that if there is to be a further development of Marxism it must lie in focusing greater attention on the significance of cultural factors.[26] Where the Marxist game theorists and the cultural theory critics differ from one another is not so much in their understanding of Marx but rather in their understanding of utilitarianism. For the former, if Marx's work could be reformulated using the theory of rational action it would finally be freed from the ballast of German philosophical profundity and could thus be preserved in a clear and rational form. For the latter, Marx's work is deficient, sociologically speaking, precisely because its core is utilitarian. For both camps, the 'rationalists' and the 'normativists' alike, everything hinges on the question of Marx's theory of action, because this forms the only possible link between Marx's critique of political economy and his political sociology. Anyone who chooses, within the framework of Marxist discussions, not to dispense with this link from the start, is therefore obliged to deal with the question of Marx's theory of action.

The very radicalism with which Alexander propounds his theory of the utilitarian character of Marx's systematic theory presents us with a salutary obligation to clarify the issue. Alexander cuts off preferred escape routes in the argument that were often resorted to when apologists tried to defend Marx against any form of criticism. He refuses to accept the claim that Marx's substantive research was superior to his own methodological interpretations: on the contrary, the charge of utilitarianism can be levelled above all at the substantive research. He also rejects the adequacy of references to Marx's political journalism and even to his historiographical works, as these may have been an expression of his world view and his tacit knowledge, but were not the systematic products of his conceptual approach. And finally, Alexander dismisses attempts to cite instances of individual cultural elements in Marx's works as evidence against the interpretation of Marx as a representative of the utilitarian tradition on the grounds that in every theory aspects which have systematically been excluded often surface in the form of residual categories, and that therefore, far from refuting such a critique, the sporadic nature of such references in Marx's work tends to confirm that it is justified.

Debating the exact form of Marx's theory of action highlights in a new way the problem of continuity and discontinuity in the development of Marx's thought. Alexander puts an earlier date on the oft-cited rupture in Marx's development than anyone else hitherto: 1842–3. He sees the very young Marx as a 'normative idealist' and claims that Marx's earliest writings can only be understood in terms of the conflict between the dictates of a universalist morality and the institutionalized norms of the Prussian-dominated Germany of the day. The rupture then came as a result of Marx's (purported) recognition of the futility of moral critique. Such a form of critique had no effect at the time; the only model, Alexander continues, that Marx believed could help to foster an understanding of the world and appropriate action within it was that developed by classical political economy, which conceived of mutually competing subjects engaged in utilitarian-egoistic action. According to this view, Marx's reception of this form of political economy and his break with normative idealism more or less coincided – if we disregard the lack of clarity and the ambivalences of a brief intermediary period. In theoretical terms, this means that Marx had not overcome utilitarianism at all, but on the contrary had fully accepted it as applying to the age of capitalism. More specifically, Alexander asserts that Marx adopted the utilitarian theory of action, but not the utilitarian theory of order. On this second level, says Alexander, Marx's emphasis on the class structure of the capitalist order and on the class conflicts that take place within it differs radically from the notions of the classical utilitarians. Here too, then, the crux of the matter is whether the 'utilitarianism versus normativity' model is at all sufficient for an understanding of Marx. It is, after all, conceivable that this model does not allow us fully to reconstruct Marx's point of departure and the nature of his reception and critique of political economy. A rough sketch of an alternative interpretation of Marx's development is therefore indispensable.

It is undoubtedly true that Marx's starting point was the moral protest of a young bourgeois intellectual against the rift that had opened up between the 'citoyen' and the 'bourgeois', against the failure of bourgeois-capitalist society to put its ideals into practice. Yet from the outset this moralistic political motive was to be of theoretical significance, in particular because it expressed itself as a critique of an attempt to fuse these parts back together again: namely Hegel's attempt to portray the Prussian monarchist state and its caste of government officials as the embodiment of the idea of a whole, a 'moral totality'. In his critique of Hegel's philosophy of right and in particular the sections referring to constitutional law, Marx takes issue with the idea that the state could successfully 'sublate' the antagonisms within bourgeois society. On the contrary, if such sublation is the goal, it can only be achieved by overcoming both bourgeois society *and* the state. This is no 'normative idealism', but rather the activistic adaptation of an attempt precisely to transcend a normative critique which views contemporary society in terms of a confrontation between the 'is' and the 'ought' and to conceive of existing institutions as an expression of ethical life. Admittedly, Marx is obliged to go beyond the horizons of his time in search of a social force capable of overcoming that age, and so arrives by a philosophical route at the proletariat as the class capable of overcoming class society as such. Yet the ambition behind his attempt is shaped by Hegel's ambition and thus by a thinker whose understanding of the state was derived from concepts he had found in expressivist anthropology.

It is only against this background that the particular character of Marx's reception of political economy can be understood. What was involved was not a switch from a normative idealism to a utilitarianism relativized only in terms of a philosophy of history, but rather an attempt to form a synthesis of various heterogeneous traditions. One way of expressing the synthesis he was searching for would be to say that Marx was trying, by means of Ludwig Feuerbach's anthropology, to link the concept of labour, as developed by British political economy, to the concept of 'mind' [*Geist*] that had evolved from the expressivist theory of classical German philosophy. It is this which explains the significance of the production model of action. The key text which most clearly reveals this bold attempt to link traditions is to be found in the collection of Marx's Paris manuscripts of 1844.

These manuscripts not only contain the first traces of a systematic analysis of the economic theories of Adam Smith and David Ricardo, but also make clear – albeit in fragmentary form – Marx's endeavours to reinterpret the relationship between human beings and nature on the basis of modern economic theory in terms of a world view shaped by Hegel and Feuerbach. Our reference to a synthesis requires further explanation.

It was, above all, British social philosophy – starting with John Locke but particularly following Adam Smith's foundation of modern political economy – that put human labour on an equal footing as a major factor of production alongside land and capital and declared labour the only measure of economic value. Specifically following Ricardo, early British socialists honed this economic theory of value into an economic critique of exploitation. Their concept of labour remained as sober as it had been throughout the tradition of British economics. Now Marx placed this sober concept of human toil for the purpose of securing a livelihood and producing goods in relation to the idea of a self-positing mind [*Geist*], which is what the expressivist model had by then developed into. Starting from the sphere of aesthetic 'production', the idea of a 'productive' power of imagination that did not merely duplicate its environment but created a new environment had been developed into the concept of 'mind'.[27] This concept increasingly became the linchpin of classical German philosophy, particularly since features were attributed to this 'mind' that the Christian tradition had assigned to the divine creator. Establishing a link between the economic concept of labour and the philosophical concept of 'mind' promised a more profound insight into the historical significance of economic activity and at the same time a concretization of philosophy.

The ground for this attempted amalgamation had already been prepared by the anthropological interpretation of Hegel's concept of mind by several left-wing Young Hegelians, in particular by Ludwig Feuerbach. In his critique of religion and his programme for an anthropological philosophy of the future, Feuerbach had protested against the alienation of religious world views and against the emanationism of a philosophy of mind. With the intention of uncovering the human origins of the achievements that were being attributed to 'mind', Feuerbach's position was, unwittingly, not far removed from the older expressivist anthropology and some of the themes addressed by the early Hegel.

In his Paris manuscripts, Marx praises Feuerbach as the inaugurator of the greatest theoretical revolution since Hegel. Marx also regards the Hegel of the *Phenomenology of Mind* as having adopted 'the standpoint of modern political economy'.[28] The positive aspect of Hegel and Feuerbach in Marx's eyes was the intention common to both – although it led to different results – to conceive of all things human as having a human cause. For Marx, Hegel had already conceived of labour as the essence of human beings, not only as the process of creating value but as a manifestation [*Entäußerung*] of essential powers.

> The importance of Hegel's *Phenomenology* and its final result – the dialectic of negativity as the driving and producing principle – lies in the fact that Hegel conceives the self-creation of man as a process, objectification as loss of object [*Entgegenständlichung*], as alienation and as supersession of this alienation; that he therefore grasps the nature of *labour* and conceives objective man – true, because real man – as the result of his *own labour*.[29]

Immediately following this acclamatory statement – and the connection is not entirely clear – Marx qualifies his opinion by stating that Hegel's concept of labour is too narrow: 'The only labour Hegel knows and recognizes is *abstract mental* labour.'[30] Hegel consequently exaggerates the claim of philosophy because he declares 'the *alienation of man who knows himself* or *alienated* science that *thinks* itself' to be the essence of philosophy. In opposition to this, Marx seeks anthropological support in Feuerbach's critique of Hegel. Feuerbach had brought to light the tacit assumptions that lay behind the presumption of a 'thinking self' and interpreted the self as a corporeal self, a self with needs, including the need to relate to others.[31] Marx finds a basis in Feuerbach's 'sensualistic' and 'altruistic' anthropology, yet criticizes it for not being sufficiently consistent. The *Theses on Feuerbach*, written in early 1845, that is, after the Paris manuscripts, criticize Feuerbach for understanding human sensuality not as a practical activity in itself but merely as a form of contemplation [*Anschauung*]. Here Marx links the idea of self-production and creativity, taken from the philosophy of mind, with the anthropological thrust of Feuerbach's thought. Marx charges the terms 'labour', 'object-related activity' and 'production' with pathos without truly clarifying the concepts. He insists on regarding human labour as an object-related activity, and object-related activity in turn as a manifestation of essential human powers and as 'pro-duction', the bringing forth of something new in the world. In so doing he imbues all human creativity with the pathos which in Romanticism and classical philosophy seemed to be reserved for aesthetic creativity or for the mind realizing itself in history. Throughout the Paris manuscripts one can sense Marx's enthusiasm at this conceptual possibility. In the 'Excerpts from James Mill's *Elements of Political Economy*' also written in 1844, Marx paints in glowing colours a utopian picture of the kind of society which would correspond to the thus conceived human being. Here we also see that Marx is thinking not only of the fulfilment of the individual actor through his action, but also of the productive activity of all interlocking to form a producing and self-enjoying community:

> Let us suppose that we had produced as human beings. In that event each of us would have *doubly affirmed* himself and his neighbour in his production. (1) In my *production* I would have objectified the *specific character* of my *individuality* and for that reason I would both have enjoyed the *expression* of my own individual *life* during my activity and also, in contemplating the object, I would experience an individual pleasure, I would experience my personality as an *objective sensuously perceptible* power *beyond all shadow of doubt*. (2) In your use or enjoyment of my product I would have the *immediate* satisfaction and knowledge that in my labour I had gratified a *human* need, i.e. that I had objectified *human nature* and hence had procured an object corresponding to the needs of another *human being*. (3) I would have acted for you as the *mediator* between you and the species, thus I would be acknowledged by you as the complement of your own being, as an essential part of yourself. I would thus know myself to be confirmed both in your thoughts and your love. (4) In the individual expression of my own life I would have brought about the immediate expression of your life, and so in my individual activity I would have directly *confirmed* and *realized* my authentic nature, my *human, communal* nature.[32]

Rarely did Marx paint such a broad tableau of his utopia. Yet here too, and in all these early writings, the utopia is only the bright background against which he intends his picture of the present to appear all the more gloomy. For Marx, what characterizes the present is precisely the fact that human labour is not free expression, but merely a means to life. Under conditions of private ownership, labour is no more than alienation, leaving the creator no chance to recognize himself in what he has created. Yet this means that labour can no longer be a process of formative education for the worker. His essential powers may be expressed, but they develop independently of him to become a force in their own right.

> the object that labour produces, its product, stands opposed to it as *something alien*, as a *power independent* of the producer. The product of

labour is labour embodied and made material in an object, it is the *objectification* of labour. The realization of labour is its objectification. In the sphere of political economy, this realization of labour appears as a *loss of reality* for the worker, objectification as loss of and bondage to the object, and appropriation as estrangement [*Entfremdung*], as alienation [*Entäußerung*].[33]

Thus the cycle of expression and appropriation is broken. Labour under conditions of private ownership makes the worker not richer but poorer. The more production increases, Marx claims, the more the worker becomes a commodity, while the alienated powers of human beings become increasingly concentrated in the hands of fewer and fewer capitalists. In the fragment on 'Alienated Labour' ('Die entfremdete Arbeit'), which is among the Paris manuscripts, Marx again portrays alienation not only in the relationship between the creator and his product, but under the fourfold aspect of alienation from nature, from one's own activity, from the nature of the species and from other human beings. Marx thus places assumptions based in economic theory in a historico-philosophical context. The present, although an age of progressive alienation, at the same time opens up the prospect of an end to this alienation, which may be brought about by the workers sweeping aside the rule of private property and ultimately establishing the utopia of communal production under communism.

The genius shown by Marx in his ability to forge not only a synthesis of these currents in early nineteenth-century thought but also close links between these abstract ideas and the social movements of the age is surely beyond dispute. Yet in a sense Marx's synthesis may also have been too ingenious! The decisive move – namely to interpret labour in the economic sense in terms of an anthropologically conceived self-realizing mind – may also have allowed problems to be concealed and postponed which then re-emerge at unexpected places in the theoretical edifice. A whole series of such problems are worth mentioning. Firstly, the equation of labour with production in the sense of bringing forth new objects is open to question. It is by no means true that all work follows the pattern of craft (or industrial) production. The structure of action underlying peasant farming does not fit the pattern any more than do numerous other activities which perform a mediating, protective or serving function in the production cycle.[34] The typical domain of housework, by which care and order are provided, is equally at odds with the production model of labour.[35] If this is already enough to expose Marx to the charge that his theory of action from the start rested on overly narrow foundations, then this negative impression is strengthened still further if we take into account the absence of any model of action other than that of labour.[36] The expressivist interpretation of the concept of labour is clearly not up to the task of covering the full diversity of forms of action.

Furthermore, there is a profound ambiguity in Marx's approach when he interprets not only the labour of the individual but also that of the whole human species in terms of self-realization. This ambiguity arises when predicates referring to the 'mind', which in Hegel is singular, are transferred to what must necessarily be regarded as a plural, to the multitude of individual subjects that make up humankind.

> For, if the development of the human species as a whole is an objectification of their essential being, then none of the individual self-objectifications through which the human species is to objectify itself will be a self-objectification of the essential being of humankind as such, even though the individual, as a member of the species, has its being as his being. On the contrary: if individual labour is already a self-objectification of human essential being, then the development of the human species as a whole cannot be this self-objectification.[37]

Since Marx uses the metaphors of alienation and reappropriation of essential powers at one and the same time to apply to both an individual and a universal collective level, the question as to the relationship between individual and collective emancipation does not constitute a problem for him. The two aspects appear, as it were, intrinsically to coincide. This creates a whole series of further ambiguities and problems. Thus, for example, it appears to be a self-evident fact that the emancipation of the proletariat is tantamount to universal emancipation. All other needs for emancipation must then appear to be parts of this one great revolutionary process of emancipation. At the same time, we are given no clear picture of this one agent of the universal process of emancipation: the relationship between the pro-letariat as a concept of the philosophy of history, on the one hand, and the actual members of society who could be described as proletarian, with their wishes and orientations, on the other, remains extremely unclear.

The greatest inherent lack of clarity is the route which the alienated proletarians are supposed to take in order to form themselves into the revolutionary class. One can imagine two possibilities. Either the proletarians could be driven to revolution by the total expropriation of all essential powers and absolute impoverishment. I have the impression that, at the time he wrote the Paris manuscripts, Marx considered this a probability. Or, alternatively, the perverted experience of labour could provide the inspiration for the formation of critical, revolutionary consciousness. If that is what Marx was thinking of, he certainly did not provide an indication of how such a process could take place in the real world. If Marx imagined that total alienation would switch over into total reappropriation of expropriated powers, then here, too, one could wish for some empirical evidence of the connection between impoverishment or alienation, on the one hand, and radicalization, on the other.

Thus, the brilliant synthesis of strands of thought that lies behind the production model of action at this initial stage clearly amounts to no more than an almost mythological historico-philosophical construct, with a narrow basis in action theory. For normative reasons, the insight into the creative nature of production is extended to all actions of labour and is taken as the point of departure for sweeping claims about the present and the future. With his concept of labour, Marx undoubtedly developed the tradition of an expressivist anthropology in a direction which saved it from being restricted to the narrow domain of aesthetics. Yet he, too, equates the creativity of action with only one particular form of action, namely that of productive labour. The problems his theoretical edifice posed could have given him the opportunity to draw a sharper distinction between the technical questions of economic theory and the normative sense of the expressivist anthropology. However, it was not Marx's intention to draw such a distinction, which, although not exonerating political economy as a science and the reality of capitalist society it describes from any kind of normative evaluation, would none the less have meant that some of its individual institutions and mechanisms could be regarded as successful or acceptable. Nor was he content to stop short at a merely philosophical reinterpretation of economics. His path therefore led him not to a self-critical examination of the step which the genesis of this concept of production constituted, but rather to the full development of a comprehensive paradigm of production in the *German Ideology* of 1845–6.

In this extensive text, which also remained unpublished during Marx's lifetime, he took on the Young Hegelian thinkers, including Feuerbach; it is rich in ideas but often exaggerated in its use of polemics. It marks the point in Marx's thought where he clearly turned towards the social sciences. No longer content merely to combine economics and philosophy to form an abstract historical construct, he now wanted to get away from precisely such constructs and down to the investigation of actual history. For this empirical research into actual history the philosophy of history could only serve as a heuristic tool. At this stage in his development, what Marx regards as crucial for such historical research is the correct choice of a starting point. Marx declares this to be the *fact* of the existence of living human individuals with a specific corporeal organization and, inherent therein, a specific relationship to their environment. The starting point for an analysis of history is therefore anthropological. Yet it is a very specific anthropology, which, says Marx, can be deduced from the actual behaviour of human beings, and that is an anthropological compulsion to *produce*.

> Men can be distinguished from animals by consciousness, by religion or anything else you like. They themselves begin to distinguish themselves from animals as soon as they begin to *produce* their means of subsistence, a step which is conditioned by their physical organization. By producing their means of subsistence men are indirectly producing their material life.[38]

Marx is very definitely making use of the 'materialist' connotation of the concept of production, and it is from this initial historical act that he derives further assumptions on which to base his theory of history. According to Marx, the satisfaction of needs via production leads to the creation of instruments of satisfaction, changes the nature of the needs and transforms the relations between human beings. Marx paints in broad strokes a picture of the history of the world and its main phases, which are distinguished from one another according to the state of development of production. We are not concerned here with the details of the historical materialist conception of history. The important point at this stage is simply that Marx, without revising the production model of action and also retaining his conception of alienation,[39] portrays a society which could be described as a systemic totality subject to the functional primacy of production. His basic concepts still have something of that exuberant ring of the production model of action. The central concept of productive power is still meant to signify the productive power of human beings and not a technology divorced from humankind. Precisely where such a divorce has occurred Marx believes we are dealing with a symptom of alienation. In that case

> first the productive forces appear as a world for themselves, quite independent of and divorced from the individuals, alongside the

individuals; the reason for this is that the individuals, whose forces they are, exist split up and in opposition to one another, whilst, on the other hand, these forces are only real forces in the intercourse and association of these individuals.[40]

At this time Marx referred to the institutional forms of production as 'forms of intercourse' – only later did he introduce the term 'relations of production'. The original term makes very clear the connection with human beings interacting with one another; yet it is not possible to deduce from Marx's text exactly what he means by this human 'intercourse' in terms of action theory.[41] If procreation is redefined as production of new life, and if Marx speaks of the production of consciousness and the production of the forms of intercourse themselves, then the term 'production' becomes very blurred. Everything then falls under the category of production – intentional and unintentional, self-realizing and estranged activities alike. Obviously, 'production' then covers activities which cannot be classified as labour. Linguistic and cultural aspects, which were decisive for the development of the expression model, are now relegated to an epiphenomenal position by Marx's transformation of the expressivist model into the production model. Marx is not interested in reflecting on the applicability of the production model. He takes advantage of its normative undertones, yet develops it chiefly into a conception of society and history in which everything is characterized by the functional primacy of production. Although less markedly evident than in subsequent works, there is already a discernible tendency in *The German Ideology* to curb the power of the production model by turning it into a technological-deterministic theory based on the development of the productive forces. Yet the idea that all social phenomena, including cultural activities, are essentially the result of labour for the purpose of guaranteeing survival is in itself a theory that is very difficult to defend. It alters the question as to the possibilities of overcoming alienation. Previously Marx had argued as if only a revolutionary act of self-awareness and reappropriation of the essential powers in timeless space was capable of creating the preconditions necessary to overcome alienation. Now, all that was needed was the continued development of the productive forces and their conflict with the existing relations of production, a conflict in which, admittedly, one class becomes actively engaged in the attempt to change these relations and thus make way for the further development of the productive forces.

Marx's later oeuvre is characterized by an ever broader development of his critical reinterpretation of political economy and by an

impressively comprehensive set of analyses of individual historical
and political topics. In particular, his seminal work, *Capital*, is a
fundamental restructuring of his critique of capitalism. Whereas in his
writings mentioned hitherto the impossibility of self-realization
through labour under conditions of private ownership was the central
tenet of Marx's theoretical construction, in *Capital* itself (although not
yet in the *Grundrisse*) the idea of a self-positing mind is taken up in a
completely different form. It is no longer the individual producer but
rather capital upon which he now bestows the predicates of the 'mind'
and its development. Expressed in these abrupt terms, such a restructuring is bound to appear incomprehensible. Yet for Marx it meant the
possibility of appearing no longer as a moralizing critic of capitalism,
arguing from some external standpoint, but instead as a rigorous
investigator of the intrinsic laws of capitalism; and such an investigation of intrinsic tendencies would prove in all the more convincing
fashion that capitalism gives birth to its own gravedigger and is
therefore doomed to perish. The predicates of subjectivity and creativity are now no longer based in anthropology but, in imitation of
Hegel's dialectical logic, are transposed onto a subject, namely capital,
that positively destroys the subjectivity of the individuals subsumed
under capitalist relations. The analysis centres no longer on the self-
positing mind or the human essence that posits itself in labour, but
rather on self-realizing value. Thus, even this fundamental restructuring of Marx's theory fails to reflect on the problems of the production
paradigm – indeed it even exacerbates them.

The polemical intention behind the interpretation of capital as a
subject is quite obvious; of course capital is not the emphatic subject
which the anthropologization of the idea of 'mind' had aimed to
establish. Yet by applying these features to capital, not only is Marx
dramatically emphasizing in a crass manner the fact that social
processes become independent of the intentions and wishes of the
actors, but he also makes it conceptually difficult, if not impossible, to
grasp the sources of a subjectivity that is directed against capital. The
more consistently the theoretical edifice treats capitalism as a self-
producing and reproducing system, the less consistent becomes the
expectation that real human protagonists could change or abolish this
system – yet this is precisely the expectation towards which the
performative intention of the text is directed. *Capital* therefore opened
the way for interpretations which saw capitalism as a hermetically
self-contained universe of oppression and alienation and consequently
could only envisage a total revolution as the means of destroying this
universe.[42] For the new age it then becomes possible to conceive of the

total control of social development by way of the 'free association of the producers'. Yet if we do not accept such a Manichean interpretation of history, preferring more cautiously to oppose the subsumption *tendencies* that arise from capitalist relations of production to the resistant subjectivity of actors everywhere,[43] then the analysis of capital can only form a part of a social theory based on Marx – and certainly cannot provide the paradigm for it. Regardless of the logical status which Marx himself may have accorded his *Capital*, the means which he supplied transformed the technological determinism of the production paradigm in the *German Ideology* into a determinism rooted in the logic of capital. Strangely shifted though the constituent parts of a model of creative action might appear here, the influence of such creativity-oriented ideas remains constitutive for the theory, even if the form it takes is a description of the logic of capital. The specific nature of Marx's critique of political economy in its various versions as opposed to the original political economy cannot be understood without taking this influence into account.

Whereas the production model of action contained the normative idea of a free self-realization of all individuals through their labour, this idea was no longer clearly identifiable either in the technological or in the economic determinism of later versions of Marxism. It was therefore quite justified that the humanistic protest of Marxist intellectuals against the loss of utopia in the Marxist-inspired parties and their version of Marxism was repeatedly articulated by appealing to the passionate content of the concepts developed by the young Marx. The first attempts in this direction date back even as far as the interwar years; they received an additional boost when some of the hitherto unknown early works of Marx were published. And particularly in the period after the Second World War we find anti-Stalinist intellectuals in Yugoslavia, Hungary, Poland and Czechoslovakia, and also in Western Europe, renewing Marxism on the basis of a 'philosophy of praxis'. The philosophy of praxis was seen not so much as a continuation of ancient practical philosophy but rather as a theory which made Marx's production metaphors the ideal of all successful action and developed a normative yardstick for judging societies on the basis of whether or not their structures could rightly be regarded as the result of the will of the members of those societies.

The danger of attempts to renew Marxism from the point of view of the philosophy of praxis was always that they might degenerate into mere humanistic proclamations and tend to smooth over rather than expose the inherent contradictions of Marx's development in order to protect their own claim to present the true Marx in opposition to the ideology of Marxism-Leninism.[44] In particular, some of Lukács' students in Budapest attempted, by means of a relativization and internal differentiation of the production paradigm, to remain true to the claims of the philosophy of praxis and avoid the danger mentioned above. For example, several of Agnes Heller's works[45] contain attempts to draw a sharp distinction between a labour paradigm and a production paradigm in Marx. She defends the paradigm of work because on an anthropological level it contains the Romantic and emancipatory aspects of Marx's thought, that is, it formulates the claim that human work should be meaningfully fulfilling and creative. She rejects the paradigm of production, which she now takes to mean the whole complex of a theory of history in which social developments are analysed in terms of the level of development of the productive forces or the logic of the production and capital-realization process. She believes that by means of this distinction, the normative substance of Marx's idea of labour can be defended against the productivist philosophy of history, which, especially in our contemporary world when the ecological consequences of the growth of the productive forces can no longer be ignored, appears less tenable than ever. She is undoubtedly right to use this distinction to draw our attention to the fact that Marx's theory of history does not necessarily follow from the idea that labour is potentially creative action. Yet her solution appears unconvincing, both as an interpretation of Marx and as a contribution to theory formation. Heller's distinction, justified though it may be, is not reflected in Marx's own writings, from which precisely this distinction is absent and which alternate ambiguously between the various uses of the concept of production.[46] With regard to theory, Heller admits – under Habermas' influence – that a paradigm of labour is also flawed, because it does not adequately account for the intersubjective structure of human action; yet it seems that she, like the later Lukács, whose ontology she regards as an attempt to revive the paradigm of labour, is content to define the action of labour itself as the teleological posting of a goal of labour and setting in motion the causally requisite sub-actions.[47] Thus, Heller pays a high price for adhering to the idea of non-deformed purposive activity: she is forced to interpret all actions vis-à-vis objects – as is usual in the Marxist tradition – in terms of the labour model.

Another attempt to develop the motifs of the Marxist philosophy of praxis is that presented by György Márkus, a former Budapest colleague of Agnes Heller.[48] In opposition to Habermas' abrupt distinction between labour and interaction, Márkus sets out to demonstrate that Marx's concept of labour has potential on the level of both action theory and social theory which cannot be realized exhaustively if labour is interpreted merely as instrumental action. On the level of action theory he is above all concerned to point out that the products of human labour reflect, according to Marx, not only the inner essential powers of the workers but also rules of appropriate use and norms of social distribution. Therefore, on the level of social theory, Márkus argues, Marx's approach allows us to conceive of the labour process and the reproduction of social relationships as a single unity, a unity which is in danger of getting lost in Habermas' translation of his basic action-theoretical distinction into a differentiation between social spheres.

Jóhann Arnason, on the other hand, who in many respects is influenced by Kosík and the Budapest Circle, attempts to bring out the ambiguity of the production paradigm in Marx and Marxism.[49] In opposition to structural Marxism and to Habermas he undertakes to mobilize the meaningful substance of Marxian concepts such as appropriation, personal activity and association (or free intercourse) which are present in Marx's works but which cannot be integrated into the production paradigm in its typical form. Here Arnason uses these concepts to open up horizons – appropriation in relation to the world of material objects, personal activity in relation to the subjective world and association in relation to the social world – horizons that remained important in Marx's underlying thoughts on anthropology and which do not fit in with the model of a purposive rationality that gradually comes to be regarded as an absolute.

And finally, Axel Honneth, drawing on research in industrial sociology, develops

> the difference between an instrumental act in which the working subject structures and regulates his own activity on his own initiative, according to his own knowledge, in a self-contained process, and an instrumental act, in which neither the accompanying controls nor the object-related structuring of the activity is left to the initiative of the working subject.[50]

Honneth thus tries to keep the focus both on the genesis of feelings of alienation in the experience of labour, that is, the experience of one's own working conditions being expropriated, and also on the emancipatory perspective of a liberation from alienated working conditions.

Although all these attempts to build on the production paradigm may be cited as proof that its fertility has not yet been exhausted, it is possible to raise objections to each one. One could object to Márkus' proposal by arguing that the goal of an integrated reconstruction of various partial actions or social spheres does not preclude analytical differentiation; indeed, that, on the contrary, such differentiations are often the only possible way of achieving a convincing integrated reconstruction. Arnason could be faulted for tending to over-interpret comments by Marx that were not central to the development of his concepts, and thus placing the accent on precisely those features of Marx's underlying ideas that were not incorporated into his theory. In connection with Honneth we could ask whether normative demands relating to the organization of labour should have a status in normative logic different from that of other normative demands. If not, then his critical concept of work would merely point to an empirical dimension of the origin of normative demands, not to the existence of different grounds on which these norms are based. Surely no one who sympathizes with the motives of these authors has nevertheless argued more vehemently against the production paradigm and the philosophy of praxis and all its contemporary extensions than Jürgen Habermas. For an assessment of the significance today of Marx's production metaphor of the creativity of action, it is therefore essential to conclude this section by examining the objections raised by Habermas.

In his various writings[51] on the subject, Habermas bases his discussion on what at first glance seems a surprisingly broad conception of the philosophy of praxis. Not only does he include all those 'versions of Western Marxism that go back to Gramsci and Lukács' which referred to themselves as 'philosophies of praxis', but also others such as Critical Theory, and even 'the radically democratic kinds of American Pragmatism (G. H. Mead and Dewey) and of analytic philosophy (Charles Taylor)'.[52] At least Habermas does not parcel them all together as proponents of the production paradigm; here he distinguishes precisely those versions – derived from Lukács and Max Weber – of a conception of rationality and rationalization which do not rely on the production paradigm, above all the Critical Theory of Horkheimer and Adorno, from the phenomenological attempts to revive the production paradigm, as are found for example in the works of the early Marcuse, as well as in the writings of Sartre and Merleau-Ponty, where – according to Habermas – the intrinsic relationship between 'praxis' and 'rationality' is lost. This distinction, however, leaves us in the dark as to where the pragmatists and analytical philosophers fit in, not to mention the more recent advocates of a synthesis of phenomenology and Marxism. The extremely broad definition of what it is that Habermas is attacking makes it difficult to refer the arguments to the respective authors, as some criticisms apply to just a few representatives of this general current, but not to all. What clearly emerges, none the less, is Habermas' intention of showing that none of the approaches listed is capable of overcoming the shortcomings of the other versions he criticizes. Habermas thus subsumes under one single category various heterogeneous theories whose only apparent common denominator is that they do not regard the *Theory of Communicative Action* as having incorporated comprehensively the normative claims of earlier strands in the tradition of action theory.

Yet what are Habermas' main objections to the philosophy of praxis in general and the production paradigm in particular? Habermas puts forward three main arguments against the philosophy of praxis. Firstly, he claims that its idea of labour is characterized by a Romantic idealization of artisanal activity. (It is surprising that this should be treated as a feature not of the production paradigm but of the philosophy of praxis, to which pragmatism is also said to belong!) Secondly, all philosophy of praxis tends, says Habermas, to reject out of hand 'all structural differentiations that cannot be brought into the acting subject's horizon of orientation'[53] and thus to show a naive preference for de-differentiating complex societies, if not indeed to foster in a dangerous way the creation of hyper-macrosubjects which lay claim to social control. Thirdly, it is, according to Habermas, extremely unclear and dubious whether justifications can be provided for the normative postulates embedded in the concept of praxis. In specific opposition to the production paradigm, Habermas claims that it does not yield any conceptual tools which can help shed light on the relationship between productive labour and other forms of cultural expression. Here, too, he censures its lack of clarity. Finally, Habermas declares the production paradigm to be outdated, and this for empirical reasons, as it 'loses its plausibility with the historically foreseeable end of a society based on labor'.[54] These various objections can be examined systematically by placing them under three headings. They are clearly empirical, normative and, in the narrow sense, action-theoretical objections.

The empirically grounded objection has its origins in Habermas' claim that the production paradigm was linked to the age of the 'work society'. If the production paradigm is to be understood as pointing up craft labour, then the gradual disappearance of that mode of production, the failure of attempts to reform industrial labour along handicraft lines, as advocated by John Ruskin and William Morris, and certainly the dwindling importance of labour for the individual that comes with the shortening of the working week and the concomitant change in values mean that the production paradigm no longer has the earth-shattering significance it once had, or is reduced to the mere demand for a humanization of the work environment. This empirical argument can of course only be tested by empirical means, and this is not the proper place to do so. However, let us note the two possible kinds of objection to this assertion. Firstly, talk of an end to a society based on labour may be premature after all. Work-centred values and physically demanding labour are on the retreat in only a few highly developed industrial societies; if we consider the future of labour on a world scale, we find little cause for such optimism. Yet even in the most advanced industrial societies, new forms of work are developing, to which the question whether we can realize ourselves in labour is just as appropriate as it was in connection with the replacement of craft manufacture by early forms of industrial labour. Yet even if we accept Habermas' contention that the end of the labour-based society is foreseeable, it still remains unclear why the demand for the chance to be creative should not focus more strongly on the sphere of leisure-time activities. It is only because Habermas does not understand 'production' as a metaphor for the creativity of all action that he fails to see the present-day possibility of disengaging 'creativity' from productive labour. The end of a labour-based society does not necessarily mean that the idea of creativity loses its significance.

There is a certain parallel between this line of argumentation and objections at the normative level. Habermas is, in my opinion, correct to insist that normative claims of all kinds can only be given justifications in discursive processes. However, Habermas seems to consider that three conclusions drawn from this are automatically justified. Firstly, it may be true that the idea of 'production' or more generally 'creativity' contains a normative substance which cannot be brought to bear merely by establishing discourses which are justified by norms. Secondly, it cannot be denied that the application of norms in action situations may itself be governed by normative rules, which do not necessarily coincide with the rules which provided the justifications for the norm.[55] Thirdly and finally, it is not legitimate to conclude that the lack of clarity on the normative implications of the concepts of 'praxis' and 'production' means that these concepts are of no value in terms of action theory. Only if the action theory is designed from the very beginning on the basis of a correspondence between a (communicative) type of action and the necessity of a communicative version of the concept of rationality does the argument hold that the lack of normative clarity in the concept of action as used in the philosophy of praxis tradition is an action-theoretical reason for not taking into account the definition of action on which the tradition hinges.

This in itself is already the beginning of a verdict on Habermas' action-theoretical arguments against the philosophy of praxis and the production paradigm. Habermas defends – rightly, in my opinion – the necessity of strictly distinguishing between action directed towards objects and that towards fellow-subjects. Equally justified is his insistence that it is necessary for a social theory to link various types of action with one another. However, this argument does not justify the rejection of approaches which precisely do not blur, or try to dismiss as unimportant, the difference between instrumental and communicative action, but instead set out to identify the characteristics common to *all* kinds of action, both instrumental and communicative. And these common characteristics must exist if the subsumption of both types under the common genus 'action' is to have any meaning at all. Viewed in this light, then, the production model of action should be regarded not as an alternative to communicative action, but rather as a – problematical – attempt to grasp in metaphorical terms the central determining property underlying all action, namely its creativity.

Correctly understood, the empirical, normative and action-theoretical arguments against Habermas' critique, therefore, all have the same thrust. Even if the idea of 'production' in Marx led to an untenable conception of society and history, and even if the majority of Habermas' objections are valid in themselves, it is not valid to conclude that these traditions of thought should simply be broken off. Rather, it is necessary and possible to take the idea of creativity contained within them, independently of the Marxist connotations, and develop it further in order to arrive at a general theory of action and thus to contribute to a social theory based upon it. The only writer to be consistent in taking this step beyond the intrinsic paradoxes of western Marxism towards a creativity theory has been Cornelius Castoriadis.[56] His theory overcomes the tradition of the production paradigm 'from within'. He is able to do so, however, primarily because he draws additionally on a very different thread of Marx's action theory, namely Marx's idea of 'revolutionary' action.

2.3 Revolution

The works in which Marx pays particular attention to the inner dynamics of revolutionary processes and thus revolutionary action are those in which he refers directly to the revolutionary events of his time. These writings are not some detached historiography, but rather an evaluation of what has occurred with a view to drawing conclusions for political strategy. The most important studies of this type were written in response to events in France: firstly, the period starting with the revolution of February 1848 in Paris and ending with the seizure of power by Napoleon III in 1851; and later the insurrection that established the Paris Commune in 1871. However, the relationship of these historiographical works to the political-economic core of his oeuvre is by no means clear cut. Marx and Engels themselves appear not to have seen this as a problem. For them it seemed self-evident that the elaboration of a critique of political economy and the analysis of contemporary 'class struggles' were complementary processes. They may indeed be complementary if the premises underpinning both fields of analysis do not contradict each other. In this case, historical analyses may be seen as the application – and, if the application is successful, as confirmation – of the conception of history used, with its roots in the production paradigm. The purpose of historiography then becomes the production of evidence for the class nature of political parties and ideologies, and indeed ultimately of all political acts and decisions. Thus, in his 1885 preface to the third edition of the most important of these works, Marx's *The Eighteenth Brumaire of Louis Bonaparte*, Engels describes the work as a test of the correctness of the great law of motion of history that Marx had discovered,

> the law according to which all historical struggles, whether they proceed in the political, religious, philosophical or some other ideological domain, are in fact only the more or less clear expression of struggles of social classes, and that the existence of and thereby the collisions, too, between these classes are in turn conditioned by the degree of development of their economic position, by the mode of their production and of their exchange determined by it.[57]

In canonized Marxism, the relationship between the two fields of analysis is largely assumed to be unproblematical. Yet 'praxis philosophy' Marxism, in its pathos of human self-creation, also bundled together these two very different categories of action: on the one hand, the production of material objects and, on the other, the bringing about of a revolutionary change in society.

In more recent discussions of Marxism, however, a number of writers have clearly established the contrast between the action-theoretical assumptions contained in Marx's analyses of 'class struggles' and those contained in the production model. Thus Habermas, in his investigation of the interests on which knowledge rests, stresses the difference between a 'self-creation by productive activity and formation (Bildung) by critical-revolutionary activity';[58] it is Marx's lack of clarity on precisely this point, says Habermas, that lies at the root of Marxism's misconception of itself to the extent that inherent in this difference is 'the difference between strict empirical sciences and critique',[59] and that it therefore burdens Marx's science of humankind with the misconception of itself as a natural science.

Castoriadis, in his assessment of Marxism, is even more pointed in the distinction he draws between the economic determinism of the materialist conception of history and the doctrine of class struggle. To assume that a simple complementary relationship obtains between the two is for him quite out of the question. If the materialist conception of history is really valid, this reduces classes to mere agents of the course of history. He concludes:

> If they are actors, they are so in exactly the same sense as actors in the theatre who recite a text given to them in advance and who make predetermined gestures, and whether they play well or poorly, they cannot prevent the tragedy from moving on to its inexorable conclusion.[60]

However, if the doctrine of class struggle is to be salvaged, then this can only be done, according to Castoriadis, if it can be proven that the economic laws formulated by Marx were only given their full meaning by the class struggle. This means, for example, that an idea so central to Marxism as the value of labour power as a commodity would be logically incomplete unless it could be shown that this value were determined not by recourse to some science but by the conflict between capitalists and workers. The economic categories are then no longer the basis of all other social processes, but are to a certain extent indeterminate, an indeterminacy which is only ended in the struggle to determine those categories. By privileging the concept of class struggle in this manner, Castoriadis takes a route which leads him to completely reject Marxism while at the same time adhering to the pathos of revolution.

The common denominator behind the sensitivity shown by both Habermas and Castoriadis to this inconsistency in Marx's thought can be found, I believe, by studying Maurice Merleau-Ponty's philosophical interpretation of Lenin's and Trotsky's conception of revolution.[61]

Under the conditions prevailing in Russia at that time, the revolutionary will undoubtedly collided even more violently with the evolutionary theory of history than it did in the works of Marx and Engels themselves. Whereas Lenin tended to overemphasize the influence of capitalism in Russia to detract attention from the backwardness of the country he was attempting to revolutionize,[62] Trotsky, inspired by Marx, developed a theory of permanent revolution.[63] The idea which was trying to find a form for itself was that even in societies which could by no means be assumed to have reached the stage of fully developed capitalism in the Marxist sense, a proletarian, socialist revolution was none the less possible, or indeed that any revolution in these societies had a tendency to develop into a socialist revolution because all societies developed not in isolation from one another according to some uniform pattern of stages, but in interconnection with one another.

> The idea of a transtemporal revolution – anticipated before its objective conditions come together, always to be remade, even when these conditions are not joined everywhere in 'embryonic' form and never completed anywhere, history's continual obsession, and the permanent justification of the will which provides the basis for renewed purgings by giving them the stamp of truth – this is nothing other than the Marxist idea of a world incomplete without praxis, of a praxis which is part of the definition of the world.[64]

According to this idea, which Lenin came close to embracing in the context of the October Revolution, the origins of a revolution are to be sought not only within one particular society, and revolutions are assumed to tend intrinsically to expand and change their goals. These notions certainly provide interesting food for thought for a historical sociology of revolutionary processes. In the present context, however, all that concerns us are their consequences with regard to action theory. Whereas in Soviet Russia the ideology of Marxism-Leninism stifled any meaningful development of an action theory,[65] many Marxist intellectuals responded to the Russian Revolution by developing a theory of revolution based on an anti-evolutionist interpretation of the Marxian heritage. The victory of the Bolsheviks and the question as to the conditions under which revolution could succeed in the West led both Lukács and Gramsci to embark on a far-reaching and independent reinterpretation of historical materialism. Merleau-Ponty, on the other hand, who coined the term 'western Marxism' to refer to such attempts, reflects – a generation later – on the link between the horrors of Stalinism and the fact that even western Marxism, including Sartre's existentialist philosophy, was at least in part an apology for Stalinism. These reflections lead him to pinpoint an autonomous 'paradigm of revolution' and to go even further in demythologizing revolution. Merleau-Ponty thereby prepares the ground for the presentation of a second action-theoretical model in Marx, one which was present only in embryonic form but unmistakably present none the less, and also for an attempt to interpret the idea of revolution as another metaphor of creative action, rather than interpreting all creative action in terms of revolution.[66]

In terms of its literary brilliance and the richness of objective information it provides, the *Eighteenth Brumaire*, Marx's analysis of the development leading up to the *coup d'état* which brought Napoleon III to power, was the best piece of historiographical writing he ever produced. Its literary form is in itself an indication of the fact that Marx was anxious to give a dramatic portrayal of a struggle in order to highlight the interlinking of the actions and the relations of a large number of different actors to one another amidst rapidly changing circumstances. The text is imbued with theatrical metaphor. That this was the result of a very conscious decision on Marx's part[67] is shown by his desire to distance his portrayal from those of Victor Hugo and Proudhon.[68] He accuses Victor Hugo, notwithstanding the latter's opposition to Napoleon III, of committing a subjectivist error by exaggerating the triggering function of the leader of the *coup d'état*. Proudhon, on the other hand, is charged with having committed the opposite error of 'objectivism' in portraying the coup as an inevitable result of preceding developments, which also elevates the importance of its leader. Marx's own concern, in contrast, is to show 'how the *class struggle* in France created circumstances and conditions which made it possible for a mediocre and grotesque person to play the role of a hero'.[69] The question we therefore have to ask of Marx's text is whether this intention was fulfilled or whether his own theory undermined his empirical reconstruction of a complex process of collective action.

The interpretation of events in terms of class struggle ascribes a meaning to them which they do not necessarily have for the actors themselves. This immediately begs the question as to which classes Marx treats as being involved in the struggles and how he defines the relationship of concretely identifiable collective actors to these classes. The second question which arises is how Marx believes collective actors and their goals in general, and acting classes in particular, come into existence and what the relationship is between these goals and the historical purpose imputed by Marx. Thirdly, we must examine whether Marx assigns the arena in which the struggle takes place the role of a contingent framework only or instead accords it constitutive significance for the meaning of the struggles.

It is possible to deduce from Marx's writings on political economy – although here we find no more than the rudiments of a class theory – that Marx assumed that only two classes existed, namely the bourgeoisie and the proletariat – indeed not only in the society of the future but already in his own day. However, his historical writings adduce no evidence to support this view. At least five[70] classes can be identified in the *Eighteenth Brumaire*. Alongside the bourgeoisie we find the petty bourgeoisie, alongside the proletariat stands the *lumpenproletariat*, and finally the class of peasants takes on a crucial role in Marx's analysis. Furthermore, Marx depicts each of these classes not as a homogeneous group with a uniform orientation, but as conglomerates of opposing factions. Thus the interests of the financiers among the bourgeoisie are, in Marx's view, by no means identical to those of other segments of this class. Marx also sees other collective actors as being involved in the class struggle, groups to which the term 'class' is not so readily applicable: state officials and the military, for example. In other words, Marx paints a differentiated picture of the wide variety of actors who are involved in the class struggle.

None the less, because he interprets the events in terms of class struggle, he is forced to conceive of the fragmentation of the classes into sub-classes and its reflection in the spectrum of political parties in terms of his model of economic interests, thus according all cultural preconditions and consequences the significance of a mere epiphenomenon. In a characteristic passage, Marx examines the deeper significance of the split in the Party of Order into rival factions, one supporting the house of Bourbon, the other the house of Orléans. For Marx, the lines of demarcation are clearly drawn:

> Under the Bourbons, *big landed property* had ruled, with its priests and lackeys; under the July monarchy, it had been high finance, large-scale industry, large-scale trade, i.e. *capital* with its retinue of advocates, professors and fine speech-makers. The legitimate monarchy was simply the political expression of the immemorial dominations of the lords of the soil, just as the July monarchy was only the political expression of the usurped rule of the bourgeois parvenus. It was therefore not so-called principles which kept the fractions divided, but rather their material conditions of existence, two distinct sorts of property; it was the old opposition between town and country, the old rivalry between capital and landed property.[71]

Marx applies a similar analytic method at other points in the text. He reduces democratic demands to an expression of the economic interests of the petty bourgeoisie, which he sees as 'a *transitional* class in which the interests of two classes meet and become blurred'.[72] In other words he evidently assigns a higher degree of reality to the main classes, the bourgeoisie and the proletariat, than he does to the petty bourgeoisie. Only when he has ruled out all the other classes as a possible class base of Napoleon III's regime does the peasant class make an appearance in Marx's analysis. Thus the differentiation into a variety of actors clearly runs counter to the intention to define all actors in terms of an economic structure which consists ultimately of only two large interest groups struggling against one another.

Moving on to the second question, namely how the goals of these collective actors are formed, we find the same ambiguity on Marx's part. On the one hand, he takes account of very widely ranging elements of the self-understanding process as mediated through symbols, or of conflict conveyed by symbol. He knows very well that the interests of a class cannot be translated directly and mechanistically into goals of action, but that possible interests can give the class a subjectively felt sense of purpose only through a process of self-definition and identity formation. The main reason why his analysis of the French peasants has become so famous is that it identifies the specific conditions of communication between these peasants, who live scattered about the countryside in relative isolation from one other, as the key factor behind their political orientation. Yet at the same time, all these insights into the role of symbolic and cultural processes are not given a chance to develop further, but are instead nipped in the bud. Thus, immediately following on from his analysis of the Orléanists and Legitimists we read:

> Who would deny that at the same time old memories, personal enmities, fears and hopes, prejudices and illusions, sympathies and antipathies, convictions, articles of faith and principles bound them to one or the other royal house? A whole superstructure of different and specifically formed feelings, illusions, modes of thought and views of life arises on the basis of the different forms of property, of the social conditions of existence. The whole class creates and forms these out of its material foundations and the corresponding social relations. The single individual, who derives these feelings etc. through tradition and upbringing, may well imagine that they form the real determinants and the starting-point of his activity. ... A distinction is made in private life between what a man thinks and says of himself and what he really is and does. In historical struggles one must make a still sharper distinction between

the phrases and fantasies of the parties and their real organization and real interests, between their conception of themselves and what they really are.[73]

It is, of course, undeniably true that people can deceive themselves or others as to the true motives behind their actions. However, Marx uses this fact to deride all subjective motives as being of secondary significance and to claim that economic interest is the ultimate determining factor. It is not clear exactly how Marx conceives of this ultimately pervasive force of economic interest. After all, there is a world of difference between, on the one hand, actively deceiving a partner by pretending to pursue noble goals although in fact one is driven by base material interests and, on the other, self-deception as to intentions that one does not admit to oneself because they contradict one's self-image or one's own moral code. Moreover, it is not clear whether Marx's hypothesis is supposed to imply that there is normally no such thing as action which does not correspond to one's own economic interests.

At any rate, Marx's formulations certainly make it possible to interpret his concept of class struggle in terms of strategic action. In this case, a merely utilitarian model of action would coexist alongside the expressivist concept of labour in Marx. However, such a model of action cannot explain how Marx, following Hegel, came to conceive of the constitution of classes as a path to self-consciousness. After all, Marx perceives 'interest' precisely not as lying in the goals which the subjects themselves would name if asked, but as involving something true that underlies these goals. This true interest in turn can, however, be defined only within the framework of his concept of history, which has a clearer understanding of where people's true interests lie than the people themselves. Now it is certainly legitimate for a scientific theory to set itself the goal of understanding the actors better, and explaining their actions better, than they themselves could. Yet in that case the decisive point is whether the theory succeeds not simply in claiming this superiority as an *a priori* fact but in showing how it is linked to the self-understanding of the actors. It is my impression that Marx, in reducing all political action to an expression of economic interests, is not saying what he would really like to say. His intention in thus reducing the various political programmes and ideologies is to dispel illusions and to enlighten, in order to give the proletariat – a class he has arrived at via philosophical means and given a prime position in his philosophy of history – a clear conscience by convincing them that they, too, should simply pursue their own economic interests. And these, according to Marx's theory, consist in bringing about the downfall of capitalism. Yet the two intentions which thus meet in his analysis are mutually contradictory. If all action is in any case economically determined, then the actions of the proletariat should automatically follow the course desired by Marx – assuming, that is, that his economic theory is correct. There are, in other words, only two reasons why the proletariat might need encouragement: either because the pursuit of economic interest is precisely not something that is self-evident for all to see or because the economic interest of the proletariat does not necessarily lie in the overthrow of capitalism. In Marx's historiography, this unresolved contradiction is reflected in the fact that whereas the political actions of the revolutionary class are described in terms of self-discovery and the creation of new institutions, the analysis of the historical significance of these actions is based on a viewpoint that is rooted in the production paradigm. The bridge between the two is formed by an expressivist–utilitarian hybrid, the so-called 'expression of interests'.

The same dilemma is again encountered in the third dimension of our original question. In many passages of the *Eighteenth Brumaire*, Marx describes the state and the public sphere as an arena in which actors combat one another. He is interested in the role of symbolic elements which provide legitimation and then themselves become bones of contention between the parties. Thus the question as to who, in revolutionary periods, is best able to guarantee public order and safety takes on a significant role in his analysis. In the history of the workers' movement, the *Eighteenth Brumaire* has probably been the most influential of Marx's works because it contains – in the shape of the so-called 'theory of Bonapartism' – the notion that it is possible for the power of the state to be relatively independent of each of the individual classes, thus seeming to argue against an oversimplified reduction of the state to the interests of a ruling class. However, on closer inspection it soon becomes clear that Marx arrives at these insights *in spite of* his actual programme, and he is visibly at pains to play down their significance. In order to explain the seeming independence of Bonapartist state power, Marx retrospectively hauls in the peasants to give it a class base. In countless variations on a theme, Marx repeatedly interprets the terms 'republic' and 'democracy' as representing the mere form in which the actual events of the class struggle take place, or even as mere slogans, as weapons deployed in that struggle. The relationship between 'democracy' and 'class struggle' is by no means one of equal-ranking categories, but one between the surface and underlying depth. Despite taking empirical account of political action in all its individual forms, Marx does not develop any concepts to describe them that could match the power of the distinctions inherent in his economic theory.

In Marx's historical analyses of revolutionary processes, therefore, the revolutionary action-type puts in an appearance, but without it being developed further. As with Marx's work, in Marxism we repeatedly encounter historical studies – such as Trotsky's *History of the Russian Revolution*[74] – or strategic analyses – such as Rosa Luxemburg's theses on the mass strike[75] – which develop ideas that point in this direction but which the author, or the codified doctrine, does not have adequate conceptual means to deal with. In western Marxism it was Georg Lukács who formulated what has undoubtedly been the most influential theory of the genesis of revolutionary class consciousness.[76] Marx himself already treats the consciousness of the proletariat not as an empirical fact but as something derived from a philosophy of history, and this normative, anti-empirical approach veritably blossoms in the work of Lukács. Still within the Marxist tradition, a more appropriate method of analysing the specific qualities of political action appears to be that adopted by Gramsci.[77] Gramsci's political theory is aimed at interpreting political action not according to the pattern of the rational pursuit of interests nor as the mere execution of historical imperatives, but as an attempt to create a normative consensus within and between social groups. Such a consensus cannot be brought about by the use of force, but requires creative achievements. Political programmes must be acceptable and it must be possible to put them into practice, that is, they require intersubjective consent to proposed new ways of acting. Only on the basis of this capacity for legitimation and innovation can political forces succeed in forging alliances between classes. Gramsci thus becomes the crown witness for critiques of the instrumentalist conceptions of the state and politics and the functionalist reductions of legality, morality and ideas that are to be found within Marxism.

Castoriadis again breaks with Marxism in order to retain the idea of revolutionary action. With regard to action theory, this enables him to consider the capacity of human action to create institutions as a type of creativity in its own right. From a political point of view, this leads him to raise expectations for change to a degree which it is difficult to justify given the present-day course of political events. The agents and the goals of the desired revolution no longer have clear contours.[78] In this respect Castoriadis' political philosophy somewhat resembles – if only partially in political terms, albeit very strongly in terms of a theory of action – that of Hannah Arendt. In her study *On Revolution*,[79]

Arendt traces the history of revolution as both an idea and a phenomenon. She shows[80] that it was not until the eighteenth century that the
concept of revolution, which had initially and for a long time been
used to refer to any kind of upheaval and which as late as 1688 could
still mean a restoration of monarchical power (as in the 'Glorious
Revolution'), took on the meaning which we associate with the term
today. This meaning refers to new social conditions being brought
about via the free action of the members of the society. In order to
arrive at this definition it was necessary both to break with the
traditional concept of time and to reach a new understanding of the
scope of human action. The concept of revolution contains the idea of
a new beginning: 'it is obvious that only under the conditions of a
rectilinear time concept are such phenomena as novelty, uniqueness
of events, and the like conceivable at all.'[81] Arendt argues that the
Christian concept of history, even that influenced by St Augustine,
recognized only one new beginning, namely that of Christ's life, but
that elsewhere it reproduced notions of eternal cycles. Even the
newness of life in the newly discovered continent of America was seen
as a gift of providence. However, revolution not only implies the
notion of a radical new beginning in history, but also, and above all,
the idea that human beings themselves are the makers of this new
beginning. Not until the eighteenth century do we find an awareness
of the possibility of creativity not only in science and the arts, but also
in the political sphere.

> These two things together – a new experience which revealed man's
> capacity for novelty – are at the root of the enormous pathos which we
> find in both the American and the French Revolutions, this ever repeated
> insistence that nothing comparable in grandeur and significance had
> ever happened in the whole recorded history of mankind.[82]

In this understanding of the term, revolutionary action means acting
in freedom. It can signify both the creation of that freedom and also
action taken under conditions of already created freedom. Consequently, Arendt is interested not only in the history of the idea of
revolution, but also in the history of the institutions of political
freedom. By drawing on American traditions, Arendt liberates the
idea of revolutionary action from its Marxist one-sidedness and thus
protects it from having overly great positive or negative mythological
importance attached to it as the historical advent of salvation or
disaster. Thus Arendt, to an even greater degree than Merleau-Ponty,

prepares the way for an understanding of revolutionary action as creative collective political action.

2.4 Life

There is one deficiency common to all three 'metaphors of creativity' discussed thus far, and that is what might be called, to use the phrase coined by Whitehead and Parsons, the 'fallacy of misplaced concreteness'. They all attempt to grasp the creativity of action by attributing creative features to a certain concrete type of action. This is very clearly the case with Marx's concepts of production and revolution; with Herder's expressivist anthropology the fault lies more in the reading of his ideas than in Herder's own intention. According to Herder's and Marx's models, then, poetry, the self-determined exercise of craft skills, and the revolutionary act are respectively made to appear creative. An inevitable consequence of this approach is that other concrete types of action are denied all vestiges of creativity and perceived as the very opposite of creativity. It thus follows that persons who are unable to express themselves in poetic form appear as dull, narrow-minded philistines whose forms of expression do not merit further attention; that persons who do not find self-fulfilment in the handling and processing of objects must be alienated; and that persons who do not actively contribute to paving the way for a revolution can be nothing more than a part of a homogeneous universe of repression. The concretist tendency to equate a particular type of action with the term 'creativity' thus leads to the depreciation of other types of action and encourages the extension of the concrete typological concept to metaphorical uses that lie beyond the proper limits of its applicability. The alternative to this undesirable form of conceptualization is to regard creativity as an analytical dimension of all human action. It then becomes possible, firstly, to view all action as potentially creative and not only one particular concrete type of action, and, secondly, to ascribe structural features to human action as such which can be summarized under the label of 'creativity'.

The philosophy of life [*Lebensphilosophie*] in Europe and pragmatism in the United States are two competing ways of conceiving of creativity without falsely equating it with one particular concrete type of action. The key ideas or metaphors which these two intellectual currents bring to bear on the problem of creativity are, on the one hand, the concepts of 'life' and 'will' and, on the other, the concepts of (creative) 'intelligence' and of 'reconstruction'. At this stage we should ask which of the two traditions yields the more convincing solution from the point of view of a theory of the creativity of action.

The philosophy of life is a somewhat opaque term used to describe a number of not clearly delimited philosophical movements which existed primarily in Germany and France between 1880 and 1930.[83] These movements were by no means confined to the realm of academic philosophy, but exerted a powerful influence on the arts of their day and were a source of ideas for the nascent German Youth Movement and the emergence of education reformers. They expressed the revolt against what was felt to be an ossified culture, a rebellion which in many respects was reminiscent of the *Sturm und Drang* movement of the late eighteenth century, but which now had something more closely resembling a mass base. Above all Nietzsche and Bergson, as well as to a lesser extent Dilthey and Simmel and a host of other less important thinkers, are considered to have provided the intellectual inspiration for these movements. The concept of 'life' which gave this current its name had more than one meaning, and it would probably not do these philosophers an injustice to claim that this ambiguity was intentional and that it contributed to the success of the concept, which increasingly became a catchword. We can distinguish between at least three layers of meaning. At the first level, life is contrasted with a form that has become devoid of content. 'Life is a symbol of opposition to what is dead and ossified, to a civilization that has become intellectualistic and inimical to life, a symbol which stands for a new feeling of life, for "authentic experiences", for "authenticity" per se: for dynamism, creativity, directness, youth.'[84] A second meaning is that a philosophy of life is precisely not intended as a philosophy for philosophers but as one which appeals to the concrete way in which every individual conducts his or her life. A third level of meaning is that of the biological concept of life, which, since Darwin's discoveries and the fundamental change they had brought about in the way people saw the world, had become a major issue. By merging these different meanings, the philosophy of life was able to claim that it offered an intellectual orientation which was at once both a cultural critique and a guide to individual conduct that was grounded in the latest scientific developments. The common point of departure for most of the philosophers of life was a thinker who had received little attention in his own day but whose posthumous reputation was all the more spectacular: Arthur Schopenhauer. It has been said with some justification that the history of the philosophy of life is more or less equivalent to the history of Schopenhauer's reception. The best method of approaching these philosophers' conception of creativity is therefore to study Schopenhauer's concept of the 'will'. And certainly, in contrast to the vagueness of the concepts used by many philosophers of life, Schopenhauer's deductions are very much transparent.

Schopenhauer's concept of 'willing' marks a break with a centuries-old tradition of European thought. According to traditional thinking, goals of action exist that are of greater or lesser value, and the decision to pursue them requires a separate act of the will on the part of an actor in order for action to take place. The worthy goals of action were perceived as themselves possessing a power capable of inducing decisions of the will. Admittedly, the will is often too weak, or misled, thus leaving the worthy causes unfulfilled; none the less, in principle the realm of values remains unaffected by the nature of the will. For Schopenhauer, this approach was flawed even at the methodological level. He felt that to think of the will in such a rationalistic manner was to take a philosophical concept of the will as simply given, without attempting to root it in experience. But how do we experience our will? The elementary experience of our will, according to Schopenhauer, lies in our corporeality, or more precisely in our ability to move our bodies. We perceive our bodies as something different from every other thing in the world by dint of experiencing it. To be sure, it is true that the body, as a material thing like every other thing, is present in the world and as such must be conceived of in terms of space, time and causality. In Schopenhauer's terminology, influenced by Kant, this means that the body is also a 'representation' [*Vorstellung*], a part of the world of phenomena. However, whereas with all other things in the world we can never penetrate – to use Kant's term – the 'thing in itself', but must make do with their external appearance [*Erscheinung*], the body affords us the one opportunity we have to lift the veil on a thing in itself. This is because in our experience of self we experience the movements of our body not as the mere relocation of a physical object in the world, but as the results of our will. It should be noted here that Schopenhauer conceives of the act of the will not in the traditional way as a separate decision to move, but as something identical with this movement.

> Every true act of his will is also at once and inevitably a movement of his body; he cannot actually will the act without at the same time being aware that it appears as a movement of the body. The act of will and the act of the body are not two different states objectively known, connected by the bond of causality; they do not stand in the relation of cause and effect, but are one and the same thing, though given in two entirely different ways, first quite discreetly, and then in perception for

the understanding. . . . Only in reflection are willing and acting different;
in reality they are one. Every true, genuine, immediate act of the will is
also at once and directly a manifest act of the body; and, correspondingly, on the other hand, every impression on the body is also at once
and directly an impression on the will. As such, it is called pain when it
is contrary to the will, and gratification or pleasure when in accordance
with the will.[85]

Strictly speaking, however, it would be possible to argue that our
experience of the will itself also remains in the realm of representation,
but even then this experience would still be the juncture at which we
came closest to a thing in itself. Thus, taking the self-experience of the
body as his – indubitably productive – starting point, Schopenhauer
draws bold analogies by which he constructs his philosophical system.
If the movements of our bodies, as seen from within, are acts of the
will, then we should assume that the same is true of the movements
of animals; in that case their movements, too, would be not simply of
a mechanical nature, but the result of will power. However, Schopenhauer does not stop there, but extends this idea beyond the animal
kingdom and even beyond the world of all living creatures when he
attributes not only the growth of plants but even the movement of
inorganic bodies – such as the movements of the planets or falling
motion due to gravity – to the power of what he speculatively
conceives of as a Will which his philosophy of nature sees as ruling
the whole cosmos. This enables him to gain significant insights, for
example into the correspondences between the organic constitution of
animals and their environment, because he interprets the bodies of
animals themselves as the objectification of this Will, but it also leads
him to adopt an attitude of uncontrollable and untenable philosophical
condescension towards the natural sciences. Only by over-stretching
the idea of a self-experience of the will in this speculative manner is
Schopenhauer able to present the will as the fundamental metaphysical principle. Here the will is precisely not restricted to the domain of
human action and conceived of as the energy that facilitates the
attainment of goals, but seen rather as a primal force that pre-exists
all action and is not directed towards a particular goal. Schopenhauer's
'will' is thus not one phenomenon among others, but rather precedes
all phenomena of this world.

This metaphysical exaggeration of the will has a retroactive impact
on his understanding of human action. If all phenomena are an
expression of a metaphysical will, then this is also true of human
actions. It thus follows that what we experience in the self-experience

of our bodies is not really our personal will but the effect of a pre-personal will acting in us. In his examples Schopenhauer devotes considerable space to human sexuality. In misanthropic tones he describes sexual attraction as human beings being overwhelmed by a natural force whose goal is the reproduction of the species, a force which deceives human beings and leads them astray. However, sexuality is not the only area in which we can be surprised by the ideas and desires that emerge from within ourselves. Others have already pointed out that Schopenhauer's line of thought could be seen as a precursor of a concept which psychoanalysis was to term the 'unconscious'.[86]

At any rate, the status of consciousness in human action is changed radically by the metaphysical interpretation of the will. In complete contrast to the tradition of thought which conceived of the will as a means to achieve consciously determined goals, Schopenhauer turns consciousness into an epiphenomenon and the intellect into a mere means of which the will avails itself. Conscious goals of action are not accepted as the true causes of action, but are regarded – to use the psychoanalytical terminology current today – as 'rationalizations' of the true determining force, the will. The conscious mind aids the will in the achievement of its goals, and deludes the actor into believing that the attainment of the goal will make him happy. In fact, however, the metaphysical will can never be satisfied, so that after each goal has been reached, new goals emerge, or the original goals suddenly lose their value by dint of having been accomplished. Schopenhauer's ethics and aesthetics revolve around the question how human beings should behave towards the world once they have realized the futility of the striving of the will. He sees art, compassion and asceticism as ways in which human beings can free themselves from the will. Persons of true genius, according to Schopenhauer, are thus precisely not the pseudo-titanic heroes of the will that were idealized in the *Sturm und Drang* period, but rather those who were best able to relinquish their fixation on their own self and its actions:

> Genius is thus the ability to behave purely contemplatively, to lose oneself in contemplation and to unyoke the knowledge, which originally was only there to serve the will, from that service, i.e. to focus not at all on its interest, its wanting, its goals, and thus to externalize one's personality to the time in which one is, in order to remain a *purely cognitive subject* with a clear view of the world, and to achieve this not for a moment, but enduringly and with as much clearheadedness as is necessary in order to repeat what has been grasped in the form of

considered art and 'establish fast, in thought that shall endure, all that life in floating semblance holds'.[87]

By virtue of this orientation towards liberation from the will, Schopenhauer becomes a thinker who is able to give a sympathetic hearing to the world-renouncing ethical systems of Asian cultures.

The concept of genius, which in the 'expressivist' tradition played such an important role in attempts at grasping phenomena of creativity, thus seems to have had its meaning turned on its head by Schopenhauer. But what does Schopenhauer's metaphysics of the will have to say about the idea of creativity? Charles Taylor labels Schopenhauer an expressivist 'with the value signs reversed'.[88] In doing so, and in his characterization of Nietzsche as a 'Dionysian' and Heidegger as a 'radical anti-subjectivist' expressivist,[89] Taylor is, in my opinion, stretching the concept of the expressivist anthropological tradition too far, thus ignoring some key differences between that tradition and the ideas of the philosophy of life, that is, between Herder and Schopenhauer. The latter construes human action in a manner fundamentally different from that of the 'expressivist' tradition. His metaphysics of the will, like Schelling's philosophy of nature, admittedly builds on attempts which had emerged since the Renaissance to see the productivity experienced in aesthetic creation as something which is also at work in nature. However, inasmuch as Schopenhauer sees this creative force not as Mind or as a pre-form of Mind, but as blind will, it is accurate to say that the values have undergone an inversion of emphasis here. Yet Schopenhauer's concept of the will reverses not only value signs but also the relation between different domains of reality. Whereas Herder, in his anthropology, was already looking for a conceptual system which would avoid or overcome Cartesian dualisms by taking the holistic nature of human expressive actions as its guiding principle, Schopenhauer could be described as an 'inverted Cartesian'.[90] Schopenhauer does not overcome the Cartesian dualisms,[91] but turns them on their head. However, just as a theory of action cannot be founded on dualisms such as body and mind, or the Self and the Other, in that the concept of action requires precisely the integration of the dualistically divided components, it is equally impossible to construct a convincing theory of action simply by inverting these dualisms.

To demonstrate this we need go no further than Schopenhauer's methodological starting point, namely the self-experience of the body. Here, almost unnoticed, Schopenhauer makes two assumptions which are by no means self-evident. Firstly, he assumes that we experience the body directly. If this is intended to mean that we experience our own bodies differently from those of other people, then this assumption is undoubtedly justified; if, on the other hand, he is saying that we are capable of gaining cognitive insights from the self-experience of the body without the mediation of a symbolic medium, then this is a highly problematic assumption.[92] In order to construct his line of argument, Schopenhauer has, of course, to rely on such cognitive substance as can in no sense be regarded as given in purely subjective and unmediated form. Secondly, Schopenhauer assumes that in our direct experience of the body we actually experience our bodies as such in pure form. However, this assumption itself implies the Cartesian separation of body and mind; it would be more logical here to say that human beings experience themselves as actors and to conceive of the body as such as a product of abstraction derived from this experience. It is presumably Georg Simmel's intention to make a similar point when, in his masterly book *Schopenhauer and Nietzsche,* he criticizes Schopenhauer's metaphysics for having no place for the concept of personality. 'It is important to note that Schopenhauer's metaphysics leaves no room for the concept of personality, which is simply lost between the ego as imagination and the ego as will.'[93] Everything that Schopenhauer has to say about the human body therefore suffers from a tendency to see false similarities between humans and the animal kingdom – or from a Cartesian concept of the animal. However, the human body is not an animal substratum for pure intellect, nor is it – to take up the inversion of the idea of mind that controls the body so typical of Schopenhauer – the strong blind creature which bears a seeing but lame fellow; rather it is utterly the body of a human personality. Schopenhauer's pessimistic philosophy of history is also based on the fact that he dualistically tears apart a conceivable evolutionary continuity between animal accomplishments and the human mind. However, a more important point in the context of questions of action theory is that Schopenhauer's metaphysical exaggeration of the will starts from what is precisely an incorrect analysis of the role of the will in action. It is again Simmel who draws our attention to the fact that the claim that the 'will as such' is purposeless is based on a logical fallacy. Rather, every single voluntary action is oriented towards a purpose, and it naturally follows that action as such is not oriented to any particular purpose.

> The end of an act of will and the particular definition of that act are equivalent concepts. If one eliminates the particularity of will in order to achieve a concept of the generality of willing, then one must eliminate

all ends. And there is no use in lodging pessimistic complaints about the fact that the general, undifferentiated, and uniform will lacks any end.[94]

Simmel is certainly not using his perceptive objection to claim that a pessimistic value judgement on the world has thus been proved invalid, but is simply asserting that to derive such a judgement from the analysis of action is indeed inadmissible. Two things happen when the will is interpreted in metaphysical terms. Firstly, the will is once again – as in traditional rationalist psychology – given the character of a substance per se, and, secondly, it is detached from its situational context. The substantialization of the will consists precisely in the fact that it is conceived of not as an abstraction derived from action but as a primal force which realizes itself in action. According to this view, it is possible to think of the conscious mind as an instrument of this primal force. If we compare this with William James' reflections on psychology,[95] then it becomes clear that it is precisely the destruction of a substantialistic concept of the will that makes it possible to conceive of all aspects of consciousness as being related to action. In this respect, Schopenhauer comes much closer to embracing the very ideas he was trying to combat – the old psychology that considered the will as a separate faculty – than he would have wanted to believe. Yet his metaphysical exaggeration also treats the will as if it were not only present in given situations in the form of an always particular will that is necessarily linked to the self of an individual actor; instead, Schopenhauer gives the impression that these are only situational contexts in which a non-situational will is active. We can certainly regard Schopenhauer's thought, in that it provides the starting point for the 'philosophy of life' movement, as an important contribution to an understanding of creativity. The intention behind my line of argumentation here, however, was to show that Schopenhauer ascribes attributes of creativity to a metaphysical will that is not only more universal than the concrete types of action – expression, production or revolution – but indeed more universal than all human action. I would even go so far as to claim that the way in which Schopenhauer grounds the concept of the will in human self-experience fails to grasp its character as action. This conception of creativity without action theory becomes particularly virulent when taken up by Friedrich Nietzsche and given an activistic slant. Would it be accurate to describe Nietzsche's conception of creativity, again based in a philosophy of life, as an activistic turn of a metaphysics of the will devoid of an action-theoretical base?

Nietzsche himself gave a very complete account of Schopenhauer's significance for his own thought and his own process of self-discovery. One of his earliest works – the third of the 'Untimely Observations' ('Unzeitgemäße Betrachtungen') – is dedicated to 'Schopenhauer as a Teacher' ('Schopenhauer als Erzieher')[96] and he repeatedly returns to Schopenhauer in later works. Yet even the tone of Nietzsche's early writings, and certainly that of his later works, is different from the timbre of suffering and pessimism that pervades Schopenhauer's thought. Despite all the horrors of the world, Nietzsche's quest is, right from the start, to find an alternative to Schopenhauer's morality based on the renunciation of the will. Later his rejection of pessimism and asceticism intensifies, and he comes to view these attitudes as a perversion of the life-determining force. Nietzsche, like Schopenhauer, abandons all belief – even philosophical belief – in a rational principle running through history. Yet there are two immediate differences between Nietzsche's approach and that of Schopenhauer. Whereas for Schopenhauer the absence of an absolute value sphere means that life appears to be no more than the meaningless drive of the metaphysical will to achieve unattainable satisfaction, Nietzsche seeks to interpret life as a value in and of itself. In order to do so, he draws on the conception of life as a process of development, a view which was inaugurated after Schopenhauer's time, and for which Darwin was chiefly responsible. This renders it possible to view life itself as an immanent process of enhancement. The second respect in which Nietzsche modifies Schopenhauer's assumptions consists in his rein-terpretation of the will not as blind desire but essentially as the capacity to control desire and as an ability to act – thus returning it closer to the self-experience of the actor. These two amendments to Schopenhauer's thought enable Nietzsche to interpret all life as the result of a 'will to power' which, similarly to Schopenhauer's meta-physical will, instrumentalizes the faculties of consciousness and articulates itself in all actions. Of course, the brevity of this description makes Nietzsche's development appear more linear than it actually was. It would be quite wrong to think that Nietzsche had produced his philosophy out of Schopenhauer's hat as if by using some simple magic simple formula. On the contrary, in painstaking work, always closely orienting his work to experience, he strove to interpret phenomena, eventually reaching the conclusion that the will to power was their key.[97] He then used this key as a master to open doors in epistemology and ethics, in psychology and metaphysics. In all these fields, he finds a supra-subjective will to power at work, or holds the character of these fields to be the result of a perversion of this will to power. Nietzsche's own 'free-thinking' morality, therefore, calls not for a renunciation of the will, but, on the contrary, for the maximum possible intensification of subjectivity. And here he means a subjectivity which, like Schopenhauer's 'will', is detached – or should detach itself – from any kind of contextual constraint. The 'free spirit' is creative because it rises above all intellectual constructs hitherto; Dionysian experience separates us from all delimitation and all forms hitherto created; the idea of a 'will to power' portrays the cosmos as an eternal process of self-production and self-destruction. In the concept of 'life', all these connotations of un-delimitation converge to what Jürgen Habermas has called 'apparently concrete but structureless productivity'.[98] This 'life' can then itself be elevated to the status of a post-religious myth.

An analysis of Schopenhauer and some brief remarks on Nietzsche cannot, of course, do justice to the internal variations and also the richness of the philosophy of life. Thus not all of the arguments I have put forward here also apply to the French philosopher of life Henri Bergson,[99] whose thought is in many respects very similar to that of Schopenhauer. Bergson also sets out to discover a cosmological principle (the '*élan vital*') by means of an analysis of self-experience. And he, too, ascribes attributes of creativity to macrocosmic processes, albeit precisely not to human action. Bergson embeds rationality and action in functional contexts, but precisely in these creativity, he thinks, plays no part. The thinking of Wilhelm Dilthey,[100] on the other hand, is quite different in these respects, so that in the sense of the term 'philosophy of life' used here he does not belong in this category at all but should clearly be treated as standing in the tradition of expressivist anthropology. For Dilthey uses the term 'life' to describe human experience and action, and not some metaphysical principle. Furthermore, this outstanding German scholar refuses to join the trend typical of the philosophy of life and contrast life to science. His works on the methodological basis for the humanities [*Geisteswissenschaften*] are, on the contrary, the most mature achievement of the 'expressivist' tradition.

The concepts of the 'will' and 'life' in Schopenhauer and Nietzsche are meant to address phenomena of creativity. Ignoring completely for the moment the implicit value judgements involved, both thinkers can be criticized for treating creativity in isolation from the intersubjective and objective contexts of human action. From an empirical point of view, the attempt to describe the interplay between the conscious and the unconscious, the rational and the non-rational in creativity therefore remains unsuccessful. The development of individuals is conceived of as self-production sealed off from the context of intersubjectively defined and objectively delineated situations. From a normative point of view, it is possible to use Nietzsche's thought as the basis of an ethos of creativity that centres on the self-enhancement of the creative person himself. The impressive feature of such an ethos is the radical willingness to accept an obligation to adhere to self-imposed values. However, in the light of the non-contextual understanding of creativity, the works of the creative person appear of secondary importance by comparison with the self-enhancement of the creator. Nietzsche tries by direct means to strive for the development of the personality, something which may only be attainable by indirect means, that is, by actually applying oneself to a task or a problem that needs solving. The values professed by a person whose orientation is towards self-enhancement are therefore always flawed by their arbitrary origin – playful arbitrariness in the case of sympathetic figures, violent arbitrariness in the case of more terrifying examples. None the less, the metaphor of life preserves, albeit in more or less unsatisfactory form, the idea that creative acts and the process of giving individual meaning over and above collectively accepted meaning have their roots in a pre-reflective realm. To apply this metaphor in the form in which it was used by the philosophy of life would, however, merely be to counterpose a metaphysics of creativity devoid of any action-theoretical foundations to classical sociology's conception of action, which is so barren when it comes to a notion of creativity.

2.5 Intelligence and Reconstruction

The philosophy of life, although it came to dominate European intellectual life, was not the only current in the second half of the nineteenth century to attempt to put forward a theory of creativity. The genuinely American current of thought known as pragmatism can also be regarded as the articulation of a specific understanding of creativity. Pragmatism contains not a single metaphor that resembles 'expression', 'production' or 'revolution', nor does it operate with concepts that go far beyond all things human, such as 'life', in order to enable us to grasp the meaning of creativity. Rather, the pragmatist conception of creativity lies in the pragmatist understanding of human action itself. This understanding of action is pivotal to a whole series of concepts which very frequently recur in pragmatist writings: the concepts of problem and problem-solving, the ideas of intelligence and reconstruction, the concepts of abduction and the constitution of meaning. If these concepts and ideas are not seen in relation to the central phenomenon of action in the pragmatist sense, then misreadings and distortions are the inevitable consequence. Such difficulties were particularly in evidence in the contemporary European reception of American pragmatism;[101] yet they were also one of the reasons why pragmatism, having enjoyed decades of relative intellectual hegemony in the United States, saw its influence largely wane there too, especially after the Second World War; indeed, it is only now beginning to experience what appears to be a renaissance. The distorted renderings of pragmatism are so common that for some readers the very mention of the term 'pragmatism' in connection with a discussion of theories of creativity is likely to arouse scepticism. The everyday use of the word 'pragmatic' and in particular its use in political life is less likely to prompt associations with the pathos of creativity than with a kind of unprincipled 'muddling through' without any great ambitions to creativity. Should we not regard pragmatic adaptation to existing conditions as the polar opposite of the creative production of something new? And even if pragmatism is seen as more than a philosophy of adaptation, does it not reduce human creativity to the solution of given problems or to coping with emergencies? In order to clarify these misunderstandings it is necessary to go back and remind ourselves of the initial thrust of the pragmatist movement.

The philosophical point of departure for pragmatism was a critique of a strand of Cartesian thought which was of decisive importance for the development of modern philosophy. The emancipation of the individual from the self-evident validity and authority of received institutions and ideas that took place in the early modern period attained its most extreme and uncompromising expression in the thought of René Descartes. He took the individual's right to doubt as the very programme of philosophy and raised the self-certainty of the thinking and doubting ego to the status of firm foundation of a new philosophy. Needless to say, this simply eradicated any notion of the world being taken-for-granted as existing vis-à-vis the individual consciousness, including notions of the body of the thinking ego as a component of this world and of the other thinking subjects in the world. An epistemologically oriented philosophy was thereby able to substantiate its claim to being the foundation of all sciences. At the same time, though, it had to take on the difficult – or impossible – tasks of constituting the world, the body and the 'you' on the basis of the thinking ego. It was against this entire programme, which had such a huge impact on post-Cartesian European thought, that the central idea of pragmatism was directed. The pragmatist places in doubt the meaningfulness of Cartesian doubt.

> We cannot begin with complete doubt. We must begin with all the prejudices which we actually have when we enter upon the study of philosophy. These prejudices are not to be dispelled by a maxim, for they are things which it does not occur to us *can* be questioned. Hence this initial skepticism will be a mere self-deception, and not real doubt; and no one who follows the Cartesian method will ever be satisfied until he has formally recovered all those beliefs which in form he has given up.... A person may, it is true, in the course of his studies, find reason to doubt what he began by believing; but in that case he doubts because he has a positive reason to do so, and not on account of the Cartesian maxim.[102]

This critique of Cartesian doubt by Charles Sanders Peirce, the founder of pragmatism, is anything but a retrogressive defence of unquestionable authorities against the emancipatory claim of the thinking ego; it is, however, a plea in defence of *real* doubt, that is, in defence of the anchoring of cognition in real-life problem situations. Right from its earliest beginnings, pragmatism supplants Cartesianism's guiding notion of the solitarily doubting ego with the idea of a cooperative search for truth for the purpose of coping with real problems encountered in the course of action. One could be tempted to attribute to this transformation the same historical significance as that accorded to the philosophy of Descartes.

None the less, reference to the fact that pragmatism's initial impetus was anti-Cartesian is obviously not enough in itself to dispel the scepticism surrounding this current of thought. The emphasis on real doubt immediately throws up the question as to the circumstances under which such doubt arises. The typical pragmatist schema anchors doubt in action, which is conceived in terms of a model of periodically recurring phases. According to this model, all perception of the world and all action in the world is anchored in an unreflected belief in self-evident given facts and successful habits. However, this belief, and the routines of action based upon it, are repeatedly shattered; what has previously been a habitual, apparently automatic procedure of action is interrupted. The world reveals itself to have shattered our unreflected expectations; our habitual actions meet with resistance from the world and rebound back on us. This is the phase of real doubt. And the only way out of this phase is a reconstruction of the interrupted context. Our perception must come to terms with new or different aspects of reality; action must be applied to different points of the world, or must restructure itself. This reconstruction is a creative achievement on the part of the actor. If he succeeds in reorienting the action on the basis of his changed perception and thus continuing with it, then something new enters the world: a new mode of acting, which can gradually take root and thus itself become an unreflected routine. The pragmatists therefore maintain that all human action is caught in the tension between unreflected habitual action and acts of creativity. This also means that creativity here is seen as something which is performed within situations which call for solutions, and not as an unconstrained production of something new without any constitutive background in unreflected habits.

This rough sketch of the basic model of action in pragmatism is, of course, still much too imprecise to ward off accusations that it reduces human creativity to mere skilful problem-solving or even adaptive behaviour. In the main, five serious objections were levelled against the key assumptions of pragmatism; I am not referring here to the nationalistically motivated polemical attacks on pragmatism by those who claimed that American thought was by definition incapable of producing anything of serious value, and who believed they saw the anti-cultural influence of the all-powerful dollar in everything that came from the United States.

The first serious objection focused on the *momentary* nature of consciousness in the pragmatist model of action. A secondary motive for rejecting Cartesian thought was, after all, precisely to destroy the notion of 'consciousness' as a non-material substance and instead to anchor in action the achievements we call 'consciousness'. In pragmatism's basic model it may therefore appear as if consciousness is only ever present in the phases in which previous certainties are shaken and the creative search for new possibilities of action takes place. And indeed it is true that the pragmatists reserve the concept of consciousness in its full meaning for precisely these phases. However, it does not follow that they therefore conceive of routine action that is not shattered at some point as being completely free from conscious achievements. The end of a cycle, when the new mode of acting slowly takes on the form of a changed routine, is the simplest example of how pragmatism conceives of the relationship between consciousness and action. The creatively developed solutions to a problem of action are precisely not stored in consciousness but instead themselves become new modes of action, new 'habits'. Thus a problem solution leads to a form of action which will not balk at the same problem or which contains its own routine for dealing with problems. It is not the actor's knowledge of his actions which increases, but the appropriateness of the actions themselves.

The second objection was that the pragmatist tendency to anchor all the achievements of consciousness in action over-stretched an idea which is productive only when applied to early cognitive development. Pragmatism, it is argued, thus takes *sensorimotor* learning as the model of all human learning, which is a serious reduction of 'higher', culturally more valuable forms of cognition and action. The third objection accuses pragmatism of an *objectivistic* conception of the constitution of problems for the actor. These critics maintain that the pragmatists deny the actor any scope for defining problems and solutions. Instead they are charged with erroneously believing that the problem inevitably forces itself upon the actor, and in a quite specific form, leaving no scope for the creation of solutions: the actor merely searches for what are in reality predetermined possibilities. The fourth objection takes issue with the ostensibly *individualistic* character of the pragmatists' basic model. It remains completely unclear whether action vis-à-vis fellow subjects, instead of objects, should also be conceived of in terms of this schema, and how these two aspects can be interlinked in concrete actions. The fifth and final important objection relates to the danger that pragmatism reduces all action to an *'instrumentalized'* variant, by leaving room neither for non-purposive action in art and play, nor for sensitive receptivity, nor states of imperturbability that are distanced from actions.

All of these objections were often raised with the intention of showing the limitations of pragmatism and of rejecting outright its programme for a new philosophy grounded in action rather than consciousness. However, they were also all used by pragmatists themselves as a starting point for advances in pragmatism from within. Thus one could say that while many of the objections were justified with respect to early formulations of the pragmatist programme by William James and also Charles Sanders Peirce, they lost their validity in the face of innovations by John Dewey and George Herbert Mead. This is not the place for a systematic presentation of the history of pragmatism, a history which could be described as the process of overcoming these imprecisions or flaws in the basic model. Instead, we must confine ourselves to indicating the directions in which the pragmatists were driven in order to respond to the objections.

Thus the pragmatists' works on developmental psychology are proof that they did not set out to reduce all human learning to sensorimotor processes, but that they did indeed argue that the concept of intelligence should not be regarded as an independent mental faculty of human beings merely based on animal foundations. This was a radical claim in that it placed even the highest forms of thought in a direct line of continuity with the most primitive forms of cognitive and motor adaptation to the environment. This was not, therefore, a reduction of human intelligence, yet nor was it a dualistic separation of mind from body, but an investigation of the phases of that developmental process which leads from the primitive to the higher forms: that is, the psychological consequence of the pragmatist programme.[103]

The charge of objectivism no longer holds water if applied either to John Dewey's psychology of thinking and his logic, or to the methodology of William Isaac Thomas, the first 'principal' of the Chicago School of Sociology, whose ideas were grounded in pragmatism.[104] Dewey inserts an additional stage into the pragmatists' basic model, namely that of problem definition. That is to say, he takes as his point of departure not a simple collision between habitual actions and reality, but rather the diffusely problematic quality of an action situation as a whole, which must first be recognized as problematic by the actor himself before the problem can be defined as such and before specific problematic qualities can be attributed to elements of it. And it is this definition of the problem that determines the direction in which the actor will look in order to find solutions. Thomas, for his part, made a valuable contribution to giving this conception of the definition of situations more concrete form in sociological terms. Thomas inquires both into the social role of those who define situations not only for themselves but also for others, and into the degree to which an individual actor's situation-definitions are consistent and the way in which they fit into a more or less coherent interpretational system. Thus, although it is no longer justified to talk of an objectivist concept of situation, it would also be incorrect to describe it as a subjectivist version. While full recognition is given to the subjective components involved, the emergence of problems is none the less not construed as the result of subjective caprice because the actors – whether they like it or not – are confronted by problematical qualities of the world which provoke them into performing definition work.

The charge that the pragmatists' basic model was individualistic was, of course, only levelled against James and could not be upheld against Peirce. Peirce had claimed not only that cognitive problems were born out of real action situations, but also that the solitary Cartesian ego could not be expected to solve them. Rather, this was the task of a community of scientists who conduct experiments together and discuss the results with each other. This 'social' aspect to

Peirce's pragmatism was inherently bound up with the model of
action insofar as Peirce claimed that all knowledge was conveyed by
signs and symbols which were not a matter for private definition but
rather constituted a public medium. Admittedly, Peirce did not
develop a theory of communication as such. The pragmatist analysis
of situations of social interaction – and also of the communication of
the actor with himself in the form of self-reflection – is George Herbert
Mead's contribution to the pragmatist system of thought.[105] Mead
seeks to discover what is specific to interpersonal problems of action
and deduces the basic structures of symbolically mediated interaction
from the functional imperatives that lead to their solution. Mead's
entire social psychology rests on these foundations and can be
regarded as the refutation of a narrowly individualistic interpretation
of the pragmatists' basic model.

And finally, the charge of instrumentalistic reduction, which is
apparently lent weight by the fact that for a time John Dewey referred
to his own thought not as pragmatism but as instrumentalism, rests
on a misunderstanding. Dewey's intention was never that this term
should describe the character of action, but rather that it should refer
to the relationship between consciousness and action. In his conception, a decisive role was always played by those types of action – from
a child's play to art – which are certainly not instrumental, that is,
which do not merely serve the attainment of external goals.

> I have from time to time set forth a conception of knowledge as being
> 'instrumental'. Strange meanings have been imputed by critics to this
> conception. Its actual content is simple: Knowledge is instrumental to
> the enrichment of immediate experience through the control over action
> that it exercises.[106]

Dewey and the other pragmatists were concerned not to interpret all
action according to the model of instrumental action, but, on the
contrary, to offer a critique of the overly narrow 'practical' orientation
of American life. Thus, to regard action as the dimension on which all
else rests precisely did not mean to conceive of the world as mere
material for the intentions of actors. What it did mean was that human
beings discovered and appropriated the world through their actions.

These advances and modifications gave the pragmatist understanding of creativity clearer contours. It is indeed true that the pragmatists
attempt to anchor creativity in the actions of human beings in their
natural and social environment. The natural conditions of the environment figure just as strongly in this way of thinking as do the physical

attributes of the human being. All action is embedded in anthropological structures of communication. Yet creativity is more than
merely one of the necessities for the survival of an organism. A
problem of action is not only given when the organism is in fundamental danger. Action constantly encounters unexpected obstacles: goals
show themselves to be unattainable; simultaneously pursued goals
prove to be mutually exclusive; attainable goals have doubts cast
upon them by other actors. In these various crises of habitual action,
the action situations have to be *redefined* in a new and different way.
This involves defining that which is as yet undefined, rather than
simply making a different selection from a reservoir of situation
components that are either already defined or have no need of
definition. According to the pragmatists, every situation contains a
horizon of possibilities which in a crisis of action has to be rediscov-
ered. Hypotheses are put forward: suppositions about new ways of
creating bridges between the impulses to action and the given circumstances of a situation. Not all such bridges are viable. However, when
the actor succeeds in building a new bridge, this serves quite concretely to enhance his capacity for action. In fact, it even changes the
goals he sets himself. For the pragmatists, action consists not in the
pursuit of clear-cut goals or in the application of norms, and creativity
is not the overcoming of obstacles along these prescribed routes.
Anchoring creativity in action allows the pragmatists to conceive of
creativity precisely as the liberation of the capacity for new actions.
John Dewey regarded this as the very core of pragmatism:

> The pragmatic theory of intelligence means that the function of mind is
> to project new and more complex ends – to free experience from routine
> and from caprice. Not the use of thought to accomplish purposes
> already given either in the mechanism of the body or in that of the
> existent state of society, but the use of intelligence to liberate and
> liberalize action, is the pragmatic lesson.[107]

This is no artificial exaggeration of a secondary motif of pragmatism.
On the contrary, pragmatism is, put succinctly, a *theory of situated
creativity*. It deserves a place in a history of the idea of creativity just
as much as in a history of action theory, for it is a theory of the
creativity of human action.

This can easily be demonstrated in the work of all the leading
representatives of pragmatism. Until now the rich and vastly complex
work of Charles Sanders Peirce, whose genius was only recognized
posthumously, has been characterized here only in terms of its

negative thrust, namely its critique of Cartesianism. Peirce's positive
contribution to overcoming Cartesianism lies in the elaboration of
ideas on the intersubjectivity of the use of signs, on the one hand, and
on the creative character of the formation of hypotheses, on the other.
His idea of intersubjectivity is at the root of the notion of discourse,
an idea which has taken on such importance in the German readings
of his work by Habermas and Apel. Much less attention, however, has
been paid to the fact that Peirce's interest in science and research
centres not so much on discourse, but on the question as to the *origins*
of those explanatory hypotheses which may then become the topic of
argumentative debate among experimenting scientists. It is for this
reason alone that Peirce's ideas on science and – from the mid-1890s
onwards – also on art, on the one hand, and his speculative philosophy
of nature, with its theistic core, on the other, are reciprocally enlightening.[108] The decisive factor here is Peirce's introduction of a concept
of 'abduction'. Alongside induction and deduction, the two forms of
conclusion known since the logic of antiquity and which serve as a
means of proceeding from individual cases to universally valid laws
or vice versa, Peirce posits a third type, namely that of the production
of new hypotheses in a creative act. For many years, the task of
analysing the specific nature of this third type and describing what
distinguishes it from the other two types, and in particular from
induction, was a major concern in Peirce's work. Clearly, for Peirce
abduction was only a necessary, but not a sufficient, condition for the
advance of science; that is, unless new hypotheses are generated, no
progress is imaginable, but of course every new hypothesis still has to
prove its worth in testing. Unlike many later proponents of a theory
of science, notably Popper, Peirce does not relegate the generation of
new hypotheses to the psychology of thought, a domain of only
marginal relevance to logic, nor does he treat it as random variation,
but instead considers it as an integral part of logic itself.

> Abduction is the process of forming an explanatory hypothesis. It is the
> only logical operation which introduces any new idea; for induction
> does nothing but determine a value, and deduction merely evolves the
> necessary consequences of a pure hypothesis.[109]

If this were not the case, argues Peirce, there would be no point in our
taking the formation of hypotheses into consideration at all when
assessing the worth of a scientist. Only because we assume there to be
more than mere chance involved in the creative act of forming
hypotheses do we give the scientist credit for it. Therefore, according

to Peirce, this creativity must be subject somewhere to control by the scientist. Abduction stands precisely between merely passive absorption of sensory impressions and communication with others about explanatory hypotheses. In abduction the scientist frees himself from the yoke of former perceptions and received interpretations and creates a free relationship to both. This free relationship is precisely one of acquired freedom, that is, what characterizes abduction is not regression to a pre-reflective relationship to the world as such, but rather the use of self-control and experience for the purpose of liberation to enable the free play of ideas and perceptions to take place. It is therefore not free association as such, which is merely being dressed up as 'creativity', but an active form of release in which sight is never completely lost of the problem at hand that is calling for explanation. Peirce describes how this enables the scientist to find a promising idea for a hypothesis which then, if nurtured with loving care – as opposed to applying force and determination – unfolds according to its own logic until it is finally ripe for testing. Peirce's ideas on artistic creativity and, above all, on divine-cosmological creativity show that his contribution to the theory of creativity does not deserve to be criticized for being all too narrowly limited to science.

For William James, the second famous representative of pragmatism, the relationship between the self-experience of the free will and science's image of the world posed a much more dramatic problem than it did for Peirce. Modern though Peirce's insights were in the fields of semiotics and the philosophy of science, later generations find something pre-modern in his unremitting trust in an optimistic understanding of natural history as the work of a creator-god, something reminiscent of the American transcendentalists' romantic philosophy of nature. By contrast, the relationship between a religiously grounded belief in the free will of a person acting morally and the view of the world offered by the sciences as a universe governed throughout by causality led to a crisis in the young William James, for he consequently felt that the meaning of life itself had been cast into question. If everything were causally determined, he reasoned, then human actions and decisions could have no influence on the course of the world; and that meant that even one's own life could not be planned or designed. This crisis did not simply emerge out of the problematic relationship between religion and science but was already inherent in the understanding of science itself. It was thanks to Peirce that the actions of the scientist could now be interpreted as creative acts; however, the popular view was that the natural laws revealed by science seemed precisely to preclude human creativity. James' personal way out of this crisis, which he experienced not merely as a philosophical problem, but as a paralysing depression, took on representative significance for the subsequent generation of American intellectuals. This solution consisted in considering that the human ability to consciously direct attention to the contents of the imagination and to choose between alternative actions itself fulfilled a function – to ensure the survival of the human organism in its environment. In the second half of the nineteenth century, Darwin's theory of evolution was one of the most spectacular success stories in the search for scientific explanations. Thanks to James, the theory of evolution and the assumption of the free will no longer appeared to be antithetical concepts, for it now seemed possible to synthesize them in the concept of a 'functionalist' psychology, that is, a psychology which defined all operations of the mind in terms of their function for the organism's active mastery of its environment. James' *Principles of Psychology* of 1890, the final product of more than ten years' intellectual development, is a milestone in the development of this approach in psychology. Subsequently James felt compelled to elaborate the epistemological and cosmological-ontological implications of the position he had struggled to attain in *The Principles of Psychology*. The epistemological strand led James to propagate 'pragmatism' and its theory of truth, which caused Peirce and others to throw up their arms in horror at James' conceptual imprecision, and which caused an outrage in Europe.[110] The cosmological strand led to a philosophy which portrayed the world as non-determined and thus open to human determination, as a field of possibilities in which something new can evolve. The crucial advance on the position formulated in 1890 in *The Principles of Psychology*, however, was made in *The Varieties of Religious Experience*, which appeared in 1902. Whereas *The Principles of Psychology* had centred on the function of the human psyche in actively grappling with the environment, James now turned his attention to religious experience as the dimension in which the life of the psyche is constituted in the first place. If James' entire thinking was based on the strength of a feeling of self, a conviction that it was possible to design one's life, he was now inquiring into the processes which enabled this feeling of self to come about. This question, too, can be described as an inquiry into the function of religious experience, but James is attempting much more than simply to relativize the cognitive claims or social impact of religion by means of ideology critique. He is striving for a self-reflection of the fundamental feeling of life had by persons who are able to experience their own creative abilities as part of a suprapersonal creative life context, or as its opposite. In his psychology of religion, James thus comes closest to the issues addressed by the philosophy of life. Yet even here the specific nature of human creativity is not subsumed under a general concept of 'life'; rather, attention is focused on the constitution of a creative feeling of life in the pre-conscious experience of the world.

George Herbert Mead's thought continues the process, begun by James, of translating pragmatist themes into a programme of empirical social science with biological foundations. Remnants of a traditional concept of the soul and inconsistent ideas of a parallel between the physical and the psychical, still present in James' work, are overcome by a consistent 'definition of the psychical'[111] in a functionalist sense. Mead's decisive contribution, however, lay in his proceeding to focus on the way in which personality structures are constituted in the dynamics of interpersonal relationships. For Mead, the assumption of a pre-social substantial self was one of the cornerstones of the possessive individualism which he was combating on both a moral and a political level and which made societies appear to be groupings of atomistic individuals with predefined interests. He believed that the influence of this individualism was still at work in James' psychology, which, although recognizing the role of the perception of others and of self-images in human action, did not assign constitutive significance to them. In this respect, Mead found stronger inspiration in the traditions of classical German philosophy, in particular the writings of Hegel, and in neo-idealist works of the late nineteenth century. However, unlike these thinkers, Mead did not seek to discover an inner logic according to which the self unfolds, but wanted instead to gain a radical new understanding of this self as constituted by the structures of communication. His concept of the human person and human action is 'constructivistic' in the sense that even the interaction of the person with himself is regarded as the result of the social structures of interaction between different persons. Here, how-ever, the pre-personal core of a person is not conceived of as passive, which would mean that the person was a mere result of social expectations. The crucial significance of the idea of creativity for Mead's model of the personality can be gauged from his concept of the 'I', which he regards as the source of unanticipated spontaneities that surprise the actor himself no less than his partners. Personality formation does not reduce this core of spontaneity, but what does happen is that the focus of conflict between it and the judgements and expectations of others is shifted to within the person himself. Mead developed this idea as the basis for a social psychology and a system

of ethics. He was also interested in the consequences of this idea for
the cognitive development of abilities which were not directly social,
such as the constitution of permanent objects in perception and the
constitution of temporal structures.

The broadest exposition of the idea of creativity contained in, and
characteristic of, pragmatism was that presented by John Dewey.
Alongside James he was particularly frequently the butt of anti-
pragmatist attacks which accused him of reducing all action to mere
acts of adaptation. And, like James, for a long time he could only see
these attacks as no more than a grotesque misreading of his intentions.
After all, his motif was not adaptation, but growth, self-enhancement,
creativity.

> Thus his logic is a logic of research and discovery, and not one of a pre-
> existent reality, his ethics is an ethics of the character in the process of
> formation and not what might be called a 'theory of values', his social
> philosophy is a philosophy of a communal life that opens up new future
> horizons and not a doctrine of social forms, his aesthetics is a theory of
> artistic creation and not a doctrine of beauty, and finally his philosophy
> of living beings is a doctrine of the ascending process of life and not a
> theory of the organic.[112]

Likewise, his theory of education was precisely not a pedagogics of
adaptation, but rather the attempt to allow the child to grow in
problem situations of absorbing interest by dint of his own creative
problem-solving behaviour. Yet it was not until the 1920s that Dewey
went further than merely refuting misinterpretations and intimating
at a pragmatist theory of values, art and religion. The first step in this
direction was marked by *Experience and Nature*, an elaboration of
Dewey's metaphysics, to be followed in the thirties by monographs
on each of these three major themes.[113] Dewey's theory of art is
particularly comprehensive, and in many respects deserves to be
regarded as the highpoint in an oeuvre spanning so many themes. The
pragmatist precursors of this book – an essay by Mead and Peirce's
approach towards a theory of qualitative immediacy, which Dewey
studied, not by coincidence, at the same time as working on *Art and
Experience* – cannot compare with the scope of Dewey's book on the
subject.[114] And it is this book which shall serve as the basis for a
concluding discussion of pragmatism's contribution to a theory of
creativity.

In *Art and Experience*, Dewey is concerned to re-establish a relationship between art and everyday life. He dismisses with almost polemi-

cal vigour the idea that an aesthetic theory should take as its starting point works of art in their final state, already hanging in museums.

> When artistic objects are separated from both conditions of origin and operation in experience, a wall is built around them that renders almost opaque their general significance, with which esthetic theory deals. Art is remitted to a separate realm, where it is cut off from that association with the materials and aims of every other form of human effort, undergoing, and achievement. A primary task is thus imposed upon one who undertakes to write upon the philosophy of the fine arts. This task is to restore continuity between the refined and intensified forms of experience that are works of art and the everyday events, doings and sufferings that are universally recognized to constitute experience.[115]

Yet Dewey not only sets out to shift the focus away from a separate sphere of artworks and onto aesthetic experience in general, but takes the even more radical step of emphasizing the aesthetic dimension of all human experience. In order to understand what he means by this we need to remind ourselves of the basic pragmatist model of situated creativity, the idea, namely, that new variations of action are generated by the tension of problems contained in situations. Dewey now adds a new distinction to this basic model. Whereas all actions involve experiences of some kind, he talks of experiences of a special quality as *'an* experience'. His aim in so doing is to bring out the holistic, coherent nature of certain experiences which seem almost of themselves to stand above the flow of multifarious experiences. In normal actions, various aspects are simply placed next to one another, without being integrated, and actions which have already commenced are, for no immanent reason, not pursued further.

> There is distraction and dispersion; what we observe and what we think, what we desire and what we get, are at odds with each other. We put our hands to the plow and turn back; we start and then we stop, not because the experience has reached the end for the sake of which it was initiated but because of extraneous interruptions or of inner lethargy.[116]

However, we are also familiar with cases where the opposite occurs and something whole is created. This refers not to the wholeness of a work, but to the holistic nature of an experience.

> A piece of work is finished in a way that is satisfactory; a problem receives its solution; a game is played through; a situation, whether that of eating a meal, playing a game of chess, carrying on a conversation,

writing a book, or taking part in a political campaign, is so rounded out
that its close is a consummation and not a cessation. Such an experience
is a whole and carries with it its own individualizing quality and self-
sufficiency. It is *an* experience.[117]

Thus for Dewey the contrast is not between art and everyday life but
between rounded versus fragmented experience. Every kind of practical action can have the aesthetic quality of being 'rounded out'.
'Roundness' is not meant to be a formal quality, but rather implies
that each partial action is comprehensively laden with meaning for the
actor. The same action – for example, cooking – can be experienced as
a meaningless chore or as a meaningful contribution to a life shared
with others. Dewey also refers to sexual experiences,[118] which may be
experienced as something brutish or as a meaningful expression of
love. Without holding out the utopian prospect of a perfect society in
which art as a separate category will become obsolete, Dewey criticizes
the reduction of art to a merely compensatory or ornamental role in
everyday life. He wants more, and thus lines up alongside those who
stand in the romantic tradition of criticizing the conditions of industrial labour and commercial civilization, for

in a better-ordered society than that in which we live, an infinitely
greater happiness than is now the case would attend all modes of
production. We live in a world in which there is an immense amount of
organization, but it is an external organization, not one of the ordering
of a growing experience, one that involves, moreover, the whole of the
live creature, toward a fulfilling conclusion.[119]

Dewey's theory of the aesthetic dimension that is potentially inherent
in all experience thus serves at the same time as a yardstick for his
cultural and social critique. He is striving for a society in which actors
are able to perform meaningful actions, that is, action in which all
partial actions are imbued with the meaning of the overall action and
where the individual action is experienced as part of a supra-
individual action. Thus for Dewey, the concept of creativity approxi-
mates to that of the self-created meaningfulness of what one does.
This is something which is not the preserve of geniuses, but is
accessible to all actors to the extent that every human being has unique
experiences which, if only he has confidence in himself, he can share
with others. Dewey stressed, as Hannah Arendt was later to do, that
the basis of individuality was 'natality', the very fact that the person
had been born.

We are given to associating creative mind with persons regarded as rare and unique, like geniuses. But every individual is in his own way. Each one experiences life from a different angle than anybody else, and consequently has something distinctive to give others if he can turn his experiences into ideas and pass them on to others. Each individual that comes into the world is a new beginning; the universe itself is, as it were, taking a fresh start in him and trying to do something, even if on a small scale, that it has never done before.[120]

Admittedly, the shift of emphasis from art to the creativity of all experience now begs the question as to what it is that none the less makes art stand out as a distinct form of human action and enjoyment. According to Dewey, the specific nature of art lies in the fact that it takes as its goal that which in all other forms of human action can never be more than an unintentional or secondary by-product. In the creation of an artwork, roundedness and meaningfulness of experience become the immediate goals. Dewey rejects the notion that art is on a par with dreams, play or expression. A key to understanding the pragmatist conception of creativity is the difference between Dewey's understanding of expression and that inherent in more traditional conceptions. The decisive point for Dewey is that we do not imagine artistic creation as the objectification of contents of meaning which are already present in finished form in the inner world of the creative subject. This model of expression would be irreconcilable with the basic pragmatist model of situated creativity. Rather, Dewey sees art as evolving out of a collision between sedimented, pre-cognitive experiences and reality.

On the side of the self, elements that issue from prior experience are stirred into action in fresh desires, impulsions and images. These proceed from the subconscious, not cold or in shapes that are identified with particulars of the past, not in chunks and lumps, but fused in the fire of internal commotion. They do not seem to come from the self, because they issue from a self not consciously known.[121]

Like James' theory of religion, Dewey's theory of art is aimed at experiences in which the self is not master in its own domain. 'Expression' presupposes resistance. Dewey chooses a mechanistic sounding metaphor: 'Unless there is com-pression nothing is expressed. The turmoil marks the place where inner impulse and contact with environment, in fact or in idea, meet and create a ferment.'[122] Expression in this pragmatist sense, then, is not an explosion – or, as Dewey terms it in his *Theory of Valuation*, an ejaculation – but is tied to a medium of expression. The latter is formed such that something new emerges which cannot be reduced either to reality or to the mood which precipitated it. Artistic creation transforms pre-cognitive experiences into something with a new shape; the creative process brings out new aspects of reality, explores new avenues of experience which then gel to a new totality of meaning.[123] Thus the process of artistic creation, the striving for *an* experience, for the wholeness of action pervaded with meaning, leads to works which bring into the world new modes of sensory experience not only for the artist himself but also for other people.

Dewey does not allow his idea of creativity to degenerate into a metaphysics of art. The most striking proof is a comparison with Dewey's book on religion, *A Common Faith*, which was written at roughly the same time as *Art and Experience*. Whereas in the book on art Dewey is concerned to show that creativity is related to the fact that all action is potentially pervaded with meaning, viewing art from this angle as an exemplary case of the possibility of such an experience, *A Common Faith* focuses on the question of how ideals are constituted in human action and what role they play in that action. Dewey pursues a parallel line of argument in both books insofar as he describes religion as something that cannot simply be equated with its institutionalized forms, such as the life of the church and the dogmatic forms of religious doctrines, just as he resisted attempts to portray art as something that could only be found in museums. Dewey is interested in religious experience, and here again his treatment culminates in the assertion that potentially there is a religious side to all experience. In order to clarify what he means by the religious dimension of experience, he distinguishes between three interrelated but different concepts: accommodation, adaptation and adjustment. The simplest form is accommodation, which implies the passive accommodation to an environment in particular aspects of action. Adaptation, by contrast, is what a person does who actively reshapes the world to serve the purposes of life. In this instance, it is we who change our environment to suit ourselves, rather than changing ourselves to suit our environment. The third type, which goes beyond either of these two, is what Dewey calls 'adjustment'. Here it is not a matter of individual desires and the possibility of satisfying them, but rather the constitution of the person himself in his fundamental strivings. 'It is a change *of* will conceived as the organic plenitude of our being, rather than any special change *in* will.'[124] All religions claim to affect personality in such a fundamental way. Yet Dewey turns this idea on its head by asserting that such a profound influence is not

attributable to some essential quality of religions; instead, he understands the profundity of influence as a criterion for defining what is
religious. 'It is not a religion that brings it about, but when it occurs,
from whatever cause and by whatever means, there is a religious
outlook and function.'[125] Thus he defines as religious those experiences
in which a person's unquestionable binding values, his ideals, come
about.

Dewey's theory of religion is an attempt to develop an empirical
philosophy of the role played by ideals in action. He rejects philosophies which either neglect the role of ideal values or conversely
treat them as transcendental givens which precede all action. In
contrast to materialism and idealism, he asks what 'function' ideals
have in action, that is, what is the significance and the origin of value
commitments and the unquestionable status of value presuppositions.
Ideals are not something we decide freely to set ourselves; rather they
take hold of us and are at the root of our individual wishes and goals.
'Conviction in the moral sense signifies being conquered, vanquished,
in our active nature by an ideal end; it signifies acknowledgment of
its rightful claim over our desires and purposes.'[126] If we are conquered by an ideal in this sense, it exercises a unifying, integrating
influence on our person and the way we see the world. Although the
self is not a whole, a person can indeed have wholeness as an ideal.
Nothing meaningful can be said about the wholeness of the world,
but what we know for certain, according to Dewey, is that a holistic
self tends to sublate the rapid sequence of different scenarios that is
our reality into a totality. It is through their creative powers of
imagination that human beings gain access to the ideals. This does not
mean that ideals are mere fantasies. Just as the artist creates a new
work out of the possibilities inherent in the world, so – according to
Dewey – does the inventor and the prophet of a new morality.
Imagination is creative because it recognizes the possibilities contained in the world and contributes towards their being made reality:
'The new vision does not arise out of nothing, but emerges through
seeing, in terms of possibilities, that is of imagination, old things in
new relations serving a new end which the new end aids in creating.'[127]

In the shape of his theory of religion, Dewey touches on various
groups of issues which he does not deal with exhaustively. One
certainly cannot claim that he analysed the dynamic collective action
processes that constitute ideals, as did Durkheim in *The Elementary
Forms of Religious Life*. Nor did he pay anything like sufficient attention
to the individual specification of ideals in concrete action. Yet for all
that, it does become clearer what his idea of action pervaded with

meaning is intended to signify. What he is referring to is a kind of action that does not satisfy the actor only when the goal has been attained, but which is inherently and in all partial actions oriented towards the realization of ideals, these being voluntarily accepted as having greater importance than immediate desires and urges. This is the articulation – albeit often in implied form – of a line of thought which permits us to apply the idea of creativity to the full spectrum of human action. The task of the following chapter will therefore consist in presenting, more systematically than has been attempted here hitherto, the essential dimensions of a revised action theory, based primarily on the pragmatist understanding of human action as situated creativity. This serves at the same time as the foundation for deliberations on social theory, which are oriented normatively, as was Dewey's work, towards the ideal of a 'creative democracy'.

3

Situation – Corporeality – Sociality
The Fundamentals of a Theory of the
Creativity of Action

The thrust of my argumentation so far has been, firstly, to show that
the idea of creativity has occupied a marginal position in the sociological tradition to date, and, secondly, to highlight in the form of a
typologizing review the various attempts at a theory of the creativity
of action which have been undertaken outside the domain of sociology. I shall now address the task of choosing the most advantageous
starting point for such a theory. It would be wrong to infer that the
intention of my argument so far has been merely to add yet another
type of action, namely creative action, to the list of possible types of
action. As my discussion of Weber, Durkheim, Tönnies and Simmel
has shown, my criticism of the sociological theory of action is clearly
not that it contains no reference to the creativity of action whatsoever,
but rather that theoretical fragments such as the concept of 'charisma',
which are obviously relevant to the question of creativity, have not
been consistently integrated into the overall theory. Moreover, I have
argued that some approaches towards a conceptualization of human
creativity have actually drawn an artificial rift between creative action
and the totality of human action. My intention is therefore to provide
not a mere extension to, but instead a fundamental restructuring of
the principles underlying mainstream action theory. It is not that
common typologies of action are simply incomplete; rather, I am
calling into question the very principle on which these typologies are
based. Any typology of action can be said to be complete, formally
speaking, if it overtly or covertly deploys a residual category into
which all those phenomena fall which it cannot explicitly grasp
conceptually. It by no means follows, however, that such a typology
actually has the power to reveal phenomena.

There are three reasons why one should not follow those economic, sociological, psychological and analytical-philosophical theories of action which take 'rational action' as their starting point.[1] Firstly, the very concept of *action* isolates the individual action from its context in a way that is by no means a matter of course. Context here has the double meaning that every action, firstly, takes place in a certain situation and, secondly, presupposes an actor who performs not only this one action. This choice of starting point may thus itself already involve a theoretically problematical extraction of action from its situational and biographical contexts. There is, however, an un-intended effect of taking *rational* action as the starting point which weighs even more heavily than these two reasons. All theories of action which proceed from this point automatically create a non-rational counterpart. In doing so they create an evaluative framework into which they force the multiplicity of action phenomena. This is true irrespective of the definition each theory of action gives to the concept of rationality. It could, as we know, be conceived of in a very narrow sense, as the maximization of efficiency in goal achievement, which then leaves the way open for various interpretations of the relationship between the goals themselves and individual or collective self-interest. In this narrow conception of rationality, clearly dis-tinguishable forms of deviation from strictly goal-oriented action are lumped together, for example spontaneous emotional action and reflective moral action. We encounter the same problem if, in contrast to this narrow conception of rationality, precisely this circumspect moral action is defined in true Kantian manner as rational per se, from which it follows then that emotions and spontaneity are excluded from rationality, and an amoral orientation towards self-interest can then itself be judged irrational. Even the most daring conception of rationality to emerge in our time, namely Habermas' theory of communicative rationality, suffers from this dilemma. There, various types of rationality are defined as stages towards the full concept of communicative rationality; however, applied to a theory of action, this merely allows us to delineate different types of action in line with these types of rationality. It is therefore possible to find the concept of communicative rationality convincing as a theory of rationality and yet resist accepting the way in which Habermas proceeds to develop a theory of action out of the same train of thought as gave birth to his theory of rationality.[2]

Yet what alternative is there to the procedure outlined above? There can be no doubt that microsociological researches into factual action in terms of specific contexts and sequences, as practised by phenomenological sociology, ethnomethodology and conversation analysis, are capable of producing a wealth of empirical data. Yet they cannot in themselves provide us with an alternative theory of action. They may quite correctly admonish the purely conceptual work done by, for example, Parsons in developing a categorial framework in action theory, for being bereft of any empirically verifiable characteristics of real human action. However, in the process they risk losing touch completely with the topic of rationality. The true alternative to taking rational action as the starting point, and thereby creating a residual category, therefore lies, I would suggest, in the *reconstructive introduction* of the concept of rational action.[3] By reconstructive introduction I mean here the process of shedding light on the tacit assumptions behind ideas of rational action. All theories of action which proceed from a type of rational action – irrespective of whether they are based on a narrower or broader, a utilitarian or a normative concept of rationality – make at least three assumptions. They presuppose firstly that the actor is capable of purposive action, secondly that he has control over his own body, and thirdly that he is autonomous vis-à-vis his fellow human beings and environment. According to this view, if the actor shows a low degree of concentration on purposive action, a loss, or low level, of body control, a loss or an abdication of autonomy as an individual, then he will appear less rational or indeed non-rational and there will be less likelihood of his actions being classified as rational. The proponents of such conceptions are well aware that the preconditions assumed by the model of rational action are frequently not to be found in empirically observable action. However, these writers are forced to claim that the limited degree to which these preconditions obtain is not a deficiency of their particular theory but a fault of the actors themselves. A similar fate befalls the common-sense insight that human beings do not enjoy such preconditions from birth. From the perspective of advocates of rational models of action in the broad sense, childhood development is merely the process of acquiring the capacity for rational action. Such theorists discount the possibility that a study of this developmental process can teach us anything about the structure of action and the capacity for action itself. Indeed, empirical knowledge of the capacity for action and its development can add nothing to an analytically defined and fixated type of rational action.

I am not in any way denying the empirical usefulness of rational models of action when it comes to analysing certain social phenomena. What I do question, however, is the claim that because of its usefulness this model of rational action, with all its tacit assumptions, can be

applied to an ever increasing number of fields of study without a
thorough reflection of precisely those intrinsic presuppositions. What
follows is therefore an analysis of *the intentional character of human
action, the specific corporeality and the primary sociality of all human
capacity for action.* I am convinced that this analysis of the tacit
assumptions inherent in theories of action based on concepts of
rational action ineluctably also alters our whole understanding of
(instrumental) rationality and normativity.[4] What emerges is a picture
of the creativity of human action. Such an analysis enables us to
introduce the relevant aspects of notions of creativity developed by
pragmatism and that expressivist anthropological tradition, of which
hermeneutics is the purest form, into the development of a theory of
action in the social sciences.

3.1   A Non-Teleological Interpretation of the Intentionality of Action

'Every serious contemplation of the ultimate components of meaningful human action is initially bound to the categories of "ends" and
"means".'[5] Talcott Parsons took this famous remark by Max Weber,
which expresses the latter's indebtedness to a modern economic theory
of action, as the motto for his *Structure of Social Action*. As the debates
on this work and Parsons' later oeuvre have shown,[6] Parsons did not
in fact orient his work so clearly towards this means–ends schema as
the choice of motto would suggest. However, the motto did enable
him to proclaim from the outset of the book his opposition to two
other theoretical strands in the social sciences. On the one hand, the
means–ends schema contradicts the stimulus–response schema put
forward by behaviourism and by other, often older forms of determinism, which reduce human action to the mere effect either of causes
rooted in situations or the natural endowments of human beings
themselves. On the other hand, he also had his sights fixed on the
idealistic-historicist tradition which interpreted the world in terms of
meaning and expression, conceiving of human action as the execution
of the intentions of some suprapersonal spirit. Compared with both of
these theoretical tacks, the means–ends schema appears more suitable
for a theory of action. It is intended there to integrate the role played
by conditions and means of action in situational-deterministic thought
and the role played by ends and the values constitutive of such ends
in idealistic approaches. This, of course, raises the question whether
such an integration can succeed. This is not to ask whether it is really

true that all action phenomena can be interpreted in terms of means and ends – neither Weber nor Parsons ever claimed that they could. Rather, the question is whether the means–ends schema does not in fact *prevent* us from reaching an understanding of the preconditions for goal-setting and goal-oriented action in that it treats these phenomena as given and self-evident.

In the field of sociological theory, no one has questioned more explicitly than Niklas Luhmann the uncritical use of the means–ends schema to interpret human action, in particular organized cooperation.[7] Luhmann compiles a mass of empirical findings from studies in organizational and industrial sociology, and uses them to dispel the notion that organizations can be understood simply in terms of their organizational purpose. At the same time, he draws together on the level of action theory the objections which various currents of thought have raised against a teleological interpretation of human action. His main authority in this connection is the pragmatist John Dewey. Luhmann's own ambition here is to show that there is a limit to the extent to which organizations can be analysed in terms of action theory, in order then to justify his adoption of models derived from systems theory. Our aim in the present context is the opposite of Luhmann's, namely to realign the theory of action in order precisely to avoid the necessity of resorting to instruments of systems theory in order to solve the problems of social order.[8] After all, the fact that widely disparate theoretical projects attach so much importance to the legitimacy of the means–ends schema indicates that we are dealing here not with mere quibbles, but with a problem of crucial significance to the strategy of sociological theory construction.

The foil for Luhmann's critique is provided by Max Weber's theory of action and model of bureaucracy, and Luhmann is particularly interested to show how the two are interconnected. No one would dispute that Weber's typology of action was based on purposive-rational action. It is equally obvious that Weber's model of bureaucracy was based on the claim that this type of organization is rational. Did Weber, therefore, believe that rational organizations presuppose the rational action of all participants? Luhmann's answer to this question is a qualified yes. He correctly observes that when analysing forms of social order, Weber switches from the concepts of his action theory to concepts associated with a theory of domination.

The ends/means schema is not abandoned as the underlying form of action rationality, but Weber takes account of the fact that most social systems, and political systems in particular, are not bound to specific ends and specific means but are capable of altering their ends and means. He judges them to be rational to the extent that they find the means which correspond to their *respective* ends. Therefore, in order to provide a theoretical account of such systems, he does not proceed from a characterization of their special ends, but from a means which is so generalized as to be able to serve various, changing ends: namely that of domination.[9]

In other words, the rationality of the (bureaucratic) form of organization lies precisely in its applicability to a variety of different ends. It is a means for those who are able to determine ends. In theory, of course, this latter category potentially includes all the members of the organization. As a rule, however, it is restricted, in Weber's view, to the entrepreneurs, the rulers, the leaders, that is, to those who are able to assert their will by issuing orders and instructions that determine the actions of others. Thus, the ways by which the right to define goals and to issue orders are justified, the ways, in other words, by which more or less limited domination is legitimated, are of decisive importance.

Empirical sociological studies of organization have not borne out this model of bureaucracy. Neither is a clear purpose for the organization the decisive factor on which action in organizations is actually based, nor are orders and instructions the only, or indeed necessarily the most effective, form of communication within organizations. Frequently, the purposes of organizations are not clear but are stated merely as general values which are more suitable as an external legitimation than as a guide to action itself. In order for them to take on this second function, they must first be actively specified by the individuals concerned. The pursuit of the organization's goal is typically only one of many purposes of action within organizations; it is therefore most certainly possible that the maintenance of the organization over time and the legitimation of its actions play an independent role in the orientation of an organization's actions. The goals of an organization can change without threatening, either internally or externally, the continued existence of the organization. The organization's goals can be subdivided into contradictory secondary objectives, or they may even be inherently contradictory from the outset. The relationship between the purpose of the organization and the motivation of the members can take on very different forms. It would be misleading simply to derive the individual actor's own ways of determining goals from the purpose of the organization. There are equally numerous objections to the notion that the most rational form of organization is one with a hierarchical command structure. Arguments which have been brought forward to refute the reality and viability of the command-hierarchy model include reference to the specialized expert knowledge of subordinates, to their independent interaction with the outside world, to the stimulation of their ability to learn, to horizontal cooperation and to the need to encourage autonomous action.

What is decisive about these research developments is that they have not merely produced new additions to the list of already familiar phenomena. In each case, the point has not been to establish the existence of a second, informal organizational structure alongside the formal structure as determined by the purpose of the organization, nor to augment the command principle with additional aspects, such as the public servant's commitment to duty or the willingness to take personal responsibility. The substantive importance of these research findings is rather that they suggest the necessity of taking an entirely new perspective. In many cases, if an organization were oriented exclusively towards an explicit goal or built entirely on a command hierarchy, it would be doomed to failure. The empirical evidence points up not just the discrepancy between the rational model and the reality – the existence of this discrepancy would also be conceded by the advocates of the rational model themselves – but the sheer impossibility of realizing the rational model and the fact that taking this model as a starting point would bear no empirical fruit. Given these circumstances, Luhmann's own conclusion is to invert the question. He no longer seeks to discover how organizational structures are derived from a goal, but asks instead what function the setting of goals has for organizations. Taking up the thread of system functionalism which Parsons developed in the late 1950s, he sees the function of goals as consisting in 'denoting the tribute which the system must pay to its environment in order to survive'.[10] Thus defining goals is subordinated to system maintenance. Expanding on this idea in a highly productive manner, Luhmann succeeds in providing a consistent account of all those findings which, according to the rational model of organization, appear to be mere aberrations.

Admittedly, even if we accept this critique of the means–ends schema, it does not necessarily follow that we are then obliged to subordinate it to a system model, and indeed Luhmann makes no attempt to give the impression that there is any logical compulsion to do so. After all, what has been demonstrated thus far is simply that there is an affinity between the rational model of action and the rational model of the organization, and that this rational model of the organization is flawed from an empirical point of view. The only direct conclusion to be drawn is that a different interpretation of action from that provided by the rational model may help us to overcome this difficulty. And indeed, at the same time, Luhmann's argumentation also operates on an action-theoretical level. Like Dewey, he returns to action as a process which, in everyday experience, is by no means structured in terms of ends and means, not even of chains of ends and means in which ends can serve as means for higher ends. However, not only the social scientist is capable of applying a teleological interpretational model to the natural flow of his actions, but also the actor himself. Luhmann describes the means–ends schema as that branch of a causalistic interpretation of action – whereby action is explained in terms of cause and effect – in which the Ego of the actor himself is cast in the role of the cause. If we compare this with the ideas of the Ancient Greeks, such as Aristotle's philosophy of action, it soon becomes apparent that a causalistic interpretation of action is anything but self-evident. However, the modern mind has great difficulty in accepting the Ancient Greeks' idea of the 'telos' as a moment of maturation and completion intrinsic to an action. In the transition from antiquity to modernity, the concept of purpose has acquired a radically subjective meaning. Common to modern interpretations is the extraction of a stable goal from the flow of action. The causalistic interpretation is given a more liberal form when we say that numerous causes underlie all action, and that every action causes numerous effects. Yet this leaves the interpretational model used virtually unchanged. The distinguishing feature of Luhmann's reformulation is that his inquiry is directed towards the function of a causalistic interpretation of action in general, and of the means–ends schema in particular, *in relation to human action.*

In both cases, he sees the function as being to provide the actor with an overview of events. With reference to the causalistic interpretation of human experience in general, this means that its function consists in 'systematizing the experiential and behavioural potentialities that manifest themselves in natural experience and interpreting them in such a way that they become available for the purposes of comparison and thus accessible to rationalization'.[11] With reference to the interpretation of action according to the schema of means and ends, Luhmann claims this schema fulfils a selective function for perceiving and evaluating the consequences of actions. He begins by disputing the usefulness of the idea that actors orient themselves towards a uniform value system which is divorced from reality. Like the pragmatists and the phenomenologists, Luhmann too goes back to the dynamics of natural experience, which tell us very clearly that the significance of values for our action depends on the degree to which they can be realized and on the level to which other values are satisfied. This enables him to regard it as the function of the concept of purpose to evaluate the consequences of actions:

> The concept of purpose denotes that effect, or complex of effects, which is supposed to justify action, i.e. it always describes no more than a part of the total complex of effects. Its 'subject' is not to bring about these specified effects, but rather purpose denotes their value in relation to the value of the secondary effects (including the effects of other possible actions, which we must pass up once we have committed ourselves to something else). To set a goal is to state that the value of the intended effects is sufficient to justify the action, *regardless of the value or non-value of the secondary or forgone effects* of other actions. The concept of means describes the same value-relationship from the other side of the dis-advantaged values. It starts from the causes which are appropriate to the achievement of the intended effect, and states that we can afford to ignore the value implications of those consequences of these causes that are extraneous to the purpose.[12]

In pursuing this line of thought, Luhmann focuses his functionalistic gaze not only on organizations but also on the dynamics of human action. The question as to the function of ends within systems of action applies to both the one and the other. It is therefore vital that we now direct our attention to the difference between Dewey's critique of the means–ends schema and Luhmann's use of these critical arguments.

In the first instance, this difference consists in the fact that, unlike Dewey's critique of the means–ends schema, Luhmann's functional analysis of this schema in action is not based on some positive concept of action that in some way evades the critique of the means–ends schema. Dewey's critique of the teleological interpretation of action is based on the possibility of '*genuine instrumentality*'; there is no counter-part to this ideal in Luhmann's theory. The critique of the rational model of organization is, however, compatible with both forms of relativization of the rational model of action.

Dewey put forward his critique of the means–ends schema of the interpretation of action in numerous writings, though his argumenta-tion is not always entirely clear and free of contradictions.[13] The starting point for his critique is precisely the contrast between action in pursuit of *externally set* goals and the ideal of action infused with meaning, as described here in the context of Dewey's theory of art and religion. This critique takes the form of an immanent critique to the extent that Dewey shows the categories 'ends' or 'goals' and 'means' to be far less self-evident than they appear to be. His first step is to claim that it is necessary to distinguish between the goals and the results of actions. This may sound trivial, as any actor knows that many of his goals remain unfulfilled, or that the results of his actions may differ considerably from goals he was actually pursuing. However, Dewey means more than this simple difference between goals and results. In his world view with its radical 'presentistic' metaphysics,[14] the results of present actions do not exist because they still lie in the future. The conception of goals as anticipated future states does not describe adequately their role in present action precisely because, as anticipations, they belong to the present. If we only dream of the future, we are not acting. Dewey therefore introduces the concept of the 'end-in-view' in order to define the role of goals in the organization of present action.

The significance of this conceptual innovation becomes clear when we consider the second step of the critique. Dewey speaks of a reciprocal relationship between an action's end and the means involved. In other words, he does not presuppose that the actor generally has a clear goal, and that it only remains to make the appropriate choice of means. On the contrary, the goals of actions are usually relatively undefined, and only become more specific as a consequence of the decision to use particular means. Reciprocity of goals and means therefore signifies the interaction of the choice of means and the definition of goals. The dimension of means in relation to the dimension of goals is in no way neutral. Only when we recognize that certain means are available to us do we discover goals which had not occurred to us before. Thus, means not only specify goals, but they also expand the scope for possible goal-setting. 'Ends-in-view' are not, therefore, vaguely conceived future situations, but concrete plans of action which serve to structure present action. They guide us in our choice between various possibilities of action, yet they themselves are also influenced by our perception of these possibilities. Dewey therefore defines an end as:

> the foresight of the alternative consequences attendant upon acting in a given situation in different ways, and the use of what is anticipated to direct observation and experiment. A true aim is thus opposed at every point to an aim which is imposed upon a process of action from without. The latter is fixed and rigid; it is not a stimulus to intelligence in the given situation, but is an externally dictated order to do such and such things.[15]

This rounds off his argumentation. Externally determined goals are excluded from the reflective processes that are intrinsic to action. Instead they are fixed at a level above the processes of action and it is this which degrades the means of action to the status of pure means. In Dewey's writings on ethics it becomes clear that his critique of fixed goals applies not only to external but also to self-imposed compulsion. Every sacralization of an end as a value per se conceals from the actor the further consequences of his definition of goals and choice of means, as though in some miraculous way these would not occur or could be ignored.[16] Dewey's orientation is not, however, towards a blind respect for values and a blinkered pursuit of goals, but rather a pragmatic participation in collective action in which all values and all goals are potential objects of reflection and discussion. Despite the significance his educational theory attaches to the role of play, Dewey rejects the common tendency to distinguish play from work on the grounds that the former is goal-free. According to Dewey, play most certainly does involve goals in the sense of an inner regulation of action. It does not consist of random movements, but often requires exceptionally sharp concentration and deeply preoccupies the child. However, the goal orientations involved in play are not fixed externally and maintained irrespective of inner resistance to them. Those who play can be said to be free because they are able to abandon or redefine the current goals if their actions no longer promise fulfilment. The goals of actions do not stand for something to be preserved beyond the limits of the play situation. In a psychological sense, this description can also apply to work, no matter how protracted the chains of means and ends may be here.

> Both (work and play) are equally free and intrinsically motivated, apart from false economic conditions which tend to make play into idle excitement for the well to do, and work into uncongenial labor for the poor. Work is psychologically simply an activity which consciously includes regard for consequences as part of itself; it becomes constrained labor when the consequences are outside of the activity as an end to which activity is merely a means. Work which remains permeated with the play attitude is art . . .[17]

Dewey's critique of the means–ends schema as a tool for interpreting human action is, in other words, motivated by his refusal to accept a form of action (like work) carried out under external or self-imposed compulsion as the prototype for a theory of action. For Dewey the crucial issue is the difference between goals which are external to the action and prescribed, and goals which emerge in the course of the action itself but which can also be revised or abandoned. The pragmatist's scepticism regarding any blurring of this distinction coincides here with the objections to the means–ends schema raised by thinkers influenced by the philosophy of life.[18] Thus Tönnies also addressed himself to the problem of the universal applicability of this schema, and concluded that there were two cases in which it stood in obvious contradiction to the actor's own experience: when a person acts on an inclination or a whim, he or she no more distinguishes between means and ends than when performing ingrained habitual actions. Both cases correspond exactly to the pragmatist's ideas on action permeated with meaning and action that has descended to the level of unreflected routine. Georg Simmel goes even further. In his metaphysical work, written towards the end of his career, Simmel views human freedom as lying precisely not in humankind's capacity for purposive action but rather in our capacity to break with purposiveness. Indeed, he defines humans as 'non-purposive' beings, as beings delivered from purpose. But it was Heidegger who provided the most radical demonstration of the impossibility of defining human life as a whole in terms of a chain of means and ends. After all, Heidegger argues, we do not rush from one action to the next in order to reach the goal we have been striving for at the end of our lives. If we wish to understand our relationship to ourselves and to our lives as a whole we need to invoke categories of a totally different nature, categories which Heidegger defines as 'for the sake of', as opposed to 'in order to', and which he attempts to grasp more fully via his analysis of our relationship to death. If we summarize these admittedly quite discrete arguments showing the limited applicability of the means–ends schema, we find that neither routine action nor action permeated with meaning, neither creative nor existentially reflected action can be accounted for using this model. Nothing remains, therefore, of the apparent self-evidence of taking this model as the starting point for developing a theory of action. What we must still clarify, however, is from what assumptions this apparent self-evidence arose and how – once we have dispensed with these assumptions – we can develop an alternative understanding of goal-setting and goal-orientation in human action.

The idea that human action can best be understood as the pursuit of preconceived goals is linked to other tacit assumptions which are deeply rooted in the traditions of western philosophy. Although it cannot be claimed that these assumptions have remained unchallenged – indeed, they have been the target of polemical attacks by some of the greatest thinkers of our century, such as Dewey, Heidegger, Merleau-Ponty, Wittgenstein and Ryle – they have none the less established themselves as cultural truisms. Ironically, at the same time as these assumptions were increasingly being banished from philosophy, they began to receive support from a new quarter in the shape of attempts to simulate human thought in computer programs.[19] I am referring here to assumptions whereby human cognition is conceived of in terms of a contemplative relationship of a cognizing subject to a world of facts and in which it is taken to be the task of cognition to select and classify these facts. These assumptions on cognition are, in a certain sense, merely the obverse of the idea that goal-orientation plays a central role in human action. Common to both ways of thinking is the idea that *first* orientation is found through cognizance of the world, only *then* to be followed by action. According to this view, which seems to assume that lethargy is the natural human state, action is initiated only after meaningful goals have been set in the cognized world and then – in a separate act of will – the decision to pursue such goals has been taken. Under these assumptions, an action conforms most closely to the ideal of rational action when its goal has been defined in complete independence of the action and as clearly as possible. The rational actor does not allow received modes of action, or his own habits, or the range of means of action which happen to be currently available, to induce him to define his goal less clearly or to select technically less appropriate or less economical means. In other words, concealed behind the notion that an act of goal-setting must precede action is the assumption that human cognition is independent of action or that it could and should be made independent of action.

The teleological interpretation of the intentionality of action necessarily implies that cognition is divorced from action. Within the theories of action put forward in the various disciplines, there are several variations on this teleological interpretation. Let us ignore for the moment whether they regard unambiguously defined, preconceived intentions, or clearly identifiable motives, or internalized values that are unambiguously applicable to specific situations as the stimulus for action. It can be claimed of all of them that they repeat the Cartesian distinctions between self and world, between mind and body – distinctions which the pragmatists, and others who accorded the category of action a central role in their theories, assumed had been eliminated by proceeding in their theories from a concept of action. Intentions, motives and values appear here as elements of an internal world which can only influence the external world by a separate conscious act of decision. What they encounter then is a world the cognizance of which is influenced by them. An alternative understanding of goal-setting is therefore compelled to conceive of intentionality no longer as a non-corporeal, purely intellectual faculty. The means–ends schema cannot be overcome until we recognize that the practical mediacy of the human organism and its situations precede all conscious goal-setting. A consideration of the concept of purpose must ineluctably involve taking account of the corporeality of human action and its creativity.

The alternative to a teleological interpretation of action, with its inherited dependence on Cartesian dualisms, is to conceive of perception and cognition not as preceding action but rather as a phase of action by which action is directed and redirected in its situational contexts. According to this alternative view, goal-setting does not take place by an act of the intellect *prior to* the actual action, but is instead the result of a reflection on aspirations and tendencies that are pre-reflective and have *already always* been operative. In this act of reflection, we thematize aspirations which are normally at work without our being actively aware of them. But where exactly are these aspirations located? They are located in our bodies. It is the body's capabilities, habits and ways of relating to the environment which form the background to all conscious goal-setting, in other words, to our intentionality. Intentionality itself, then, consists in a self-reflective control which we exercise over our current behaviour.

If this non-teleological and instead self-reflective conception of intentionality does justice to the matter at hand, then it changes our picture of all action-related phenomena. Probably the most spectacular change would be that of our understanding of human perception, which can now be interpreted as an action-related phenomenon.[20] According to this view, our perception of the world appears to be structured by our capacities for, and experiences of, action. Even when we are not pursuing any immediate intention of action, the world exists not simply as an external counterpart to our internal self, but in the form of possible actions. Our perception is directed not towards the properties of the world as such, but rather towards our being able to use in practice in the context of our actions that which we perceive. In our perception of reality, what we experience is not a subjective tailoring of reality, but reality as such. Given that the fundamental forms of our capacity for action lie in the intentional movement of our body in connection with locomotion, object-manipulation and communication, our world is initially structured according to these dimensions. We divide the world into categories such as accessible and inaccessible, familiar and unfamiliar, controllable and uncontrollable, responsive and unresponsive. If these action-related expectations inherent in our perception of the world are not met, we do indeed dissociate ourselves from a part of the world which now surprisingly transpires to be inaccessible and unfamiliar, uncontrollable or unresponsive, and accord it the status of an external object. Yet this external object with which we are confronted is atypical of our ongoing relationship to reality – it remains embedded in a world which we access and which is familiar to us by virtue of our capacity for action.

Human perception, as founded in our capacities for intentional physical movement, differs from the traditional picture of perception – from Descartes right down to notions of 'artificial intelligence' – in three respects.[21] Firstly, our corporeal–practical relationship to the world allows us to face the world with relatively unspecified expectations rather than with a clear, thoroughly defined value system, since our ability to come to terms with reality in a practical sense is an adequate criterion by which to gauge the validity of our expectations. Then, for the same reason, the world need not be subdivided into exhaustively defined data, but can be perceived globally. As long as no problems of action arise, human interaction with reality consists in a flexible interrelationship between global expectations and global perceptions. When such problems do arise, however, the expectations and perceptions become more specific in these individual cases, yet this does not entail a complete readjustment of expectations and perceptions in order to fit them into a precisely defined framework. And finally, the third difference lies in the fact that the body permits us to choose between various modes of perception and action, to switch from one mode to another and to substitute one for another. If, for example, simply by looking at an object we are unable to gain sufficient information about its practical significance, it may perhaps be useful in addition to resort to touch. It is therefore not necessary to exhaust the full analytical range of one mode of perception; rather it is possible to arrive at a satisfactory result for the practical purposes of action by a flexible application of various sensory organs and the experimental combination of modes of action. If these arguments are correct, then the superiority of human perception over attempts to simulate it does not arise from some 'higher' quality of the human intellect which is beyond the reach of computer programs, but rather by the fact that our perception is founded in the corporeality of human life.

Likewise, our ideas on the regulation of action are affected by dropping a teleological interpretation of the intentionality of action.

Every action takes place in a situation. If we adopt a teleological approach, then this fact is of interest only to the extent that in order to realize our preconceived intentions we need to take into account the conditions prevailing, and use such means as are available, in the given situation. In Parsons' classic version of the action frame of reference, the situational components are indeed limited specifically to conditions and means. What is missing, and what becomes immediately obvious the moment we adopt a non-teleological approach, is that it is not sufficient to consider human action as being *contingent* on the situation, but that it should also be recognized that the situation is *constitutive* of action. In order to be able to act, the actor must pass judgement on the nature of the situation. Every habit of action and every rule of action contains assumptions about the type of situations in which it is appropriate to proceed according to the particular habit or rule. In general, our perception of situations already incorporates a judgement on the appropriateness of certain kinds of action. This explains why situations are not merely a neutral field of activity for intentions which were conceived outside of that situation, but appear to call forth, to provoke certain actions already in our perception.

Thus defined, the concept of 'situation' is a suitable replacement for the means–ends schema as the primary basic category of a theory of action. Dietrich Böhler provides us with a convincing formulation of this idea:

> By 'situation' we – that is, 'we' as human beings who act and who know about action – understand a relationship between human beings and to objects, or between a human being and objects, which already precedes the particular action under consideration and which is therefore in each case already understood by the person or people concerned as a challenge either to do or alternatively not to do something. In colloquial speech we talk about 'getting into' situations: they 'befall' us, 'happen to' us and we find ourselves 'confronted' by them. These are ways of expressing that a situation is something which precedes our action (or inaction) but which also provokes action because it 'affects' us, 'interests' us, or 'concerns' us.[22]

Böhler coins the term 'quasi-dialogical' to express a non-teleological conception of the relationship between action and situation. This implies that actions should be thought of as responses to situations; situations are not mute, they demand that we take action. He is well aware that by emphasizing this situation-relatedness as constitutive of action we run the risk of overreacting to the one-sidedness of the teleological interpretation of action by advocating a kind of behaviour-istic reductionism. If the situation alone were regarded as constitutive of action, then the idea of intentionality would lose all meaning. The only way out of this dilemma is to posit the idea that the teleological and the quasi-dialogical nature of action operate as reciprocal precon-ditions of each other.

> Situational orientation and goal-orientation are interlinked with one another from the outset. For if we did not have certain *dispositions towards goals*, no matter how vague, which are given *ante actu* in the form of needs, interests and norms, an event would not occur for us as a situation we are in, but would remain devoid of meaning and mute.[23]

In other words, we must again refer to the corporeality of action. For, as we have seen, these vague dispositions towards goals, which are constantly at work even when we have not set ourselves any immedi-ate goals, are located in the personal body of the human being. The claim that situation-relatedness is constitutive of action and the definition of intentionality is the self-reflective control of current behaviour are merely two different ways of addressing the same state of affairs. Situations do not trigger our actions, but nor do they merely provide the terrain on which we carry out our intentions. Our perception of the situation is predefined in our capacities for action and our current disposition for action. Our reflective response to the challenge presented to us by the situation decides which action is taken.

The realization that situation-relatedness is constitutive of all action also changes our ideas about the role of motives and plans for action. According to the teleological view, motives appear to be the cause of action and plans are seen as preconceived structures of the course to be taken by action and on which action is then continuously based. Once we conceive of action as something founded in pre-reflective situational contexts, however, these assumptions can no longer be taken for granted. For action then no longer necessarily presupposes planning, and even if plans have been drawn up, the concrete course which the action takes has to be determined constructively from situation to situation and is open to continuous revision. Plans may place us in situations, but do not in themselves provide a comprehen-sive answer to the challenges of these situations. Our pre-reflective, practical ways of relating to action situations do not cease to obtain when we have devised a plan; the plan is never the sole focus of orientation for our action. As a consequence, even in the case of purely individual action the concrete course taken by the action can never be fully traced back to some specific intentions. These may have been the decisive factors behind the particular plan, but they certainly do not determine the actual course the action takes. Yet even drawing up a plan is not, as a rule, dependent on singly identifiable intentions. If, therefore, intentionality is to be thought of as a self-reflective realization and assessment of pre-reflective quasi-intentions in concrete situations, then motives and plans must be seen as the products of such reflections and not as the factual causes of action. Reflection on pre-reflective quasi-intentions depends, however, on a medium. C. Wright Mills forged a classic link between the model of action as formulated by pragmatist philosophy and the empirical practice of sociological research into motives.[24] According to his theory, what is stated as a motive is always already based on a standardized vocabulary of possible and legitimate motives. Even when we try to clarify our motives in the solitude of self-reflection, we still cannot escape having to couch them in a common language. Ethnomethodological research raises the same claim in connection with the concrete role of plans of action.[25] Whenever we devise plans or attempt to understand our motives, this always takes place in a language which is barely capable of penetrating the alien nature of even our most personal aspirations.

Finally, breaking with the teleological interpretation of the intentionality of action influences the image we have of the very act of setting and creating goals. According to the teleological view which we are attempting to overcome here, this act appears to be so free that it could be called arbitrary. The actor designs his goals independently, or so the argument runs, of any influence from the outside world. If we adopt the understanding of intentionality that I am putting forward here, however, goal-setting becomes the result of a situation in which the actor finds himself prevented from continuing his pre-reflectively driven forms of action. In this situation he is forced to adopt a reflective stance on his pre-reflective aspirations. Values or ideals defining a successful personality or a successful community can be used here as a yardstick for assessment. Parsons believed he could refute the claim that choice of goal was a random process by proving that the actor oriented himself towards commonly held values. In so doing, he failed to address the question how, in that case, actors oriented their actions towards their internalized values. If these values function as unequivocal signposts, then action is independent of the situation and inflexible. This is what Garfinkel meant when he criticized Parsons' actors for being 'cultural dopes'.[26] We can arrive at an adequate theoretical understanding here only if the relationship between values in human action and situations is thought to be as open as the situation-relatedness of the pre-reflective aspirations. We must establish in concrete action-situations what satisfies our aspirations and what accords with our values. Both the concretization of values and the satisfaction of needs depend on exercising powers of creativity. Dreyfus illustrates this idea elegantly by using the example of falling in love.

> When a man falls in love, he loves a particular woman, but it is not that particular woman he needed *before* he fell in love. However, after he is in love, that is after he has found that this particular relationship is gratifying, the need becomes specific as the need for this particular woman, and the man has made a creative discovery about himself. He has become the sort of person that needs that specific relationship and must view himself as having lacked and needed this relationship all along. In such a creative discovery the world reveals a new order of signification which is neither simply discovered nor arbitrarily chosen.[27]

Human action is therefore characterized not simply by the interplay of values and impulses, but by the creative concretization of values as well as the constructive satisfaction of impulses. No creative action would be possible without the bedrock of pre-reflective aspirations towards which the reflection on the concretization of values is oriented. Thus corporeality shows itself to be the constitutive precondition for creativity not only in perception but also in action itself.

The critique of the teleological interpretation of the intentionality of action put forward here, together with the outline of an alternative interpretation and the consequences thereof, are designed to introduce via reconstruction the tacit assumptions inherent in theories of rational action – in the present case, the imputed capacity for goal-orientation and goal-setting. This objective is not accomplished simply by advancing general theses on the role of ends in human action. Rather, we must direct our attention to the emergence of the capacity to set goals and thus uncover the preconditions for this essential component of the creativity of action. I am referring here not to the knowledge yielded by developmental psychology on the extension of means–ends chains in action, but rather to a more fundamental question: namely, what actually takes place when we proceed from *mere wishing to goal-setting*? Anyone who sets goals is just as aware of the fact that reality is independent of his wishes, as he is of the possibility of changing reality through his wishes via the medium of appropriate action. The creative act of setting goals therefore requires both the constitution of a reality that is independent of the subject and at the same time the retention of the ability to dream and desire. However, that which can simply be assumed within a Cartesian world view requires a hypothesis to explain its development now that we have entered anti-Cartesian terrain.

The most plausible hypothesis on this problem is, in my opinion, Donald Winnicott's theory of transitional objects and children's play.[28] It may not seem particularly original to place child's play at the focal point of an analysis of the development of the capacity for action. All sorts of theories frequently do precisely this, indeed so does everyday parlance. However, opinions differ widely as to the exact significance of play. Connecting creativity and play is also nothing unusual. Winnicott's outstanding achievement, however, is to have focused on an area of phenomena which occur at an earlier stage of development than play proper, a sphere which he terms that of transitional objects or transitional phenomena. What does he mean by this?

Winnicott inquires into the origins of the child's readiness to accept the existence of an objective reality. This is a basic achievement which is not restricted to childhood, but still has to be performed in later life. For the task of 'keeping internal and external reality separate and yet reciprocally linked to one another'[29] is one that confronts human beings throughout their lives, and many a psychopathological condition is the result of a failure to perform this function. Winnicott therefore means more than merely the cognitive construction of reality in the development of the small child. Like Freud, he sees the constitution of reality as a process which is *also* affective in nature, although of course to separate cognition and affects in the context of a newborn baby is to impose an artificial pattern on the actual experience of the child at this early stage when no such distinction exists. Winnicott is not prepared to go along with Freud, however, in ascribing the child's acceptance of the 'reality principle' simply to experiences of frustration, suffering and deprivation. Such experiences can, after all, lead to destructive rage, and the same experiences as are cited here as constitutive of reality are declared elsewhere to be the cause of fantasies.

Winnicott consistently proceeds from the suckling infant's experience of self and world as an indistinguishable whole. This experience of self and world is echoed by the mother, who has released the child from her body at birth. 'From a psychological point of view, the child drinks from a breast that is part of its self, and the mother feeds an infant that is part of her self.'[30] Thus, it is not only in a practical sense that the newborn child is helpless and utterly dependent on care and attention; in terms of its experience of self too, the child is indistinguishable from the environment which guarantees its survival. However, I feel it is misleading to express this state of affairs in such a way as to imply that the baby understands the attention it receives to be the result of its own omnipotence. After all, this redefinition would suggest that the baby already had the ability to distinguish between itself and its surroundings. It is probably more accurate to say that the baby experiences the connection between its desires and their satisfaction – which does, after all, stem from some external source – as some kind of magical causal relationship. It helps to have desires, as this enables the child to exercise control over the world and fosters the illusion that the world is something that can be placed at its command.

The transition from this original inseparability of self and world to the recognition of the existence of a world that is autonomous, that is, independent of desires, cannot of course be made in a single leap. The child ventures gradually and cautiously out of its subjective world, always ready to recoil. And Winnicott's theory of transitional objects applies precisely to these stages of the transition from an undifferentiated feeling of oneness with the world to the development of true object relationships. Transitional objects are those objects which are no longer classified as part of the baby's own body, nor that of the mother, yet neither are they at this stage objects which are already conceived of as parts of the external world. Winnicott is referring here to the relationship of the child to objects such as the indispensable teddy bear or the 'security blanket'. These objects possess a whole range of functional characteristics which distinguish them not only from the autoerotically enjoyed parts of the body, such as the thumb, but also from toys used for play as such. Their most important characteristic is that these transitional objects take on heightened importance for the child in those situations where it feels that it has left its original secure environment behind it and thus that excessive demands are being placed on it. Situations like being alone, falling asleep or going on a journey underline the child's intense relationship to transitional objects with particular clarity. With them at its side, the child feels confident enough to risk a step out of its secure surroundings and into the world, or to approach the threshold of the frightening world of dreams, without panicking. This explains why the loss of such an object is such a disastrous event in a child's life. Winnicott goes on to elaborate a second feature, namely the fact that the child treats these transitional objects with extremely intense but by no means always positive emotions. They are also the object of hatred and destructive rage. Winnicott's concern is not, however, to interpret these emotions; instead, he concentrates on the fact that the child is able to vent such emotions on the transitional object and yet ascertain that the object 'survives'. Even more so than towards the mother, the child is free to express the full range of its emotions in the presence of these objects, and yet the objects do not disappear. It is precisely this discovery which is such a crucial step towards recognizing that there is a world whose existence is independent of our desires and emotions. The third characteristic, as Winnicott sees it, is that only the child is allowed to alter the transitional object. Many parents respect the wishes of the children that these objects should not be interfered with, not even cleaned, as this would threaten their significance for the child. And finally, the fourth feature lies in the unspoken agreement between the adult and the child not to bring up the question: '"Did you think of that yourself, or was it suggested to you from outside?" The important point is that the child is not expected to come to a decision on this matter. The question is simply never raised in the first place.'[31] It is as though a feel for the oppressive nature of Cartesian dualisms prevents the adults from forcing the child to accept this rigid picture of the world.

As the child develops further, the significance of the individual transitional objects gradually becomes diffuse. In other words, more and more close and familiar objects – such as the child's home environment or immediate surroundings – begin to take on the function of providing security, which the child for its part comes to require ever less urgently. Children's play comes to replace the 'transitional phenomena'. According to Winnicott's analysis, play constitutes an intermediate sphere between internal and external, or shared, reality, in which it is possible both to vent emotions and to test reality at the same time. The child at play lives 'with certain dream potentials from within and in a scenario that it has chosen itself from fragments of external reality'.[32] Playful action is thus defined as that action which does not allow itself to be bound by the distinction between dream and reality, between internal and external reality. Paradoxically, it is precisely when absorbed in play that a child develops the ability to integrate internal and external reality. Winnicott considers that individuals who harbour illusions that are divorced from reality, or whose behaviour is characterized by unimaginative conformism to the pressures of the external world, in both cases require therapy in the form of the liberation in them of that intermediate realm of experience that is play. Dispersed throughout his work are indications that he regards the production and reception of culture as the adult equivalent of the child's play. For him, culture is not merely an optional supplement to a realistic conception of reality. Rather, creativity is a special 'toning of a person's whole attitude towards external reality'.[33] Thus play, as the elemental form of human action, instils in human beings the ability to set goals in a creative way, yet this ability is not a feature of human action that can simply be taken for granted; it is a merely potential trait that is contingent on numerous factors for its realization.

3.2   The Constitution of the Body Schema

The second tacit assumption in most theories of action is that actors are able to control their bodies. Unlike the means–ends schema, which is quite patently the factor that determines the thrust of rational models of action and is simply not examined any further, the assumption that the body can be controlled in the sense of its being deployed for the actor's purposes is in fact an *implicit* assumption, for the body does not appear explicitly in most theories of action. As a rule, sociological theories simply assume that the body is the factual basis of action, but pay no attention to it, as if in a fit of theoretical prudishness.[34] In sociological theory, the concept of action is usually only linked to the human condition in a biological or anthropological sense if the task at hand is to defend the identity of the social sciences against attempts to reduce them in a biologistic or psychologistic manner. Thus, thinkers often resort to biological arguments when refuting behaviourism. Biological arguments also have a certain impact on those scholars who, influenced by the pragmatism of George Herbert Mead, declare the difference between symbolically mediated interaction with other human subjects, on the one hand, and instrumental action vis-à-vis objects, on the other, to be the most important internal distinction in any concept of action. With the exception of these two debates, however, any investigation of the role of the body in action has been confined to the margins of sociology.

Apart from the significance of corporeality for a non-teleological understanding of intentionality there are at least two other reasons why we should not accept this state of affairs. Firstly, action theory must defend itself against the accusation that it intrinsically leans more heavily in favour of an *activistic relationship to the world*, which is evidently culture-specific if not gender-specific, and thus does not fulfil its claim to universality. If action theory interprets action itself as something of value, then this tends either to obscure or to downgrade both the cultivation of an aesthetic sensibility that is not linked to action and the willingness to accept fate, that is, the unintended and unexpected events of life. Action theory can square up to these accusations only if it makes use of a concept of action that also encompasses passivity, sensitivity, receptivity and imperturbability. In other words, we require a concept of action which does not describe continuous activity, the permanent generation of individual acts, but instead delineates the specific structure of the relation between the human being as an organism and his environment. If action theory is to avoid activistic undertones it is therefore necessary for it to take corporeality into account.

The second reason why the body cannot simply be taken as the tacit assumption underlying a theory of action has to do with the problems of *confining* the body to an *instrumental* role. Such a limitation occurs if the body is thought of as a permanently available instrument of pure intentionality, be it as a technical instrument in instrumental action, be it as a controllable body in the framework of normatively oriented action, be it as the mere medium for expressing intentions in the context of communicative action that is neither recalcitrant nor significant in itself. The major historical and anthropological projects, such as those undertaken by Norbert Elias and Michel Foucault, can be read as attempts to analyse the historical genesis of an instrumentalist relationship to our own bodies. They justifiably do not merely try to pinpoint the influence of cultural values on individual attitudes, but foreground the emergence and implementation of techniques for disciplining the body. Even if they tend to consider history as a more or less linear process in which the body is disciplined to an ever greater extent, so that, as Anthony Giddens has said of Foucault, all that remains are 'bodies without faces',[35] that is, the desubjectified objects of disciplining, their thought nevertheless contains substantial steps towards writing a 'cultural history of the rational actor'. Such a cultural history is the historical counterpart to a reconstructive introduction of the tacit assumptions contained in the concept of rational action. However, what this cultural history could learn from the conceptual reconstruction is that the straightforward assumption that the body can be instrumentalized, as is contained in naive models of rationality, does not necessarily result in a historical totalization of the disciplining of the body. The instrumentalization of the body by the actor or some independent 'disciplines' must never be posited as all-embracing if the ability to act is assumed at all. In other words, what is really involved is an unstable equilibrium between the body's instrumentalization and other non-instrumental relations with the body. Control of the body on the stage of life is always accompanied by the periodic relaxation of control when we go backstage.[36] Action theory must therefore concern itself not only with the emergence of control of the body but also with the development of abilities to ease that control, that is, with intentional reductions in the instrumentalization of the body.

Many approaches in pragmatism, phenomenology and philosophical anthropology have overcome the limitations innate in both a purely activistic interpretation of action and the belief that the relation between an actor and his or her body is purely instrumental in nature. Worthy of mention here is above all that interpretation of actions which relies on a notion of passive intentionality and of a meaningful loss of intentionality. The term *'passive intentionality'* refers to those forms of action in which the body is intentionally released from control. Merleau-Ponty's analysis of how we fall asleep is a famous example of this. We all know that if we intend to fall asleep – in the sense of 'active' intentionality – our efforts will be self-defeating. Nevertheless we know how to realize our intentions by allowing and promoting the presence of pre-reflective bodily intentions that want sleep:

> I lie down in bed, on my left side, with my knees drawn up; I close my eyes and breathe slowly, putting my plans out of my mind. But the power of my will or consciousness stops there. As the faithful, in the Dionysian mysteries, invoke the god by miming scenes from his life, I call up the visitation of sleep by imitating the breathing and posture of the sleeper. The god is actually there when the faithful can no longer distinguish themselves from the part they are playing, when their body and their consciousness cease to bring in, as an obstacle, their particular opacity, and when they are totally fused in the myth. There is a moment when sleep 'comes', settling on this imitation of itself which I have been offering to it, and I succeed in becoming what I was trying to be: an unseeing and almost unthinking mass, riveted to a point in space and in the world henceforth only through the anonymous alertness of the senses.[37]

What Merleau-Ponty describes so brilliantly here resembles that which the pragmatists have identified as the interim phase in problem-solving behaviour. In order to solve a problem, you must precisely not adhere rigidly to one type of action, but must rather open yourself to ideas and new types of action that result from the pre-reflective intentionality of the body. Similar examples could easily be cited from the domain of sexuality.

The *meaningful loss of intentionality* does not obtain in instances where bodily phenomena become an indicator of intentions we do not wish to admit having: for example, when we blush with shame. This does not fundamentally cast our ability to act intentionally into question; our body simply reveals other intentions than those we would have liked to communicate. Instead, we should think here of two forms of action which advocates of the rational model of action would not seriously believe come within the scope of a theory of action: laughing and crying. Laughing and crying are actions unique to humans and yet which cannot be intentionally generated in the full sense of the term. We 'have to' laugh or cry; but only we humans, as beings capable of action, know this compulsion. Helmuth Plessner had the ingenious idea of finding a real way out of this apparent paradox by attempting to grasp laughing and crying in terms of the situational loss of intentionality.[38] Whereas, on the one hand, language and gestures require intentional control of our bodies, and, on the other, facial expressions and body posture unintentionally signal to our partner in action what our emotions are (which may indeed contradict what we intend to communicate), laughing and crying cannot be subsumed under either of these two forms of expressive bodily behaviour. In language and gestural communication there is no threat to our dominance of our bodies; in unintentional expressivity the limits to this dominance emerge clearly, yet without this calling that dominance into question within the given limits. In the case of laughing and crying, by contrast, control of the body is suddenly lost: 'Bodily processes emancipate themselves. The human being is shaken by them, pushed this way and that by them and they take his breath away. He has lost his relation to his physical existence, which evades his grasp and to a certain degree does with him as it likes.'[39] The expressive value of laughing and crying consists precisely in the fact that these two acts indicate the loss of any ability to react in a controlled manner. Both occur in situations whose ambiguity places excessive demands on the subject. If an actor finds a situation to be so contradictory and ambivalent that he can no longer integrate the forms of action thereby provoked into one consistent act, then, so Plessner claims, the action thus triggered is discharged as laughter:

> The impossibility of responding to the situation owing to the (multiple) mutually exclusive possible responses is the reason for the resistance to recoiling from the situation in question, i.e. for the tension that then

dissolves into laughter. In this way, the person responds to the ambivalence of a situation to which there can be no response. In this way he
counters the vitally, spiritually and existentially 'non-sensical' by means
of a reaction that reveals self-assertion and self-sacrifice at one and the
same time. By laughing he leaves his body to its own devices, forgoes
any unity with it, any control over it. By means of this capitulation of
the mind–body unity he asserts himself as a person.[40]

According to Plessner, crying occurs, by contrast, in situations the
meaning of which is so powerful that it completely steamrollers the
actor's reflective distance to the situation and to his own actions. The
impotence that crying expresses, Plessner claims, is not simply attributable to the person being overwhelmed by superior forces, but is the
result of the loss of that distance which is a precondition of intentional
action: 'a lack of distance – not to the particular feeling but to the
substance which fills me with that feeling, which seizes me and
convulses me'.[41]

If it is legitimate at all to bring the multifarious phenomena of
human action to bear on action theory and thus to insist that the
theorist focus on phenomena such as falling asleep, laughter and
crying, then 'passive intentionality' and the 'meaningful loss of
intentionality' indicate that it is necessary to acknowledge that the
relation between the personality and that person's body is one of the
central issues of a theory of action.

However, both classical and contemporary sociological theory suffer
from a deficit of anthropology. Max Weber, for example, did not
worry about whether his basic assumptions were biologically tenable.
In a late essay, Émile Durkheim, who wrestled so strongly in his work
with the Cartesian heritage, claimed the distinction between mind and
body (presupposed by the Cartesian doctrine) resulted from a process
of social constitution.[42] However, his analysis only went so far as to
describe the body of the actor as one physical object alongside others.
Talcott Parsons did not recognize until after finishing *The Structure of
Social Action* that the human organism was of great significance as the
basis of human action. This change in orientation was the result in
particular of his study of Freudian psychoanalysis, the problems of
research into socialization and psychosomatic medicine.[43] Yet Parsons'
theory of socialization concentrates solely on what one might call the
objective side to the emergence of personality structures, and does not
face up to the task of analysing from a sociological angle the way in
which the actor's subjective relationship to his own body develops.
And his concern with psychosomatic 'disturbances' is not interested

hermeneutically in whether these phenomena have a positive meaning. The lack of an anthropological footing is equally apparent in the major contemporary theoretical projects. The German tradition of philosophical anthropology is admittedly one of the most important bases for the development of Jürgen Habermas' thought.[44] However, although he initially attempted to elaborate on it, he has since all but abandoned this tack. In the case of Niklas Luhmann, an anthropological foundation would contradict the very nature of his theory, which is based precisely not on the characteristics of human action. Although Anthony Giddens' theory of structuration continually touches on anthropological issues and occasionally enters the domain of anthropology, this involvement is more coincidental than it is systematic.[45]

There are thus two major areas that remain unclarified in action theory. On the one hand, there is the question which human biological preconditions must obtain in order for action to be possible in the first place. This is the fundamental anthropological question as to what renders human action possible. On the other, we must establish how the actor develops the ways in which his body is subjectively present for him. After all, body control is not simply present to him from the outset. Rather, it is possible only on the basis of specific qualities exhibited by the human body and emerges in the course of childhood development. The agenda for a reconstructive introduction of the tacit assumptions of models of rational action must therefore include establishing the anthropological foundations for action theory as well as reconstructing the constitution of the body schema.

A discussion of the anthropological foundations of action theory would of course go beyond the bounds of the present study. The biological literature often cannot simply be adopted for this purpose without further interpretation, particularly as its hypotheses often lead to unsubstantiated reductionist statements when applied to human beings.[46] Axel Honneth and I therefore chose Arnold Gehlen's anthropology as the starting point for our study of this problem.[47] For all the one-sidedness and exaggerations in Gehlen's oeuvre, and although it is clearly no longer the cutting edge of such research, it none the less has an incisive advantage for a theory of action. For Gehlen does not equate human action with animal behaviour, but instead inquires into the preconditions with regard to the human organism and evolution which enabled the emergence of the specific characteristics of human action. Gehlen modelled his anthropological reconstruction of the human capacity for action on John Dewey's pragmatist anthropology.[48] There are similarities here to Jean Piaget's efforts to ensure his developmental psychology had foundations in a biological theory.[49]

Common to all these theories is a belief that the human capacity for action is rooted in the fact that human behaviour is no longer controlled purely by instinct. This break with instinct regulation at the same time excludes the possibility of human action being reduced to a schema of stimulus and response.

It was above all Gehlen who (following in Herder's footsteps) focused on the break with the fact that animals were safe in their instincts; he spoke trenchantly in this regard of the human being as a 'deficient being'. He paints a broad picture[50] of the relative primitiveness of individual human organs, the lack of hair as protection against the weather, man's weak sensory organs compared with those of animals, the lack of congenital organs of attack and the extremely long period of a human child's helplessness; all these examples serve to underpin his theory that the organic deficiencies of human beings are a threat to the survival of the species. He ascribes these deficiencies in the main to evolutionary causes, construing the human being as an example of 'normalized premature birth'. The deficiencies he lists are thus interpreted as quasi-foetal characteristics. Gehlen cites the upright posture of human beings as the cause for this premature birth and the corresponding overly long period of helplessness after birth, as the conditions of pregnancy changed dramatically for the creature that then became *homo erectus*. In other words, Gehlen does not understand the human capacity for action and culture – something that was decisive for human superiority over all animal species and human dominance of the earth – as some linear, evolutionary enhancement of abilities such that human action then appears to be the most complex form of animal behaviour. Instead, he posits it as a radical break with the course of animal behaviour. The natural deficiencies proved to be a challenge and an opportunity to develop new and superior abilities – with failure punishable by extinction. Gehlen attempts to show how the original instinctive links between the three sides to the triangle of motivation, perception and movement were respectively broken and re-established by replacing instinct with cultural symbols. In place of a fixed instinct-based repertoire of impulses, diffuse and highly plastic sources of motivation arise, which become increasingly specific and unambiguous through the experience of satisfaction and through cultural influence. In the realm of perception the instinctual selection of stimuli is replaced by the construction of a field of perception by human design, a necessity for the organism in order to protect itself from being flooded with more stimuli than it can process and an achievement which opens up unheard-of opportunities for intimacy with objects. And finally, in the realm of movement, 'inherited motoricity' comes to be replaced by an 'acquired motoricity' that stems from learning movements, including the evolution of tools of all types. However, Gehlen's anthropology over-dramatizes the dangers which a break with the instinct-based safety mechanisms posed to the coherence of the social order. As a consequence, he sees humankind's only chance of survival as being to create institutions that are as absolute as animal instincts. Neither Dewey nor Piaget concurs with the overtly authoritarian political implications of the theory of institutions to which Gehlen's anthropology leads. This bears mentioning in order to show that to reject his theory of institutions does not automatically mean rejecting his 'anthropology as a theory of action'.

At least one of the deficiencies of Gehlen's anthropology of action is worthy of explicit mention here.[51] His suggestion that there is a break from the rigid instinct-directed actions of animals admittedly creates scope for elaborating a definition of the specifically human capacity for action. However, it obscures the fact that there are differences in the various stages of the development of animal behaviour and animal learning and it exaggerates the degree to which animal behaviour is characterized by rigidity, inability to learn and pre-programming. Ethological research shows that the simple notion of rigid links between stimuli and instinctive responses is no longer valid in the case of organisms that possess a central nervous system. Even prior to that stage of biological complexity, the stimulus–response schema is inappropriate, for it does not correspond to the complexity of congenital coordinated movements. Once this stage has been reached, however, it is no longer even accurate to speak of there being strict causal links between stimuli and responses. In particular Konrad Lorenz[52] proved the existence of action-specific energies and the relatively independent generation of states of arousal which, at a given level, lead to general motoric unrest, then to the automatic triggering of instinctive actions and thus to reactions which run idle. This enabled him to demonstrate that the different elements of an instinctive action are coordinated independently. Moreover, with his theory of 'appetence behaviour', that is, of spontaneous behaviour directed to finding stimuli, he pinpointed the first form of animal behaviour involving control of the animal's surroundings.

Although still entirely within the bounds of genetic programming, forms like appetence behaviour, the division of movements into individually controllable sub-movements and the formation of hierarchical chains, preparation, the formation of associations, imprinting and learning by successful doing, all enable the animal to adjust flexibly and individually to its surroundings to an ever increasing degree. In other words, the creativity of human action does after all have precursors in animal behaviour and it cannot be understood without this pre-history. But it was the 'breaking of the instincts' in the transition from animal to human being that first created the precondition for a gradual and individual transition from exploitation of the scope left by the genetic programming of behaviour to the 'constructive self-control' (as Piaget termed it) of extensive domains of action. Therefore Gehlen is wrong to suggest that rigid institutions must take up where rigid instincts left off. Instead, intelligence and creativity ensue from the emerging behavioural scope that already existed in instinct-based behavioural control. The pre-reflective intentionality of the human body is thus not some residue of animal behaviour, upon which some pure intellectuality is superimposed, but is in fact the structure of the relation between organism and environment that is typical for human beings. The assumptions of action theory are built on quicksand if they do not match our knowledge of this structure.

The reconstructive introduction of the tacit assumptions of the various models of rational action needs to be taken one step further. Just as was the case with the ability to set goals and orient oneself towards goals, now that we have uncovered the tacit assumptions themselves, have revealed that they are by no means self-evident truths and indicated what alternatives exist (in this case an anthropological conception of action), we must now move on to the actual reconstructive step. That is, we must demonstrate that on the basis of the alternative conception we can nevertheless reconstruct the intention behind the original tacit assumption. In the present case, this means showing that the actor's instrumentalization of his body must be the result of a development and it also means we need a hypothesis for that development. If we assume that the latter results not in a de-subjectified instrumentalization of the self but instead in the ability to act, then we must address the one line of scientific research which has tackled this issue, namely research into the 'body schema' or the 'body image'.

The concepts of 'body schema' or 'body image' refer to the fact that the body is subjectively present for the actor. Of course, the body is one entity among others in the world, but by virtue of being one's own body it is radically different from all other things. The body schema is usually defined as the actor's awareness of the morphological structure of his own body, its parts and its posture, its movements and its limits. Little empirical research and very few theories have been forthcoming in this field, presumably because merely to broach the issue of the body schema is to stand at odds with the basic postulates of the Cartesian view of the world. Consequently, social psychologists tend to focus more on other people's perception of a person's body than on self perception of the body, and physiological psychology usually considers the body simply to be objectively present.[53] The major part of research to date deals with pathological phenomena such as malfunctions of the ability to localize sensations on the body's surface or to distinguish between left and right as well as the phenomenon that has enjoyed such fame since the days of William James' psychological work, namely the 'phantom organs', that is, those organs which a person feels are present, although they 'objectively' no longer exist, such as an arm or leg that has been amputated.

With regard to the problem at hand, the history of interest in this phenomenon and the discussion of the concept of 'body schema' is highly instructive. The earlier history comprised the physiological research in the nineteenth century into bodily sensations: this concentrated simply on the perception of stimuli which flowed constantly from the internal organs or the surface of the body to the 'sensory apparatus'. The decisive first step towards a more profound analysis was made by neurophysiologists at the turn of the century (Head, Bonnier) who progressed beyond merely concerning themselves with the sensations of one's own body in two vital respects. On the one hand, they endeavoured to establish what caused humans to possess the ability to localize the sensations generated by their own bodies accurately. On the other, they asked what it was that enabled humans consciously to regulate their own movements and posture. They believed that the answer to both questions lay in the existence of an unconscious body schema. This was conceived of in strictly objectivist terms as a neurological mechanism which was thereby treated as the precondition for all correct movements and operations. This mechanism was assumed to be highly flexible, as only thus was it possible to explain how instruments could be incorporated into movements or how the feeling for movement could so easily be extended to include, for example, clothing. The first version of the theory of the body schema therefore already addressed the issue of a *holistic* perception of one's own body, but its proposed solution was a conception that completely disregarded the role of the conscious mind.

The second step was taken by Paul Schilder, an Austro-German psychiatrist, who, taking up the ideas suggested by gestalt psychology and psychoanalysis, published a small book on the body schema in 1923. After emigrating to the United States he expanded the volume considerably and expressly placed his work in the context of the thought of James and Dewey.[54] His contribution was an advance on previous research in three key respects. First of all, he overcame the physiological reductionism of his predecessors by focusing on the psychological representation of the body schema. Secondly, he tried to go further than some elementarist psychology of associations and thus concentrated on the prior presence of holistic perceptual schemata even in a person's perception of his own body; this was where he came close to gestalt psychology. And, thirdly, he endeavoured to construe the problem of body perception not solely in cognitive terms, but also with regard to the affective side to the question, so that psychoanalysis came to play an important role in his thought.

To Schilder's mind the psychological representation of the body schema resulted ineluctably from an understanding of the cognitive character of the body schema. The localization of a feeling is not something simply given with the feeling; rather, feelings must be identified actively or constructively in spatial terms. A dysfunction in this ability to localize feelings does not necessarily mean that the feeling itself is not felt. Schilder therefore speaks of body *image* [*Körperbild*] and not of body *schema*, because he believes the former term better captures the cognitive character involved. However, this terminological decision has a price: self-perception thus appears to be equated with *visual* self-perception.

Nevertheless, with its notion that we each have a holistic spatial image of ourselves, this conception had the advantage of departing from the established trend in the empirical psychology of the day, which held that the body existed for us as a sum of sensations. Admittedly, the founding fathers of neurophysiological research into the body schema had already alluded to the holistic nature of the body schema; however, they had located this at a level below the psychological. It was thus logical that Schilder construed the issue of the body image as a problem of the genesis of the mental representation of a holistic perception of one's own body – in the sense of an integral whole that was clearly marked off from the person's environment. He provided a wealth of illuminating examples of how all the achievements of the body image or body schema depend on this holistic perception: for instance, the full meaning of the localization of a sensation of movement depends on its relation to the whole body. At times it almost seems as if Schilder believed that the mere reference to gestalt psychology's rejection of a psychology of association suffices as an explanation of the holistic nature of the body image. In his second book on the subject, written in the United States, and following criticism of his work from among the ranks of orthodox gestalt psychologists,[55] he distinguished between his own quasi-pragmatist interpretation of the evidence and that offered by gestalt psychology.[56] He maintained that gestalt psychology underestimated the significance of the learning process during which a holistic body image develops and, above all, neglected the activistic elements in the constitution of the body schema:

> I consider that the connotations of gestalt psychology are too static and do not acknowledge sufficiently the never ceasing psychic activities. The body-image is based not merely on associations, memory, and experience, but also on intentions, will aims, and tendencies.[57]

Bringing action theory to bear on the body schema problem appears to Schilder to offer the only chance of solving the question why the body schema is holistic. In other words, he felt it necessary to show that the development of a holistic body schema and of a holistic world view must both be part of the development of a holistic personality capable of action:

> When we perceive or imagine an object, or when we build up the perception of an object, we do not act merely as a perceptive apparatus. There is always a personality that experiences the perception. The perception is always our own mode of perceiving. We feel inclined to answer with an action or actually do so. We are, in other words, emotional beings, personalities. And personality is a system of actions and tendencies to such.[58]

Thus, Schilder establishes a bridgehead for a link to psychoanalysis. For it is probable that we do not tend to relate to our bodies in a distant manner characterized by mere intellectual curiosity, but rather perceive our bodies in a manner highly charged with emotions. Accordingly, Schilder not only undertakes an extensive investigation of the physiological basis of the body image in sensory perception but also adumbrates phenomena that relate to disorders in the libidinous cathexis of our bodies or to how we treat our bodies. At the time when Schilder was writing, psychoanalytical research on issues of developmental psychology such as the genesis of the body schema mainly involved reconstructions of case histories using material from therapy sessions, rather than directly studying children.[59] Schilder was therefore not really able to achieve a synthesis of knowledge on the cognitive and affective dimensions in the development of the body image. However, his work contains ideas and problems which such a synthesis must take into account.

As a consequence, the thinker who has devoted the greatest effort to taking this issue out of its confined specialist area and relating it to comprehensive philosophical questions draws substantially on Schilder's work. I refer, of course, to Maurice Merleau-Ponty.[60] His proposed interpretations in the form of 'existential' analyses of pathological cases can justifiably be termed the third major step in the search for an understanding of the body schema. Merleau-Ponty quite clearly thought along the same lines as Schilder, but recognized more perceptively how the Cartesian dualisms influenced medical and psychological research into the body schema. Consequently, Merleau-Ponty believed that proving the superiority of his own phenomenological analyses in this area was an important test of the validity of his work in an overarching philosophical controversy. At the same time, it meant that a phenomenological analysis of the experience of the body also had to eliminate the Cartesian trends within phenomenology itself. An analysis of the body thus afforded Merleau-Ponty an opportunity to champion a new concept of intentionality which emphasized its bodily, 'incarnate' character. The underlying idea here is that the problem of the relationship of mind and body, intentionality and corporeality will never be solved if it is not addressed from the outset in a different, non-dualistic way; this led Merleau-Ponty to adopt a position which is as far removed from an empiricist psychology of sensation as it is from a rationalist psychology of consciousness. By taking the perceiving body as his point of departure, Merleau-Ponty did not exactly follow the pragmatist agenda of locating the basis of all perception in action, but the differences are very slight.[61] Here, the concept of constitution no longer has the meaning it had in Husserl's work, namely of constitution by consciousness, but rather refers to something which the body does at a pre-conscious level. Merleau-Ponty uses the terms 'pre-reflective' or 'pre-predicative' to refer to the givenness of the world prior to all acts of reflection or predication.

In order to demonstrate the superiority of his anti-dualist approach, Merleau-Ponty applies it to two examples in particular: on the one hand, the phenomenon of the 'phantom limb' and, on the other, the inability of certain patients to make 'abstract' movements such as 'pointing', despite clearly possessing the necessary motor skills (that is, the ability to lift an arm and extend a finger). He argues that a phantom arm is not the result of physiological causality in the simplistic sense that the channels of sensory stimulation continue to exist, even after the arm has been removed. Yet nor can a phantom arm simply be understood as a psychological phenomenon in the sense that the absence of the arm has not reached the consciousness of the amputee. Rather, what is involved is an act of *active* ignoring, a not-knowing based on latent knowledge:

> The phantom arm is not a representation of the arm, but the ambivalent presence of an arm. . . . To have a phantom arm is to remain open to all the actions of which the arm alone is capable; it is to retain the practical field which one enjoyed before mutilation. . . . The patient therefore realizes his disability precisely in so far as he is ignorant of it, and is ignorant of it precisely to the extent that he knows of it.[62]

In other words, what is involved is not a dualism of mind and body, but two modes of corporeality. 'Man taken as a concrete being is not a psyche joined to an organism, but the movement to and fro of existence which at one time allows itself to take corporeal form and at others moves towards personal acts.'[63] Merleau-Ponty distinguishes between a 'habitual' and an 'actual' body in order to denote the two different forms of corporeality. In many respects, his interpretation of the inability to make 'abstract' movements parallels his discussion of the phantom limb phenomenon. The inability to point to something can be adduced neither to physiological damage to an optic nerve nor to a purely psychological loss of the ability to construe symbols, but must instead be attributed to a bodily and psychological loss of the ability to distance oneself from a given situation. The patient cannot abstract from the concrete situation and explore it in a playful manner. He becomes ensnared in the confines of his own habitual body and thus forfeits all spontaneity and creativity.

Thus the theory, initiated by Schilder, of the constitution of the body schema in actions related to specific situations is taken one step further by Merleau-Ponty, who also gives it a more profound philosophical footing. He pays more attention than did Schilder to the integration of the cognitive and affective dimensions; consequently he places stronger emphasis on the permanent transformation of the body schema, that is to say, the task of constructing and destroying an acquired body schema, a task permanently imposed upon us by infirmity or the ageing process. He also uncovers a further developmental dimension that was by no means compelling given his original phenomenological point of departure, namely the intersubjective dimension. As early as his *Phenomenology of Perception*[64] Merleau-Ponty takes into consideration the subject's relation to others in a pre-linguistic sense and indeed in the pre-linguistic stage of infant development. He maintains that the basis of all experience is not just corporeality but the interrelatedness of our experience of our bodies to our experience of others' bodies, something he terms 'intercorporéité'. What he is thinking of is the mother's care of the infant by means of stance, gesture and voice, for it is this which enables the infant to advance from its original state of indifferentiation and relate to the world as a separate ego. However, at this stage in his thought, Merleau-Ponty's remarks on the intersubjective constitution of the body schema still remained rather vague. This was to change in his late writings,[65] where, influenced by Jacques Lacan,[66] he oriented himself towards the latter's interpretation of the experience of the mirror as the constitutive condition for the emergence of the body schema. Irrespective of the impact Lacan's interpretation of the mirror experience may have on psychoanalytic therapy his hypothesis is highly questionable in empirical terms. Even if one wishes to leave aside the argument on the emergence and dissemination of the mirror as a cultural phenomenon, the hypothesis tends to lead to an exaggeration of visual experience and to the importance of affective relations to others as a precondition for the development of a body schema being played down.

We must therefore take a fourth step, one that involves taking up Merleau-Ponty's notion of 'intercorporéité' but which is more consistent with regard to making pre-linguistic infant *communication* a part of the explanation of the constitution of the body schema. For this step, we can draw on insights which George Herbert Mead expressed in a manuscript found in his estate.[67]

Mead emphasized two points. Firstly, despite the fact that the infant originally focuses primarily on its inner experiences we can nevertheless not speak of the priority of self-perception, for the infant cannot originally identify these perceptions as perceptions of its own body.

> That they (the feelings) are found entirely within the organism of the form does not change their nature as objects in the experience of the form. It is not until the living individual becomes an object to himself, and until this experience becomes identified with himself, through social conduct, that the identification of these experiences with the self takes place. A pleased palate or an aching tooth is an object in experience just as a tree or a mountain is an object.[68]

In order to be able to identify a perception as originating in one's own body, one must be able to adopt a stance towards oneself that can be conveyed by signifying gestures. This implies that it has, at least in an elementary manner, become possible to experience the unity of the body. Yet how can the body ever be experienced as a unity if each perception only presents one part of it? This is Mead's second important point:

> The body of the percipient individual is not an object as a whole. Different parts of the individual are seen and felt, or are both seen and felt, but there is no experience in which the entire individual appears as an object. That there are peculiar characters that are common to these parts of the body of the individual does not constitute them as a single object, for that arises only in so far as the individual acts with reference to it as a whole. It is only as the objects are fixed in a field of contemporaneity that the individual can be fixed as a persistent whole within such a field, and only as the hypothetical content of the physical object is so identified with the attitudes of the individual that the individual presses against the body's resistance to the object, can the percipient individual become an object in the field of physical objects.[69]

We can glean from this statement that Mead relates the problem of the unity of the body to the question of the constitution of the physical thing, the permanent object. We cannot go into the full complexity of this aspect of Mead's theory here.[70] What bears stressing, however, is his key idea that the constitution of the permanent object presupposes the existence of elementary structures of role-taking, that is, identification with a person, and that only this renders possible the coordination of hand and eye and the transference onto the objects of a substance that has an active effect. To Mead's mind, the cooperation of hand and eye first forms 'things', that is, permanent objects, if we impute a substantive inner quality to the object, which then exerts the pressure which we experience as resistance in our relation to the object. This 'inner quality' is to be understood not as something that is located within the object, somewhere beneath its surface, but rather as an active, resisting quality, whose effective core is located in the object. In our practical handling of the object we assume that it has an 'inner quality', that is, that it innately, independently of us, is able to offer resistance. How do we arrive at such an assumption? Mead argues that this assumption stems from the primary reflexivity of our movements, for example our own experience of the interaction between different parts of our body, such as the interaction of our hands with each other. It would be completely mistaken to construe the constitution of the physical thing as the result of the subject's projection of kinaesthetic sensations onto the object. Mead, by contrast, insists that the organism is already tied into the structure of social interaction, even if at that point it does not yet have an awareness of the boundaries between itself and the social or physical world. It has already started to react to the gestural language of partners in interaction and to articulate itself by means of gestures, or expressions that can be understood as gestures. There is a form of communication via gestures that does not presume the prior existence of boundaries: namely, symbiotic unity or identification. This is the model Mead takes for the human being's assumption of a role vis-à-vis objects, that is, for what he terms the equation of one's own efforts with the movements of the objects. He then links the constitution of the permanent object, which is rooted in the fact that the young, pre-linguistic infant is embedded in communicative interaction, with the constitution of the body as one's own body. We first become able to treat our bodies as a unity via the social path of self-identification. The separation of mind and body, which appears self-evident, is in fact the result of a process in which inanimate objects are gradually recognized as such. Their originally 'naive' incorporation into social behaviour then becomes both habitual and is at the same time accompanied by an awareness of their not being part of the social domain. Mead calls this a 'desocializing process' and maintains that the distinction between own body and own mind or consciousness has to take place parallel to this desocialization of physical objects.

> It was not until the desocializing of physical objects had taken place or was taking place that the distinction between the active self as a social being, and of the body as a non-social i.e. purely physical being, was made.[71]

In other words, Mead consistently links the question of the constitution of the body schema to the infant's development of communicative abilities, but largely ignores questions of motivation and the emotions. Accordingly, there is clearly a need here for further theoretical and empirical research. It is also necessary to go beyond the issue of the genesis of the body schema and address the issues of the important later stages in which it is reconstructed (for example, during adolescence with the acquisition of a capacity for intimacy, or as the result of illness and old age, or during pregnancy, etc.). In the present context it must suffice to indicate the general direction that must be taken by an elaboration of how an instrumental relationship to our bodies comes about. If the hypothesis on the constitution of the body schema put forward here in connection with the thought of Merleau-

Ponty and Mead is accurate, then the relation of the actor to his body is itself already shaped by intersubjective structures. In that case, we can relate to our bodies as if we were mothers,[72] who are sensitive to all signals sent out by the child and acknowledge them benevolently. Yet again, we can also transform our body into a tool, ignore its signals or subordinate them to our conscious ends. If an actor does not perceive his own body directly as present, but rather via a body schema, and if this body schema is itself a result constituted in an intersubjective process, then any ability to act rests on a further tacit assumption, namely that there is a *primary sociality* which has not been generated by conscious intentionality but has preceded such, in other words a structure of common action which initially consists solely of our interaction with other bodies.

3.3 Primary Sociality

Today, of the various assumptions contained in the concept of rational action, the primary autonomy of the individual actor is the postulate that can probably least be termed a *tacit* assumption. Theories to date have generally not questioned the first two assumptions covered in this chapter, namely that the intentionality of action is teleological in nature and that the actor is able to make instrumental use of his body. Therefore, before we were able to introduce reconstructively the ability to set goals or to control the body, we first had to destroy the apparent self-evidence of these ideas. However, this task is far less pressing with the third assumption. Certainly, the unreflected assertion that the self-interested, autonomous individual is the natural starting point of all social theory is deeply rooted in the possessive individualism of western culture. However, the voices of those opposing this view were always audible and in fact in certain countries, at certain times or in certain spheres they even formed the majority opinion. Among the social sciences today, it is economics which is the most important domain of individualistic assumptions. Yet it is precisely in this discipline that there has been the strongest awareness of the fact that these assumptions are no more than a methodological starting point.[73] What has not yet been clarified sufficiently in that context is whether the preference for this methodological point of departure does not actually conceal a propensity for an individualistic ontology. Strong individualistic currents are also to be observed in psychology and philosophy. However, parts of social psychology, the development of socio-cognitive research and the shift in psychoanalysis away from instinct theory to a theory of object relations have all acted as a counterweight to this trend. In the domain of philosophy, individualistic assumptions are to be found above all in analytical philosophy; however, a consideration of the latter's basis in a theory of language already casts doubt on its individualistic premisses. Other philosophical schools, such as hermeneutics, pragmatism and Marxism, were, from the outset, either non-individualist or even anti-individualist, or, as was the case with phenomenology, changed from the one to the other in the course of development.

In sociology, the opposition to individualistic assumptions is to be seen everywhere. Frequently, this rejection is regarded as the only way to prevent the identity of sociology from being reduced to an (individualistic) psychology. In particular, the question as to the social conditions framing the genesis of the autonomous individual has played a constitutive role in the sociological research on 'socialization', which began to develop at the end of the nineteenth century. Therefore the assertion that the theory of rational action simply presumes the individuality of actors and can shed no light on its genesis is true of only the narrowest versions of that theory. A normativist understanding of rationality is, by contrast, linked to a theory of the formation of personality structures by the internalization of norms, and the theory of communicative rationality and communicative action is itself intended to devise a concept of primary intersubjectivity. I would be tilting at windmills if I were to devote a great deal of time to developing arguments against the idea of a presocial, substantive Self and thus pretend that theories of identity formation were widely unknown. The postmodernist polemic against the purported dominance of the idea of an integral subject is decidedly out of place in this context.[74] I shall therefore paint only a rough picture of the social basis of the individual ability to act by pointing to what is already known and paying closer attention to certain less well-known aspects.

It was not scholarly research into the formation of the ego as part of a theory of socialization that first treated the ego as an entity detached from more comprehensive wholes or as something which, after its formation, transgressed its own limits. The Romantic notion of love involved profound thoughts on the balance to be struck between symbiosis with the other person and an unconditional willingness to recognize the otherness of the other person. The ideas about self-becoming and symbiosis with the other usually went beyond the horizon of interpersonal relationships and were extended to include the person's relation to all creatures or, indeed, the whole cosmos. A knowledge of the instability of the ego's boundaries and the possibility of breaking through them ran like a red thread through the philosophy of classical German philosophy, and above all in Hegel's work we encounter the idea of the ego being formed through interchange with others. In fact, even in what is purportedly the purely individualistic intellectual heritage of Britain and North America we come across not only anti-individualistic sub-currents but also a tradition of thought on the self-transgression of the ego.[75] The key concept here is 'sympathy' and it was elaborated in classic form in Adam Smith's theory of moral sentiments in 1759.[76] However, prior to and after that book the term was used widely in all attempts to oppose Hobbes' rationalist individualism with a theory of the creative imagination. It was Shaftesbury who first challenged the natural egoism assumed by Hobbes by referring not only to the existence of equally natural pro-social feelings, but also to the ability to imagine oneself to be another person or a quite different creature altogether. This 'sympathetic' faculty afforded the ego experiences that were inaccessible within the constraints of its own experiences. The ability to sympathize may of course be unequally distributed: it is, above all, attributed to poets. Indeed, it is only in the literary and, admittedly, not in the philosophical strands of the above traditions that we encounter the ego actually evolving from such acts of putting oneself in the other person's shoes, and thus only in literature does 'sympathy' play a constitutive role for the ego as actor.

Max Scheler made a bold attempt to appropriate this tradition critically on the basis of a phenomenological approach.[77] In both his phenomenology of the forms of 'sympathy' and his doctrine of the constitution of the other person in knowledge, he went beyond the boundaries of what was, in the final instance, an *a priori* concept of the ego. Scheler pinpoints social life prior to the establishment of the ego's boundaries, or involving their dissolution, in a variety of phenomena: in totemistic rituals such as the Mysteries in classical antiquity; in hypnosis; in the 'mass'; in a mother's ecstatic identification with her newborn child; in the shared 'impassioned suspension of their spiritual personality (which serves as the basis of the actual individual Being-as-ego)' in sexual intercourse, as both partners 'seem to relapse into a *single* life-stream, in which nothing of their individual selves remains any longer distinct, though it has equally little resemblance to a consciousness of "us" founded on the respective self-awareness of each.'[78] And this is why Scheler is able, in his study of how the alien ego is perceived, to jettison the assumption that the actor is aware of his ego as a matter of course. In the stream of experiences a person makes there is initially no distinction between 'me' and 'you';

both one's own *and* the other's ego must first be constituted in that stream.[79] Scheler drew strongly on the history of the loss of an idea of 'sympathy' and 'coalescence' in western culture and on attempts by contemporary reformers to rejuvenate the idea. However, his conceptual imprecision and his inadequate reference to empirical research on socialization prevented his work from becoming a classic among scholarly investigations of the genesis of the ego.

It was instead the work of George Herbert Mead, the American pragmatist, that became the classic. He was responsible for two of the main strands of the reconstructive introduction of the autonomous ego into action theory, namely the theory of identity formation on the basis of the ability to take roles, on the one hand, and the defence of a non-individualist concept of social action, on the other. The field in which Mead developed his most important ideas was that of an anthropological theory of the specific nature of human communication.[80] Mead believed that what made human communication superior to that of animals was its use of 'significant symbols'. For each human being is able to react to his own expressions and actions as if he were the party addressed. In other words, humans anticipate the way partners in action would potentially behave in response, and create an inner representation of that response. This ability enables humans to gear their behaviour to what potentially would be that of partners. As the partner, assuming it to be a human being, also had the same ability, a completely new pattern in the history of evolution emerges for coordinating behaviour: coordination by means of a shared orientation towards patterns of mutual behavioural expectations. Mead maintained that this was the basic trait of human sociality. In human society, the group activities necessary for the survival of the species become differentiated in terms of individual actions, actions that are by no means set by nature, and these are then reintegrated into a whole through the patterns of mutual behavioural expectations as represented by 'significant symbols'. This, he says, distinguishes human sociality both from some in-born division of labour based on the biological specialization of the individuals and from the regulation of group life via instinctual modes of behaviour in a unilinear hierarchy of dominance. Mead based his developmental psychology on this anthropological theory of communication. The hinge linking the two was his concept of 'role taking', which refers precisely to the anticipation of the situation-specific behaviour of a partner in action. If an actor can objectify his own behaviour in the same manner as his partner, then what develops is an evaluative scale for spontaneous instinctive impulses, as these come to be seen in connection with anticipated reactions to the expression of these impulses. These expectations, or rather the actor's expectation of such expectations, serve both as an evaluative agency that structures instinctive impulses and as an element in the emerging self-image. Mead has a radically constructivist notion of the development of a unitary self-image; to his mind, the task for the actor is to create by himself a synthesis of the representations of the expectations, which may very well diverge from one another. The 'self' that thereby emerges is then a point of reference for unitary self-appraisal and for action orientation. It is thus by no means simply given from the outset of infant development, nor does it ever become the sure property of an individual as a product of mere maturation. Rather, Mead is interested in reconstructing an ability to create consistent behaviour within the conflict of different expectations and irregular instinctive impulses. In addition to developing these enormously influential ideas, Mead also attempted to draw conclusions from them for our understanding of cognitive, motivational and moral development. If it is true that the actor is only able to reflect upon himself as an actor once he has developed role-taking ability, and given that this is the precondition for major cognitive achievements such as the constitution of a permanent object and, of course, for the capacity to make moral judgements, Mead concludes that the development of communicative abilities is the precondition for cognitive and moral learning. More consistently than the other classic founding fathers of research into socialization,[81] Mead destroys the basis for assuming that individuality is a pre-given quality in any other sense than the purely biological meaning of the term. For the actor, individuality proves to be the result of development, a result that depends on many preconditions, and Mead provides the basic outline of a proposed theory of human development from the point of view of the *emergence* of individual autonomy.

The other classic researchers into socialization all destroy, in a less consistent manner, the basis of an *a priori* concept of the ego. Jean Piaget's developmental psychology increasingly neglects early childhood social behaviour, a strategy which means that the ability of role-taking is presented as the mere application of cognitive achievements to social objects and is therefore not seen as being itself socially constituted.[82] However much Sigmund Freud's psychoanalytic theory focused on individual development in terms of the person being caught up in affectively highly charged interpersonal relations, Freud himself was not successful in devising a conceptual apparatus for assessing this development in terms of the structures of human sociality as opposed to instinctual dynamics. Only recent developments in this tradition have changed the focus and attempted to shed light on the preconditions of the human ability to be alone.[83] Winnicott's sensitivity in this regard enables him to give a vivid demonstration of the apparently paradoxical fact that the suckling infant can develop this ability only in the presence of its mother (or the person caring for it), as its weak ego relaxes only if given reliable support and is only then able to devote itself playfully to its own impulses and to the task of exploring the world. Talcott Parsons' dependence on the orthodox version of Freud's theory has a negative impact on his thought to the extent that it leads him to declare the internalization of norms and the formation of a super-ego to be the bridge between sociology and psychoanalysis and the decisive step in the social formation of personality.[84] Like the first psychoanalytic theorists he thus neglects pre-oedipal interaction between mother and child, and indeed social interaction in general as well as the formation of ego-structures during this early phase. Without wishing to construe Mead's approach as anything more than an (albeit brilliant) *initiation* of research into the 'development of the self', it is worthy of note that without the research carried out in this field it would be impossible to introduce a reconstructed notion of the autonomy of the ego into action theory.

Mead's entire conceptual strategy is directed towards a non-individualist concept of social action. Whereas any action theory that is fundamentally individualistic would have to regard social action as a special case of something essentially construed as individual action, Mead starts from the 'social act', which he understands precisely not as individual action that refers to another person, but instead as a complex group activity, the parts of which are individual acts. It would be a crass misinterpretation to consider this an organicist or holistic attack on individualism. Mead outlines his agenda for social psychology as being to address the task of explaining 'the conduct of the individual in terms of the organized conduct of the social group, rather than to account for the organized conduct of the social group in terms of the conduct of the separate individuals belonging to it'.[85] In other words, he is interested not simply in according the whole precedence over the parts, but in developing a different type of action theory in which social interrelations are not held to be mere aggregations of individual actions. Instead, Mead wishes to expose the irreducible sociality behind all individual acts; he then describes this sociality itself as a specific type of action and of action coordination. This conceptual strategy is currently highly topical, for many different thinkers have meanwhile pointed out that the implicit and holistically structured background knowledge presupposed in all communication and collective orders, such as language, plays an irreducible role in all action.[86] Structures of social action that cannot be reduced to individual actions are thus also the precondition for the existence of interpersonal relations or social orders, although these appear to follow the pattern of being a mere aggregation of originally individual acts.[87] An action theory which does not have the conceptual means to describe the preconditions for the individual's autonomous ability to act cannot therefore be deployed as a comprehensive programme for the social sciences.

It is possible to object to this emphasis on the primary sociality of the human capacity for action by claiming that all that is involved here is the genetic precondition for the emergence or acquisition of this ability to act, rather than a dimension that is important for the structure of all action. To counter this objection, we must depart from the leisurely paths trodden by research into socialization and focus instead on those somewhat more dramatic forms of discovering sociality which call the ego's boundaries into question. For it is here that we will find clear proof that individuals or groups do not acquire the ability to act once and for all, but that this has to be refreshed periodically, something that arises from the temporary retraction of the actor's symbolic ego boundaries vis-à-vis his environment. This idea is strongly charged with deeply ambivalent emotions (oscillating between the pleasure of symbiosis and the fear of losing one's integral gestalt), and this emotional ambivalence is also reflected in the scholarly attempts to reach an understanding of the phenomena in which the boundaries of the self are transgressed. In their speculative thought the Romantics were the first to rediscover Dionysus, god of intoxication and mad ecstasy, and the increasingly disintegrating social world of western Christendom hoped that his return would rejuvenate its cohesive forces and *élan vital*. Drawing on these Romantic speculations and, above all, on Richard Wagner's art and self-conception, Friedrich Nietzsche declared that art was the modern possibility for regaining the Dionysian, and that the Dionysian was the way out of the intractable paradoxes of modernity.[88] Nietzsche felt the passionate urge of the creative person to transgress his own limits[89] and this gave him a sensitive awareness of the tension between the need for creativity and the delimiting mechanisms by which an ego-identity attempts to preserve integrity and consistency. And Nietzsche was prepared to forgo identity in favour of creativity, or, to be more precise, to claim that people who transgressed their limits in creative activity were liberating themselves from the compulsion to remain within the limits of a particular individuality. Broad sections of left-wing and right-wing cultural criticism were influenced by the stark opposition Nietzsche construed between creativity and identity. Seen in the light of this polarity, any attempt to find a form of personality in which creativity was by no means incompatible with the formation of a consistent ego-identity could be dismissed as naive conciliatory optimism, as an attempt to skirt the seriousness of the problem Nietzsche had uncovered. It is presumably for this reason that virtually no links were ever forged between, on the one hand, cultural criticism and its discourse on the transgression of the boundaries of the self, drawing on Nietzsche's ideas and, on the other, the scientific discourse, which took Durkheim as its starting point, on the revitalization of the collective in religious experience that is construed as an overcoming of the self.[90]

For the purposes of action theory, however, it is the latter approach that is more important. In his sociology of religion, Émile Durkheim provided what has since been acknowledged as a classic analysis of the emergence of new institutions and the revitalization of existing social totalities in processes of self-transgression.[91] Durkheim was interested not simply in the emergence of obligatory rules but rather in the principles which are constitutive of our world; he wished to explain what motivates people, not what disciplines them. The experiential background which he claimed is involved comprises all those influences by means of which 'society' stimulates humans. To Durkheim's mind these always influence us.

> The man who has done his duty finds, in the manifestations of every sort of expressing sympathy, esteem or affection which his fellows have for him, a feeling of comfort, of which he does not ordinarily take account, but which sustains him, none the less. The sentiments which society has for him raise the sentiments which he has for himself. Because he is in moral harmony with his comrades, he has more confidence, courage and boldness in action, just like the believer who thinks that he feels the regard of his god turned graciously towards him.[92]

In some situations, however, the force society exerts is particularly intensive and the individual feels himself uplifted and taken beyond himself. Durkheim illustrated this by referring to the 'demon of oratorical inspiration' which takes hold of a speaker who succeeds in communicating with a crowd:

His language has a grandiloquence that would be ridiculous in ordinary circumstances; his gestures show a certain domination; his very thought is impatient of all rules, and easily falls into all sorts of excesses. It is because he feels within him an abnormal oversupply of force which overflows and tries to burst out from him; sometimes he even has the feeling that he is dominated by a moral force which is greater than he and of which he is only the interpreter.[93]

Durkheim asserted that such an experience is real; the feeling of a force that takes the self beyond itself is no hallucination, but

very real; it comes to him from the very group which he addresses. The sentiments provoked by his words come back to him, but enlarged and amplified, and to this degree they strengthen his own sentiment. The passionate energies he arouses re-echo within him and quicken his vital tone. It is no longer a simple individual who speaks; it is a group incarnate and personified.[94]

These examples describe only the individual enhancing his own abilities by dint of the force of the group, and the confirmation of a group's values. Yet Durkheim was interested in something at a deeper level, namely not just the revitalization of a shared belief in something sacred but how that belief came about, and he maintained that it stems from self-transgression. These experiences, he claimed, are by no means solely an empowerment but initially an overwhelming of the ego. In the course of which types of action are such experiences made and how is the commitment to something sacred forged? In line with the evolutionist premiss that the answer to so fundamental a question is most likely to be found in primitive phenomena, Durkheim examined totemist rituals among Australian aboriginals, as these were regarded as the most elementary form of religious life available for study. He contrasted everyday life in these tribes, whose search for the basic means of subsistence causes them to spread out over a wide geographic area, with the occasions on which they gather in one place. Durkheim suggested that when many people gather together, their self-control is undermined, and that this tendency is particularly strong among less civilized peoples:

Since the emotional and passional faculties of the primitive are only imperfectly placed under the control of his reason and will, he easily loses control of himself. Any event of some importance puts him quite outside himself. Does he receive good news? There are at once transports of enthusiasm. In the contrary conditions, he is to be seen running here and there like a madman, giving himself up to all sorts of immoderate movements, crying, shrieking, rolling in the dust, throwing it in every direction, biting himself, brandishing his arms in a furious manner, etc. The very fact of the concentration acts as an exceptionally powerful stimulant. When they are once come together, a sort of electricity is formed by their collecting which quickly transports them to an extraordinary degree of exaltation. Every sentiment expressed finds a place without resistance in all the minds, which are very open to outside impressions; each re-echoes the others and is re-echoed by the others. The initial impulse thus proceeds, growing as it goes, as an avalanche grows in its advance. And as such active passions so free from all control could not fail to burst out, on every side one sees nothing but violent gestures, cries, veritable howls, and deafening noises of every sort, which aid in intensifying still more the state of mind which they manifest.[95]

Here, Durkheim conflated a wide variety of different physical metaphors: heating up, echoes, electricity, avalanches, etc., in order to describe vividly the state of ecstatic collective excitation. Any gathering of people over a longer period of time can trigger off this state, and this is all the more true the weaker the self-control of the participants. An intensification of this experience can lead to what might be called a loss of self. He continues:

One can readily conceive how, when arrived at this state of exaltation, a man does not recognize himself any longer. Feeling himself dominated and carried away by some sort of an external power which makes him think and act differently than in normal times, he naturally has the impression of being himself no longer. It seems to him that he has become a new being: the decoration he puts on and the masks that cover his face figure materially in this interior transformation, and to a still greater extent, they aid in determining its nature. And as at the same time all his companions feel themselves transformed in the same way and express this sentiment by their cries, their gestures and their general attitude, everything is just as though he really were transported into a special world, entirely different from the one where he ordinarily lives, and into an environment filled with exceptionally intense forces that take hold of him and metamorphose him.[96]

To experience loss of self is thus at the same time to experience an extra-ordinary power that holds one in its sway. Durkheim had the dialectical notion of construing such an experience as the birth of religion. Given that the immense experiences of a loss of self and of a force which causes the everyday to vanish cannot be interpreted with cool-headed reason by those involved as being the product of their gathering together, they ascribe it instead to pre-existent powers with which they came into contact at the time and place of their gathering. The affective certainty that higher powers are at work, a certainty derived from experiencing a loss of self, therefore becomes transformed into a pre-reflective bond with the attributes of religious experience. Thus begins the classification of the world into two separate domains: on the one hand, the profane and, on the other, the domain which corresponds, in however mediated a form, to an experience of the sacred. However, this does not mean that the experience of going beyond oneself is some primitive or irrational marginal phenomenon of sociality; in fact it is the constitutive precondition for all affectively charged social bonds to other individuals, collectives or values. Durkheim consequently regards the emergence of the 'sacred' as the core of social bonds. It is not accessible to reflective thought and is by no means limited to primitive cultures or times of revolutionary upheaval, but is an ongoing process. Although we cannot really derive from his work a full theory of the transformation of the 'sacred' in modern society, it nevertheless contains numerous pointers to modern equivalents of totemist rituals.

These pointers have been taken up both by Durkheim's disciples and by others who were more remotely influenced by him.[97] They have attempted to specify more closely what experiences are involved and also trace them beyond the domain of the religious. Victor Turner, for example, maintains that in all cases in which a collective is brought up against the boundaries of its interpretative abilities, rituals serve to remind the members of the collective of its common ground beyond all social and symbolic differentiation, thus absorbing the disruptive impact of deviance by reasserting the force of the collective. In the occasional dissolution of its symbolic and social structures, the collective does not dissolve into nothingness, but rather experiences that it always extends beyond what is contained in its own structures.

> An event such as twinning that falls outside the orthodox classifications of society is, paradoxically, made the ritual occasion for an exhibition of values that relate to the community as a whole, as a homogeneous, unstructured unity that transcends its differentiations and contradictions.[98]

In other words Turner not only claims that the collective experience which transcends the boundaries of the ego is the precondition for social bonds but uses it as an argument against the possibility of construing the social purely in 'structural' terms.

The reconstructive introduction of the autonomy of individuals into action theory by taking into account the formation of the ego's identity in socialization processes and its ritual dissolution and restabilization in processes of 'primary sociality' thus takes us away from the terrain of action theory and confronts us with the question as to what consequences such a revised understanding of human action has for social theory in general. After all, it is now apparent that goal-setting, body control and the formation of boundaries between subject and environment can no longer be regarded as everyday, self-evident truths. A theory of action which is aware of the extent to which these assumptions are conditional must immerse itself in the 'Dionysian' source of all rationality and sociality. The possible reward is an understanding of current structures of individual and collective action which is not to be gained via the short-cut of directly applying the established conception of rational action as it stands.

4

Creative Democracy

Three arguments have been put forward to explain why a reconstructive introduction of the tacit assumptions found in the various models of rational action is necessary.[1] Firstly, such an approach was considered the only way to prevent action theory from starting with a rigid abstraction and thus, secondly, from becoming divorced from the situational and biographical context of action. But thirdly, and above all, this way of proceeding was seen as the best safeguard against another danger: namely that the consideration of human action should be forced to adhere to the dictates of a conception of rationality to such an extent that the broad spectrum of different phenomena of action should appear primarily as examples of a lack of rationality. Not only must we move beyond instrumental and monological conceptions of rationality, and develop a 'communicative' or 'discursive' idea of rationality; but we must also change how we view the role played in human action by rationality. We can then observe the full spectrum of action phenomena without sacrificing the link to rationality altogether.

There are further advantages to this. Whereas models of rational action apply normative preconditions to the study of action, this is not the case with a theory of the creativity of action. The models of rational action – at least those that claim to be more than merely normative – inevitably force phenomena of action to fit the concepts found in the model, or else they must distinguish one concrete, rational kind of action from other concrete, less rational types of action. By contrast, a reconstructive introduction of the tacit assumptions found in models of rational action that is informed by the overarching idea of creativity is aimed from the beginning at discovering the specific characteristics of *all* human action. Such a revised theory is concerned not just with one concrete type of creative action, but with the creativity of human action as such. This, of course, does not imply that all specific human actions are said to contain the same degree of creativity in contrast to routines and habits. This cannot be so for the simple reason that every action theory that takes basic pragmatist ideas as its point of departure must assume that creatively found solutions to the action problem will be absorbed into new 'beliefs', or, more precisely, into altered routines. This means that even acts of the utmost creativity assume the pre-existence of a bedrock of underlying routine actions and external conditions which are simply taken as given.[2] There are naturally large differences between various acts and actors with regard to creativity; however, an empirical, differential psychology and sociology of creativity does not concern us here. This, too, would have to start with a general theory of action in order to examine concrete types of creative action, and here we are asserting that such a general theory should regard creativity as a dimension that is present in all human action and should interpret routine as a result of creativity. Consequently, such a general action theory would not contain value judgements on concrete instances of creativity. From this perspective, creativity in itself is neither good nor bad; there are many reasons why routine could be considered praiseworthy, and many a vision of permanent aesthetic or political creativity is a vision of terror that would overtax human capabilities. Whether a particular creative act is good or bad can only be settled in a discourse. Yet the search for a normative agency to justify validity claims is not the same as the search for a model to describe in empirical terms how new validity claims arise.

The advantages of revising the structure of action theory in this way extend far beyond the immediate bounds of action theory itself. The question whether our ideal personality should aspire to ever higher levels of rationality (however this is defined) or instead to alternating between the discipline of rationality and an easing of such rigours is of central importance to the theory of personality. In the theory of organization we can, following the model of rational action, classify the structures yielded by empirical evidence as simple deviations from the model in the direction of informal relationships. Or, conversely, empirical organizations can be analysed independently of the rational model in order to explore the unlikely and highly contingent character of the rational type.[3] In the theory of social movements we also find examples of the consequences of rationalist prejudice, such as the widespread idea that clear goals held by individual actors or the group as a whole are the driving force behind these movements.[4]

And finally, in a theory of history and the analysis of present-day society, rational models of action theory show an affinity to those interpretations which consider historical developments to be more or less linear 'processes of rationalization'. What tends to be forgotten here is that, even when trends towards rationality can be empirically observed, they should not be universalized, as there will always be some spheres of life and some individuals who do not passively submit to the rationalization process. On the contrary, their resistance sparks counter-movements, which may end up prevailing over the tendencies towards rationality.

It would clearly go well beyond the limits of our present context to explore all these aspects of the consequences of a revised action theory. We shall therefore confine ourselves to only a few relevant issues. Firstly, we shall defend the claim that action theory, especially in its revised form as described above, is useful as a basis for approaching more general questions of social theory in the first place. This view is by no means the generally received opinion. Many maintain that action theory is only suitable for analysing microsociological phenomena and that the type of explanation it uses is only intentional. Following this reasoning, it no longer even seems necessary to justify the unacceptability of intentional explanations when discussing macrosociological phenomena. As a consequence, it is frequently considered valid to bring in, especially for this macrosociological purpose, model assumptions and types of explanation which are often borrowed from fields outside the social sciences and then experimentally applied to socio-historical subject matter. In such instances, structure and system models and the logic of functional explanations are regarded as useful, if not indeed ineluctable when discussing macrosociology.

The next step in my argumentation is to refute these arguments. In a sort of pincer movement, I shall first demonstrate that where research into collective action is concerned, action theories have long since ventured beyond the frontiers of microsociology; at the same time, this will provide an opportunity to illustrate the superiority of a theory of the creativity of action over rationalistic and normativistic approaches within a particular area of research. This not only involves attaching a higher status to the claims of action theory, but also leads to the next step, which is to show that the macrosociological jump to functionalism is not only unnecessary but even inadmissible. Having thus legitimated a programme for a *non-functionalist macrosociology based on action theory*, I shall illustrate how this programme can be applied using just one point as an example, namely the *altered status of 'functional differentiation'* in such a theory. The chapter ends with a brief survey of the relevance of the idea of creativity when diagnosing our present cultural situation. The point of departure here is the idea that an understanding which stems from action theory and which is influenced by pragmatism is needed to resolve the dilemmas which have arisen from the predominance of interpretations of creativity culled from the philosophy of life in discussions on the 'postmodern' age. I propose that the conflict between Nietzschean and pragmatist versions of creativity is the key to understanding the *ambivalence of the idea of creativity in contemporary cultural trends*. The common point of reference for these exemplary applications, which in the final instance even functions as an evaluative standard, is an emphatic understanding of democracy for which John Dewey coined the term 'creative democracy'.[5]

4.1 Creativity and Collective Action

For both empirical and theoretical reasons, processes of *collective* action are increasingly becoming a focus of social scientific research. The empirical reason is the current boom in the topic of 'new social movements'. The multiplication and normalization of social movements in Europe raises questions about how they arise, their inner dynamics, and how members are recruited, questions which the old explanatory models are considered incapable of answering. In the United States it was in particular the Civil Rights Movement and the race riots of the sixties, but also the student and anti-war movements of the same period, which engendered a new interest in reviving older research into collective action or developing new research approaches, an interest which has remained alive to this day.[6] From a theoretical viewpoint, the allure of analysing collective action is that it enables us to reconcile the unproductive opposition between action theory, on the one hand, and models of social order, social systems and structures, on the other. By focusing on collective action, rather than purely individual action, it becomes much easier to proceed to issues such as the emergence, reproduction and transformation of social order. This is true in the twofold sense that not only do collective forms of action and social movements contribute significantly to developing and changing social order, but they can also be understood in themselves as models of social order in the process of self-generation.[7]

The great number of competing approaches in this field can be grouped according to various criteria. The attempt to group these approaches simply on the basis of existing schools of macrosociology is somewhat futile, because although these schools describe the character of certain social problems, they often fail to explain the dynamic process whereby such problems develop into social conflicts. What is seen as a problem from the perspective of macrosociological theory will not necessarily be perceived as an actual problem by the social actors themselves, and even if it is, this does not automatically imply that they will feel confident enough about finding a solution to join forces over it. Whether or not it is possible to predict the likelihood of an uprising or the emergence of a social movement based on given degrees of absolute or relative deprivation is a hotly debated point.[8] Therefore, it is more useful to classify approaches according to the assumptions of a theory of history on which they are respectively based. For this purpose, Charles Tilly[9] has suggested that ideal-typical models of collapse and solidarity be contrasted. The first category includes all approaches which attempt to interpret collective action in terms of the collapse of social order. In these approaches, the individuals who have been set free from the old social orders are considered the most likely agents of processes of collective action. Societies in which the dissolution process occurs quickly and extensively are considered the most probable breeding grounds for social movements. Theories of mass psychology and mass society are prototypical expressions of this way of thinking, but one can also subsume here those works which argue that there is a historical trend towards progressive individualization. Especially influential in this respect is the work of Michel Foucault, who presents an outline of history that is implicitly characterized by the gradual destruction of all autonomous, effective solidarities and their replacement by the 'disciplines', that is, the individuation techniques of the modern state. Collective action is then seen as a matter of minor skirmishes and battles of everyday life which in themselves hardly affect the course of history. Rather, history follows an intrinsic logic of progressive centralization and bureaucratization.

Such theories of the collapse of an autonomous social order can be contrasted with those approaches which are interested in collective action as a process that results in the development of new bonds of solidarity. These include Marxism, which interpreted the labour movement as the forerunner of a new order and a new era; the tradition in American sociology of the Chicago School, which considered an investigation of the reorganization of a culture – such as took place, for example, in immigrant ghettos – to be just as important as the analysis of disorganization processes; and Tilly's own research, which on the basis of substantial empirical evidence provides an appraisal of the influence of major historical processes, such as urbanization, industrialization and the consolidation of the nation-state, on the emergence and forms of collective action. Although Tilly, too, pinpoints the retreat of traditional communities in conjunction with these historical processes, he also perceives a change in the form taken by collective action as reflected in the evolution of associations with voluntary membership and a centralist organizational structure in the period from about 1830 to 1930. We can conclude from this that in contemporary society as well, collective action is more likely to undergo a transformation than to disappear altogether.

In the context of our present argumentation, one further method of classification suggests itself: Research into collective action may also be classified according to the action-theoretical assumptions on which it is based. And indeed, various models of rational action which are influenced by economic theory are also found in this area of research, as are models of normative action such as dominate the field of sociology. It is also possible to identify isolated approaches to examining collective action which rely on a theory of action informed by a concept of creativity. We shall set out to demonstrate that only this last group has the potential to integrate the different approaches on the level of action theory.

The most thoroughgoing attempt to construct a theory of collective action based on a rationalistic action theory was that put forth by Mancur Olson, a theory which has since become a virtual classic.[10] Olson asks which conditions render collective action possible if we posit the individual as a rational actor. Olson is cautious enough to treat this as just one of many possible assumptions, a fact which is often ignored by commentators on his paradigmatic work. None the less, this assumption leads him to some highly significant counter-intuitive findings. In particular, he challenges the view that when rational individuals have goals or interests in common with other rational individuals, they will automatically form a group which actively pursues these common goals, an assumption which is considered self-evident in many social theories. From this point of view, recruitment and mobilization problems are merely incidental; what needs to be explained is not the existence but the absence of organizations representing interest groups in instances where a common interest can be clearly identified.

> The idea that groups tend to act in support of their group interests is supposed to follow logically from this widely accepted premise of

rational, self-interested behavior. In other words: if the members of some group have a common interest or objective, and if they would all be better off if that objective were achieved, it has been thought to follow logically that the individuals in that group would, if they were rational and self-interested, act to achieve that objective.[11]

Olson's objection to this view is as simple as it is perspicacious: it makes even more sense for the rational individual to allow his interests to be represented by a group without investing his own time and effort in obtaining results that he can enjoy without direct participation. If this is accurate, other conditions are then necessary for the unlikely occurrence of collective action, assuming the existence of individuals who behave rationally. Olson lists three kinds of such additional conditions. On the one hand, coercion can be used in order to obtain individual contributions to a cause; for example, a tax-collecting state does not rely on its citizens' understanding of the usefulness of tax-funded state projects. The size of a group is another aspect which Olson considers to be conducive to obliging individuals to pull their weight. In small groups there is a greater chance that one member's failure to contribute will be noticed by the other members. In addition, the smaller the group, the more likely it is that one member will end up taking on sole responsibility for achieving the collective aims of the group.

> This is because in some small groups each of the members, or at least one of them, will find that his personal gain from having this collective good exceeds the total cost of providing some amount of that collective good; there are members who would be better off if the collective good were provided, even if they had to pay the entire cost of providing it themselves, than they would be if they were not provided.[12]

The third factor which will ensure individual participation in collective action is that alongside the desired collective good there exist other non-collective advantages which serve as a selective incentive for individual activity. Thus German labour unions offer fringe benefits such as insurance cover in order to get workers to join, rather than relying on them to take part solely out of a desire to pursue goals which are common to all workers. The further ramifications of Olson's theory and their empirical application by Olson himself and those who followed in his footsteps are of no significance here. From the point of view of action theory, the crucial issue is to determine how widely his theory can be applied; in other words, how empirically convincing is the initial assumption that individuals can be looked upon as rational agents? Olson himself restricts the validity of his premiss when he expressly states that it is inapplicable to the study of the 'communal groups' and of little use when considering philanthropic and religious organizations.[13] However, he lays great emphasis on the idea that rational action does not only consist in the pursuit of selfish goals, but may also include unselfish goals provided that they can be pursued using the most appropriate and effective means.[14] A second restriction on Olson's theory lies in his discussion of the extent to which individual participation can be observed. The question is whether this simply confronts rational individuals with a new problem – namely a self-presentation problem: how can I create the impression that I am making my contribution while expending the least possible effort? – or whether moralistic impulses such as shame or guilt enter into the picture. Olson is quite convinced of the effectiveness of a moral code in the constitution of collective action, but at the same time prefers to disregard moral phenomena in this particular field. This brings to a head the question of how narrow this field actually is. When do empirical individuals have clearly defined interests, and when do they pursue these interests in an individualistic fashion? Even if we start with the problematic assumption that individual action is shaped by clear goals, it does not follow that an outside observer would be able to perceive them. It is equally uncertain whether these goals would remain unchanged in the course of a complex action sequence. The plausibility of the assumption that individuals concentrate on their own goals of action also depends on whether we are willing to place examples of spontaneous or premeditated altruism outside the chosen category of rationality. There are many well-documented cases of such altruism, ranging from the process of self-organization in order to provide disaster relief, to making donations and performing charitable acts.[15]

Another example of a theory of collective action which is based on rationalist action theory is the resource mobilization school, where the organizations rather than the individuals are regarded as the rational actors.[16] The perspective here is no longer that of the single individual who reflects upon his membership in an organization or his participation in a collective act, and therefore also calculates the advantages of 'free-riding'. Rather it is the vantage point of the 'general secretary' of an interest group in a society where social movements are commonplace but have become highly professionalized and indeed partially commercialized. Studies of resource mobilization examine the strategic dilemmas which confront such groups, and determine the most advantageous courses of action in given situations. As the name of the school implies, attention is mainly given to the availability of resources such as time and money, and whether they can be mobilized in order to attain the goals of the organization in question. Aspects of this question include competition with other organizations that have comparable goals, the chances of obtaining state or public support, the most effective ways of recruiting members, and other similar tasks. From this perspective, it would be absurd to interpret social movements as irrational outbursts that result from the decay of social bonds. The idea that they can be attributed to miserable social conditions is also called radically into question; the experience of 'professional' members of such movements suggests that such conditions are often first defined and made a subject of public debate by the movements themselves. Like Olson, the proponents of the resource mobilization approach regard their theory as offering only a partial account, although what they mean by this is not completely clear. If it means that the validity of the theory is conditional on movement organizations acting like rational actors, then this is largely unproblematic. However, it then loses the thrust which sets it off from competing approaches. If, on the other hand, the claim is that social movements mostly correspond to the rational type, then empirical objections may be raised and it may also be necessary to give additional empirical reasons why this particular type should be considered representative in modern societies. Charles Tilly, whose work is undoubtedly related to that of the resource mobilization school, provides just such a supplementary, historical proof. The conditions imposed by the market economy and by a nation-state which commands important resources make it imperative for social movements to conform to the pattern of strategic rationality, he argues. This is because they are competing, on the one hand, with other collective actors for the opportunity to obtain power and influence, and, on the other, with providers of goods and services for the deployment of resources in the hands of the members of society. Yet even Tilly does not provide an answer to the question of which other theoretical means should be used to analyse both pre-modern and modern non-rational forms of social movements. Rationalist theories of collective action and social movements are undoubtedly powerful analytical tools for a whole series of phenomena. However, they start by clearly defining an area of analysis which corresponds to their own premises, and therefore cannot be developed into a comprehensive theory.

The most ambitious attempt to develop such a comprehensive

theory of collective action based on a normativist critique of the rational model of action was advanced by Neil Smelser.[17] In this undertaking, Smelser, who was a student and close collaborator of Talcott Parsons, tried to overcome one of the spectacular difficulties inherent in Parsons' theory. Admittedly, Parsons had put forth a theory of action which was much more extensive than the models of rational action, and Smelser correspondingly based his own investigation of collective action on an action-theoretical model which encompassed components such as values, norms, the mobilization of individual energy and available resources. Yet not only had Parsons made no attempt to apply his own action theory to developing a theory of collective action, but he based his macrosociology on a conception of institutions which foregrounds their contribution to the maintenance and reproduction of the social order, thus at the same time making non- or anti-institutional action appear as something that threatens order. Smelser resolutely devotes himself to such non-institutional action. He clears it of the stigma of being basically pathological or irrational, which is how it had been characterized by theories of mass psychology, yet he does not thereby simply append it to the rational model. In doing so, he breaks open the hermetically sealed world where all action conforms to institutionalized and internalized norms. However, he stops short of making collective action a necessary component of institutionalization processes, with the result that it appears to be a mere accompaniment to processes of social change rather than constitutive of them. According to Smelser, collective action occurs when social structures give rise to tensions which impair the functioning of various components of action. These structural tensions also produce generalized beliefs that interpret the crisis situation, ascribe causes and outline alternative actions. Smelser's model also suggests that the whole process can be accelerated by certain other factors, such as dramatic intensifications of conflicts, the processes of mobilizing participants and the influence of authorities of social control. He links differing action components with various types of collective action, ranging from panic and mania to outbreaks of hostility, to social movements oriented towards norms or even values. He states that underlying this approach is

> the basic principle . . . that each type of collective behavior is oriented
> toward a distinct component of social action. Thus, a) the value-oriented
> movement is collective action mobilized in the name of a generalized
> belief envisioning a reconstitution of values; b) the norm-oriented
> movement is action mobilized in the name of a generalized belief

envisioning a reconstitution of norms; c) the hostile outburst is action mobilized on the basis of a generalized belief assigning responsibility for an undesirable state of affairs to some agent; and d) the craze and the panic are forms of behavior based on a generalized redefinition of situational facilities.[18]

The result is a framework of analytic categories for the overwhelming variety of historical instances of collective action, a framework that is consistently grounded in action theory.

However, the consistency of this framework is also the reason why the deficiencies of the action theory on which it is based are so directly reflected in the theory of collection action. Smelser suggests taking economic theory's concept of the value-added process as the model for processes of collective action. This implicitly contradicts the conception of history as a progression of natural states ('natural history'), which was widely held in American sociology before Parsons. Unlike a history of natural development, the value-added logic 'implies a temporal sequence of activation of determinants, but any or all of these determinants may have existed for an indefinite period before activation'.[19] The economic model is also based on a teleological action process, that is, a progression in which each previous step is considered, at least in hindsight, to be the means for achieving a future goal. This kind of teleological analysis is highly inappropriate to the dynamics of non-institutional action because here the definitions of situations and the norms which arise out of the process, and indeed even the goals of the whole process and the choice of means to attain them, are usually unclear and unknown to the people involved; they are only elucidated as the process itself unfolds. Furthermore, Smelser incorporates social control as a phase in his model of collective action. This would be understandable if the model were to be thought of as a list of possible causes of collective action. However, by making social control part of a model of successive phases, the combative aspect of the interplay between collective outbreaks and social control is lost unless the latter is conceptualized as a counterforce whose structure is based on its own laws and which is activated by its own 'theories' on collective outbreaks. Another problem comes to light when one scrutinizes Smelser's explanation of why a particular type of collective action results as a reaction to certain structural tensions. The answer is to be found in the ensuing 'generalized beliefs', which Smelser claims are necessary components of collective action. However, his theory does not at all explain which 'generalized beliefs' actually ensue, and thus, rather than solving the original problem of explanation, merely shifts it to another level.

The difficulties in operationalizing Smelser's analytical categories are hence not the only factors which limit the value of this impressive theoretical construction in terms of its empirical application.[20] More pertinently, the reason can be found within the theory itself. Smelser's normativist model ignores the question of which categories are adequate to deal with the issue of the emergence of *new* norms and values; his theory only applies to modifications, specifications or generalizations of values that can in principle be anticipated. This is a kind of congenital defect, so to speak. Parsons' action theory, which Smelser used as his starting point, was unable to assign a place to the one quality of human action which cannot be overlooked when observing non-institutional collective action: the creativity of action.[21]

A creativity-oriented model of action forms the basis for two currents of research into collective action and social movements:[22] on the one hand, work that stands in the tradition of symbolic interactionism, and, on the other, the studies of Alain Touraine and his colleagues. The symbolic interactionists carry on the only classical tradition in sociology where collective action held centre stage – the tradition of the Chicago School. There, the early version of European mass psychology was not simply rejected out of hand. Certainly, the Chicago School repudiated mass psychology's polemical gesture of denying that social movements have any sort of intellectual content, and regarding the actions of such movements as nothing more than the destructive consequences of a loss of ability on the part of individuals to take responsibility when in a collective.[23] However, mass psychology's characterization of movements as 'blind, raging mobs' was not countered in Chicago by considering social movements now as 'well-organized interest groups'. On the contrary, the Chicago School retained the attention paid by mass psychology to specific forms of action and experience in social movements and other forms of collective action. Underlying this was the idea that institutions should be defined as the result of creative processes of institutionalization that had gained temporary stability. It is for this reason that Park and Burgess posit the process of collective action as *the* point of concern for sociology.[24] Unfortunately, even these early authors allowed their view of collective action to be coloured by deterministic concepts of a 'biotic' or 'ecological' order. Although this led to the incorporation into the theory of unplanned and unintended processes whereby the consequences of actions become interconnected and whereby functionally suitable alternatives are selected, it none the less remained impossible to integrate these divergent aspects of the theory into a coherent whole. Herbert Blumer, who picked up where the Chicago School's approaches to a theory of collective action left off,[25] extricated himself from this situation by turning his attention almost exclusively to collective action itself and simply removing the elements which Park had been unable to integrate. At the same time, this eliminated the possibility of providing a fundamental definition of sociology based on collective action, reducing it to one particular aspect of the field. The relationship between a theory of the emergence of norms and institutions, and an analysis of the structural effects of existing institutions, thus remained obscure.

In this respect, little has changed in the further history of this tradition. None the less, its empirical contribution to an understanding of the emergence of norms and institutions is indispensable. Nowhere else is the consideration of phenomena rooted so firmly in a theory of the constitution of collective actors. Its focus is not on a kind of collective action which can simply be derived from existing psychological dispositions or social problems, but rather on one in which the actors only become what they are for the movement through their involvement in it. Social movements themselves define the problems which prompt them; they create motives and identities, form new social relations and communities, give rise to far-reaching identity changes (conversion and regeneration), invent emotionally charged symbols and leave behind symbolic bonds powerful enough to structure human biographies.[26] No light is shed on these phenomena when the studies are based on a rationalistic or normative model of action. On the other hand, the special types of collective action which can be examined using these models may be understood as specific applications of this most comprehensive of action-theoretical approaches.

Alain Touraine has attempted to put forward just such a comprehensive schema of theories and types of collective action.[27] To a greater extent than in the work of the symbolic interactionists, the collective action processes on which Touraine's empirical investigations are focused are those which form the central lines of conflict in society. Thus his studies include the conflict over the use of nuclear power in France, student movements, the revived interest in regionalism, and the 'Solidarnosc' trade union in Poland. He is opposed to reducing social movements to strategic actors or to a process of pure identity development, and instead ties together the dimensions of power and culture in his definition of social movements as 'collective action aimed at the implementation of central cultural values against the interest and influence of an enemy which is defined in terms of power relations'.[28] According to Touraine, the process of defining oneself and one's goals does not occur in a power-free environment; likewise, these processes are seldom unaffected by power struggles. From the outset, Touraine rejected Parsons' theory bluntly because it overestimated the degree to which norms play a direct role in the orientation of the actors and because it was incapable of explaining the genesis of value systems. For Touraine, competing value systems do not pose a threat to the stability of societies; they are rather the form in which societal self-'production' or self-'constitution' takes place. The self-institutionalization of a society is no simple act of creation, but occurs in the context of discussions about new values and changes in consciousness, social protests and repression based on force. Touraine revives the feeling of confidence that by examining collective action one is getting to the core of macrosociological analysis, a confidence which over time had disappeared from the Chicago School. A creativity-oriented theory of action thus raises far-reaching macrosociological claims. Can it live up to those claims in the face of competition from functionalism?

4.2 Beyond Functionalism

In order to answer this question, the claims of the functionalist competitors need to be examined. In 1976, when Anthony Giddens took stock of the controversies over functionalism which had been so important for sociology in the fifties and sixties, he did so with a feeling of writing 'après la lutte';[29] in other words, after a battle in which the critics had scored territorial gains over the functionalists but did not succeed in defeating them conclusively, so that the end result was primarily fatigue on all sides. However, this impression was misleading because not only did functionalism and critiques of it go through a temporary renaissance in the following decade; they also took on board new themes and arguments. The critique of functionalism was no longer fixated on its chief opponent, Talcott Parsons, but turned its attention to disguised forms of functionalism unearthed in the works of schools and authors who would never have referred to themselves as 'functionalists'. The hidden functionalist assumptions in Marxist writers and in the works of Marx and Engels themselves were a favourite target of such criticism. In particular, Jon Elster's work[30] tied together some of the older arguments of the critique with considerable brilliance and clarity, resulting in what was a devastating attack. On the side of the defence, the attempt to find a productive continuation of the legacy of Talcott Parsons, which for a time had been all but forgotten, branched into two quite different paths. In Germany, in a profusion of programmatic and substantive writings, Niklas Luhmann developed a comprehensive functionalist social theory which, by dint of being by and large detached from an inner conflict with action theory and empirical research practice, promised to solve Parsons' unsolved problems. It is currently making waves as what one might call a scientistic parallel to post-structuralism. Even in Jürgen Habermas' main work on the theory of communicative action,[31] the influence of Luhmann's functionalism is clearly detectable. In the United States at the same time, a circle of younger sociologists led by Jeffrey Alexander tried to circumvent undeniable problems in Parsons' writings by referring to his earlier action theory or by contesting discontinuities in his work as a whole. Unfortunately the name they have chosen for this attempt is 'neo-functionalism'. There are close affinities between this work and some of the writings of Richard Münch in Germany.

The earlier critique of functionalism can be summed up using two brief formulas. On the one hand, it vigorously contests the possibility of functional *explanations*. The critics consider functionalist propositions admissible only as counterfactual statements on what conditions are necessary to produce certain possible consequences. On the other hand, the merit of using functionalist models in an essentialist way is also disputed. This does not, of course, mean that the critique simply denies that processes of regulation or self-regulation exist; however, it does deny that it is possible in the social sciences to establish clearly those systemic requirements which may act as reference points or guiding values and thus make a functionalist model both applicable and meaningful in the first place. The critique accuses functionalist *theories* of prejudging on a metatheoretical level the issue of whether self-regulatory processes exist, instead of treating this as an empirical question and thus keeping open the 'degree of systemness'.[32] Starting from a critique of Merton's famous but unclear distinction between manifest and latent functions, Giddens, for one, succeeds in proving the indispensability of taking account of the intentions and the cognitive expectations of real actors when analysing social phenomena. His general strategy is to show that in every case the concept of function is either misleading or redundant. In most cases, Giddens is able to fall back on the arguments of previous writers concerning functional explanations and the problems of the reference point in functionalist analyses. The truly original aspect of what Giddens has to say is not his critical argumentation in itself, but the fact that he does not take as his starting point the position of methodological individualism or logical positivism. Giddens claims that, by means of a theory of action which is superior to the theories of rational action, he is able to arrive at a social theory which is neither functionalist nor 'individualist'. This raises the stakes when it comes to examining new contributions to functionalism because it also indirectly prompts the question of whether there is currently a superior alternative to such an *action-theoretical foundation of a non-functionalist social theory*. We shall now attempt to answer this question with reference to the relationship to functionalism of Luhmann, Habermas and Alexander.

Nobody has taken on the criticism of functionalism as boldly and cleverly as has Niklas Luhmann. Even in his essays of the early sixties,[33] he was already dealing with the arguments that subsequently became a central part of the later critique. For all the changes that have taken place in the structure of his theory, culminating in his magnum opus, *Soziale Systeme*,[34] the basic arguments on the possibility of using a functional method remain unchanged. Because Luhmann himself draws a sharp programmatic – if not always factual – distinction between this functional method and the internal structure of systems theory, we are justified in confining our present investigation to his position on the functional method.[35]

Luhmann expressly admits that the results of functional analysis do not constitute causal explanations. He also concedes that the problem of the stability and existence of social systems is as yet unresolved and can certainly not be the ultimate reference point for functional analysis. Luhmann arrived at the latter insight in particular by way of his early research into the sociology of organization and administration. In his 1962 essay 'Funktion und Kausalität' Luhmann demonstrates that all attempts to reconcile the functional method in the social sciences with the methodologically rigorous concepts of causality have failed. Neither by referring to established or clearly identifiable needs, nor by transferring the ideas of equilibrium found in thermodynamics and biology did it prove feasible to explain causes by effects. In similarly unambiguous terms, Luhmann summarizes the problems that arise when one tries to define functions 'as the effecting of the stability and existence, or of individual preconditions of the stability and existence, of a system of action'.[36] Social systems are neither 'fixed types', that is, they are not defined once and for all by a particular identity, nor is it clear what death, which is a tangible and unequivocal problem in biology, is supposed to mean with respect to social systems. The idea of individual preconditions of stability and existence, as distinct from stability and existence in general, is also of no help in resolving the matter because they, too, have to be linked in some way to a concept of an overall system or system needs. On both of these key issues, therefore, Luhmann appears to side with the critics of functionalism. However, he draws completely different conclusions from these observations. His strategy in each case is to reverse the burden of proof. If the functional method cannot fulfil the demands of a methodologically rigorous conception of causality, it could be due to a misconception of causality in that methodology itself. If the problem of system stability can be shown to be an inadequate reference point for functional analyses, then perhaps a deeper point of view needs to be established. If difficulties arise in the empirical verification of functionalist statements, this means that other methods of verification are required. Finally, if the understanding of causality, the problem of system stability, verification procedures and other aspects need to be changed, it shows that the functional method of analysis goes against the grain of the ontological tradition of western thinking since classical antiquity, and that it is the very power of this tradition that needs to be broken.

These are, of course, very far-reaching, indeed extreme, claims. Whether or not they can be met can be tested adequately only by considering Luhmann's theory as a whole, and not in the immediate context of the controversy over functionalism as a method. The only question we need to answer here is: which positive reasons does Luhmann adduce for considering functional analysis a useful and applicable method? If functional analysis provides us with no causal explanations, what does it in fact provide? Luhmann answers:

> Functional analysis uses relationings with the aim of understanding that which exists as contingent and that which is different as comparable. It relates what is given, whether situations or events, to problem perspectives and seeks to make it clear and comprehensible that the problem can be resolved either one way or another. The relation between problems and problem solutions is not simply understood in its own terms; rather it serves as a guide in the quest for possibilities, the search for functional equivalents.[37]

According to Luhmann, the starting point for functional analysis is the relationship between problems and their solutions, and not, as in causal analyses, that between causes and effects. Thus the possible outcome of such analyses is not to establish causal linkages between causes and effects, but rather to open up a realm of possibilities for functional equivalents. This means that various combinations of causes can be identified for existing effects, and particular effects can be identified for given causes and compared with one another. The true potential of this method, which is ultimately comparative, is, Luhmann claims, that it pinpoints and eliminates functional equivalents.

It would perhaps be more useful to speak of a method of 'alienation' (to use the term in the Brechtian sense), because the point is not to compare existing states of affairs with each other, but rather to transpose the familiar into the realms of its unrealized, and perhaps in practice unrealizable, possibilities. At first glance it might seem that Luhmann is modest enough to make a merely heuristic claim for functional analysis. His forgoing of any causal claims would seem to confirm this. The opponents of functionalism would not be expected to raise objections to this, because it would very much correspond to their ideas on the construction of conceivable relations of cause and effect. However, it is precisely this 'alienating' quality of Luhmann's approach that is more than merely 'heuristic'.

In fact, his claim is problematic in two respects. First of all, this alienation is different from that used by Brecht because Luhmann is not interested in demonstrating that there are alternatives to the existing undesirable reality which are not only morally and politically appropriate but also achievable in practice. Rather, Luhmann's intention is to bring out the unreality and potentiality in *all* existing states of affairs, which may be why his ideas are more closely related to romantic irony or the theatre of the absurd than to Brecht. The second problem is that Luhmann does not actually succeed in getting around the problems of causality. In fact he has to interpret the 'different possibilities' and the 'functional equivalents' in the context of scientific causality, which means that he has no alternative but to resort to an intuitive consideration of plausible causal relationships. In scientific work, such intuitive hypotheses cannot be left untested. Luhmann readily admits that this recourse to causality is unavoidable, but says that knowledge can be obtained using functional analyses

> even if those causalities are initially no more than hypothetical assumptions that have not yet been sufficiently researched. The task, then, is not simply to forget the purely hypothetical nature of the causal assumptions, but instead to incorporate them in the comparison.[38]

This is basically the same argument as that brought forward by Gerald Cohen in his defence of functional argumentation in orthodox Marxism under the heading of 'consequence laws'.[39] However, Cohen admits unequivocally that such statements can only be regarded as heuristic orientations. In this respect, the argument of the critics of functionalism can also be applied to Luhmann, who is able to defend the heuristic value of functional propositions, but no more than that. The 'alienation effect' of his theory may have certain literary qualities and as such may offer new insights, but it has no power of scientific proof.

But how does Luhmann attempt to avoid the pitfalls of the 'system stability problem'? The only plausible answer is: by displacing or 'temporalizing' it, not once, but many times. In his early works, the solution is sought in a 'hierarchy of problem levels'. Attention should not always be focused at the primary level of a system as such; we can also identify and analyse functional problems on secondary, tertiary and other levels with a reasonable chance of success. Thus the problems resulting from problem solutions become the starting points for new functional problems at a higher level. Luhmann even believes that with this approach he has found a reasonable compromise 'between Parsons' system functionalism and Merton's problem-oriented "theories of the middle range"'.[40] However, this compromise is not at all clear. Luhmann does not explain at this stage what would lead someone to identify given states of affairs as problems, nor does he say how the problem on the primary level can be understood other than as a problem of stability. In other words, the obscurities which were condemned in the critique of functionalism remain just as unclear as before. It seems that the only way out would be for Luhmann to acknowledge the normative-analytical status of functional analyses in the sense that certain guiding values, set for analytical purposes, could serve as reference points, but that beyond this, no empirical claims would be made. This sort of modesty, however, would seem incompatible with Luhmann's far-flung ambitions.

Instead, therefore, the first way out he chooses is that of temporalization. In his 1967 essay entitled 'Soziologie als Theorie sozialer Systeme', he overcomes the problem of system stability by subjecting the change in and emergence of structures to functional analysis. This interest in structuration processes rather than simply in structures suggests an affinity to Giddens' later theory, but upon closer inspection the similarity vanishes. Luhmann simply transforms the question of the ultimate reference point of functional analyses into one of the function of structuration processes. This problem was clearly observed by Jürgen Habermas in his outstanding critique of Luhmann when he wrote:

The function of structure-formation cannot be examined without reference to a more comprehensive system, whose structures must then be
kept constant for the purposes of analysis. The asymmetry between the
system stability (structure) and the achievements which maintain the
system (process) cannot be resolved on an analytical level.[41]

Yet even at this early stage, Luhmann goes one step further and
searches for an ultimate reference point. He finds it in the reduction of
the complexity of the world, which he identified as a problem in all
systems. Habermas' objection to this was that to talk of world
complexity as such is meaningless because this concept inevitably
implies a system for which world complexity presents itself as a
problem. In defending himself, Luhmann concedes this point, but
claims that the issue of world complexity is a fundamental one that
exists independently from all specific systems, and therefore deserves
to be taken as an ultimate reference point.[42] This counter-argument is
incomprehensible, as Habermas had criticized the semantic emptiness
of the concept of 'world complexity as such', not its specific relation to
a particular system. In other words, Luhmann's formula for an
ultimate reference point of functional analyses is semantically
meaningless.

After further developing his systems theory along the lines of a
theory of self-referential, autopoietic systems, Luhmann once again
reformulated the 'problem of system stability':

> It is no longer a question of a unit with definite features, about whose
> stability or lack thereof an overall decision is made; rather the issue is
> whether the reproduction of elements will continue or be broken off
> when they are arranged relationally. System maintenance in this sense
> means the maintenance of the integrity and the incessant reproduction
> of elements, which disappear at the very moment they come into
> being.[43]

What remains completely unclear here is whether by redefining
system stability in terms of the maintenance of a reproduction process
really does anything to alter the problem. The question whether a
reproduction process has been broken off or merely interrupted raises
the same hermeneutic identity problems which Luhmann had admitted were entailed in determining the death or loss of identity of social
systems. Logically, Luhmann's last step toward defending himself
goes beyond justifying a choice of method and enters the dimension
of epistemology. In his magnum opus, *Soziale Systeme*, epistemological
theory is not the basis for his reflections, but is again a testing ground

for demonstrating the applicability of systems theory. His ideas can best be derived from the 'alienating' character of his functional analysis. When social phenomena are described using characteristics which are potential rather than actual, it becomes clear that every reality is a selective construct. However, Luhmann argues that functional analysis reflects this selectivity only when it considers precisely this need for selectivity as the crucial problem. Only then is the last reference point grounded in a self-reflective (or, as Luhmann puts it, self-referential) rather than a decisionist manner. Only thus can the reference problem be valid both for the objects under investigation and also for the system that comprises the analyst and the object of the analysis. The objection to be raised here is surely that Luhmann equates circularity with self-reflection. In no sense has he shown that other theories are not also capable of identifying their premises in a process of self-reflection. On the basis of pragmatism, for example, it is possible to suggest that scientific knowledge can be the solution to problems of action, which means that the task of the social sciences consists in studying the problems that arise in the field of social action after everyday actors have found solutions to existing problems. In this case, self-reflection would be achieved without referring to the problem of complexity or over-stretching the capabilities of functional analysis.

Critics of Luhmann always face the problem that he reformulates every objection in his own theoretical language, and, in the process, blunts their critical cutting edge. Confronted with the verification problem of functional analyses, Luhmann again ducks the issue when he boldly asserts that the applicability of his assumptions to a wide range of facts and situations is a kind of proof of their plausibility. However, whether or not the theory is applicable is evidently decided only by the theorist himself, or perhaps by supporters who have been blinded by his rhetorical brilliance. If one argues in this way, it is no longer possible to distinguish between intersubjectively verified knowledge and monological entanglement in what has become a seamless but self-deluding system.

Jürgen Habermas' early critique was the most incisive and comprehensive appraisal of Luhmann's work to date. Habermas also dedicated a detailed excursus in his book *The Philosophical Discourse of Modernity*[44] to Luhmann's *Soziale Systeme* (published in 1984). In view of this fact, and the subtitle to Volume II of the *Theory of Communicative Action* – 'A Critique of Functionalist Reason' – it may be a surprising twist to group Habermas with the functionalists and pose the question of whether the criticism of functionalism can be applied to Habermas as well. Yet one ironic upshot of the controversy between Habermas and Luhmann was that Habermas revised certain points in his own theory under Luhmann's influence, or used elements of Luhmann's theory to provide the revisions which he considered necessary and proven, even though other options were available. Of course, there is nothing inherently wrong with this in an abstract sense; reciprocal enlightenment is a desirable result of all scientific debate. We therefore need to formulate more specifically the question as to the meaning of this instance of borrowing. Does Habermas really succeed in overcoming the self-acknowledged weaknesses in his conceptions with the aid of Luhmann's works, or does Luhmann's theory lure him into new and even deeper water? Had he sufficiently considered other conceivable alternatives and the problems of functional analyses before he attempted to integrate Luhmann's theory with his own?

Various authors have asked this question with reference to the *Theory of Communicative Action*. For example, Thomas McCarthy[45] analysed the dangers for Habermas arising from the 'seducements of systems theory'. I myself have attempted to describe Habermas' theory as 'the unhappy marriage of hermeneutics and functionalism'.[46] Axel Honneth has identified a conflict between two tendencies which already existed in Habermas' writings of the late sixties and claimed that only the one which more or less corresponded to Luhmann's ideas was pursued.[47] Anthony Giddens expressed his ambivalent judgement of Habermas on this point in a sort of 'methodological schizophrenia' by praising Habermas' attempt to combine systems theory and conceptions of the lifeworld to form a theory of modernity, and yet in the next breath accusing him of not being critical enough of functionalism,[48] and therefore of paying insufficient attention to the contingent results of the historical battles of individuals and groups. Because Habermas has since replied to these objections,[49] the question of his current relationship to the critique of functionalism, including his own early critique, can now be posed on a new footing.

According to Habermas, one informative aspect of Luhmann's theory was the convincing proof of the limits of all sociological action theory.[50] Describing the deciding factor which convinced him of the need to supplement his action theory approach with elements taken from systems theory, Habermas tells us:

> Given that the collective subject of a meaningfully constituted lifeworld, a concept borrowed from transcendental philosophy, has shown itself to be a misleading fiction, at least in the context of sociology, the concept of system provides a promising alternative. Social systems are units

which can solve objectively presented problems through meta-subjective learning processes.[51]

This, therefore, is the motive behind the search for a conceptual framework which does not conceive of a whole society as a kind of self-enlightening subject writ large. Habermas was pressured into this search from several quarters at once. The understanding of history had to be liberated from the fiction of a continuously developing subject, the 'human species'; the category of self-reflection needed to be reconciled with the forever incomplete transparency of human life-situations; the politically normative utopia had to be stripped of the idea of reorganizing all social processes along participatory lines; and the path towards progress had to be cleared of the legitimation of autonomous super-subjects, as in Lukács' conception of the commu-nist party. Introducing the systems concept appeared to be useful as a means to all of these ends, as long as it was integrated with Habermas' own theory of communication, and substantiated by a theory of evolution. Habermas' writings of the following decade contain vari-ous, sometimes divergent attempts to provide this theoretical agenda. The variation set forth in the *Theory of Communicative Action* consists in keeping systems theory under control by asserting the primacy of lifeworld analysis. In doing this, however, the distinction between system and lifeworld is used simultaneously on so many different levels of logic that confusion is the inevitable result. Thus, the distinction is used to express the methodological difference between the perspective of the participant and that of the observer, the difference between social integration via orientations to action and system integration via the consequences of action, the difference between the symbolic and material reproduction of societies; and finally it is used to express a basic structure of history in the sense of a progressive separation of lifeworld from system. McCarthy has demonstrated impressively the mutual incompatibility of this profu-sion of goals. In particular he shows that in the political arena Habermas uses the concept of system in an effort to counter at a metatheoretical level certain demands for the democratization of economy and state. The reason is not that Habermas has disavowed his radical democratic political convictions, but that he confounds the general justification of the need for methods and techniques of social 'steering' in the economic and political arena with establishing bound-aries between lifeworld and the 'monetary–bureaucratic complex'. In my characterization of the 'unhappy marriage of hermeneutics and functionalism', the central idea was that Habermas was impelled to take this step both by his failure to recognize the status of action theory and by the particular construction of his own theory. The failure can already be identified at the point where Habermas concurs with Luhmann in presuming the limitations of all action theory.

In his reply to these widespread criticisms, Habermas undertakes a number of clarifications and self-corrections, both implicit and explicit. For example, he expressly denies the exclusive applicability of systems theory to the area of material reproduction. At heart, though, Habermas defends the attempt to provide a synthesis between his ideas, based on hermeneutics and action theory, with Luhmann's functionalism, employing two main arguments in favour of the use of functional analyses and models. Firstly, he vehemently defends the essentialist use of the concept of system against the simply analytical one. As is well known, Luhmann differs from Parsons in that he unequivocally takes the idea 'that systems exist'[52] as a starting point for his theory. Secondly, he distinguishes between a descriptive and a critical use of the concept of system. The 'critical' use implies the elaboration of a currently acceptable version of the Marxian idea of the reification or independence of social relations in which areas of the lifeworld can be shown to be irreconcilable with media-led interactions.

The critique of functionalism can find no objections to the descriptive use of a functionalist model, merely pointing out the need to clarify in advance the 'degree of systemness' as a prerequisite for an empirical application of these models. From this perspective, systems do exist, but by no means every social phenomenon fulfils the preconditions for the application of systems theory. In many cases, these preconditions are given to such a limited extent that functional analysis is bound to have a distorting effect on its subject. Functional analysis requires that many preconditions be fulfilled, and its application makes sense only when the phenomenon has the attributes of a real system in the functionalist sense.

The purpose of Habermas' 'critical' use of a functionalism defined in essentialist terms is to express both the pathos of Marx's critique of reification and simultaneously the radical break with the idea of the 'philosophy of praxis' conception of a society which has become completely transparent to itself. On the face of it, there is no difference here between the respective goals of Habermas and Giddens. Giddens' programme for a sociological transformation of the philosophy of praxis takes into account the totalitarian dangers of a social utopia which does not incorporate into its conceptual apparatus the problems of excessive centralization and lack of pluralism. Through his reading of structuralism, Giddens has also learned the lesson of the 'de-

centring' of the subject. In his view, however, it does not necessarily
follow from his programme that the prospects for change are limited
to a defence of the lifeworld against the functional imperatives of the
economy and the state. On the contrary, it carries the issue of
democratic socialist alternatives into the realm of economics and state
politics. These alternatives need not imply the abolition nor the
withering away of money, market and state; however, one effect will
certainly be to open up, rather than curtail, discussion on the right
relationship between participation and control by the media.

Jeffrey Alexander and Richard Münch follow a quite different path
from Luhmann in continuing the Parsonian tradition. Both authors
deserve great credit for achieving a more accurate picture of Parsons'
theory after the many years of crass misrepresentation and its widespread labelling as conservative, incapable of explaining conflict and
change, conformist in its personality theory, formalistic, and imper-
vious to empirical verification. In emphasizing the continuity and
homogeneity of Parsons' work, Münch even goes so far as to deny
flatly that there are internal tensions between the differing tendencies
that exist within it. This is also true of the status of functional methods
of explanation in Parsons' theory. Münch believes that these methods
never possessed a 'systematic importance in Parsons' action theory in
the methodological sense of Hempel's explanatory model for *concrete
systems*'.[53] Surely the crucial question here is what is meant by a
'systematic' importance. If it means that, when constructing his theory,
Parsons was constantly aware of the exclusively analytic character of
his concept of system, then Münch is contradicted by what Parsons
actually wrote, even in those passages which Münch himself cites. For
example, Münch correctly points out that Parsons employs multiple
system reference points and thus moves beyond the perspective of
simple systems functionalism and allows the simultaneous consideration of cultural, social and personal systems. However, this does not
mean that Parsons overcame or refuted systems functionalism, he
merely refined it. Münch's interpretation makes Parsons out to be less
ambiguous than he is and fails to explain what use there is, if any, in
a functionalist interpretation of systems and subsystems which exist
only at an analytical level.

Alexander's approach to this subject is both more differentiated and
more radical. He shares with Münch an appreciation of the enduring
significance of Parsons' action theory and he, too, defends Parsons'
normative view of the evolution of action in the sense of an increasing
level of individual personal responsibility. Among the most important
accomplishments of Alexander's theory-oriented interpretations of the

classical sociologists, which are problematic in many other respects,[54] is undoubtedly to have extricated the famous AGIL schema of the interchange between the respective functional subsystems from the shackles of its functionalist reading. For Alexander this model is untenable as a functionalist model of society: it merely formulates a metatheoretical taxonomy of analytic abstractions. He shows how Parsons tried from around 1945 onwards to specify his metatheoretical assumptions by resorting to a functionalist system model. He takes care to emphasize that this was a specific decision by Parsons which can be seen in isolation from the metatheoretical level itself. Parsons believed that, in adopting a functionalist system model, it would be possible to avoid the dangers of biological reductionism or of an identification of social totalities with 'cultural totalities'. And indeed, up until his incorporation of cybernetics, Parsons applies the system model cautiously and sparingly. None the less, Alexander demonstrates with great acumen in just how many respects and to just how large an extent Parsons himself reified the assumptions inherent in the model, thereby even contradicting other parts of his own theory. Alexander's judgement of Parsons appears scathing:

> It was with interchange ... that Parsons' methodological confusion reached its highest point. .... Each of the interchange model's key terms – the 'dimensions' of interchange, the 'boundaries' between systemic dimensions, the 'inputs' and 'outputs' between different dimensional structures – is now presented as if it were derived from some inherent logic of systems rather than from Parsons' effort to model his analytic synthesis of instrumental-normative order.[55]

However, Alexander does not intend this to sound scathing because, for him, neither the continuity nor the merits of Parsons' work are to be found in the latter's recourse to functionalist models. This allows Alexander to disentangle what is for him a doubly false identification, namely the identification of supra-individual relations with conflict-free social orders and of the latter with systemic states of equilibrium, and still remain a Parsonian.

Yet why does Alexander, in the name of the circle of young American sociologists he founded, cling to the term 'neo-functionalism'? Alexander gives his reasons for doing so with due clarity when he explains that 'functionalism' has proved itself to be neither precise nor tenable as a term for a particular framework of concepts, a method, a model or an ideology. None the less, it still serves as a sign of recognition for an extremely pluralistic tradition that is worth continuing.[56] Yet this means that all attempts to define the features common to various strands in this tradition are extremely vague and, as Alexander himself admits, these features are not always limited to this particular tradition. Alexander claims that there is no other tradition in which all these features are present *simultaneously*, but does not provide conclusive evidence to support this assertion.

If one asks, therefore, whether the critique of functionalism still applies to this 'neo-functionalism', the conclusion must surely be that the critique no longer finds a target in neo-functionalism only because the latter has voluntarily stepped out of the line of fire. As far as the points raised by the critique are concerned, neo-functionalism is simply no longer a kind of functionalism. Other themes must therefore be considered if we are to be able to decide on the validity of neo-functionalism and its relationship, say, to Giddens' theory of structuration. We may then find that all of the vaguely defined common features of a so-called functionalist tradition are also present in Giddens' theory. Put positively, this means that a constructive dialogue between sophisticated versions of Parsonianism, such as those of Eisenstadt or Alexander, and Giddens' own theory, is possible. Put negatively, this means that Alexander's characterization of 'neo-functionalism' as the continuation of a tradition loses all its analytical sharpness outside the context of American sociology.

To summarize: The arguments used in the critique of functionalism are tacitly accepted in Münch's and Alexander's neo-Parsonianism. Luhmann's attempts to justify functional analysis and his systems-theoretical cosmology are unconvincing, and Habermas' use of Luhmann's work creates more problems than it solves. However, both neo-Parsonianism and the theories of Habermas and Giddens show that the critique of functionalism does not necessarily lead to the adoption of methodological individualism or its restrictive action theory. The common task is therefore to develop a social theory which is based on action theory, does not conflate functional analyses and causal explanations, yet contains the benefits of a controlled use of system models.

In this respect the leading contemporary theoretical schools of social theory point in divergent directions. What seems desirable is a 'realistic' use of a systems model which is based on a theory of individual and collective action. By 'realistic' I mean in this context that systems analysis is restricted to the real reciprocal effects of the interactions between social actors. This was the approach outlined twenty years ago by Amitai Etzioni, an approach which deserved further development but has been virtually ignored. He wrote:

'Constituting a system' is treated as a proposition subject to empirical test; any two units do not necessarily form a system. When the actors are less related, when there is no feedback effect or only a sporadic and inconsequential one, we shall refer to the relationship as a 'situation'. Societal units ... often 'behave' as if they were linked in a system fashion. ... But unlike the analytical system, which is composed of variables, this system is composed of collectivities, organizations, movements, and government agencies.[57]

In contrast, from Parsons to Luhmann and Habermas *analytical* systems were interpreted in an *essentialist* manner. Etzioni, Touraine and Giddens, on the other hand, have established the preconditions for an application of systems theory exclusively for the empirically controllable interactions between individual and collective actors. Consistent with this approach, Giddens defines systems as 'reproduced relationships between actors or collectivities, organized as regular social practices'.[58] The issue of the extent to which the word 'function' as such should be avoided, as Giddens suggests, then becomes a merely terminological question. Indeed only this sort of 'realistic' use of systems theory allows us to tackle one of the most urgent desiderata of current social theory, namely a consideration of the effects of processes within societies on the natural environment of social units. In the same way that preventing a metaphorical use of the concept of system is a precondition for its empirically productive use, avoiding a metaphorical use of the concept of environment is a precondition for a meaningful incorporation of ecological outcomes and effects into the analysis of social processes. Human society will not become an 'ecological system' by means of terminological sorcery, but only through far-reaching social reforms.

4.3 Differentiation and Democratization: Perspectives for a Non-Functionalist Theory of Social Development

The theory of differentiation is at the core of functionalist theories of macrosocial interrelations and social change. In order to test the validity of the claim that such theories cannot be formed without incorporating functionalist components, we must begin by considering differentiation theory. Following a discussion of what can be achieved by applying differentiation theory, and of where its shortcomings lie, we shall contrast it with a group of theoretical approaches which have been used to map out a theory of social development in line with the principles of action theory rather than using functionalist constructs. And finally, we shall elicit the prospects for a fruitful dialogue between these two theories.

The idea of a *theory of differentiation* dates back to attempts, inspired by Darwin, to transplant evolutionist models into the domain of human sociality and history. No doubt, in retrospect, the discourse on the impact of the division of labour can be seen to have prepared the ground for the theory of differentiation. This discussion, which was begun by the early political economists, focused on the fact that, while the progressive division of labour tended to raise productivity, it also had a potentially deleterious impact on society. However, Herbert Spencer was the first to treat the subject on a high level of generalization: he perceived differentiation as a developmental trend, permeating the entire cosmos, whereby unconnected homogeneity became connected heterogeneity, and it was he who first raised the problem of integrating the progressively more differentiated parts. Whereas Spencer's obviously speculative work was for the most part destined to fall into oblivion – and all the more so that of his contemporary disciples – Durkheim's ingenious normativistic critique of Spencer in his study of the division of labour became the point of departure for attempts to identify the specific qualities of modern societies by means of the concept of differentiation. Durkheim added a normative dimension to a naturalistic notion of social development in that he endeavoured to elaborate the normative foundations for the functioning of differentiated societies, and consequently declared normative integration to be the essential precondition for all social integration.

It was, in particular, Talcott Parsons who took up these ideas and developed them into a sociological theory which, in the decades that followed the Second World War, came to dominate our understanding of how societies develop. Parsons' work appeared to lend the theory of differentiation a foundation in a theory of action; the logic of functional explanations and the incorporation of elements of systems theory made it possible to extend this theory to generate universally applicable theorems which could even be used as a practical guide to action, for example for the 'modernization' of societies in the context of development policy. Parsons believed the decisive stages of modern history were marked off from one another by three 'revolutions' which he defined as the differentiation of three societal subsystems. According to this schema, the industrial revolution involved differentiation of the economic system – which had the functional advantage of making society better able to adapt to its environment. In the 'democratic' revolution it was the political system, and in the 'educational' revolution it was the cultural system which became differentiated as the process of world history advanced in bursts. Admittedly, Parsons' fully developed theory of social change can no longer be described as merely a theory of differentiation, for it incorporated the added dimensions of improved control over the environment, progressive generalization of values and a comprehensive 'inclusion' of the members of society under a single value system. None the less, even the identification of these dimensions is based on a schema of the basic functions common to all systems and of differentiation in the fulfilment of these basic functions.

Initially, Parsons believed the ongoing process of differentiation was a cultural problem and associated, for example, the rise of National Socialism in Germany with the difficulties of finding integrative solutions to the problems created by differentiation. However, in the post-war years he increasingly came around to the view that the consequences of the differentiation process were entirely desirable and ruled out the possibility of tension between various dimensions of social change. In the ideological battle between the superpowers during the Cold War, it was assumptions about modernization derived from the theory of differentiation which were regarded as *the* superior alternative to the Marxist understanding of history. And indeed, such a conception *was* superior to economic determinism, for the latter construed social developments as a mere derivative of the development of the productive forces. And the former alternative was also more appropriate to its subject than was an understanding of history in terms of class struggle, in that it took account of the role of values and the independent significance of the political and cultural spheres. However, this predominance did not remain unchallenged. Its critics were influenced by the social problems and movements that emerged during the sixties. In terms of a sociology of knowledge, the argument had been voiced that the modernization theories were

> a reaction of America's intellectual elites to the post-1945 role of the United States as a world power, to the rivalry between East and West, and to developments in the Third World, before the profound impact of the Vietnam War, civil rights problems, urban decay, increased violence and poverty in America made itself felt and led to a marked reduction in the range and attractiveness of modernization theories.[59]

As might be expected, the critique was at least in part politically motivated, and was often highly polemical. None the less, there is some point in bringing to mind the substance of the objections raised to differentiation theory.[60] Let us begin with the objections to the very *concept* of differentiation and to its *logical status*. The concept, it was argued, subsumes highly diverse phenomena under one umbrella, and there are no clear rules for its application. What may be true of one process may not necessarily be true of other processes which are also characterized as examples of differentiation. At the very least, so the critics demanded, a clear distinction needed to be made between various types of differentiation. As for the logical status of the concept of differentiation, the problem was the lack of clarity as to whether its function was merely descriptive or whether it could be claimed to be an explanatory law. If a process could be described as differentiation, did this mean we had adequately explained it?

This brings us to the serious objections raised in connection with the complex of the *causes* of differentiation processes. How do differentiation processes come about in the first place? The oldest explanation, which dates back to the earlier discussion on the division of labour, explains differentiation in terms of the increased productivity it facilitates. Here we are prompted to ask whether it is indeed true that differentiation necessarily leads to increased efficiency. Even in the case of differentiation within organizations, the empirical facts do not automatically support this conclusion, as was shown with reference to rising coordination costs and loss of flexibility and motivation. And the assumption becomes all the more suspect when applied to relations that exist between organizations and outside them. Furthermore, even if such a correlation between differentiation and increased efficiency did obtain, we would still have to answer the additional question why the more efficient structure came into being.

With the development of mainstream differentiation theory another argument came to the fore. It focuses on evolutionary mechanisms which ostensibly lead to differentiation. The argument appears in two guises. On the one hand, it is assumed that differentiation – that is, the formation of specialized structures – is the means by which systems respond to internal problems or difficulties in their relationship to their environment. Selection mechanisms then determine which of the solutions thus found actually gains acceptance. However, the argument again rests on the assumption that differentiated system structures are functionally superior to others, and is similar in this respect to the simplistic efficiency argument. If we were to abandon this at least implicit assumption we would have to accept that less differentiated structures would be selected if they were found to be functionally superior. Thus the problem shifts from ascertaining what the causes of differentiation are to elucidating the reasons why differentiated systems should enjoy a comparative advantage in the selection process.

The second variant of the evolutionary argument avoids this problem. Here all systems are assumed to have an innate tendency to become increasingly complex. This engenders a constant need for differentiation, which in turn only precipitates a new process of increasing complexity within the new subsystems thus created. However, this is an answer based on speculation rather than empirical fact. Here, too, the question as to the causes of differentiation is merely deferred – namely to the question of the causes of universally increasing complexity.

If the problem of causes remained unsolved, so, too, in the eyes of the critics, did the problem of the *effects* of differentiation. Even at an early stage in the discussion of differentiation theory, Georg Simmel, for one, opted for a position characterized by caution and scepticism.[61] He believed that the effects of differentiation were ambiguous and that they by no means always constituted a higher stage of evolutionary development. In opposition to Parsons' optimistic interpretation, Shmuel Eisenstadt considered there to be four possible reactions to differentiation:[62] the absence of any institutional solution; a regression to a lower level of differentiation; partial differentiation; and successful integration via new institutions. For example, one possible outcome of differentiation is a structure in which certain interest groups evolve which actively oppose any further continuation of the differentiation process.

Whether it is the causes or the effects we are seeking to identify, in both cases the question of the *agents* of differentiation comes into view. Should differentiation processes be conceived of as something which unfolds, so to speak, merely through the agency of the actors' intentions and which therefore takes place independently of them? Or do differentiation processes require actors who set themselves the goal of differentiation as a means of improving efficiency or for some other reason? Why, after all, should actors set themselves such a goal: because they feel it is of intrinsic value or because it serves certain of their interests? As soon as the differentiation theory takes on board actors as agents of differentiation processes, it becomes bogged down in all the tasks which have to be performed by any theory of social change which takes the actions of the members of society as its starting point. Differentiation theory then has no choice but to confront the problem of determining the relative importance of 'ideas' and 'interests' for action.

In other words, just as we can conceive of differentiation processes as being carried out by agents with their own value systems and interests, so, too, *resistance* to differentiation processes may arise among individual or collective actors based on their different sets of values and interests. Indeed, it is conceivable that the differentiation process is itself what generates resistance in the first place, thus creating new interpretations of values and forming new interest groupings. One need only think of the emergence of fundamentalist, anti-modernist movements – from the American middle classes to the Middle East.[63]

A further lack of clarity in differentiation theory concerns the *time-scale* of the differentiation processes. By ignoring the time-scale, differentiation theory can immunize itself against objections based on empirical evidence. It then becomes possible to interpret every regression in the differentiation process, and every differentiation that fails to materialize, as a mere detour in the developmental process which does not cast serious doubt on the validity of the 'master trend'. This lack of a specific time frame could indeed be seen as merely the first step towards a critique of the great distance between this theory of social development and the real *history of events with all its contingencies and problems*. Differentiation theory has frequently paid little attention to national peculiarities or major historical events such as wars or revolutions, or reinterpreted them as mere delays, diversions or crises of the differentiation process. In such a view, developmental variations between societies are explained by saying that change in all societies follows the same basic pattern, but that the process takes place at different rates in different places. No, say the objectors, the history of colonialism and imperialism, indeed of wars and international politics in general, demonstrates irrefutably that a differentiation-induced efficiency gain in one society can have a decidedly retarding effect on the development of another. Societies do not proceed parallel along the same path, though at varying speeds, but rather they exist in varying degrees of cultural, political, economic, military and ecological dependence on one another. The lead of one country changes the conditions for all the other countries.[64] One country can try to force other countries into the periphery of backward and subordinate nations. Conversely, countries facing this threat can develop defensive innovations, thus foiling the attempts to press them into subservience. Even within a single society, differentiation-induced tension can arise between various regions or between sectors at different stages of development.[65] Regardless of the actual manifestations of these trends, the point is that differentiation theory typically failed to address the structure of world society as a whole, but referred merely to the *parallel existence* of individual societies, for which it proposes an *evolutionary* model. This model rests exclusively on endogenous causes of development or reduces international relations to the unspecific heading of 'environmental' problems faced by the individual social systems.

One critique which was presented in a particularly fiery form focused on the fact that this evolutionary model portrayed the institutional and cultural structures of the West, and, in particular, those of the United States, as the evolutionary optimum, and promised the whole world salvation if it developed in the same direction. In such a critique, differentiation theory appeared to be a form of *Eurocentric* or '*Americanocentric*' cultural arrogance.

The criticisms outlined here were raised, on the one hand, by commentators who wished to deny that differentiation theory had any validity at all. The alternative to the patently inadequate differentiation theory they proposed was often either to adopt a Marxist position or to dispense altogether with macro theories of social development in favour of mere historiography, mere microsociology or mere middle-range theories. On the other hand, there were also self-critical attempts from within the Parsonian school to improve on differentiation theory. Neil Smelser's project of developing a theory of collective action based on Parsons' action theory[66] simultaneously attempted to incorporate the dimension of the actors into differentiation theory. Robert Bellah, an expert on Japan and a specialist in the sociology of religion, analysed religions along the lines of Parsons' evolutionary model, but at the same time contributed successfully to a more extensive account of the cultural conditions of non-western societies.[67] Yet it was the Israeli sociologist Shmuel Eisenstadt who went further than probably any other follower of Parsons in linking the ideas of differentiation theory with the processes of collective action and the contingent events of real history. Eisenstadt treats differentiation no longer as a gentle progression but as a process which, at least in part, is initiated, or at any rate accompanied, by innovative elites and social movements, and the results of which can be interpreted as *intentional* differentiation or at least as the effects of actions directed towards very different purposes.

Jeffrey Alexander and his circle of American 'neo-functionalists' are now attempting to merge these self-critical revisions and their own reactions to the other critical objections in order to be able to go on the offensive again with differentiation theory.[68] They concede virtually all the points raised by the critics, yet do not admit that these strike to the core of differentiation theory. A key element in this argumentation is the normative quality of differentiation theory, which not only describes a developmental trend but also presents it as something desirable.[69] The collapse of most of the socialist systems has lent considerable plausibility to this view. Insufficient social differentiation can indeed be counted as one of the reasons for this collapse. The current renaissance of conceptions of differentiation and modernization is in itself a reason not to be too hasty in our dismissal of this theory.[70] None the less, the price paid by the neo-functionalists for their self-critical efforts towards revision is that the contours of differentiation theory become increasingly blurred. If differentiation theory has to concede that the causes and effects, the agents and contingencies of differentiation need to be identified and taken into account, then it becomes more and more difficult to use differentiation theory as a universal explanatory key for analysing social change. In other words, by becoming more open and 'liberal', differentiation theory loses its explanatory power. For all their reflections, the neo-functionalists end up reducing the theory to a mere schema which may sharpen our attention to certain aspects of the processes of social development, but which cannot explain them.

Remarkably, despite losing its explanatory edge, differentiation theory is still at the forefront of neo-functionalist thought. Regardless of the precise nature of the contingent processes that lead to differentiation, the result, namely differentiation itself, appears to be beyond question.[71] However, improving the extent to which actors and real history are taken into account could lead to a different conclusion: namely, that differentiation should no longer be regarded as the 'master trend' of historical change. The neo-functionalists fail to conceive of the possibility that the degree and direction of differentiation, or indeed the very fact of further differentiation, can be made the object of collective action and social movements, in short of the social formulation of objectives. In that case, differentiation would no longer be the inevitable outcome of an evolutionary process, but a stake in the processes of social change that have an indeterminate outcome. This would be a view that would call differentiation theory into question in a more radical manner than the mere admission of the existence of de-differentiation processes as intermezzi in the grand overall differentiation process. Yet only by taking this more radical step would the primacy of action theory be re-established. And this step is strategically crucial when it comes to deciding whether a non-functionalist macrosociology based on action theory is possible.

I propose the label *'constitution theories'* as a generic term for describing the increasingly frequent current attempts to pose an alternative to functionalism.[72] This term denotes all those sociological theories which set out to make social processes intelligible in terms of the actions of the members of a society without assuming there to be some underlying transhistorical developmental trend and without borrowing – except for merely pragmatic reasons – from models that are foreign to the social sciences. Admittedly, 'to make intelligible in terms of the actions' is a formulation that is open to misinterpretation. It is frequently taken to mean that the explanation of all social processes should be based on the intentions of the actors concerned. Yet it is, of course, naive even on a microsociological level – and on a macrosociological level it is utterly absurd – to want to conceive of social processes as being completely intentional. Common sense alone tells us that the results of actions are likely to deviate from the intentions behind the actions. In any case, an explanation based on intentions can never have the final word, as the question can immediately be extended to include the origins of those intentions. Unintended consequences of actions are not simply rare instances of action gone wrong and thus an exception; instead, they are the inevitable rule. Even if the intended consequences of an action do indeed ensue, these in turn have further consequences which were not part of the original intention and which may correspond to our original intentions in a manner we had not intended or, alternatively, may run counter to those very intentions. Indeed, for cognitive reasons alone, our capacity for picturing in our minds the consequences of actions for large numbers of people who may be affected, and the relationship between these consequences and our intentions, is extremely limited. We can strive to improve our empirical knowledge of the likely consequences of actions and incorporate this knowledge into the process of forming intentions; but any obligation to have total foresight would be beyond the capacity of all actors, and would effectively paralyse them. If, in defence of functionalist models, the argument is put forward that they systematically take into account the utility and the regular occurrence of such unintended consequences, then this argument can be countered by pointing out that this is precisely what robs the phenomenon of its explosive force: unintended consequences of action then appear as contributions to the latent fulfilment of the functional requirements of a social system.

But the next question follows on immediately from this: does this mean that all unintended consequences of action are functional in this sense? Consequences of actions are, in the first instance, nothing more than just that: consequences of actions. Intended and unintended consequences of actions interlink to form structural patterns as well as the preconditions, both perceived and unperceived, for the next round of action. It is equally impossible to distinguish neatly between the coordination of actions via intentions and the coordination of actions via consequences of action. Coordination via intentions is highly unstable because consequences are constantly liable to occur for which no consensual interpretation can be found within the framework of the actors' systems of meaning. Conversely, coordination via consequences can never take account of all the consequences of an action, but always only of a particular kind of these consequences which is defined as legitimate. Making intelligible 'in terms of action' therefore means the attempt to relate in a transparent way all the unplanned 'systems' of consequences of actions to the real actions of real actors.[73] 'It is certainly not the case that all patterns stem from conscious action, but all patterns have to be made *intelligible* in relation to conscious action.'[74] At least this claim is common to all constitution theories.

At present it is possible to list several theoretical currents which, although taking very different points of departure, share this general thrust. The earliest and most systematic attempt to break free from the functionalist tradition with the goal of establishing a macrosociology based on a notion of action was, to my mind, Amitai Etzioni's monumental book, *The Active Society*.[75] This book was wrongly interpreted as an expression of euphoric affirmation of welfare-state planning and was so radically forgotten when that mood went out of fashion that it is completely absent from most reconstructions of the recent history of sociological theory.[76] In fact the title alone, which was not, after all, *The Active State*, should have been sufficient to ward off such misinterpretations. A second, albeit relatively inconspicuous current in this direction consists of attempts by representatives of symbolic interactionism to pick up the threads originated by the Chicago School and pragmatist social philosophy and to develop a macrosociological conception which takes as its starting point the idea of a 'negotiated order', that is, the social order as a temporarily stabilized result of dynamic and conflict-ridden negotiation processes.[77] Among the members of this group of theorists, it is probably Anthony Giddens and his theory of structuration that currently receive the greatest attention. Giddens draws together a wide variety of themes to form a comprehensive anti-functionalist and anti-revolutionist theory.[78] A fourth group consists of those present-day followers of Max Weber or Norbert Elias who, rather than primarily gleaning from the work of these classical sociologists a theory of rationalization or civilization (something which fits more closely into the evolutionism of the differentiation theories), instead develop theories of conflict and power in which social orders are presented as unstable and usually asymmetrical balances of power. Among this category are the studies, mainly by British sociologists, on a theory of power, and also those on culture and conflict put forward by Pierre Bourdieu and Randall Collins.[79] A fifth current can be identified in the shape of Alain Touraine's sociology of social movements and the political philosophy of Cornelius Castoriadis on which the former is based.[80] However, in a broader sense, this group also includes all those approaches which, although based on that of Parsons, try to free his work from the ballast of functionalism.[81]

What is the common thread linking all these approaches, which we have merely listed here; what justification is there for assigning to them the collective label 'constitution theories'? In the first instance, what they have in common is negation. They all set themselves off from functionalism *and* Marxism, the great rivals of the post-war era, by breaking with conceptions of holism or totality and by adopting a perspective which regards social order and social change as either contingent or constructed. Despite this break with the structural determinist aspirations of the tradition of grand theory, they do not fall into the trap of simply jettisoning macrosociological theories.[82] In a positive sense, what all the constitution theories have in common is the idea that a theory of action should form the point of departure for theory construction. However, there are considerable differences in how consistently they transcend the limitations of models of rational or normatively oriented action. In striving to form a macrosociological theory, their attention is focused on the creative dimension of action, which is also implicitly contained in the other models of action. After all, creativity is present even within action which is conceived of as the pursuit of utility, because, firstly, the appropriate means of action are often not immediately available but have to be created, and, secondly, the conception of a skilful strategy also requires the application of one's creative powers. Within normatively oriented action it is also possible to demonstrate the presence of creativity: action that is appropriate to the situation and conforms to norms cannot simply be deduced from the norms themselves, but often requires that the actor devise a new and unfamiliar path of action that is therefore fraught with risks. Creativity is needed not only in order to give norms and values a concrete form in practice; the existence of values depends also on there having been a creative process by which values were formed. And here it is possible to draw an analytical distinction between the creation of value content and the creation of the binding force of that specific value. All these results of creativity – means of action, new strategies for action, cultural innovations and the binding force of cultural values – become detached from the act of their creation and turn into resources for new action. The analysis of power takes into account the breadth of the spectrum of possible resources of action, and power is seen not only from the point of view of the application of the given means, but also from the point of view of the creation and creative use of these resources. Thus, power becomes part of the action processes and loses the pseudo-substantial character of being firmly bound to institutions or the stable characteristics of the actors in the interplay of forces.

The adoption of the concept of action as the foundation on which to erect theory coincides with a departure from the traditional 'holistic' concept of society. The representatives of the constitution theories refuse to accept the tacit equation of the abstract notion of 'society' with the specifics of a modern state that exists on clearly demarcated territory. Scepticism towards this equation, which is part of the very foundation of sociology, has repeatedly been expressed by individual Weberians, but also by those who subscribe to the dependency theory of the relations between highly developed countries and the 'Third World'. However, because differentiation theories – if only for the purpose of being able to use functionalist arguments – are based on the idea of a clearly delimited 'system', and because, furthermore, Marxism is based on the Hegelian idea of 'totality', these two schools of theory were left with no choice but to interpret the 'world society' as a 'world system' – if, that is, they did not wish to ignore the criticisms of the idea of societies corresponding to national states. Parsons, moreover, claimed that the normative integration of a society was the functional precondition for its continued existence. The constitution theorists share a sceptical attitude to this idea of normative integration. They point to empirically well-founded phenomena such as the vast plurality of cultures in most traditional and modern societies, the often minimal degree to which everyday life is permeated by overarching interpretational systems, and the frequency of opportunist motives for behaviour in conformity with norms. Thus, on the one hand, they play down the relative significance of the normative integration of societies by pointing to other mechanisms of social integration; on the other, they argue that the scale of social integration within a state is altogether lower than normally assumed by the functionalist tradition. The constitution theories dispense with notions of a balance of interests between rational actors that can never be stabilized and of an all-embracing and therefore impossible normative integration. They replace these notions with the idea of networks of interconnected action which span differences of space and time to various degrees. This brings phenomena such as communication and transport, information storage and control to the forefront of a discipline which had previously tended to ignore them. Networks of interconnected action appear to rule out the possibility that social processes can be explained in terms of a single sphere of societies to which all the others are functionally subordinate. Neither an economic system called the 'material base' – as in Marxism – nor a value system described as a 'supreme cybernetic instance' – as in normative functionalism – makes the task of macrosociological theory any easier. Instead, the objective is to identify in each case the relevant, institutional clusters and the ways in which they are flexibly interconnected. This is an empirical task which cannot be pre-empted by theory. Anthony Giddens, for example, distinguishes between four such complexes in the advanced societies of the present-day western world:[83] the capitalist business enterprise with its orientation towards the three marketplaces – capital, commodity and labour markets – and the concomitant asymmetrical relations between capital and wage labour; the industrialist economy and the production and utilization of technology; the nation-state and the bureaucratic-administrative and military power concentrated within it; and finally, the domain of 'surveillance', to which Giddens, following Foucault, assigns an extremely wide range of mechanisms of social control.

Of course, the validity of precisely this analysis of the essential institutional complexes is open to debate. For example, Giddens omits the complex of political participation and democratic institutions, something given particular prominence in other constitution theories. However, absent from these other versions is a consideration of the specific characteristics of the nation-state and the role of military power.[84] Important though this controversy may be, the fact remains that, for a characterization of the common ground of all constitution theories, the decisive point is not which and how many complexes of institutions are identified but the non-deterministic relationship between them. Capitalism can lead to industrialism, it is true, but non-capitalist industrialization and capitalist de-industrialization also exist. The control systems ('surveillance') may originate in the capitalist enterprise and then be adopted by the state; but there are also state surveillance techniques which are taken on by private companies. Industrialization did not lead, as Spencer assumed it would, to a peaceful type of society, but became an instrument of the nation-state and gave rise to the industrialization of war. It is, therefore, safe to conclude that the various complexes of institutions can be related to one another in very different ways. This, in turn, leads to a view of history as a contingent and discontinuous process. The emergence of typical institutions – such as the state per se or the modern state in particular – is interpreted not as an inevitable evolutionary imperative, but as a contingent innovation with unintended subsequent effects. Such institutional innovations, however, also rely on the cultural sphere. Key concepts of social development must therefore always also be conceived of as imaginary schemata: 'revolution' and 'nation', 'sovereignty' and 'democracy' are not objectively given, but are interpretations and self-interpretations of actions and the interconnection of actions on the part of the actors and their observers. Accordingly, Castoriadis criticizes concepts such as rationalization (and differentiation) for being ambiguous in a systematic way.[85] The terms are mostly used without distinguishing between what is a specific pattern of unintended development and what is an outgrowth of the imaginary schemata of western culture which contribute to the predominance of technology and bureaucracy, economic efficiency and rational science in this culture.

The dangers inherent in constitution theories are mirror images of those intrinsic to differentiation theories. Differentiation theory in its classical form ventures to make a bold assertion about the trend of all social development, only to leave itself exposed to possible contradiction by the contingencies of real history; constitution theories, in contrast, by emphasizing that all actions and all history are not deterministically defined, run the risk of embracing history so closely that they can no longer provide a meaningful theory of social development and instead offer merely an abstract and inelegant reproduction of past developments. Differentiation theories, either consciously or unconsciously, generally tend to superimpose a normative component on the empirical concept of differentiation; many constitution theorists, on the other hand, tend to draw a radical distinction between the 'realistic' observation of social change and its evaluation by the theorist. However, the greater the significance a school of constitution theory attaches to the power of cultural traditions and innovations to make history, the more inconsistent this stance becomes, as the normative substance of culture is not accessible unless one is willing oneself to take up a normative position.[86]

If it is our intention to contribute to a synthesis of the two major families of current macrosociological theory – differentiation theories and constitution theories – then we must proceed on a methodological, a normative and an empirical–substantive level. Methodologically speaking, the critique of the logic of functional explanations does not mean we must reject them completely. It can – as mentioned above in the discussion of this type of explanation[87] – by specifying their conditions of application, enable us to use them in a controlled and reflected manner as a heuristic for developing hypotheses on explanatory sub-theories. Analogously, differentiation theory, as a functionalist theory of social change, can serve as an important guide to investigating concrete forms of social change.

From the normative point of view, constitution theory must defend itself against accusations of political bias. Emphasizing the creativity of action and the constitution of social structures in this action is not logically linked either to the Leninist myth of a supersubject that can see through and control every aspect of whole societies, or to a fascistic idealization of charismatic leaders and movements, or indeed to the romantic and anarchistic notion of a permanent upheaval of all that has become established. Just as differentiation theory is opening itself to the role of individual and collective actors, so, too, constitution theory – made wiser by the experience of twentieth-century totalitarianisms – can be made to incorporate the insight that differentiation is something real, valuable and useful. The normative core of constitution theories is the idea of self-determination, as this idea expresses the desire of the actors to endorse their social orders as if these were the work of the actors' own will. However, the idea of self-determination must be made more specific by naming the individual and collective actors who should enjoy the right of self-determination and by delimiting the extent and the criteria for their self-determination. By linking it to aspects of differentiation theory, the abstract idea of self-determination can be turned into a theory of democracy. The question as to the causes, agents and effects of democratization processes and of the institutional structures of democratic societies or of a democratic world thus becomes the central axis of theory formation. For this reason, a constitution theory can undoubtedly be said to be seriously deficient if it fails to provide not only a normative clarification of the democratic ideal but also empirical clarification of the causes and effects of democratization processes. Such an omission may be motivated by the fear that the resulting theory appears to follow in the tradition of normative functionalism as it construes democratization as the result of the institutionalization of democratic values. As an alternative, both Giddens and Michael Mann lay the main emphasis on the processes of an interconnection of networks ('polyarchy'), which provide structural stimuli for democratization in complete independence of cultural traditions. In a manner that is fruitful from an empirical point of view, this brings the history of democracy and the history of nationalism closer together than is usual in a theory which regards both as the result of value commitments. None the less, such an explanation can only bring to light conditions that are necessary for democratization; it cannot elucidate all the conditions presupposed. The constitution theories cannot sidestep having to reflect normatively on the idea of democracy in order to concretize the idea of self-constitution under the conditions of a differentiated modern society.[88]

With regard to substantive questions, the synthesis of differentiation and constitution theories can take place only on a subject-by-subject basis. One example of this could be the answer to the question as to the central lines of conflict in modern, highly developed societies, for which I propose the formula 'democratization of the differentiation question'. Nothing could be further from my mind than to try to conjure up probable answers to this question with a quick flick of the wrist. My formula is intended solely to denote one specific characteristic of these lines of conflict, one which is of such particular importance because it affects the way conflicts over various topics take place.

The starting point for an understanding of this formula has to be the position of the constitution theorists who regard all social processes in modern societies as being mediated via politics. Alain Touraine, for example, characterizes present-day 'post-industrial' or 'programmed' society as one in which planning and control take on a heightened significance.[89] He, like Etzioni, is referring not to a state that has become capable of universal planning, but to an increase in the capacity of society to influence itself. As society becomes progressively detached from nature, says Touraine, it increasingly comes to appear as the product of its own actions. 'Historicity' is Touraine's concept for this 'self-production' or 'self-constitution' of society, which Castoriadis termed the 'imaginary institution'. Touraine defines this concept as 'the capacity of a society to construct its practices on the basis of cultural models and through social conflicts and movements'.[90] Nowadays, says Touraine, no economic, technical, scientific or indeed general cultural situations remain unaffected by political mediation. For this reason, the extent and nature of social differentiation themselves become the subject of political conflict in modern societies. And typically they do so not in the sense of an idea that there should be a return to a state which precedes all modern differentiations, but rather in the sense that the existing differentiation, precisely because of its constitution in action, can also be the object of action. 'Gradually, however, a theory of a new system of action is also developed, i.e. a theory of the cultural projects, the social actors, the arenas of conflict, the negotiation mechanisms, the political control and the new social and cultural forms of organization which, taken together, characterize post-industrial society.'[91] Touraine himself is interested primarily in a sociology of social movements, as he regards the existence of a multitude of social movements that cannot be reduced to the pursuit of class interests as the characteristic feature of post-industrial society.

However, we should not be so hasty in dismissing as obsolete the role of the state and the classic questions of a sociology of industrial society. Touraine's vision of a society that constitutes itself in the conflict of social movements stands in sharp contrast to other present-day sociological lines of argumentation. Firstly, it is, after all, possible that the same developments which have rendered the social order of industrial society obsolete might simultaneously ruin the conditions under which new social movements emerge.

> We assume that the dissolution of homogenous class milieus, the heterogenization of social living conditions, the individualization of life-designs and the process of cultural pluralization have become so irreversible that in the long term the formation of new, structurally distinct collective identities as the basis of social movements can no longer be expected.[92]

This diagnosis combines numerous empirical trends which Ulrich Beck has packaged together under the handy catchword 'individualization'. Beck speaks of a rapid process whereby social milieus and ways of living based on class-specific cultures disappear without anything taking their place, so that a society of isolated, individually planned biographies emerges. This process is the convergence of numerous factors, namely the unintended impact of the expansion of education on old class- and strata-based structures; the influence of welfare-state bureaucracies; the lower extent of standardization of paid work; and the increasing institutionalization of biographical patterns.

Niklas Luhmann also rejects a diagnosis which believes the future lies in the conflict of social movements, but does so by a very different route – namely, by drawing extreme conclusions from differentiation theory. Luhmann argues that the particular advantage of differentiation within the societal subsystems is precisely what prevents these systems from reacting in any other way than that prescribed by their own logic, and that this holds true even when problems occur which

pose a threat to the social system as a whole. This applies to politics
and economics, and equally to law, science, education and religion.

> It contradicts the principle of social differentiation to reestablish the
> totality of the system within the system. The whole cannot be a part of
> the whole at the same time. Any attempt of this kind would merely
> create a difference in the system: the difference of that part which
> represents the totality of the system within the system vis-à-vis all the
> other parts. The presentation of unity is a product of difference, thus the
> intention itself is already paradoxical, self-contradictory.[93]

A unified representation of the whole is only possible from some
undefined point beyond society. However, the Enlightenment put an
end to that possibility.

> This clarification reflects the transition from stratificatory to functional
> differentiation. In the new order there are no natural primacies, no
> privileged positions within the whole system and therefore no position
> *in the* system which could establish the unity *of the* system in relation to
> its environment.[94]

None the less, admits Luhmann, one cannot of course rule out the
possibility that within and between its subsystems a society observes
itself. The present-day semantics of 'self-observations', he avers, is
only defined negatively: as post-industrial, post-modern, post-capital-
ist. According to Luhmann, the basic structure of the ideology that is
reflected therein consists in the assertion that within a society bereft
of clear alternatives to its functional differentiation the losses incurred
through that functional differentiation should none the less be given
expression. 'As far as sociological observation of this observation is
concerned, it becomes attractive to imagine that all this is ultimately a
protest against functional differentiation and its effects.'[95] This protest
articulates itself in the form of social movements which try to influence
society from within, but 'as if it occurred from outside'.[96] However,
this pseudo-external position, with its paucity of experience, is in
Luhmann's view the worst conceivable, most woefully inadequate
basis for a successful self-description of the highly differentiated order
of modern societies.[97]

Touraine's theory of the transition from the industrial and class
society to a post-industrial society characterized by the conflict
between social movements is therefore challenged in two ways. On
the one hand, it is possible that the structural conditions of the new
society actually prevent the emergence of the social movements. In

this case, class society would be replaced by a multitude of indivi- dualized enclaves with specific lifestyles and anomie with respect to the question of universally binding cultural orientations. On the other, functional differentiation may have reached such an advanced stage that it is no longer possible to identify a vantage point within society that affords a view of its overall principle. In this case, although protest against this differentiation is likely, it is at the same time condemned to impotence: its only chance for development lies in taking account of the factual existence of the principles of the differ- entiated subsystems, or failing to impact on them, to the extent that the protest does not end up – albeit with good intentions – hampering the functioning of these subsystems. Even Luhmann interprets the new social movements as a protest against functional differentiation and its effects. This is not so far removed from Touraine's assumption that these movements centre on the issue of differentiation itself. Unlike Touraine, however, Luhmann reduces these movements to some protest against functional differentiation *as such*. If we follow Luhmann's logic, what we have today are two opposing camps, with the one side affirming differentiation and having no illusions as to what this means, and the other side pursuing illusory dreams of de- differentiation. If we accept Touraine's view, then we see a conflict between many voices, each calling for differentiation in various degrees and directions. If it is possible to speak at all of two opposing camps, then the line of demarcation would be drawn between those who are willing to accept the extent and nature of today's 'functional' differentiation as an iron law, and those who would like to make this differentiation the subject of social reflection and formulation of objectives.

Ulrich Beck's theory of the 'risk society' contains an interesting extension of Alain Touraine's approach. Beck argues that today the old battle lines are becoming irrelevant in the face of the overwhelm- ing threat of the enormous risks that modern industrial society is capable of producing, as witness Chernobyl. These new dangers differ from the typical risks of industrial society in several respects. They cannot be geographically, temporally or socially contained; the estab- lished rules of accountability and responsibility can no longer be made to apply; the damage they may cause is mostly irreversible; the dan- gers can never be eliminated, only minimized. However, like the risks of industrial society, they differ from natural dangers by virtue of their social constitution. Science, technology, politics and economics, as conditions for their possibility, are already a part of these new threats (as posed, for example, by nuclear technology or genetic engineering).

Beck's name for both the belief in progress and its cynical destruction is 'industrial fatalism'. By this he means that in our culture, in which after all the autonomy of subjects is given an institutionalized, important status, only a very limited range of consequential decisions are taken by individual choice or political participation. What he has in mind is not simply the democratization of the economy and certainly not its total subordination to bureaucratic state planning. However, it does remind us that the dangers of large-scale technology pose new demands on the way democratic institutions define themselves. According to Beck, the main front line is that which divides technocratic de-democratization from de-technocratized enlightenment. How can technological development as such be integrated into the democratic process of will formation? This division is made all the more dramatic by the scale of the dangers to which the civilization of modern societies sees itself exposed, not only in the sense of an impending disaster which threatens to destroy everything, but in the sense of continual self-destruction. In today's dangerous situations, the repressed causes of the dynamic of industrial societies return to their originators. 'The danger itself is alienated, concentrated, objectified subjectivity and history. ... It is a kind of enforced collective reminder – of the fact that what threatens us is the product of our own decisions and mistakes.' And Beck concludes from the scale of the dangers that we are compelled to reflect on differentiation, as the dangers remind us 'that even the greatest degree of institutional autonomy is still subject to recall, a borrowed form of action which can and must be changed if it signifies a danger to ourselves'.[98]

Unlike Luhmann, therefore, Beck believes that the scale of present-day dangers prompts us to become aware of the fact that differentiations which have already occurred are, in principle, reversible. And unlike Touraine, he thus construes the emergence of social movements not only as *releasing* individuals to participate in the conflict over value systems, but as a *compulsion* to engage in this conflict in order to ward off these dangers. And here he attempts to link the trends towards individualization, which he himself has described in such great detail, with the emergence of social movements by claiming that such movements are mainly recruited from among those milieus and cohorts in which 'individualization' has already reached an advanced stage. This is a clear empirical assertion, which of course cannot be examined in our present context. It is undoubtedly valid to inquire into the structural and institutional conditions for a growing awareness of the differentiation problematic, yet Beck's whole construction here could be understood to mean that everything can ultimately be reduced to an automatic mechanism whereby danger evolves and is brought under control. In such a reading it looks like a re-run of old Marxist ideas about the innate tendency for capitalism to collapse and its linkage to the perspective of revolution. Here, the industrial system, by incessantly producing risks, inexorably triggers a questioning of the economic, political, legal and scientific structures that are an integral part of that system. The intellectual problematization of the system and the articulation of motifs of protest in the shape of the social movements thus, in effect, come to resemble mere phases in a predetermined process.

This is not the only conclusion that could be drawn. Beck's theory can be opened up: its components can be conceived of as variable dimensions. We then face the question how likely it is that social movements will emerge whose target is the degree and direction of differentiation in modern societies. And following on immediately from this question is that of the chances of influencing the degree and direction of differentiation by such a means. Claus Offe has described this question as a modernization problem of the *second order*.[99] By this he means that the point at issue is the rationalization of the interplay between already rationalized subsystems. The only chance of a solution to this problem, as far as he can see, lies in the 'zero option', that is, the conscious choice to forgo any further increase in the option-multiplying rationalization of the subsystems, because this is the only means with which we stand a chance of increasing our power to control what we have created, or at least of avoiding new control problems. However, this is precisely the point: Offe's zero option can certainly prevent any further exacerbation of the control problems we face, but it cannot reduce their present-day extent. Between Offe's pessimistic zero option and the optimistic confidence in the 'interpenetration' of all subsystems, as expressed in Münch's neo-Parsonianism,[100] there is a third possibility, namely to give concrete institutional form to present-day types of societal self-control. Institutional imagination is called for here; and indeed, this was precisely the goal of Dewey's programme for a 'creative democracy'. 'The creation of parastatals; the delegation of governmental tasks to social groups, state action according to the subsidiarity principle . . .; active control through liberal corporatism, and loose-knit bodies of concerted action; channeling via subsidization'[101] – these are all means to this end and they all already exist today.

The phrase 'democratization of the differentiation question' implies that the increased possibilities afforded by modern societies for designing our relationship to our environment and its inner structures should not be concealed by radical pessimism with regard to controlling them, irrespective of whether it has its roots in Marxism or systems theory. Rather, all conflicts over economic, political, military and cultural issues are now taking a different form. This avails us with new opportunities for social creativity and provides a new impetus for it. The questions of the peace movements were directed not only towards military strategy itself, but also towards the continued differentiation of a military–industrial–scientific complex, and they totally undermined the classification of debates on military strategy as the domain of experts.[102] The questions of the ecology movements are not merely directed towards the defence of a natural or traditional environment, but also take the offensive in challenging the legitimacy of the continued differentiation of technological progress. The classical questions of industrial society as to the structure of the social division of labour and the distribution of wealth may still be frequently articulated by the trade unions in their traditional form; however, they now become part of something which has been declared the object of societal self-organization, namely the complex of problems comprising the differentiation of the roles of the sexes, the political design of the welfare state and the relationship between 'industrial' and 'post-industrial' lines of conflict.

If we dispense with the utopian perspective of an alternative world (such as socialism) in which these questions would simply disappear, then the only way we can make sense of them is to pose them as questions on the appropriate degree and type of differentiation acceptable. The questions of democracy are today the result of applying the idea of differentiation to itself. With regard to the democracy of a differentiated society, in the institutions of political will formation – and their differentiation is itself susceptible to communication from the members of society – the battles that are going on are being fought over the type and degree of unavoidable and desirable differentiation.[103]

4.4   Creativity in the 'Postmodern' Age

For nearly a decade now, cultural journals and the arts sections of newspapers have been bursting at the seams with articles on the ominous subject of 'postmodernism'. The same period has, by contrast, seen waning public interest in professional sociology and social research. It is therefore not without a certain degree of resentment that representatives of the discipline now look upon the works of authors who, often making little attempt to adduce empirical evidence or to come to terms seriously with the substantial contents of traditions in social theory and social history, have put forward overly daring claims about the dawning of a new epoch and the apocalyptic nature of contemporary change. There have been, and still are, perfectly good reasons why the social sciences should treat those intellectual currents sceptically which not only appear empirically weak and theoretically dubious, but which also blur the distinction between science and literature not in order to enhance their quality, but to lower standards, thus promoting the rapid success of many a charlatan. Yet such scepticism must not be allowed to degenerate into sterile disregard; and sociology should certainly not be engaging in moral or political polemics.

Rather, there are three possible approaches open to sociologists if they wish to make fruitful reference to the discussion on postmodernism. The first is to take this current of thought seriously at least as a phenomenon to be studied in terms of the sociology of knowledge or culture. The few attempts forthcoming to date are themselves very lax in their use of allegations. Their conclusion is that the postmodernism discussion is a consequence of the resignation and saturation of the protest generation of 1968,[104] or of the crisis of status and identity among intellectuals in the age of information technology.[105] What is missing here is a much more detailed inquiry into questions such as: Why did the current first emerge in France and not elsewhere? Which mechanisms of dissemination are discernible? Which modifications to the postmodern argument can be attributed to the utterly different conditions prevalent in the United States? And which protagonists, or which demarcations of cultural fields, were decisive in this context?

A second possible approach would be to conduct a sociological analysis of precisely those phenomena on which the postmodernist authors base their diagnoses. Has the significance of advertising, the mass media and information technologies really increased to the extent that reality is no longer distinguishable from simulation and only Walt Disney and Jean Baudrillard can see through this veil?[106] Have lifestyles really become so stripped of traditions and given so many different forms that it no longer makes any sense to talk of unequivocal standards of normality? Research into social structures and lifestyles has certainly begun to address these questions, and it must be said that the results so far have generally not been altogether flattering for the diagnoses which would have us believe we are witnessing epoch-breaking socio-cultural changes.[107]

In this context I shall be taking a third approach. It is possible to

view the discussion surrounding postmodernism not only as a subject
for the sociology of knowledge or as a good reason to conduct research
into social structures and lifestyles, but also as a provocation, a
challenge to sociology's fundamental theoretical concepts. I would
argue that the postmodernism discussion constitutes a radical break
with those assumptions concerning rationality and normativity which
are enshrined in the basic underlying concepts of sociological theory,
and in the theory of action in particular. This break may be fruitful in
that it opens up the perspective of a more comprehensive understanding of human action, an understanding enriched by a theory of the
creativity of these actions. However, since the postmodernist authors
utilize a concept of creativity that stems from a philosophy of life,
they instantly miss the opportunity to revise the sociological theory of
action and are unable, for their part, to forge a productive link to
sociology. This is immediately evident from their equation of sociology with a modernist belief in progress.

The present-day crisis of the belief in progress is not the first in the
history of ideas, nor is it the first in the history of sociology. The belief
in progress is frequently talked about as though there had existed
since the Enlightenment philosophy of the eighteenth century a living
tradition of unquestioned assumptions regarding the inevitability, or
at least easy realization, of progress in human living conditions and
ways of life. People who express such an opinion tend to forget that
even contemporaries of the Enlightenment – and by no means only its
conservative opponents – certainly did not interpret the epoch-making
changes taking place at that time as an unequivocal expression of
progress. The pathos of Rousseau's fundamental critique of civilization merged in Germany – for example, in Herder's thought – with a
religiously inspired antipathy towards utilitarianism and materialism
to facilitate a profound insight into the ambivalence of the transformation processes that had been set in motion. Even loyal supporters
of the demands raised by the French Revolution were worried by the
course it took and the consequences it had. The first signs of the
upheavals wrought by capitalist industrialization filled people with
a horror that can be sensed in the art and literature of Romanticism.
The nineteenth century itself, which is generally regarded as the
period when unquestioning belief in progress was at its strongest,
shows very few traces of the original ideas of the Enlightenment.
Instead, these ideas were redefined by the socialist and also the
anarchist movements to arrive at a notion of history as the battlefield
of antagonistic classes and powers. In this scheme, only the self-
confidence of emergent classes held out the possibility of perceiv-

ing progress in what was frequently seen as a radically negative present. Outside these social movements – and later, also within them – the Enlightenment philosophy ended up as a collection of evolutionist conceptions. To be sure, these now exhibited a determinist certainty regarding the mechanics of historical progress. However, this represented a departure from the original ideas of the Enlightenment to the extent that, if progress was an automatic, predetermined process, there was no longer any need for subjects with the will to enlightenment.

Yet the representative thinkers of the late nineteenth century were neither Marxist or Hegelian philosophers of history, nor were they determinist evolutionists. Most of the writers of the day treated Marx and Spencer not as model thinkers, but as whipping boys. In the decades leading up to the First World War, Germany and France were heavily influenced by cultural pessimism. In Britain and North America, where such ideas were less influential, the impact of war was to shatter a moderately optimistic world view. Cracks developed in the belief in a world that had become interdependent and, thanks to science and democracy, enlightened. The inter-war years, with their permanent economic and political crises, afforded little opportunity for a return to a belief in progress. While the self-confidence of Marxist revolutionary perspectives grew, so did the appeal of attempts to escape the nihilistic trough of progress-oriented thinking by espousing an abstract new beginning, justifiable only in terms of activism and decisionism, under the banner of the fascist movements. It was not until after the Second World War that a belief in progress echoing nineteenth-century evolutionism, or some aspects of the Enlightenment philosophy of the eighteenth century, resurfaced and started to spread. The destruction of the worst fascist dictatorships gave cause for hope that the historical future belonged to other forces. The vast economic expansion of the West and the optimistic self-appraisal of East European socialism lent credence to the notion that the remaining social problems could gradually be resolved through economic growth. As the old colonial empires disintegrated, these hopes even spread to regions of the world which until then had felt that political, economic and military power had excluded them from 'progress'. The expansion of the sciences was supported by a broad consensus of public opinion which saw this as one of the preconditions for economic growth. The social sciences, too, were able to count on sympathy and funding for their projects, which were regarded as a useful aid to researching social problems, uncovering possible ways of increasing productivity and growth, and generally rendering state planning more effective. In this light, sociology in particular appeared to be on the way to becoming a core discipline for a modern state in which everything could be planned.

Not that it would be at all true to say that the discipline developed out of a firm belief in progress. The actual founding fathers of the subject, who between 1890 and 1920 defined sociology as an object of intellectual inquiry and established its institutional forms, did not simply adopt the assumptions of Comte and Spencer lock, stock and barrel. It would be closer to the truth to say that the ideas of the early sociologists originated as a polemical defensive campaign against any kind of optimistic evolutionism and against the false certainties of an overly elaborate philosophy of history. Their oeuvres were, after all, produced in an age when the cultural and moral consequences of the rapid progress of industrial production were being fiercely debated. The philosophy of the day, which strongly influenced the classical sociologists, never tired of dissecting the belief in progress and its various aspects. The most impressive instance of this close link between sociology and cultural crisis is surely that of Germany. Of the leading exponents of German sociological thought at that time – Weber or Simmel, Sombart or Tönnies – not one of them was not deeply moved by the most ambitious and most radical critic of the belief in progress, namely Friedrich Nietzsche. For all of them, Nietzsche had utterly destroyed the simplistic correlation between individual action and historical progress. This is not to say that they accepted Nietzsche's own way of dealing with the situation he described so convincingly and so overwhelmingly. They all heard and welcomed Nietzsche's call for the destruction of illusions and a new elite of life-affirming geniuses who would develop a new feeling of self. Yet they did not allow themselves to be seduced into embracing a view of history as something that could appear only as a continuum of futile struggles which the geniuses alone were able to rise above, so that the sole discernible purpose behind history was to produce these geniuses. Weber echoed Nietzsche's tone when he described the belief in progress as a dishonest way of dealing with the death of God: 'The idea of "progress" becomes necessary only when the need arises to lend a this-worldly and none the less objective "meaning" to the course of a human destiny that has been drained of any religious content.'[108]

The situation in France was scarcely any different. Bergson's entire thought was, like the German philosophy of life, directed towards overcoming a cultural crisis. The driving force behind Durkheim's work – not only when he developed his theory of religion but from the very beginning[109] – was the wish to pinpoint the conditions under which a new morality and new institutions could emerge. Yet this question can be understood only as resulting from the insight that the foundations of existing institutions had been destroyed and that it was uncertain whether the progressive division of labour would really lead to a new 'organic' solidarity.

Even the American philosophy and sociology of the day, which were undoubtedly imbued with historical optimism and social-reforming self-confidence, did not arrive at this position by naively ignoring the ambivalent nature of the progress that had manifested itself during the preceding decades. The pragmatist philosophers, and the sociologists of the Chicago School whom they strongly influenced and who played the key role in American sociology up to and beyond the First World War, did not regard the present day as idyllic. What they did believe, however, was that the discovery of the scientific method had given society a tool which, provided that it could be comprehensively institutionalized and applied to the problems of social reform under democratic conditions, would render further progress possible. In a certain sense, pragmatism can be seen as an attempt to shift the focus away from the evolutionist and historico-philosophical remoulding of the idea of progress and back to the original Enlightenment concepts. For John Dewey, for example, the First World War was almost to be welcomed as an opportunity for people to snap out of their fool's paradise, their dream of a world in which progress was automatic and uninterrupted. 'We confused rapidity of change with advance, and we took certain gains in our own comfort and ease as signs that cosmic forces were working inevitably to improve the whole state of human affairs.'[110] It was time, said Dewey, to abandon 'laissez-faire' thinking – and here he extended the meaning of this term to include people's trust in the beneficial forces of the market, their trust in nature, providence, evolution, some national mission or 'manifest destiny'. All these attitudes opposed the willingness to assume historical responsibility; yet only such a willingness, he believed, could guarantee progress. Science, as Dewey pointed out, had demonstrated only the *possibility* of proceeding rationally.

Similarly, the bulk of George Herbert Mead's philosophy post-First World War, as presented in *Philosophy of the Present*, is devoted to opposing both a philosophy of the past, that is, a mechanistic determinism, and a philosophy of the future, that is, a teleological or finalistic determinism. A philosophy of the present, argued Mead, should conceive of the 'emergence of the new' in the universality of given determinants.

The crisis of the belief in progress is therefore seen here as a chance to forge a new link between responsible action and progress. Common to all the classics is thus the idea that only when the naive belief in progress is lost can we move forward to understanding the openness of the historical future, the risk- and responsibility-laden nature of present action. They disagree, however, on which possibilities human-kind has in the face of this undecided future. What antidotes did the classical sociologists have to offer to a darkening of all future perspec-tives? I believe it is wrong to try to answer this question by referring to the thinkers' respective political world views. Here we find a broad array of political options: from Tönnies' gradual attraction towards social democracy to Sombart's eventual support for Hitler. Often it is difficult to establish how much these decisions were based on pre-scientific preferences and commitments and how much they were the result of sociological analysis. However, sociological theorists cannot be reduced to their party-political allegiances; their theoretical con-structions cannot even be fairly judged on the basis of their usefulness as a diagnosis of the times they lived in. Therefore, to ask about their fundamental theoretical achievements is to shift the inquiry onto the level of fundamental assumptions regarding human action and social order. And here it becomes clear that it is the concept of action itself, or one of its dimensions, which forms the conceptual nub for the emergence of something new, something better in the works of these classical sociologists. After the wane of evolutionism and the philos-ophy of history, which Benedetto Croce dubbed 'the last religion of the educated', the only viable way of looking into the future – assuming that a reversion to transcendental sources of meaning was not acceptable – was to address the inherent features which character-ized the way human beings came to terms with their lives. In order to construe a way out of the cultural crisis, it was necessary to bring out the (potential) creativity of human action and sociality itself.

The marginal position granted creativity in the tradition of the sociological theory of action thus constitutes a regression behind the position attained by the classics. The discussion around postmodern-ism challenges underlying sociological concepts precisely because it makes it impossible simply to carry on in what is thus an overly narrow tradition of sociological action theory. The debate exposes the tacit assumptions behind this theory of action. *To be sceptical towards an activist attitude to the world,* to demand that people sit back and let things happen, is to challenge the presupposition that all behaviour is purposive, and forces us to break with a narrowly teleological under-standing of intentionality.[111] *To focus attention on the body, on the disciplining of the body and the resistance it offers*, is to challenge the presupposition that the body can be instrumentalized for the purposes of action and forces us to construe a non-instrumental relationship to the body.[112] *To pour scorn on the belief in a substantive self*[113] is to challenge the presupposition of autonomous individuality and forces us to accept that identity is constituted not by some static condition of a person always remaining the same, but rather by an active, indeed creative process of addressing events that befall us and impulses that are alien to the self, as well as by a willingness to be open to other identities. This is why rationalistic pathos gets one nowhere in the postmodernism debate. Instead, the sociological theory of action must show itself capable of countering the charges and of revising its own position in the light of postmodernist critique.

In the present context, this revision has been embarked upon with reference to the tradition of pragmatism. Our reconstructive introduction of the tacit assumptions at the heart of models of rational action has enabled us to address precisely those areas that have been foregrounded by postmodernist scepticism vis-à-vis a theory of action. Whereas the influence of pragmatist thought has, to this day, remained largely confined to the United States, and even there has lost ground since the Second World War, in Germany and France it was the philosophy of life which became – for some time – the dominant current of thought. What both approaches have in common is the central role they accord a notion of creativity. There is, however, a striking difference between the two traditions of thought. Whereas pragmatism locates creativity in everyday human activity and regards science as a more pronounced development of this potential, the philosophy of life draws a sharp distinction between creativity, on the one hand, and everyday life and ordinary science, on the other. In the philosophy of life, the nexus of creativity and action is severed, either in order to attribute creativity to some pre-human will – although the concept makes sense only in the context of human intentionality – or to define it as an arbitrary form of generating meanings and an uncontrolled game, rather than as a constant reorganization of our behavioural habits and institutions. Creativity in the sense of genius is thus

> not creative in the sense of positive generation. It thrives on a negative dialectic which conveys the sensation of creative freedom only by destroying all concrete positions and serves merely to open up the creative universe of possibilities by abolishing existing realities and values; indeed, it is this alone which it sets out to achieve. It is the kind

of genius that, in its abstract claim to absoluteness, is its own end. It
forgoes all actuality for the sake of unlimited potentiality.[114]

The difference between the philosophy of life and pragmatism with
regard to their understanding of creativity[115] is therefore not some
obsolete question which is of interest only to historians of philosophy,
but is in fact the very pivot around which the relationship between
the postmodernism debate and sociology revolves.

Such a theory of the creativity of action also seems best able to
account for present-day psycho-social developments. I think we can
confidently put aside the prediction of the old generation of critical
theorists that we would all become 'amphibians' or laboratory rats.[116]
Adorno used this metaphor to prophesy an ongoing reduction of
subjectivity to the level of mere patterns of stimulus and response.
This allowed him to interpret the triumphal march of behaviourism
through the American psychology of his day as a harbinger of real
psycho-social changes under 'late capitalism'. One inherent weakness
of this pessimistic view was, of course, its failure to take equal account
of notions of a psychology of creativity that were being developed
during the same period, ideas which were also to be found in the
work of Erich Fromm and were thus being articulated even by a
member of the Frankfurt School. If ever more people were developing
a self-understanding of creative individuality, this was not judged to
be an optimistic sign of a better future, but was dismissed as
ideological mystification.[117] On the level of value orientations, however, the findings of research into so-called changes in values leave us
in no doubt as to the fact that in the advanced industrial societies
post-materialist values – and in particular the value of individual self-
fulfilment – are becoming increasingly widespread.[118] With respect to
this value, nobody could say that postmodernists are totally arbitrary
towards value-related validity claims; on the contrary, the postmodernist stance implicitly lays claim to creativity – and, given the
influence of the philosophy of life, it is an exaggerated claim. Qualitative and intuitive studies tend to corroborate what research into
changing values has revealed using the quantitative methods of
empirical social research. In an original study of the children of
respondents who, in the fifties, had provided the basis for the now
classic social psychology of the 'Organization Man',[119] the authors
come to the conclusion that the divergence between these two generations is of dramatic proportions. To sum this up they have coined the
phrase: 'From the Self-Made Man to the Man-Made Self.'[120] They use
concepts expressivity, creativity and authenticity to characterize the

value orientation of the new generation. Gone is the strict divide between a purely instrumental professional life and a purely expressive private life within the framework of social conformity. It has been replaced by each individual's attempt to find his or her own lifestyle in which expressivity and instrumentality can be reconciled. This generation therefore exhibits a yearning for the kind of careers which appear to permit such a reconciliation – such as creative professions in the media – or for a redefinition of professional roles along these lines. The authors observe that wherever the career pursued by a respondent imposes narrow limits on the practical application of these values, the persons in question consistently tend to craft their private life as if it were a work of art.

An observable shift of values may, of course, be no more than a passing phenomenon and should not be allowed to engender speculations about the beginning of a new epoch. Without a more precise knowledge of the causes of this shift and the likelihood of its persisting, any statements to that effect would be unfounded. Neither would the proponents of the critical 'amphibian' prognosis consider their position to have been refuted by the mere fact that creativity-related value orientations are becoming more widespread. After all, it may be precisely this self-image of creative individuality that is arguably the new form of repression, if all it amounts to is the illusory frippery of detached 'systems' that have rendered themselves autonomous. The crucial question here is therefore whether this change in values fails to affect social reality or whether it is capable of permeating and changing the latter. Moreover, this being the case, is social reality in turn even encouraging its development?

For all the question-marks and problems that remain,[121] research into changes in values does at least provide numerous indications of the structural conditions necessary for realizing these values and of the likelihood that they will prevail. Shorter working hours, a higher level of formal education, female employment, team-based organization structures and the spread of flexible links between career work and other activities – all these developments have created a wide range of possibilities for realizing these changed values in the design of one's own biography. It goes without saying that this must not divert our gaze from the perpetuation, or indeed exacerbation, of forms of social discrimination, nor blind us to the fact that we are tacitly assuming the stable underlying existence of a democratic welfare state and the rule of law. Suffice it to state at this point that there is some basis in reality for the claim that the significance of the idea of creativity for an understanding of our present is growing.

In part, the concept of 'individualization' owes its enormous impact on public discourse to the fact that the notion that people are increasingly basing their lives on the value of personal autonomy has in some vague way become connected with an utterly different phenomenon, namely the fear, rooted in the sociological tradition, that community ties and binding value systems are rapidly falling apart – in short, the fear of anomie. In reality, of course, these conceptually discrete processes may indeed by interlinked. Today, the anomization processes which have characterized the dynamics of capitalism since its origin occur in a cultural environment in which the highest priority is attached to the value of personal autonomy. However, 'anomization' is not a consequence of 'autonomization'. This sharp conceptual distinction is vital to the diagnosis here because the right choice of therapy depends on it. If the problem is 'individualization', then the only possible remedy for the present crisis of culture is to place individualism under normative constraints – irrespective of whether the phenomenon we are trying to deal with is the utilitarian or the expressive variety of individualism, or both at once.[122]

Diagnoses of contemporary society may be right to dispute the plausibility of life being increasingly reduced to *one* form of action, arguing instead for a plurality of types of action and for tension or compromise between them. Yet when they propose a form of therapy such as that just mentioned, all they succeed in doing is to play into the hands of representatives of 'postmodernism'. The normative critique of expressive individualism is the foe that the postmodernist propagandists of normatively uninhibited self-creation have always set their sights on. A satisfactory sociological diagnosis of the present day therefore has no choice but to take seriously also the *normative* provocation of the postmodernist discussion. In other words, sociologists must be prepared to draw on insights into the creativity of human action in order to revise the ideas concerning norms and morality that are fundamental to sociology. Striving for creativity is itself not inherently limited to individualistic forms. The conflict between utilitarian and expressive individualism is not a necessary outcome of these forms of action themselves, but rather the result of specific historic settings. In this sense, the conflict is of a secondary order in that it presupposes that trends towards comprehensive creativity have already been diverted into the domain of the individual.

My understanding of such a comprehensive creativity can best be explained using the concepts developed by Abraham Maslow in his 'humanist psychology'.[123] Maslow distinguishes between primary, secondary and integrated creativity. Primary creativity refers to the release of 'primary processes' of fancy, imagination, playfulness and enthusiasm. He applies the term 'secondary creativity' to the rational production of something new in the world, a solution to a technical or scientific, an artistic or indeed an everyday practical problem. The crisis of the belief in progress can be interpreted as a crisis of this secondary creativity. The point was not and is not that people doubt the possibility of further technical, scientific or economic progress. Rather, there is a feeling that the advances in these specific areas do not add up to a valuable whole worthy of the generic name 'progress'. This failure to achieve progress by means of secondary creativity then leads to a revaluation of primary creativity. Yet two possibilities emerge here. On the one hand, this may produce a longing for primary creativity which despises all forms of secondary creativity. This is the path of irrationalism in the narrow sense. On the other, however, it is possible to conceive of an integration of primary and secondary creativity. And precisely that is Maslow's third type of creativity. Here the distance from secondary creativity leads to a higher creativity, one which does not spurn rational and critical control. The great work

> needs not only the flash, the inspiration, the peak-experience; it also needs hard work, long training, unrelenting criticism, perfectionistic standards. In other words, succeeding upon the spontaneous is the deliberate; succeeding upon intuition comes rigorous thought; succeeding upon daring comes caution; succeeding upon fantasy and imagination comes reality testing.[124]

In this concept of 'integrated creativity', the openness of self-articulation is wedded to the responsibility of self-control. A psycho-social diagnosis of the present age based on an action theory that emphasizes the role of creativity must therefore inquire into the potential for just such an 'integrated creativity' in today's society. In other words, we would have to look for evidence of the preconditions for autonomous personality that have not been achieved at the price of moral regression. We would then have to analyse the individualistic remoulding of creativity through commercialization and status struggles and decipher the forms in which suppressed creativity expresses itself. What follows is no more than a first step towards such a diagnosis, using the concepts 'participation', 'yuppification' and 'violence'.

Today, the concept of participation refers to the desire for public, tangible sociality and serious creative activity within the community – a desire which the tendency towards privatization has not yet completely silenced. By participating in the organizations and institutions of democratic politics and culture, as well as in the social movements which form the fluid substratum of democracy, people are able to experience a rational pursuit of interests, moral commitment and creative self-fulfilment in a form in which these three are not separated from each other. Participation can be said to be a practical form of integrated creativity only if it is not exclusively the pursuit of one's own interests or a merely normative obligation, uncoupled from the self-fulfilment that takes place in the private sphere. Conversely, those who would instrumentalize participation for purposes of an individualized conception of self-fulfilment also defeat their own object. Much as participation may be a key word to describe a creativity that is not limited narrowly to a privatistic understanding, so, too, we must be wary of overemphasizing it and thus making it synonymous with a successful life. Not only should we not forget the domain of work which exists alongside it, but we must also be mindful of the fact that not all questions of how to lead a meaningful life can be answered in terms of public and political action.[125] Participation has its place within each person's individual balance of modes of action.

The concept of 'yuppification' is intended, by contrast, to denote the silencing of the tension between normativity and creativity which arises from the radical loss of morality inherent in both utilitarian and expressive individualism. The 'yuppie',[126] a term which came into everyday parlance during the mid-1980s, is conceived of as the type of person who feels no pangs of conscience, whether he be ruthlessly deploying any means that promise business and career success, or enjoying the beauties of luxury and pleasure in his lifestyle and leisure time. Monetary greed and careerism are just as devoid of any morality as are wasteful self-indulgence and conspicuous consumption in the face of social inequality. What characterizes 'yuppyism' here, as I see it, is the indeterminate hunger for novelty with regard to experiences for novelty's sake, and the lifestyles that emerge without any claim to being universally valid. While it is true that democratic culture demands that tolerance be shown towards the various lifestyles and the broadest freedom be given to choose autonomously between them, and just as these lifestyles, of which many necessarily exist, cannot be equated with universalizable demands on the commonality as a whole, so, too, they must nevertheless claim some sort of validity for others. If this residual claim disappears, then cultural innovation degenerates to the level of privatistically forming cultural enclaves, leaving the public sphere open to those who would seek to use it as a means to impose their own principles. The postmodernists never tire of repeating the idea that rigid consensus stifles the creative potential of difference. Yet this creative potential is also wasted if the difference exists free of any tension because none of the parties any longer feels bound to that which is specifically its own, because none experiences the Other as a potentially salutary provocation, a stimulus to serious self-transformation, and because all orientation towards a possible consensus – even if it is only a consensus on agreeing to differ – has disappeared.

When individual or collective 'violence' is committed spontaneously, it is an expression of barriers to integrated creativity. This is, of course, not the only form which violence takes. It is often used in utilitarian sobriety or with a feeling of moral obligation. Yet wherever participation is impossible or creativity cannot be integrated meaningfully into the personal balance of a meaningful life, the potential that is denied expression slowly builds up. Wherever the postmodern coexistence of heterogeneous lifestyles is not a source of intellectual pleasure but is experienced as an excessive, anxiety-producing strain, we witness an increase in the potential for violence against outsiders, foreigners and anyone else who is perceived as threatening to destabilize the already unsteady value systems still further. In their euphoria over multiculturalism and liberation from concrete communities, the postmodernists show an utterly inexcusable disregard for the consequences of the excessive strain that many people may be undergoing as a result of this development. Indeed, in contemporary Germany today we need only look as far as the periphery of the student population to find the obverse of xenophobia and racism: the self-enactment of the so-called 'autonomists', that is, militants obsessed with struggle and violence.

I make no apologies for having been normative in these cursory allusions and observations on the subject of a phenomenology of creativity today and thus on the application of a theory of action revised to accommodate the idea of creativity to a diagnosis of contemporary society. There is no denying that even the concept of 'integrated creativity' is by no means value-free. Do I not therefore leave myself open to the charge that ultimately I am trying to counter the alleged moral indifference of the postmodernists by resorting to normative pathos? This question can be answered only if we have a clear understanding of the ambiguity that lies at the heart of the *normative* provocation posed by the postmodernism discourse. On the one hand, it may be understood as a carefree dismissal of all morality or indeed a 'fascination for amorality',[127] in which case normative pathos is an entirely appropriate response. On the other hand, it may also be seen as jolting us into a profound revision of our ideas of morality and normativity. Such a revision becomes necessary when the idea of creativity is given centre stage. This holds true, irrespective of whether it is the 'philosophy of life' or the pragmatist version of this idea which is dominant.

Nietzsche's critique of Christianity was already an object-lesson in the meaning of inauthentic morality. It is possible to understand freedom from the excessive pressure of moral ideals as constituting the end of all morality. Yet this liberation can also point the way to an authentic morality. Ideals become destructive when they prevent us from being open to the positive and negative tendencies of our own pre-linguistic being and from accepting ourselves and our fellow human beings. Certainly, morality demands that we distance ourselves from these tendencies; yet creativity demands also that we distance ourselves from morality. The question to be asked of moral theory from the standpoint of a theory of creativity does not necessarily challenge the substance of morality, but addresses the way morality is rooted in personality. And it is here that the two competing conceptions of creativity part company again. One route leads to an aestheticization of life and is associated today, despite the existence of numerous precursors, mainly with the names Foucault, Lyotard and Rorty.[128] These and similarly minded authors sing a panegyric to the ongoing acquisition of new kinds of experience and of new idioms in order constantly to be able to describe these experiences in a new way. For no reason at all, a lifestyle that limits its own options, that allows firm bonds, that is capable of asceticism and is coherent, is thus devalued by a one-sided understanding of what is aesthetic.[129] Those who take the other route maintain that the tension between creativity and normativity cannot be overcome.[130] However, precisely this insistence on some claim to creativity can itself result in the moralization of social life in a new guise.[131] This applies not only in the sense – current since Herder and the Romantics – of collisions between claims to individual self-fulfilment and the limiting parameters of the social order, collisions which are the potential source of demands for social change. It also applies in the post-romantic, perhaps even 'postmodern' sense to the question of what the social order would look like that *we* should create, and want to create, *for ourselves*. Now that there are no longer any metasocial guarantees to underpin the creation of social orders, reflection causes us to turn to the creativity of human action itself.

Notes

Introduction

1 Richard Bernstein, *Praxis and Action* (University of Philadelphia Press, Philadelphia, 1971).

Chapter 1   The Emergence of the Theory of Action

1 Paul Nolte, 'Optimist der liberalen Gesellschaft: Talcott Parsons', *Merkur*, 41 (1987), pp. 579–89.
2 Talcott Parsons, *The Structure of Social Action* (McGraw Hill, New York, 1937), p. 344.
3 Ibid., p. 64. Charles Taylor, 'What is Human Agency?', in his *Philosophical Papers I* (Cambridge University Press, Cambridge, 1985), pp. 15–44, here p. 29.
4 Harold Bershady, *Ideology and Social Knowledge* (Blackwell, Oxford, 1973).
5 Jeffrey Alexander, *Theoretical Logic in Sociology, Vol. I: Positivism, Presuppositions and Current Controversies* (University of California Press, Berkeley, 1982); Richard Münch, *Theory of Action* (Routledge & Kegan Paul, London, 1987) and *Understanding Modernity* (Routledge & Kegan Paul, London, 1988).
6 Harald Wenzel, *Die Ordnung des Handelns. Talcott Parsons' Theorie des allgemeinen Handlungssystems* (Suhrkamp, Frankfurt/Main, 1991).
7 Parsons, *Structure*, p. 476.
8 Ibid., pp. 697–8.
9 Ibid., p. 709.
10 For a useful critical overview of these attempts see Manfred Trapp, 'Utilitaristische Konzepte in der Soziologie. Eine soziologische Kritik von Homans bis zur Neuen Politischen Ökonomie', *Zeitschrift für Soziologie*,

15 (1986), pp. 324–40. For a view that strongly sympathizes with recent trends to make the model of rational action the epitome of a reconstruction of the contingency of action as such, see the excellent article by Helmut Wiesenthal, 'Rational Choice. Ein Überblick über Grundlinien, Themenfelder und neuere Themenakquisition eines sozialwissenschaftlichen Paradigmas', *Zeitschrift für Soziologie*, 16 (1987), pp. 434–49.

11 See the foreword to the 1949, second edition of *The Structure of Social Action* and above all Parsons' essay, 'Cooley and the Problem of Internalization', in *Cooley and Sociological Analysis*, ed. Albert Reiss (University of Michigan Press, Ann Arbor, 1968), pp. 48–67.

12 R. Jackson Wilson, *In Quest of Community. Social Philosophy in the United States 1860–1920* (Wiley, New York, 1968), p. 155.

13 Louis Wirth, 'Review of Parsons's "The Structure of Social Action"', *American Sociological Review*, 4 (1939), pp. 399–404.

14 Roscoe Hinkle, 'Antecedents of the Action Orientation in American Sociology before 1935', *American Sociological Review*, 28 (1963), pp. 705–15.

15 See Parsons' preface to the second edition of *The Structure of Social Action*.

16 Donald Levine, *Simmel and Parsons* (Arno, New York, 1980). In the introduction (pp. iii–lxix) Levine provides a first, excellent appraisal of the debate on *The Structure of Social Action*. Meanwhile a more comprehensive and thorough study has appeared: Charles Camic, '"Structure" after 50 Years: The Anatomy of a Charter', *American Journal of Sociology*, 95 (1989), pp. 38–107. There can clearly be no talk of the discussion having come to an end. Cf. Wenzel, *Die Ordnung*, and Mark Gould, 'Voluntarism versus Utilitarianism: A Critique of Camic's History of Ideas', *Theory, Culture & Society*, 6 (1989), pp. 637–54.

17 Letter from Talcott Parsons to Jeffrey Alexander of 19 January 1979, quoted in Levine, *Simmel*. See also on this issue the more recent essay by Donald Levine, 'Simmel and Parsons Reconsidered', *American Journal of Sociology*, 96 (1991), pp. 107–116.

18 Jeffrey Alexander, *Theoretical Logic in Sociology, Vol. III: The Classical Attempt at Synthesis: Max Weber* (University of California Press, Berkeley, 1983).

19 Also of seminal importance in this respect is Habermas' interpretation of Weber. See Jürgen Habermas, *Theory of Communicative Action*, vol. 1, tr. T. McCarthy (Beacon Press, Boston, 1984; Polity Press, Cambridge, 1991), pp. 143–272.

20 Best known is Whitney Pope, 'Classic on Classic: Parsons' Interpretation of Durkheim', *American Sociological Review*, 38 (1973), pp. 399–415.

21 Reinhard Bendix, 'Two Sociological Traditions', in Reinhard Bendix and Günther Roth, *Scholarship and Partisanship* (University of California Press, Berkeley, 1971), pp. 282–98.

22 Above all Charles Camic, 'The Utilitarians Revisited', *American Journal of Sociology*, 85 (1979), pp. 515–50.

23 Münch, *Understanding Modernity*, p. 273, fn. 58.

24 Albert Hirschman, *The Passions and the Interests: Political Arguments for Capitalism Before its Triumph* (Princeton University Press, Princeton, 1977).

25 *The Theory of Social Action: The Correspondence of Talcott Parsons and Alfred Schütz*, ed. R. Grathoff (University of Indiana Press, Bloomington, 1978). Stephen Warner, 'Toward a Redefinition of Action Theory: Paying the Cognitive Element its Due', *American Journal of Sociology*, 83 (1978), pp. 317–49. Niklas Luhmann, *Zweckbegriff und Systemrationalität: Über die Funktion von Zwecken in sozialen Systemen* (Mohr, Tübingen, 1968). Alain Touraine, *Sociologie de l'action* (Seuil, Paris, 1965).

26 Talcott Parsons, 'Review of Bershady', *Sociological Inquiry*, 44 (1974), pp. 215–21. In this context, Charles Camic provides an important interpretation of this early phase in Parsons' work: 'The Making of a Method: A Historical Reinterpretation of the Early Parsons', *American Sociological Review*, 52 (1987), pp. 421–39. Only after I had completed my manuscript did Camic publish: 'Introduction: Talcott Parsons before *The Structure of Social Action*', in Talcott Parsons, *The Early Essays* (University of Chicago Press, Chicago, 1991), pp. ix–lxix.

27 The article he published using material from his thesis appeared as '"Capitalism" in Recent German Literature: Sombart and Weber', *Journal of Political Economy*, 36 (1928), pp. 641–61 and 37 (1929), pp. 31–51; also in Parsons, *The Early Essays*, pp. 3–38.

28 Parsons, *Structure*, p. 768.

29 Wenzel, *Die Ordnung*, has tackled this task. Given that he strongly emphasizes the presence of a 'philosophy of analytical realism' indebted to Whitehead in Parsons' work, he attaches decidedly less weight than Camic or myself to the importance of the economic controversies for an understanding of Parsons' early development.

30 I shall return to pragmatism in the second chapter of this book, see chapter 2.5.

31 Parsons, *Structure*, p. 733.

32 Parsons, 'The Place of Ultimate Values in Sociological Theory', *International Journal of Ethics*, 45 (1935), pp. 282–316; also published in *The Early Essays*, pp. 231–58.

33 Parsons, *Structure*, p. 297.

34 Talcott Parsons, *The Social System* (Free Press, Glencoe, Ill., 1951).

35 Göran Therborn, *Science, Class and Society. On the Formation of Sociology and Historical Materialism* (New Left Books, London, 1976), see esp. pp. 240–315; Simon Clarke, *Marx, Marginalism and Modern Sociology. From Adam Smith to Max Weber* (Macmillan, London, 1982).

36 For a convincing new interpretation of these developments see Peter Wagner, *Sozialwissenschaften und Staat* (Campus, Frankfurt/Main, 1990).

37 Vilfredo Pareto, *Compendium of General Sociology* (University of Minnesota Press, Minneapolis, 1980).

38 Arnold Gehlen, 'Vilfredo Pareto und seine "neue Wissenschaft"', in his

Studien zur Anthropologie und Soziologie (Luchterhand, Neuwied, 1963), pp. 149–95.

39 Max Weber, 'Basic Sociological Categories', in *Economy and Society*, tr. Günter Roth and Claus Wittich (Bedminster Press, New York, 1968), p. 3.
40 Ibid., pp. 63–211.
41 Wilhelm Hennis, *Max Weber: Essays in Reconstruction*, tr. K. Tribe (Allen & Unwin, London, 1988).
42 Weber, *Economy and Society*, p. 248.
43 See Wolfgang Schluchter, *Die Entwicklung des okzidentalen Rationalismus* (Mohr-Siebeck, Tübingen, 1979), p. 192.
44 Christopher Prendergast, 'Alfred Schütz and the Austrian School of Economics', *American Journal of Sociology*, 92 (1986), pp. 1–26.
45 For example, Charles Horton Cooley, 'The Institutional Character of Pecuniary Valuation', *American Journal of Sociology*, 18 (1913), pp. 543–55.
46 Émile Durkheim, 'La science positive de la morale en Allemagne', in his *Écrits*, vol. 1 (Presses Universitaires de France, Paris, 1975), pp. 267–343 (published in English as *Ethics and the Sociology of Morals*, tr. R. T. Hall, Prometheus Books, Buffalo, NY, 1993).
47 See, for example, Mead's review of B.M. Anderson Jr., *Social Value. A Study in Economic Theory*, *Psychological Bulletin*, 8 (1911), pp. 432–6.
48 Georg Simmel, *The Philosophy of Money*, tr. T. Bottomore and D. Frisby, 2nd enlarged edn, (Routledge & Kegan Paul, London, 1978).
49 Ibid., p. 66.
50 Ibid., p. 72.
51 Weber, *Economy and Society*, pp. 400ff.
52 Ibid., p. 17.
53 Ibid., pp. 241 and 711ff, etc.
54 The remark was made orally by Erik Erikson; see Robert C. Tucker, 'The Theory of Charismatic Leadership', *Daedalus*, 97 (1968), pp. 731–56.
55 Shmuel Eisenstadt, 'Charisma and Institution Building: Max Weber and Modern Sociology', in Max Weber, *Selected Papers* (University of Chicago Press, Chicago, 1968), pp. ix–lvi; Wolfgang Mommsen, 'A Notion of Universal History and Political Thought', *International Social Science Journal*, 17 (1965), pp. 27–45; Edward Shils, 'Charisma, Order, and Status', *American Sociological Review*, 30 (1965), pp. 199–213; Jóhann Páll Arnason, *Praxis und Interpretation* (Suhrkamp, Frankfurt/Main, 1988). See also Arthur Mitzman, *The Iron Cage. An Historical Reinterpretation of Max Weber* (Knopf, New York, 1969); Charles Camic, 'Charisma: Its Varieties, Preconditions and Consequences', *Sociological Inquiry*, 50 (1980), pp. 5–23; Thomas Dow, 'An Analysis of Weber's Work on Charisma', *British Journal of Sociology*, 29 (1978), pp. 83–93; Stefan Breuer, *Max Webers Herrschaftssoziologie* (Campus, Frankfurt/Main, 1991), pp. 33–67 and 215–21.
56 Jeffrey Alexander, *Theoretical Logic, Vol. II: The Antinomies of Classical Thought: Marx and Durkheim* (University of California Press, Berkeley, 1982). For a later, more condensed version of this interpretation, see

Alexander, 'Rethinking Durkheim's Intellectual Development', *International Sociology*, 1 (1986), pp. 91–107 and 189–201. On Alexander's approach see my essay 'The Antinomies of Neofunctionalism: A Critical Essay on Jeffrey Alexander', *Inquiry* 31 (1988), pp. 471–94 (now also in Joas, *Pragmatism and Social Theory*, tr. J. Gaines, R. Meyer and S. Minner [University of Chicago Press, Chicago, 1993], pp. 188–213).

57 Robert Nisbet, *Émile Durkheim* (Prentice Hall, Englewood Cliffs, NJ, 1965); Anthony Giddens, *Émile Durkheim* (Fontana, London, 1978).

58 René König, *Kritik der historisch-existenzialistischen Soziologie. Ein Beitrag zur Begründung einer objektiven Soziologie* (Piper, Munich, 1975). Among his numerous other writings on Durkheim, of particular interest is: 'Émile Durkheim. Der Soziologe als Moralist', in *Klassiker des soziologischen Denkens*, ed. Dirk Käsler, vol. 1 (Beck, Munich, 1976), pp. 312–64.

59 Bernard Lacroix, *Durkheim et le politique* (Presses de l'Université de Montréal, Paris and Montréal, 1981).

60 Stjepan G. Mestrovic, 'Durkheim, Schopenhauer and the Relationship between Goals and Means: Reversing the Assumptions in the Parsonian Theory of Rational Action', *Sociological Inquiry*, 58 (1988), pp. 163–81 and his *Émile Durkheim and the Reformation of Sociology* (Rownam & Littlefield, Totowa, NJ, 1988).

61 André Lalande, 'Allocution', *Centenaire de la naissance de Durkheim. Annales de l'Université de Paris*, 1 (1960), pp. 20–3, here p. 23.

62 Hans Joas, 'The Classics of Sociology and the First World War', *Thesis Eleven*, 27 (1990), pp. 101–24.

63 Durkheim, *Ethics*.

64 Ibid., p. 127.

65 Émile Durkheim, *Division of Labour in Society*, tr. W. D. Halls (Macmillan, London, 1984), pp. 5–6.

66 Durkheim, *Ethics*, p. 69.

67 For example, ibid., p. 81.

68 Émile Durkheim, review of Jean-Marie Guyau, *L'irréligion de l'avenir* (1887), in Durkheim, *Textes*, vol. 2 (Minuit, Paris, 1975), pp. 160–1.

69 Durkheim, *Ethics*, p. 103.

70 Ibid., p. 117.

71 Émile Durkheim, review of Ferdinand Tönnies' *Gemeinschaft und Gesellschaft* (1889), in *Émile Durkheim. On Institutional Analysis*, ed. Mark Traugott (University of Chicago Press, Chicago and London, (1978), pp. 115–22, here p. 121.

72 The posthumous writings of Ferdinand Tönnies in the Schleswig-Holstein State Library in Kiel contain a copy of Durkheim's review with Tönnies' marginal notes. These notes indicate that Tönnies felt misunderstood, especially with regard to his alleged centredness on the state.

73 Jean Piaget, *The Moral Judgement of the Child*, tr. M. Gabain (Penguin, Harmondsworth, 1977), p. 328.

74 This idea is fully elaborated in Michael Schmid, 'Arbeitsteilung und

Solidarität. Eine Untersuchung zu Émile Durkheims Theorie der sozialen Arbeitsteilung', *Kölner Zeitschrift für Soziologie und Sozialpsychologie*, 41 (1989), pp. 619–43.

75 Hans-Peter Müller, 'Durkheim's Political Sociology', in *Émile Durkheim. Sociologist and Moralist*, ed. Stephen Turner (Routledge, London, 1993), pp. 95–110, here p. 100.

76 Durkheim's book on 'rules', which certainly smacks more of positivism than do any other of his works, also conforms with the interpretation proposed here as long as we recognize that in it Durkheim was asserting his own programme: in devoting a great amount of space to the distinction between the normal and the pathological, he was concerned with the question as to how the pathological could be cured by means of a new morality. Durkheim's typology of suicide also assumes the turn which I shall seek to elucidate here.

77 Ernest Wallwork, *Durkheim, Morality and Milieu* (Harvard University Press, Cambridge, Mass., 1972); see also his 'Durkheim's Early Sociology of Religion', *Sociological Analysis*, 46 (1985), pp. 201–18.

78 Émile Durkheim, *Moral Education*, tr. E.K. Wilson and H. Schnurer (Free Press, Glencoe, Ill., 1961), p. 9.

79 See my essay 'Durkheim and Pragmatism', in Joas, *Pragmatism*, pp. 55–78.

80 Gregory Stone and Harvey Farberman, 'On the Edge of Rapprochement: Was Durkheim Moving Towards the Perspective of Symbolic Interaction?', *Sociological Quarterly*, 8 (1967), pp. 149–64.

81 See Jürgen Habermas, *Theory of Communicative Action*, vol. 2, tr. T. McCarthy (Beacon Press, Boston, 1987 and Polity Press, Cambridge, 1987), pp. 77–112.

82 Robert T. Hall, *Émile Durkheim. Ethics and the Sociology of Morals* (Greenwood, London, 1987) regards Durkheim's studies of socialism and the history of education as investigations that are also studies of the emergence of new ideals.

83 Émile Durkheim, 'Introduction to "Morality"', in *Émile Durkheim. On Institutional Analysis*, pp. 191–202, here p. 193.

84 Parsons, *Structure*, pp. 686–94.

85 I do not know Pareto's work well enough to be able to judge whether the theme is just as important there. The point of departure here would no doubt have to be the often cited similarity between Pareto's and Nietzsche's thought. An energetic attempt to bring Pareto's thought to bear against mainstream sociological theory today, as influenced by Weber and Parsons, has been made by Alan Sica in his *Weber, Irrationality and Social Order* (University of California Press, Berkeley, 1988). In the case of the classical American sociologists neglected by Parsons, suffice it to point to the importance of pragmatism if this itself is understood as a theory of creativity. See chapter 2.5 of the present study and my *Pragmatism*.

86 Thus the picture he painted of himself in *Philosophie der Gegenwart in*

Selbstdarstellungen, ed. Raymund Schmidt, vol. 3 (F. Meiner, Leipzig, 1922), pp. 199–234; in the foreword to *Der Nietzsche-Kultus. Eine Kritik* (Reisland, Leipzig, 1897). On the importance of Nietzsche for Tönnies see also the controversial essays by Zander and Alwast: Jürgen Zander, 'Ferdinand Tönnies und Friedrich Nietzsche', in *Ankunft bei Tönnies,* ed. Lars Clausen and Franz Urban Pappi (Mühlau, Kiel, 1981), pp. 185–227 and Jendris Alwast, 'Die Wertung der Philosophie Nietzsches bei Tönnies', ibid., pp. 228–40.

87 Tönnies, *Nietzsche-Kultus,* p. 10.

88 Ibid., p. 102.

89 Cf. also Cornelius Bickel, 'Ferdinand Tönnies' Weg in die Soziologie', in *Simmel und die frühen Soziologen* (Suhrkamp, Frankfurt/Main, 1988), pp. 86–162.

90 Ferdinand Tönnies, *Community and Society* (1887), tr. C. P. Loomis (Harper & Row, New York, 1957), p. 156.

91 Correspondence between Tönnies and Höffding, p. 40, quoted here from Rolf Fechner, '"Der Wesenwille selbst ist künstlerischer Geist". Ferdinand Tönnies' Geniebegriff und seine Bedeutung für den Übergang von der Gemeinschaft zur Gesellschaft', in *Hundert Jahre 'Gemeinschaft und Gesellschaft',* ed. Lars Clausen and Carsten Schlüter (Leske und Budrich, Opladen, 1992), pp. 453–62.

92 The best study on this issue is Klaus Lichtblau's 'Das "Pathos der Distanz". Präliminarien zur Nietzsche-Rezeption bei Georg Simmel', in *Georg Simmel und die Moderne,* ed. Heinz-Jürgen Dahme and Otthein Ramstedt (Suhrkamp, Frankfurt/Main, 1984), pp. 231–81.

93 Georg Simmel, 'Bergson und der deutsche "Zynismus"', *Internationale Monatsschrift für Kritik, Wissenschaft und Technik,* 9 (1914), pp. 197–200.

94 Georg Simmel, *Schopenhauer and Nietzsche,* tr. H. Loiskandl, D. and M. Weinstein (University of Massachusetts Press, Amherst, 1986).

95 Georg Simmel, 'The Conflict in Modern Culture' (1918), in *Georg Simmel on Individuality and Social Forms,* tr. D. Levine (University of Chicago Press, Chicago, 1971), pp. 375–93, here p. 377.

96 Although hard to prove philologically, the evident importance of Nietzsche for Weber has been established by a number of authors in recent years (e.g. Hennis, *Max Weber;* Georg Stauth and Bryan Turner, 'Nietzsche in Weber oder die Geburt des modernen Genius im professionellen Menschen', *Zeitschrift für Soziologie,* 15 [1986], pp. 81–94; and, at an earlier date, Eugène Fleischmann, 'De Weber à Nietzsche', *Archives européennes de sociologie,* 5 [1964], pp. 190–238).

Chapter 2   Metaphors of Creativity

1 I refer here to the distinction drawn by Jürgen Habermas, roughly based on ideas developed by Popper and others. See Jürgen Habermas, *Theory*

of Communicative Action, vol. 1, tr. T. McCarthy (Beacon Press, Boston, 1984 and Polity Press, Cambridge, 1991), pp. 75–102.

2 Niklas Luhmann, 'Vom Zufall verwöhnt. Eine Rede über Kreativität', *Frankfurter Allgemeine Zeitung*, 10 June 1987; Allan Bloom, *The Closing of the American Mind* (Simon & Schuster, New York, 1987), pp. 180ff.

3 James Engell speaks of a self-transformation of the Enlightenment 'from an age of reason to an age of imagination' and not of a Romantic anti-Enlightenment. See James Engell, *The Creative Imagination. Enlightenment to Romanticism* (Harvard University Press, Cambridge, Mass., 1981). Raymond Williams actually opens his treatise on the subject with the following sentence: 'No word in English carries a more consistently positive reference than "creative".' Raymond Williams, *The Long Revolution* (Chatto & Windus, London, 1961), p. 3.

4 Bernhard Fabian, 'Der Naturwissenschaftler als Originalgenie', in *Europäische Aufklärung. Festschrift für Herbert Dieckmann*, ed. Hugo Friedrich and Fritz Schalk (Fink, Munich, 1967), pp. 47–68.

5 See Isaiah Berlin, *Vico and Herder* (Hogarth, London, 1976), and Charles Taylor, *Hegel* (Cambridge University Press, Cambridge, 1975), part I.

6 As examples of attempts in this direction, see: Vinzenz Rüfner, 'Homo secundus Deus. Eine geistesgeschichtliche Studie zum menschlichen Schöpfertum', *Philosophisches Jahrbuch der Görres-Gesellschaft*, 63 (1955), pp. 248–91; Edgar Zilsel, *Die Entstehung des Geniebegriffs* (Mohr, Tübingen, 1926); Zilsel, *Die Geniereligion. Ein kritischer Versuch über das moderne Persönlichkeitsideal mit einer historischen Begründung* (Braumüller, Vienna and Leipzig, 1918) (reprinted Suhrkamp, Frankfurt/Main, 1990); John Hope Mason, 'The Character of Creativity: Two Traditions', *History of European Ideas*, 9 (1988), pp. 697–715; Mason, 'Thinking about Genius in the Eighteenth Century' (unpublished manuscript, London, 1990).

7 See J.G.A. Pocock, *The Machiavellian Moment. Florentine Political Thought and the Atlantic Republican Tradition* (Princeton University Press, Princeton, 1975).

8 Rüfner, 'Homo secundus Deus', p. 280.

9 Charles Taylor, 'Action as Expression', in *Intention and Intentionality. Essays in Honour of Gertrude E. M. Anscombe*, ed. Cora Diamond and Jenny Teichman (Harvester, Brighton, 1979), pp. 73–89. Charles Taylor has been prominent in taking up the ideas first put forward by Isaiah Berlin in speaking of an 'expressivistic' tradition that begins with Herder. In doing so, he not only reconstructs one of the important points of departure for Hegel and the whole of classical German philosophy, but also uses the tools of linguistic analysis to defend the linguistic theory of the '3 H's' (Hamann, Herder, Humboldt) contained within it. Cf. the essays 'Language and Human Nature' and 'Theories of Meaning' in Taylor, *Philosophical Papers*, vol. 1 (Cambridge University Press, Cambridge, 1985), pp. 215–47 and pp. 248–92; and most recently 'The Importance of Herder', in *Isaiah Berlin. A Celebration*, ed. Edna

and Avishai Margalit (University of Chicago Press, Chicago, 1991), pp. 40–63.

10 Johann Gottfried Herder, *Abhandlung über den Ursprung der Sprache* (Berlin, 1772). (I quote here from the five-volume Aufbau edition of Herder's works [Berlin and Weimar, 1982]rb, vol. 2, pp. 89–200.)

11 In particular, Arnold Gehlen developed his ideas as a direct extension of Herder's. See Arnold Gehlen, *Man, His Nature and Place in the World* (1940), tr. C. McMillan and K. Pillemer, with an introduction by K. S. Rehberg (Columbia University Press, New York, 1988). On the tradition of philosophical anthropology, see Axel Honneth and Hans Joas, *Social Action and Human Nature*, tr. R. Meyer (Cambridge University Press, Cambridge, 1988).

12 Herder, *Ursprung der Sprache*, p. 110.

13 An excellent presentation of Herder's theory of art is given in a book which I have found useful in many respects: Jochen Schmidt, *Die Geschichte des Genie-Gedankens in der deutschen Literatur, Philosophie und Politik 1750–1945*, vol. 2 (Wissenschaftliche Buchgesellschaft, Darmstadt, 1985), pp. 120–49.

14 Johann Gottfried Herder, 'Vom Erkennen und Empfinden der menschlichen Seele' (1774/5), in *Werke*, vol. 3, pp. 341–405, here. p. 393.

15 Cf. Herman Wolf, 'Die Genielehre des jungen Herder', *Deutsche Vierteljahresschrift für Literaturwissenschaft und Geistesgeschichte*, 3 (1925), pp. 401–30.

16 Johann Gottfried Herder, 'Von Kunstrichterei, Geschmack und Genie' (1800), in Herder, *Kalligone* (Arion, Weimar, 1955), p. 166.

17 Ibid., p. 164.

18 Ibid., p. 169. On this interpretation, see also Schmidt, *Geschichte des Genie-Gedankens*, p. 149.

19 Note how John Dewey, using the means of pragmatism, pursues this idea to its logical conclusion in his *Art as Experience* (1934) (Putnam's, New York, 1980). See also section 2.5 of the present chapter.

20 In many respects, there is no better account of the interwoven history of philosophy and literature than Hermann August Korff, *Geist der Goethezeit*, 4 vols (Koehler & Amelang, Leipzig, 1966). Needless to say, the influence of Herder's thought extends far beyond this period; it is the determining factor behind the hermeneutic tradition.

21 We have Charles Taylor to thank for the most impressive expositions of this development viewed from the standpoint of the problem of expressivism. See in particular Taylor, *Hegel*, and now also *Sources of the Self. The Making of the Modern Identity* (Cambridge University Press, Cambridge, 1989). The attempt to interpret classical German philosophy in terms of action theory, which is referred to only in passing in the text here, obviously comes close to efforts to make not one single type of action, such as communicative action and a formal procedure based upon it, the principle of practical philosophy, but instead a structure encompassing all forms of action. One present-day example of such an attempt

is the reconstruction of the idea of recognition, drawing on Fichte and in particular Hegel. While Ludwig Siep moves within the context of the institution-theory debate, Axel Honneth uses these tools to overcome certain problems in Jürgen Habermas' theory. See Ludwig Siep, *Anerkennung als Prinzip der praktischen Philosophie. Untersuchungen zu Hegels Jenaer Philosophie des Geistes* (Alber, Freiburg, 1979); Axel Honneth, *The Struggle for Recognition*, tr. J. Anderson (Polity Press, Cambridge, 1995).

22 The most influential and impressive of these authors is Jon Elster. See his essay 'Marxism, Functionalism and Game Theory', *Theory and Society*, 11 (1982), pp. 453–82, and in particular his book *Making Sense of Marx* (Cambridge University Press, Cambridge, 1985). In the present section I shall reiterate formulations which first appeared in an essay by Axel Honneth and myself which was written as a contribution to the discussion of Marxism in the GDR: Axel Honneth and Hans Joas, 'War Marx ein Utilitarist?', in *Karl Marx und Friedrich Engels. Ihr Einfluß und ihre Wirksamkeit in der Geschichte und Gegenwart der soziologischen Theorie*, ed. Helmut Steiner (Institut für Soziologie und Sozialpolitik, East Berlin, 1987), pp. 148–61. Axel Honneth has also expanded on this text in his brief evaluation of Marxism: Honneth, 'Logik der Emanzipation. Zum philosophischen Erbe des Marxismus', in *Wege ins Reich der Freiheit. André Gorz zum 65. Geburtstag*, ed. Hans Leo Krämer and Claus Leggewie (Rotbuch, Berlin, 1989), pp. 86–106.

23 For a representative example of this departure, see Anthony Giddens, *A Contemporary Critique of Historical Materialism* (Macmillan, London, 1981).

24 Louis Dumont, *From Mandeville to Marx. The Genesis and Triumph of Economic Ideology* (University of Chicago Press, Chicago, 1977).

25 Jeffrey Alexander, *Theoretical Logic in Sociology, Vol. II: The Antinomies of Classical Thought: Marx and Durkheim* (University of California Press, Berkeley, 1982).

26 David Lockwood, *Solidarity and Schism: The Problem of Disorder in Durkheimian and Marxist Sociology* (Clarendon Press, Oxford, 1992).

27 An extremely informative article on this subject is 'Geist' in *Historisches Wörterbuch der Philosophie*, ed. Joachim Ritter, vol. 3 (Schwabe, Basel and Stuttgart, 1974), columns 154–204. With his accustomed brilliance, Odo Marquard describes the rise and fall of the 'mind' concept as follows (see col. 188): 'That mind already became the ruling fundamental principle before him [= Hegel, H. J.], already in 1795–97, was therefore – so it seems – the product of an amalgamation of aesthetics and theology; yet if the two elements were no more than engaged in the Tübingen Seminary or Jena, their marriage not taking place before 1800, "mind" is in this respect a child born prior to wedlock, that was soon expelled from the house of romanticism, adopted by Hegel and re-educated to be no longer a 'view' but a 'concept' in order to be able to play its part as a grown-up in the philosophy of history and in philosophical systems, until it was sent into retirement by the Young Hegelians and finally – when *Geist*

gave up the ghost – was put to rest in the graveyard of systems, to the intensely felt sympathy of its surviving descendants: the *Geisteswissenschaften* (humanities).'

28 Karl Marx, 'Economic and Philosophical Manuscripts', in Marx, *Early Writings* (Penguin, Harmondsworth, 1977), pp. 279–400, here p. 386.

29 Ibid., pp. 385–6. I endorse the view of R.N. Berki that Marx and many a Marxist, in particular Georg Lukács, overestimated the similarity between the concepts of 'labour' used by Hegel and Marx respectively. The interesting affinity is that between the Marxian concept of 'labour' and Hegel's concept of 'mind'. See R. N. Berki, 'On the Nature and Origins of Marx' Concept of Labor', *Political Theory*, 7 (1979), pp. 35–56; Georg Lukács, *The Young Hegel*, tr. R. Livingstone (Merlin, London, 1975). For an important study on the Romantic sources of Marx's concept of labour, see Petra Röder, 'Von der Frühromantik zum jungen Marx. Rückwärtsgekehrte Prophetie eines qualitativen Naturbegriffs', in *Romantische Utopie – Utopische Romantik*, ed. Gisela Dischner and Richard Faber (Gerstenberg, Hildesheim, 1979), pp. 149–73. A wealth of stimulating ideas are to be found in Axel Honneth, 'Work and Instrumental Action: On the Normative Basis of Critical Theory', *Thesis Eleven*, 5/6 (1982), pp. 162–84.

30 Marx, 'Economic and Philosophical Manuscripts', p. 386.

31 On the relationship between Feuerbach and Marx, see Honneth and Joas, *Social Action*, pp. 12–25. Ludwig Feuerbach, 'Grundsätze der Philosophie der Zukunft', in Feuerbach, *Kleine Schriften*, ed. Karl Löwith (Suhrkamp, Frankfurt/Main, 1966), pp. 145–219.

32 Karl Marx, 'Excerpts from James Mill's *Elements of Political Economy*', in Marx, *Early Writings*, pp. 259–78, here pp. 277–8.

33 Marx, 'Economic and Philosophical Manuscripts', p. 324.

34 This point was established in, for example, Hans Freyer, *Theorie des gegenwärtigen Zeitalters* (Deutsche Verlagsanstalt, Stuttgart, 1956), pp. 15ff.

35 Important here is the distinction between 'labour' and 'producing' in Hannah Arendt, *The Human Condition* (University of Chicago Press, Chicago, 1958).

36 Jürgen Habermas, 'Arbeit und Interaktion. Bemerkungen zu Hegels Jenenser Philosophie des Geistes', in Habermas, *Technik und Wissenschaft als Ideologie* (Suhrkamp, Frankfurt/Main, 1968), pp. 9–47. The most advanced attempt to identify a theory of communication in Marx based on an awareness of present-day theoretical problems has been presented by Hans Peter Krüger, *Kritik der kommunikativen Vernunft. Kommunikationsorientierte Wissenschaftsforschung im Streit mit Sohn-Rethel, Toulmin und Habermas* (Akademie-Verlag, Berlin, 1990), esp. pp. 99–143.

37 Ernst Michael Lange, *Das Prinzip Arbeit. Drei metakritische Kapitel über Grundbegriffe, Struktur und Darstellung der 'Kritik der politischen Ökonomie' von Karl Marx* (Ullstein, Berlin, 1980), esp. pp. 62–3. Lange has made this point particularly vigorously. – I am unable to endorse the rest of Lange's argumentation, however, as he interprets Marx's ideas on labour exclu-

sively in terms of an expression (i.e. externalization) of previously made plans and not in terms of the interaction between vague intentions and the circumstances of the world. This is the price Lange pays for not going far enough back into the tradition of expressivist anthropology.

38 Karl Marx and Friedrich Engels, 'The German Ideology', in *Marx–Engels Collected Works*, vol. 5, tr. W. Lough (Lawrence & Wishart, London and New York, 1976), p. 31.

39 Ibid., although there is a touch of self-irony about its use here: 'This "alienation", to remain comprehensible to philosophers. . . .'

40 Ibid., p. 86.

41 But see also Krüger, *Kritik der kommunikativen Vernunft*, pp. 100ff.

42 A classical example of this view is Georg Lukács, *History and Class Consciousness*, tr. R. Livingstone (Merlin, London, 1971).

43 Jóhann Páll Arnason, *Zwischen Natur und Gesellschaft. Studien zu einer kritischen Theorie des Subjektes* (Europäische Verlags-Anstalt, Frankfurt/Main, 1976).

44 This is true even of what is arguably the most brilliant attempt by an East European author: Karel Kosík, *Dialectics of the Concrete*, tr. K. Kavanda and J. Schmidt (D. Reidel, Dordrecht, 1976). On this point of criticism, see also Jean Cohen, *Class and Civil Society. The Limits of Marxian Critical Theory* (University of Massachusetts Press, Amherst, Mass., 1982), p. 235, fn. 39.

45 Agnes Heller, 'Paradigm of Work – Paradigm of Production', in Heller, *The Power of Shame* (Routledge, London, 1985), pp. 57–70; also Heller, 'Habermas and Marxism', in *Habermas. Critical Debates*, ed. John B. Thompson and David Held (Routledge, London, 1982), pp. 21–41. For Agnes Heller's own formulation of a philosophy of praxis, see in particular her book *Everyday Life*, tr. G. L. Campbell (Routledge, London, 1984); the German edition (Suhrkamp, Frankfurt/Main, 1978) contains my introduction (pp. 7–23).

46 On this point, see Jóhann Páll Arnason's arguments in Arnason, *Praxis und Interpretation* (Suhrkamp, Frankfurt/Main, 1988), here p. 315, fn. 34.

47 Georg Lukács, *The Ontology of Social Being, Part 2: Marx's Basic Ontological Principles*, tr. D. Fernbach (Merlin, London, 1978); Lukács, *The Ontology of Social Being, Part 3: Labour*, tr. D. Fernbach (Merlin, London, 1979). The background to my criticisms of this model will not become clear until the third chapter of the present book, which is a critique of a teleological understanding of intentionality. (See chapter 3.1.)

48 György Márkus, 'Die Welt menschlicher Objekte. Zum Problem der Konstitution im Marxismus', in *Arbeit, Handlung, Normativität*, ed. Axel Honneth and Urs Jaeggi (Suhrkamp, Frankfurt/Main, 1980), pp. 12–136.

49 Jóhann Páll Arnason, 'Die Mehrdeutigkeit des Produktionsparadigmas', in Arnason, *Praxis und Interpretation*, pp. 11–53.

50 Honneth, 'Work and Instrumental Action', p. 180.

51 Addressed to Agnes Heller: Jürgen Habermas, 'A Reply to My Critics', in

Habermas. Critical Debates, pp. 219–83, here pp. 220–5. See also his refutation of Honneth's position, p. 225, fn. 11. In more general form, and in opposition to Márkus: Habermas, *The Philosophical Discourse of Modernity,* tr. F. Lawrence (Polity Press, Cambridge, 1987), pp. 60–69 and pp. 75–82. And finally, this time in direct refutation of criticisms of his *Theory of Communicative Action* raised by McCarthy, Honneth and myself: Habermas 'A Reply', in *Communicative Action,* ed. Axel Honneth and Hans Joas (Polity Press, Cambridge, 1991), pp. 214–64.

52 Habermas, *Discourse,* p. 62, fn. 15.

53 Ibid., pp. 66f.

54 Ibid., p. 79.

55 I have already dealt briefly with a number of these questions concerning the normative implications of the theory of action in the polarity between discursive and pragmatic ethics. See my 'The Creativity of Action and the Intersubjectivity of Reason – Mead's Pragmatism and Social Theory', *Transactions of the Charles Sanders Peirce Society,* 16 (1990), pp. 165–94 (now also in my *Pragmatism and Social Theory,* tr. J. Gaines, R. Meyer and S. Minner [University of Chicago Press, Chicago, 1993], pp. 239–61). A very important book in this context is Klaus Günther, *Der Sinn für Angemessenheit. Anwendungsdiskurse in Moral und Recht* (Suhrkamp, Frankfurt/Main, 1988).

56 Cornelius Castoriadis, *The Imaginary Institution of Society,* tr. K. Blamey (Polity Press, Cambridge, 1987). For an assessment of the specific contribution made by Castoriadis' political philosophy, see my essay: 'Institutionalization as a Creative Process', *American Journal of Sociology,* 94 (1988/9), pp. 1184–99 (now also in my *Pragmatism,* pp. 154–71). – Habermas attempts to subsume Castoriadis under his critique of the philosophy of praxis; see Habermas, *Discourse,* pp. 327–35.

57 Frederich Engels, preface to the third German edition of 'The Eighteenth Brumaire of Louis Bonaparte', in Karl Marx and Frederich Engels, *Selected Works in One Volume* (Lawrence & Wishart, London, 1970), pp. 94–5, here p. 95.

58 Jürgen Habermas, *Knowledge and Human Interest,* tr. J. Shapiro (Polity Press, Cambridge, 1987), p. 55.

59 Ibid., p. 62.

60 Castoriadis, *Imaginary Institution,* p. 29.

61 Maurice Merleau-Ponty, *Adventures of the Dialectic,* tr. J. Bien (Northwestern University Press, Evanston, Ill., 1973).

62 Vladimir Ilyich Lenin, 'Die Entwicklung des Kapitalismus in Rußland', in Lenin, *Werke,* vol. 3 (Dietz, East Berlin, 1963). Bernd Rabehl presents an interesting critique of Lenin's theory of capitalism and imperialism in Rabehl, *Marx und Lenin. Widersprüche einer ideologischen Konstruktion des 'Marxismus-Leninismus'* (Verlag für das Studium der Arbeiterbewegung, Berlin, 1973).

63 Leon Trotsky, *The Permanent Revolution* (New Park, London, 1962).

64 Merleau-Ponty, *Adventures*, p. 87.

65 This remark is not intended to conceal the fact that the so-called 'cultural-historical school' of Soviet psychology and in particular its founder, Lev Wygotski, made valuable contributions to psychological action theory.

66 In recent years these contradictions inherent in Marx's work have been examined by a number of authors, each concentrating on a different aspect. I found their ideas very helpful. On class theory, see Cohen, *Class and Civil Society*. On the theory of class consciousness, see Rainer Paris, *Klassenbewußtsein und lutersubjektivität, Zur handlungstheoretischen Reformulierung des Klassenbewußtseinskonzepts* (Campus, Frankfurt/Main, 1984). On historical methodology, see Gerhard Kluchert, *Geschichtsschreibung und Revolution. Die historischen Schriften von Karl Marx und Friedrich Engels 1846–1852* (Frommann-Holzboog, Stuttgart, 1985). On aspects of modern social theory, see John F. Rundell, *Origins of Modernity. The Origins of Modern Social Theory from Kant to Hegel to Marx* (Polity Press, Cambridge, 1987). In a broad sense, the works of – mainly British – Marxist historians and cultural sociologists also fall into this category.

67 On the literary character of Marx's piece, see John Paul Riquelme, 'The Eighteenth Brumaire of Karl Marx as Symbolic Action', *History and Theory*, 19 (1980), pp. 58–72.

68 Karl Marx, 'Vorwort' (1869), in Marx and Engels, *Werke*, vol. 8, pp. 559–60. Marx refers here to Victor Hugo, *Napoléon le petit* (Vizetelly, London, 1852) and Pierre-Joseph Proudhon, *La révolution sociale démontrée par le coup d'état du 2 décembre* (Garnier frères, Paris, 1852).

69 Marx, 'Vorwort', p. 560.

70 Cohen finds mention of five classes (*Class and Civil Society*, p. 116), while Rundell discovers six (*Origins of Modernity*, p. 150).

71 Marx, 'The Eighteenth Brumaire of Louis Bonaparte', in *Survey from Exile*, tr. B. Fowkes (Penguin, Harmondsworth, 1973), p. 173.

72 Ibid., p. 179.

73 Ibid., pp. 173–4.

74 Leon Trotsky, *History of the Russian Revolution*, tr. M. Eastman (Victor Gollancz, London, 1934).

75 Rosa Luxemburg, 'The Mass Strike, the Political Party and the Trade Unions' (1906), in *Rosa Luxemburg Speaks*, ed. Mary-Alice Waters (Pathfinder Press, New York, 1970), pp. 153–218.

76 Georg Lukács, 'Reification and the Consciousness of the Proletariat', in Lukács, *History and Class Consciousness*, pp. 83–222.

77 Antonio Gramsci, *Prison Notebooks*, ed. Quintin Hoare and Geoffrey Smith (Lawrence & Wishart, London, 1973). Gramsci was influenced by one of the most confusing figures in the history of the idea of creativity: Georges Sorel. His strange blend of production paradigm, revolution mythology and philosophy of life would be an interesting topic for a separate investigation. See Georges Sorel, *Reflections on Violence*, tr. T. E. Hulme (Allen & Unwin, London, 1916). For a brief but cogent appraisal of Sorel's

oeuvre, see Isaiah Berlin, 'George Sorel', in Berlin, *Against the Current: Essays in the History of Ideas* (Clarendon Press, Oxford, 1977), pp. 296–332.

78 For my debate with Castoriadis, see my 'Institutionalization as a Creative Process'. Essential reading for a discussion of Castoriadis' overall oeuvre is 'Pour une philosophie militante de la démocratie. Autonomie et autotransformation de la société', ed. Giovanni Busino, *Revue européenne des sciences sociales*, 27 (1989).

79 Hannah Arendt, *On Revolution* (Faber, London, 1963).

80 An important history of the concept of revolution which Arendt draws upon is Karl Griewank, *Der neuzeitliche Revolutionsbegriff* (Böhlau, Weimar, 1955). A history of the tradition of revolutionism from the late eighteenth century onwards is presented by James H. Billington, *Fire in the Minds of Men. Origins of the Revolutionary Faith* (Temple Smith, London, 1980).

81 Arendt, *Revolution*, p. 19.

82 Ibid., p. 27.

83 Still worth reading is the overview presented in Max Scheler's essay of 1913: 'Versuche einer Philosophie des Lebens, Nietzsche–Dilthey–Bergson', in Scheler, *Gesammelte Werke*, vol. 3 (Francke, Berne, 1955), pp. 311–39. Unsurpassed as a brief résumé is Otto Friedrich Bollnow, *Die Lebensphilosophie* (Springer, Berlin 1958). Another stimulating assessment is that of Eugene Rochberg-Halton, 'On the Life-Concept in Social Theory', *Comparative Social Research*, 11 (1989), pp. 319–43.

84 Herbert Schnädelbach, *Philosophy in Germany 1831–1933*, tr. E. Matthews (Cambridge University Press, Cambridge, 1984), p. 139.

85 Arthur Schopenhauer, *The World as Will and Representation*, tr. E.F.J. Payne (Falcon's Wing, Colorado, 1958), pp. 100–1.

86 See for example – although admittedly here the main emphasis is on Schelling – Odo Marquard, 'Über einige Beziehungen zwischen Ästhetik und Therapeutik in der Philosophie des neunzehnten Jahrhunderts', in Marquard, *Schwierigkeiten mit der Geschichtsphilosophie* (Suhrkamp, Frankfurt/Main, 1973), pp. 85–106, 185–208. I shall refrain in this context from considering the question as to the extent to which the tradition of psychoanalytic theory contains thoughts on the subject of creativity which go beyond the ideas of the philosophy of life and which come close to the ideas of pragmatism (which I shall cover in section 2.5 of the present chapter).

87 Schopenhauer, *The World* (our translation, JG and PK). Schopenhauer is alluding here to Goethe, *Faust*, Part One, lines 348–9.

88 Taylor, *Sources of the Self*, p. 442.

89 On Nietzsche see Taylor, *Hegel*, p. 562; on Heidegger, see Taylor, *Philosophical Papers*, vol. 1 (Cambridge University Press, Cambridge, 1985), p. 239.

90 I owe this term to Walter Schulz, *Philosophie in der veränderten Welt* (Neske, Pfullingen, 1984), p. 401.

91 In making this claim, I categorically reject Gehlen's interpretation of

Schopenhauer. Gehlen believes that the seeds of his own approach and that of the pragmatists were already present in Schopenhauer. See Arnold Gehlen, 'Die Resultate Schopenhauers' (1935), in Gehlen, *Philosophische Anthropologie und Handlungslehre*, complete edition, vol. 4 (Klostermann, Frankfurt/Main, 1983), pp. 25–49.

92 I shall develop the counter-hypothesis in greater detail in chapter 3.2.

93 Georg Simmel, *Schopenhauer and Nietzsche*, tr. H. Loiskandl, D. and M. Weinstein (University of Massachusetts Press, Amherst, Mass., 1986), p. 40.

94 Ibid., p. 50.

95 This instructive comparison is easily made by referring to the chapter entitled 'The Will' in William James, *Talks to Teachers on Psychology* (Longman, London, 1899), pp. 169–96. Unlike the many writers who regard Schopenhauer's concept of the will as in some way proto-pragmatist, Schelsky clearly recognizes the non-pragmatist character of the metaphysics of the will. See Helmut Schelsky, *Thomas Hobbes Eine politische Lehre* (1941) (Duncker und Humblot, Berlin, 1981), p. 37.

96 Friedrich Nietzsche, 'Schopenhauer als Erzieher', in Nietzsche, *Werke*, I (Hanser, Munich, 1969), pp. 287–366.

97 Walter Kaufmann, in particular, was concerned to deliver proof of this view in his book *Nietzsche. Philosopher, Psychologist – Antichrist* (Princeton University Press, Princeton, 1974).

98 Jürgen Habermas, 'Motifs of Postmetaphysical Thought', in Habermas, *Postmetaphysical Thinking: Philosophical Essays*, tr. W.M. Hohengarten (MIT Press, Cambridge, Mass., 1992 and Polity Press, Cambridge, 1992), pp. 35–60.

99 See, for example, Henri Bergson, *Creative Evolution*, tr. A. Mitchell (Macmillan, London, 1964).

100 See in particular *Einleitungn die Philosophie des Lebens*, i.e. Volumes 5 and 6 of Dilthey, *Gesammelte Schriften* (B.G. Teubner, Leipzig and Berlin, 1924), and also Dilthey, *Introduction to the Human Sciences*, tr. R. Betanzos (Harvester, Hemel Hempstead, 1989) and *Der Aufbaü der geschichtlichen Welt in den Geisteswissenschaften* (Suhrkamp, Frankfurt/Main, 1970).

101 See my essays 'Durkheim and Pragmatism', 'An Underestimated Alternative' and 'American Pragmatism and German Thought', in Joas, *Pragmatism*, pp. 55–121. There are thinkers within the German tradition of 'philosophical anthropology', notably Arnold Gehlen, who come very close to pragmatism. The definition of human action as the 'mastering of a situation by means of creative inspiration' is most clearly espoused by Erich Rothacker. See his essays: 'Das Wesen des Schöpferischen', *Blätter für deutsche Philosophie*, 10 (1937), pp. 407–29; 'Vom Geist des Erfindens', *Stahl und Eisen. Zeitschrift für das deutsche Eisenhüttenwesen*, 57 (1937), pp. 1–5 (which is the source of the above quotation, p. 2).

102 Charles S. Peirce, 'Some Consequences of Four Incapacities', in Peirce, *Collected Papers*, ed. C. Hartyshorne and P. Weiss, vol. 5 (Harvard

University Press, Cambridge, Mass., 1934), pp. 156ff. – In this section I have relied on formulations similar to those used in my *Pragmatism*.

103 In this respect, Jean Piaget applied the pragmatist programme more comprehensively and more consistently than anyone in the immediate vicinity of pragmatism itself. See, for example, Jean Piaget, *Psychology of Intelligence*, tr. M. Piercy and D.E. Barlyne (Routledge, London, 1950).

104 John Dewey, *How We Think* (Heath & Co., London, 1910). William I. Thomas and Florian Znaniecki, *The Polish Peasant in Europe and America*, 2 vols (Knopf, New York, 1926). See in particular the preamble on methodology.

105 See my book: *George Herbert Mead: A Contemporary Re-examination of His Thought*, tr. R. Meyer (Polity Press, Cambridge, 1985).

106 Dewey, *Art as Experience*, p. 290. The notion of 'control' which occurs in this passage is of course also in danger of being misinterpreted as a sign of 'instrumentalism'.

107 John Dewey, 'The Need for a Recovery of Philosophy', in Dewey et al., *Creative Intelligence. Essays in the Pragmatic Attitude* (Henry Holt, New York, 1917), pp. 3–69, here p. 63.

108 Following on from the writings of Carl Hausman on creativity, this idea has been elaborated in particular by: Douglas R. Anderson, *Creativity and the Philosophy of Ch. S. Peirce* (Nijhoff, Dordrecht, 1987).

109 Peirce, *Collected Papers*, vol. 5, p. 172 ('Lectures on Pragmatism', no. 1).

110 I refer here in particular to the following of James' writings: *The Principles of Psychology*, 2 vols (Henry Holt, New York, 1890); *Pragmatism* (Longman, New York, 1922); *The Varieties of Religious Experience* (Fontana, London, 1982). My interpretation is based on the following outstanding German critiques: Eduard Baumgarten, *Die geistigen Grundlagen des amerikanischen Gemeinwesens*, vol. 2 (Deutsche Verlagsanstalt, Frankfurt/Main, 1938), pp. 99–211; Eilert Herms, *Radical Empiricism. Studien zur Psychologie, Metaphysik und Religionstheorie William James'* (Mohn, Gütersloh, 1977); Herms, epilogue to James, *Die Vielfalt religiöser Erfahrung* (Walter, Olten, 1979), pp. 481–521.

111 George Herbert Mead, 'The Definition of the Psychical', in *Decennial Publications of the University of Chicago*, First Series, vol. 3 (Chicago, 1903), pp. 77–112.

112 This remarkable assessment is contained in Karl-Heinz Brandenburg, 'Kunst als Qualität der Handlung. John Deweys Grundlegung der Ästhetik' (dissertation, Königsberg, 1942), here p. 10.

113 John Dewey, *Experience and Nature* (1925) (Open Court, London, 1958); Dewey, *Art as Experience*; Dewey, *A Common Faith* (1934) (Yale University Press, Yale, New Haven, Conn., 1980); Dewey, *Theory of Valuation* (University of Chicago Press, Chicago, 1939).

114 George Herbert Mead, 'The Nature of Aesthetic Experience', in Mead, *Selected Writings*, ed. Andrew Reck (Bobbs-Merrill, Indianapolis, 1964), pp. 294–305. – John Dewey, 'Peirce's Theory of Quality', *Journal of*

Philosophy, 32 (1935), pp. 701–8. Here Dewey bases his ideas on Peirce's category of 'firstness' and his conception of a 'phenomenology', as used for example in the second of the 'Lectures on Pragmatism' of 1903. Cf. Peirce, *Collected Papers*, vol. 5, pp. 41ff.

115 Dewey, *Art as Experience*, p. 3.
116 Ibid., p. 35.
117 Ibid.
118 Ibid., p. 77.
119 Ibid., pp. 80–1.
120 John Dewey, 'Construction and Criticism', in Dewey, *Later Works*, vol. 5 (1929/30) (Southern Illinois University Press, Carbondale, Ill., 1988), pp. 127–43. The aphorism I have chosen as a motto for the present volume is taken from this essay (p. 143).
121 Dewey, *Art as Experience*, pp. 65–6.
122 Ibid., p. 66.
123 An excellent and comprehensive description and discussion of Dewey's theory of art is to be found in Thomas M. Alexander, *John Dewey's Theory of Art, Experience and Nature: The Horizons of Feeling* (SUNY, Albany, NY, 1987). A recent description, written more from a historical perspective than as an examination of Dewey's ideas as a philosophical system, is Westbrook's superb portrait. See chapter 11 ('Consummatory Experience') in Robert B. Westbrook, *John Dewey and American Democracy* (Cornell University Press, Ithaca, NY, 1991). – Of the sparse German literature on the subject, mention should be made of Thomas Baumeister, 'Kunst als Erfahrung', *Zeitschrift für philosophische Forschung*, 37 (1983), pp. 616–24. Cursory reference to Dewey is also made in a whole series of recent German works on aesthetics and literary theory. See, for example, Wolfgang Iser, *The Act of Reading* (Johns Hopkins University Press, Baltimore, 1978), pp. 216ff; Hans Robert Jauss, *Aesthetic Experience*, tr. M. Shaw (University of Minnesota Press, Minneapolis, 1982); Martin Seel, *Die Kunst der Entzweiung. Zum Begriff der ästhetischen Rationalität* (Suhrkamp, Frankfurt/Main, 1985). A more comprehensive study which attempts to redress the one-sidedness of other authors is the doctoral thesis by Ulrich Engler, *Kritik der Erfahrung. Die Bedeutung der ästhetischen Erfahrung in der Philosophie John Deweys* (Königshausen & Neumann, Würzburg, 1992).
124 Dewey, *A Common Faith*, p. 17.
125 Ibid.
126 Ibid., p. 20.
127 Ibid., p. 49. – Dewey's theory of religion positively cries out to be compared systematically with the corresponding conceptions in Durkheim and Weber. However, I am unaware of any such comparison in the literature.

Chapter 3   *Situation – Corporeality – Sociality*

1 In contemporary German philosophy two authors particularly have shown an awareness of the problems of such an approach. The one author's work is not far removed from Karl-Otto Apel's 'transcendental pragmatics', but goes a decisive step further in the respect which is of interest here; the other thinker has his roots in phenomenology, in particular that of Maurice Merleau-Ponty. See Dietrich Böhler's book *Rekonstruktive Pragmatik. Von der Bewußtseinsphilosophie zur Kommunikationsreflexion: Neubegründung der praktischen Wissenschaften und Philosophie* (Suhrkamp, Frankfurt/Main, 1985), which has to date not received the attention it merits, particularly as it provides fruitful insights for action theory. The other thinker is Bernhard Waldenfels; see his book *Ordnung im Zwielicht* (Suhrkamp, Frankfurt/Main, 1987), pp. 41–2 and pp. 212–13 on Böhler.

2 Sociological discussions about Habermas, which concentrate entirely on his distinction between lifeworld and system, almost completely ignore this point; for me, it is the major issue behind my rejection of Habermas' position. See my essay, 'The Unhappy Marriage of Hermeneutics and Functionalism', in *Communicative Action*, ed. Axel Honneth and Hans Joas, tr. J. Gaines and D. Jones (Polity Press, Cambridge, 1991), pp. 97–118, reprinted in my *Pragmatism and Social Theory*, tr. J. Gaines, R. Meyer and S. Minner (University of Chicago Press, Chicago, 1993), pp. 125–53. The anti-critique put forward by Thomas Saretzki in defence of Habermas and attacking my critique rests on a misunderstanding of my intentions here. See Thomas Saretzki, 'Collective Action versus Functionalism? Some Remarks Concerning Hans Joas's Critique', *Praxis International*, 8 (1988), pp. 52–72.

3 As the references in this chapter will make clear, such a reconstructive introduction is approximated by various thinkers in the phenomenological tradition, despite their different historical point of departure. For an application of this theory in philosophy, see Kiyokazu Washida, 'Handlung, Leib und Institution – Perspektiven einer phänomenologischen Handlungstheorie', in *Japanische Beiträge zur Phänomenologie*, ed. Yoshihoro Nitta (Alber, Freiburg, 1984), pp. 319–49. For an overview from a sociological point of view see John Heritage, 'Ethnomethodology', in *Social Theory Today*, ed. Anthony Giddens and Jonathan Turner (Polity Press, Cambridge, 1987), pp. 224–72. There remains, admittedly, a difference between the phenomenological programme of Alfred Schütz and the procedure I have adopted here. It is the difference that obtains between a phenomenologically informed analysis of the constitution of action which takes consciousness as its starting point, and a pragmatist method, which, taking action as its starting point, brings to light the assumptions that underlie specific models of action. See Alfred Schütz, *The Phenomenology*

of the Social World, tr. G. Walsh and F. Lehnert (Northwestern University Press, Evanston, Ill., 1967) and *Collected Papers*, 3 vols (Nijhoff, The Hague, 1971/2). For an interpretation of Schütz, I recommend the excellent work by Ilja Srubar, *Kosmion. Die Genese der pragmatischen Lebenswelttheorie von Alfred Schütz und ihr anthropologischer Hintergrund* (Suhrkamp, Frankfurt/ Main, 1988), which builds numerous bridges to non-phenomenological thought.

4 One of the few places where I have discovered a similar programme is in the feminist theory of Dorothy Smith. Cf. Dorothy Smith, 'A Sociology for Women', in *The Prism of Sex. Essays in the Sociology of Knowledge*, ed. J. A. Sherman and E. T. Beck (University of Wisconsin Press, Madison, 1979), pp. 135–87, esp. pp. 149ff. Unlike others, Smith does not call for a theory of emotional action to supplement a theory of rational action, but rather criticizes the implicit assumptions that lie behind an orientation towards the model of rational action, as exemplified in the work of Talcott Parsons and Alfred Schütz. For an example of the demand for a theory of emotional action as a supplement to rationalistic and normativistic models, see Helena Flam, 'Emotional Man', *International Sociology*, 5 (1990), pp. 39–56 and pp. 225–34.

5 Max Weber, 'Die "Objektivität" sozialwissenschaftlicher und sozialpolitischer Erkenntnis', in Weber, *Gesammelte Aufsätze zur Wissenschaftslehre* (Mohr, Tübingen, 1973), pp. 146–214, here p. 149.

6 See chapter 1 of the present study, and Charles Camic, '"Structure" after 50 Years: The Anatomy of a Charter', *American Journal of Sociology*, 95 (1989), pp. 62ff.

7 Niklas Luhmann, 'Zweck – Herrschaft – System. Grundbegriffe und Prämissen Max Webers', in *Bürokratische Organisation*, ed. Renate Mayntz (Kiepenheuer & Witsch, Cologne, 1968), pp. 36–55; Luhmann, *Zweckbegriff und Systemrationalität. Über die Funktion von Zwecken in sozialen Systemen* (Mohr, Tübingen, 1968). Jürgen Habermas must, needless to say, also be included among the critics of an exclusively teleological interpretation of action inasmuch as he draws a sharp distinction between communicative action and 'success-oriented', teleological action. Yet in so doing, he excludes non-communicative action from the critique of the teleological interpretation of action which interests us here. This criticism of Habermas has been raised by Ernst Tugendhat, albeit on the basis of an unproblematized understanding of teleological structure. See Tugendhat, 'Habermas on Communicative Action', in *Social Action*, ed. Gottfried Seebass and Raimo Tuomela (Reidel, Dordrecht, 1985), pp. 179–86.

8 For a critique of Luhmann's justification and application of functional statements, see chapter 4.2 of the present study.

9 Luhmann, 'Zweck', p. 37.

10 Ibid., p. 48.

11 Luhmann, *Zweckbegriff*, p. 29.

12 Ibid., p. 44.

13 Typical in this respect: John Dewey, *Democracy and Education* (1916) (Macmillan, New York, 1969) pp. 117ff; Dewey, *Theory of Valuation* (University of Chicago Press, Chicago, 1939), esp. pp. 33ff. For secondary literature on this point, see in particular the following works: Eduard Baumgarten, *Die geistigen Grundlagen des amerikanischen Gemeinwesens*, vol. 2 (Deutsche Verlagsanstalt, Frankfurt/Main, 1938), pp. 288ff; Aldo Visalberghi, 'Remarks on Dewey's conception of Ends and Means', *Journal of Philosophy*, 50 (1953), pp. 737–53; and now also J. E. Tiles, *Dewey* (Routledge, London, 1988), pp. 154ff.

14 See esp. John Dewey, *Experience and Nature* (1925) (Open Court, London, 1958); but also, in the same vein: George Herbert Mead, *Philosophy of the Present* (Open Court, La Salle, Ill., 1932).

15 Dewey, *Democracy*, p. 129.

16 Cf. Dewey, *Valuation*, p. 42.

17 Dewey, *Democracy*, pp. 241–2.

18 Cf. Ferdinand Tönnies, 'Zweck und Mittel im sozialen Leben', in *Hauptprobleme der Soziologie. Erinnerungsgabe für Max Weber*, vol. 1 (Duncker und Humblot, Munich and Leipzig, 1923), pp. 235–70; Georg Simmel, *Lebensanschauung. Vier metaphysische Kapitel* (Duncker und Humblot, Munich and Leipzig, 1918), esp. pp. 37–45; Martin Heidegger, *Being and Time*, tr. J. Macquarrie and E. Robinson (Blackwell, Oxford, 1987), pp. 114 and 279ff.

19 For what is probably the most accomplished critique of such attempts on the basis of modern philosophy, see Hubert L. Dreyfus, *What Computers Can't Do – The Limits of Artificial Intelligence* (Harper and Row, New York, 1979). Another excellent work which directs the discussion towards a theory of meaning that is compatible with the theory of the creativity of action is: Mark Johnson, *The Body in the Mind. The Bodily Basis of Meaning, Imagination, and Reason* (University of Chicago Press, Chicago, 1987).

20 Alongside the works of the pragmatists and Heidegger's analysis of the present-at-hand and ready-at-hand in *Being and Time* stands the classic text: Maurice Merleau-Ponty, *Phenomenology of Perception*, tr. C. Smith (Routledge, London, 1982). – For an excellent concise interpretation which fits exactly into the line of thought we have been developing here, see Charles Taylor, 'Embodied Agency', in *Merleau-Ponty. Critical Essays*, ed. Henry Pietersma (University Press of America, Washington, DC, 1990), pp. 1–21.

21 Cf. Dreyfus, *What Computers*, esp. pp. 231–85.

22 Böhler, *Rekonstruktive Pragmatik*, p. 252.

23 Ibid., pp. 272–3.

24 C. Wright Mills, 'Situated Action and Vocabularies of Motive' (1940), in Mills, *Power, Politics and People. Collected Essays*, ed. I.L. Horowitz (Oxford University Press, London, 1967), pp. 439–52.

25 For example, Lucy Suchman, 'Representing Practice in Cognitive Science', *Human Studies*, 11 (1988), pp. 305–25. Within analytical philosophy we

find an interesting approximation to this view in John Searle's distinction, so crucial to his theory of intentionality, between intentions which
precede action and intentions in action. Searle also establishes that
actions may be intentional, even though no intention preceded them.
Conversely, even if an intention did precede the action, that action
may still involve many partial or secondary actions which were not
included in the intention. Despite the fact that Searle comes a step closer
to a non-teleologial interpretation of action here, the thrust of his theory
as a whole is still dependent on a 'Cartesian' separation of intellectual
and physical processes. See John Searle, *Intentionality. Essays in the
Philosophy of Mind* (Cambridge University Press, Cambridge, 1983). For a
critique, see, inter alia, Bernhard Waldenfels, 'Mens sive cerebrum.
Intentionalität in mentalistischer Sicht', *Philosophische Rundschau*, 31
(1984), pp. 22–52.

26 Cf. Harold Garfinkel, *Studies in Ethnomethodology* (Polity Press, Cambridge, 1984), p. 66.

27 Dreyfus, *What Computers*, p. 277.

28 Donald W. Winnicott, *Playing and Reality* (Penguin, Harmondsworth,
1974). For an interesting comparative study of Winnicott's theory of
children's play and that of George Herbert Mead, see Robin Das and
Doyle McCarthy, 'The Cognitive and Emotional Significance of Play in
Child Development: G. H. Mead and D. W. Winnicott', *Sociological Studies
of Child Development*, 1 (1986), pp. 35–53. This comparison emphasizes
that whereas Mead stresses the social origins of self-awareness, Winnicott
foregrounds the constitution of the differentiation between the inner and
the external worlds. In many respects, Cornelius Castoriadis' argument is
similar to that of Winnicott. See Castoriadis, *The Imaginary Institution of
Society*, tr. K. Blamey (Polity Press, Cambridge, 1987), pp. 273ff.

29 Winnicott, *Playing*, p. 2.

30 Ibid., p. 12.

31 Ibid.

32 Ibid., p. 51.

33 Ibid., p. 65.

34 In a multifaceted book, Bryan Turner shows, if somewhat unsystemati-
cally, that this is the case: *The Body and Society. Explorations in Social Theory*
(Blackwell, Oxford, 1984).

35 Anthony Giddens, *The Constitution of Society* (Polity Press, Cambridge,
1984), p. 157.

36 Cf. Erving Goffman's analysis of 'front stage' and 'back stage' in various
points in his oeuvre, e.g. in *The Presentation of Self in Everyday Life*
(Edinburgh University Press, Edinburgh, 1956).

37 Merleau-Ponty, *Phenomenology of Perception*, pp. 163–4. Jon Elster treats
this and similar phenomena under the heading of 'states that are
essentially by-products' in the framework of his conception of rational
action, which stretches the notion to its very limits. Cf. Elster, *Sour Grapes*.

Studies in the Subversion of Rationality (Cambridge University Press, Cambridge 1983), pp. 43–108.

38 Helmuth Plessner, 'Lachen und Weinen' (1941), in his *Philosophische Anthropologie* (Suhrkamp, Frankfurt/Main, 1970), pp. 11–171. For an interpretation of Plessner's anthropology, see also Axel Honneth and Hans Joas, *Social Action and Human Nature*, tr. R. Meyer (Cambridge University Press, Cambridge, 1988), pp. 70–90.

39 Plessner, 'Lachen und Weinen', p. 74.

40 Ibid., p. 153.

41 Ibid., p. 154.

42 Émile Durkheim, 'The Dualism of Human Nature and Its Social Conditions', in *Émile Durkheim on Morality and Society*, ed. Robert Bellah (University of Chicago Press, Chicago, 1973), pp. 149–63.

43 For example, Talcott Parsons, *Social Structure and Personality* (Collier-Macmillan, London, 1970). For a critique of his approach see Karola Brede, *Sozioanalyse psychosomatischer Störungen. Zum Verhältnis von Soziologie und psychosomatischer Medizin* (Athenäum, Frankfurt/Main, 1972).

44 Jürgen Habermas, 'Anthropologie', in *Philosophie*, ed. Alwin Diemer and Ivo Frenzel (Fischer, Frankfurt/Main, 1958), pp. 18–35.

45 I have attempted to show this in my essay 'A Sociological Transformation of the Philosophy of Praxis: Anthony Giddens's Theory of Structuration', *International Sociology*, 2 (1987), pp. 13–26 (now also in my *Pragmatism*, pp. 172–87).

46 A favourable exception to this rule is Vernon Reynolds, *The Biology of Human Action*, 2nd edn (W.H. Freeman, San Francisco, 1980).

47 See Honneth and Joas, *Social Action*.

48 John Dewey, *Human Nature and Conduct* (Allen & Unwin, London, 1922).

49 Jean Piaget, *Biology and Knowledge*, tr. B. Walsh (Edinburgh University Press, Edinburgh, 1971).

50 Arnold Gehlen, *Man, His Nature and Place in the World* (1940), tr. C. McMillan and K. Pillemer, with an introduction by K. S. Rehberg (Columbia University Press, New York, 1988).

51 The other failing, namely an insufficient consideration of the sociality of action, is something Axel Honneth and I have already endeavoured to show (*Social Action*, pp. 64ff). On the proposition that the ability to act has a primarily social origin, see section 3.3 of this chapter. – I first became aware of the failings of Gehlen's theory with regard to his conception of instincts from a reading of Markus Kaiser's 'Individuelle Vergesellschaftung in naturhistorischer Sicht. Ein Beitrag zur soziologischen Anthropologie' (Philosophical dissertation, Free University of Berlin, 1987).

52 Konrad Lorenz, *Über tierisches und menschliches Verhalten*, Gesammelte Abhandlungen, 2 vols (Piper, Munich, 1965).

53 I found the best survey of research to date in Michel Bernard, *Le corps* (Éditions Universitaires, Paris, 1976). See also Peter Paulus, *Zur Erfahrung*

des eigenen Körpers (Beltz, Weinheim, 1982); Douwe Tiemersma, '"Body-Image" and "Body-Schema" in the Existential Phenomenology of Merleau-Ponty', *Journal of the British Society for Phenomenology*, 13 (1982), pp. 246–55.

54 Paul Schilder, *Das Körperschema. Ein Beitrag zur Lehre vom Bewußtsein des eigenen Körpers* (Julius Springer, Berlin, 1923) and his *The Image and Appearance of the Human Body. Studies in the Constructive Energies of the Psyche* (Kegan Paul & Co., New York, 1935).

55 A glance at this critique of Schilder is an instructive case of how his innovative ideas were then compressed back into a Cartesian framework. See Klaus Conrad, 'Das Körperschema. Eine kritische Studie und der Versuch ihrer Revision', *Zeitschrift für die gesamte Neurologie und Psychiatrie* 147 (1933), pp. 346–69.

56 Schilder, *Image*, esp. pp. 286ff.

57 Ibid., pp. 287–8.

58 Ibid., p. 15.

59 With regard to the issue that is of interest to us here, the following example of later psychoanalytic research is especially important: Margaret S. Mahler, *The Birth of the Human Infant* (Hutchinson, London, 1975).

60 Merleau-Ponty, *Phenomenology*, esp. pp. 98ff. He appears to have taken only Schilder's first book, the one in German, into account.

61 See chapter 2.5 of the present study.

62 Merleau-Ponty, *Phenomenology*, pp. 81–2.

63 Ibid., p. 88.

64 See ibid., pp. 346–65.

65 Above all Merleau-Ponty, 'Les relations avec autrui chez l'enfant', *Bulletin de psychologie*, 18 (1964), pp. 295–336. For an interesting discussion of the achievements and shortcomings of Merleau-Ponty's approach see, among others, Herman Coenen, 'Leiblichkeit und Sozialität. Ein Grundproblem der phänomenologischen Soziologie', *Philosophisches Jahrbuch*, 86 (1979), pp. 239–61; Martin C. Dillon, 'Merleau-Ponty and the Psychogenesis of the Self', *Journal of Phenomenological Psychology*, 9 (1978), pp. 84–98; Käte Meyer-Drawe, *Leiblichkeit und Sozialität. Phänomenologische Beiträge zu einer pädagogischen Theorie der Inter-Subjektivität* (Fink, Munich, 1984), esp. pp. 133ff.

66 Jacques Lacan, *Écrits. A Selection*, tr. A. Sheridan (Tavistock, London, 1980).

67 George Herbert Mead, untitled manuscript, starting with the words 'The human individual has as part of his self the physical organism', University of Chicago, *Mead-Papers*, Box 1, Folder 4.

68 Ibid., p. 5. Strictly speaking, Mead probably does not mean here that a palate is an object of experience, but that it is a source of stimuli like a tree or a mountain, because he is interested precisely in exploring the specific quality of a person's own body as an object.

69 George Herbert Mead, *Philosophy of the Act* (University of Chicago Press, Chicago, 1938), p. 266.

70 See chapter 7 of my *George Herbert Mead: A Contemporary Re-examination of His Thought*, tr. R. Meyer (Polity Press, Cambridge, 1985).

71 Mead, 'The human individual', p. 20.

72 Bernard, *Le corps*, pp. 102ff.

73 See chapter 1 of the present study, particularly chapters 1.2 and 1.3.

74 For an excellent refutation of this polemic and a discussion of concepts such as 'patchwork-identity' see Jürgen Straub, 'Identitätstheorie im Übergang?', *Sozialwissenschaftliche Literaturrundschau*, 23 (1991), pp. 49–71.

75 See James Engell, *The Creative Imagination. Enlightenment to Romanticism* (Harvard University Press, Cambridge, Mass., 1981), pp. 143–4.

76 Adam Smith, *Theory of Moral Sentiments* (Clarendon Press, Oxford, 1976).

77 Max Scheler, *The Notion of Sympathy*, tr. P. Heath (Routledge, London, 1979).

78 Ibid., p. 73 and p. 25.

79 Ibid.

80 George Herbert Mead, *Mind, Self and Society* (University of Chicago Press, Chicago, 1934) and also his *Selected Writings*, ed. Andrew Reck (Bobbs-Merrill, Indianapolis, 1964). For a description of Mead's importance for research into socialization, see my 'Role Theories and Socialization Research', in *Perspectives on Sociological Theory, Vol 2: Micro-sociological Theory*, ed. H.J. Helle and S.N. Eisenstadt (Sage, London, 1985), pp. 37–53 (reprinted in an abridged version in my *Pragmatism*, pp. 238–61); Lothar Krappmann, 'Mead und die Sozialisationsforschung', in *Das Problem der Intersubjektivität*, ed. Hans Joas (Suhrkamp, Frankfurt/Main, 1985), pp. 156–78. In the following I shall take up remarks I have made elsewhere.

81 A good survey is offered by Dieter Geulen in his *Das vergesellschaftete Subjekt. Zur Grundlegung der Sozialisationstheorie* (Suhrkamp, Frankfurt/Main, 1977).

82 For trenchant criticism of Piaget in this respect see Werner van de Voort, 'Die Bedeutung von Vorformen des kommunikativen Handelns für die Entwicklung der vorsprachlichen Intelligenz beim Kinde', in *Ansätze zur materialistischen Sprachtheorie*, ed. Anton Leist (Scriptor, Kronberg, 1975), pp. 206–33; Monika Keller, *Kognitive Entwicklung und soziale Kompetenz. Zur Entstehung der Rollenübernahme in der Familie und ihrer Bedeutung für den Schulerfolg* (Klett, Stuttgart, 1976).

83 An exemplary analysis of this ability is given in Donald W. Winnicott's *The Maturational Processes and the Facilitating Environment* (Karnac, London, 1990); good surveys are to be found in Morris N. Eagle, *Recent Developments in Psychoanalysis* (McGraw Hill, Maidenhead, 1984); Wolfgang Mertens, 'Psychoanalytische Theorien und Forschungsbefunde', in *Neues Handbuch der Sozialisationsforschung*, ed. Klaus Hurrelmann and Dieter Ulich (Beltz, Weinheim, 1991), pp. 77–98.

84 Cf., in particular, the essays in Parsons, *Social Structure and Personality*.

For an interesting critique of Parsons from precisely this present vantage point, see Hans-Joachim Busch, *Interaktion und innere Natur* (Campus, Frankfurt/Main, 1985).

85 George Herbert Mead, *Mind, Self and Society* (Chicago University Press, Chicago, 1934), p. 7.

86 For what will no doubt go down as a classic attempt to synthesize different currents in this regard, see Jürgen Habermas, *Theory of Communicative Action*, and in particular his introduction of the concept of lifeworld in vol. 2, tr. T. McCarthy (Beacon Press, Boston, 1987 and Polity Press, Cambridge, 1987), pp. 113–198.

87 For a discussion that takes up Mead's work and opposes Elster's position, see Aanund Haga, 'Interaktion und Intentionalität. Bemerkungen zum Versuch, die Sozialwissenschaften spiel- und entscheidungstheoretisch zu rekonstruieren', in *Die pragmatische Wende*, ed. Dietrich Böhler, Tore Nordenstam and Gunnar Skirbekk (Suhrkamp, Frankfurt/Main, 1986), pp. 91–109.

88 Nietzsche did this in a manner still deeply indebted to the objects of the scholarly classics in his *The Birth of Tragedy*, tr. R. Hollingdale (Anchor Press, New York, 1988). For a superb reconstruction of the development of these ideas, see Jürgen Habermas, *The Philosophical Discourse of Modernity*, tr. F. Lawrence (Polity Press, Cambridge, 1987), above all in the chapters on Nietzsche and Bataille. Strangely enough, however, Habermas leaves out the treatment of the phenomena in question by the positivist sciences, with which I will deal in the following part of this chapter.

89 See chapter 2.5 of the present study.

90 This is not true of thought in France, in which there was constant contact between the two domains. See Georges Bataille, *Eroticism*, tr. M. Dalwood (Calder, London, 1962); Michel Maffesoli, *L'ombre de Dionysos – Contribution à une sociologie de l'orgie* (Méridiens/Anthropos, Paris, 1982); Georges Balandier, *Le désordre* (Fayard, Paris, 1988).

91 On the background to this, see chapter 1.5 of the present study.

92 Émile Durkheim, *The Elementary Forms of the Religious Life*, tr. J.W. Swain (Allen & Unwin, London, 1976), p. 211.

93 Ibid., p. 210.

94 Ibid.

95 Ibid., pp. 215–16.

96 Ibid., p. 218.

97 Victor Turner's work is of major importance here, although he only mentions in passing the degree to which he is evidently indebted to Durkheim's theory of religion. See Victor Turner, *The Ritual Process* (Cornell University Press, Ithaca, NY, 1969); *From Ritual to Theater* (PAJ Publications, New York, 1982). He writes there (*From Ritual*, p. 57) explicitly about the experience of a loss of the ego.

98 Turner, *Ritual Process*, p. 92.

Chapter 4   Creative Democracy

1 See the introduction to the third chapter of this book, esp. p. 146.
2 Charles Camic has adduced comprehensive evidence to remind us that not only pragmatism, but also the classical sociologists (Durkheim, Weber), unquestioningly resorted to using concepts like 'habit' etc. It was only when behaviourist psychology gave a reductionistic meaning to these concepts of 'habits', and when Thomas, Park and the early Parsons took care to distance sociological action theory from behaviourism, that this dimension disappeared from sociological writings. The development of a theory of the creativity of action does not contradict the rediscovery of the routine dimensions of action; on the contrary, these two dimensions complement each other in their joint critique of rationalist and normativist action models. See Charles Camic, 'The Matter of Habit', *American Journal of Sociology*, 91 (1986), pp. 1039–87.
3 See (among others) Luhmann's critique of the notion of purpose in the sociology of organization; cf. chapter 3.1 above.
4 This line is pursued in a very interesting essay by Klaus Peter Japp, based on the ideas of Charles Perrow. See Japp, 'Selbsterzeugung oder Fremdverschulden: Thesen zum Rationalismus in den Theorien sozialer Bewegungen', *Soziale Welt*, 35 (1984), pp. 313–29.
5 John Dewey, 'Creative Democracy: The Task Before Us', in *The Philosopher of the Common Man. Essays in Honor of John Dewey to Celebrate His Eightieth Birthday*, ed. Sidney Ratner (Greenwood Press, New York, 1940), pp. 220–8.
6 The best overviews that I know of are: Gary T. Marx and James L. Wood, 'Strands of Theory and Research in Collective Behavior', *Annual Review of Sociology*, 1 (1975), pp. 363–428; James B. Rule, *Theories of Civil Violence* (University of California Press, Berkeley, 1988); Joachim Raschke, *Soziale Bewegungen. Ein historisch-systematischer Grundriß* (Campus, Frankfurt/ Main, 1985); Ron Eyerman and Andrew Jamison, *Social Movements. A Cognitive Approach* (Polity Press, Cambridge, 1991), chapter 1, pp. 10–44.
7 In particular it is Piotr Sztompka who has contributed significantly to this point of view in recent years. See, for example, Sztompka, 'Social Movements: Structures in Statu Nascendi', *Revue internationale de sociologie*, 2 (1989), pp. 124–55.
8 The most important proponent of the 'relative deprivation' theory of processes of collective action is Ted Robert Gurr, *Why Men Rebel* (Princeton University Press, Princeton, 1970). For a critique on Gurr, see Rule, *Civil Violence*, pp. 200–23.
9 Charles Tilly, Louise Tilly and Richard Tilly, *The Rebellious Century* (Harvard University Press, Cambridge, Mass., 1975).
10 Mancur Olson, *The Logic of Collective Action* (Harvard University Press, Cambridge, Mass., 1965).

11 Ibid., p. 1.

12 Ibid., p. 33.

13 Ibid., p. 6.

14 Ibid., p. 65.

15 The entire argumentation of the first chapter about the importance of normative orientations and the reconstructive introduction of rational action in the third chapter are naturally relevant here – an excellent critique has been presented by: Ralph H. Turner, 'The Use and Misuse of Rational Models in Collective Behavior and Social Psychology', *Archives européennes de sociologie*, 32 (1991), pp. 84–108.

16 For example, John D. McCarthy and Mayer N. Zald, 'Resource Mobilization and Social Movements: A Partial Theory', *American Journal of Sociology*, 82 (1977), pp. 1212–41.

17 Neil Smelser, *Theory of Collective Behavior* (Routledge & Kegan Paul, London, 1962).

18 Ibid., p. 9.

19 Ibid., pp. 18–19.

20 One need not go so far as James Rule, who accuses Smelser of providing no more than a definition: 'Smelser's theory of collective behavior is an elaboration of a definition. It provides a showcase for empirical materials studied under the rubric of collective behavior' (*Civil Violence*, p. 167).

21 An approach which is empirically stimulating but theoretically unsatisfying is that taken by Offe and Wiesenthal, which involves a simple interlinking of the rational and norm models of collective action, so that, for example, the organizational problems of the employers are analysed according to the rational model, but those of the employees according to the norm model. This does not resolve the issue of a comprehensive theory on collective action which may, under certain conditions, be simplified in the direction of the norm or the rational model. See Claus Offe and Helmut Wiesenthal, 'Two Logics of Collective Action: Theoretical Notes on Social Class and Organizational Form', *Political Power and Social Theory*, 1 (1980), pp. 67–115.

22 Additional mention should be made of Francesco Alberoni's original sketch: *Movement and Institution* (Columbia University Press, New York, 1984).

23 Especially informative here is Robert Park's German doctoral thesis: Robert Park, *The Crowd and the Public*, tr. C. Elsner (Chicago University Press, Chicago, 1972).

24 Robert Park and Ernest Burgess, *Introduction to the Science of Sociology* (University of Chicago Press, Chicago, 1921). For a history of this tradition in research, see also my 'Symbolic Interactionism', in *Social Theory Today*, ed. Anthony Giddens and Jonathan Turner (Polity Press, Cambridge, 1987), pp. 82–115. Now also to be found as 'Pragmatism in American Sociology', in Joas, *Pragmatism and Social Theory*, tr. J. Gaines, R. Meyer and S. Minner (University of Chicago Press, Chicago, 1993), pp. 14–51.

25 Especially important are two extensive summaries by Herbert Blumer: 'The Field of Collective Behavior', in *Principles of Sociology*, ed. Alfred McClung Lee (Barnes & Noble, New York, 1951) (1st edn 1939), pp. 165–222; and 'Collective Behavior', in *Review of Sociology*, ed. Joseph Gittler (John Wiley & Sons, New York, 1957), pp. 127–58.

26 Of significance for the further development of this theory: Ralph Turner and Lewis Killian, *Collective Behavior* (Prentice Hall, Englewood Cliffs, NJ, 1972). An excellent overview is: Louis Zurcher and David Snow, 'Collective Behaviour: Social Movements', in *Social Psychology*, ed. Morris Rosenberg and Ralph Turner (Basic Books, New York, 1981), pp. 447–82.

27 Alain Touraine, 'An Introduction to the Study of Social Movements', *Social Research*, 52 (1985), pp. 749–87.

28 This formulation can be found in Touraine's response to Dieter Rucht's analysis of his research, which is probably the most thorough to date: Dieter Rucht, 'Sociological Theory as a Theory of Social Movements? A Critique of Alain Touraine', in *Research on Social Movements. The State of the Art in Western Europe and the USA*, ed. Dieter Rucht (Campus, Frankfurt/Main, 1991), pp. 355–84. For Touraine's reply, see: 'Commentary on Dieter Rucht's Critique', ibid., pp. 385–91, here p. 389.

29 Anthony Giddens, 'Functionalism: Après la lutte', *Social Research*, 43 (1976), pp. 325–66.

30 Jon Elster, *Ulysses and the Sirens* (Cambridge University Press, Cambridge, 1979); Elster, 'Marxism, Functionalism, and Game Theory', *Theory and Society*, 11 (1982), pp. 453–82.

31 Jürgen Habermas, *Theory of Communicative Action*, 2 vols, tr. T. McCarthy (Beacon Press, Boston, 1984/1987 and Polity Press, Cambridge, 1991/1987).

32 Anthony Giddens, *The Constitution of Society* (Polity Press, Cambridge, 1984), p. 283.

33 Niklas Luhmann, *Soziologische Aufklärung*, vol. 1 (Westdeutscher Verlag, Opladen, 1970). See esp. pp. 9–53.

34 Niklas Luhmann, *Soziale Systeme* (Suhrkamp, Frankfurt/Main, 1984).

35 Correspondingly, an evaluation of Luhmann's justification of the functional method is not tantamount to an evaluation of the accomplishments of his theoretical work as a whole. Particularly since its 'autopoietic' turn, his systems theory has incorporated many motifs which have their roots in creativity. As in the tradition of the philosophy of life, however, Luhmann places creativity on a deeper level than that of human action. For a discussion of Luhmann, see also chapters 3.1 and 4.3 of the present volume.

36 Luhmann, *Soziologische Aufklärung*, vol. 1, p. 18.

37 Luhmann, *Soziale Systeme*, pp. 83–4.

38 Ibid., pp. 84–5.

39 Gerald Cohen, 'Functional Explanation, Consequence Explanation, and Marxism', *Inquiry*, 25 (1982), pp. 27–56.

40 Luhmann, *Soziologische Aufklärung*, vol. 1, p. 22.
41 Jürgen Habermas and Niklas Luhmann, *Theorie der Gesellschaft oder Sozialtechnologie* (Suhrkamp, Frankfurt/Main, 1971), p. 153.
42 Ibid., p. 299.
43 Luhmann, *Soziale Systeme*, p. 86.
44 Jürgen Habermas, *The Philosophical Discourse of Modernity*, tr. F. Lawrence (Polity Press, Cambridge, 1987), pp. 368–85.
45 Thomas McCarthy, 'Complexity and Democracy: or the Seducements of Systems Theory', in *Communicative Action*, ed. Axel Honneth and Hans Joas, tr. J. Gaines and D. Jones (Polity Press, Cambridge, 1991), pp. 119–39.
46 Hans Joas, 'The Unhappy Marriage of Hermeneutics and Functionalism: Jürgen Habermas's Theory of Communicative Action', in *Communicative Action*, pp. 97–118 and reprinted in Joas, *Pragmatism*, pp. 125–53.
47 Axel Honneth, *The Critique of Power*, tr. K. Baynes (MIT, Cambridge, Mass., 1991).
48 Anthony Giddens, 'Reason without Revolution? Habermas' *Theorie des kommunikativen Handelns*', in *Habermas and Modernity*, ed. Richard Bernstein (Polity Press, Cambridge, 1985), pp. 95–121, here p. 119.
49 Jürgen Habermas, 'A Reply', in *Communicative Action*, pp. 214–64.
50 Habermas and Luhmann, *Gesellschaft oder Sozialtechnologie*, p. 270.
51 Ibid., p. 271.
52 Luhmann, *Soziale Systeme*, p. 30.
53 Richard Münch, 'Teleonomie und voluntaristische Handlungstheorie. Replik auf Helmut Fehr', *Soziale Welt*, 31 (1980), pp. 499–511, here p. 503.
54 Hans Joas, 'The Antinomies of Neofunctionalism. A Critical Essay on Jeffrey Alexander', *Inquiry*, 31 (1988), pp. 471–94 (now also in my *Pragmatism*, pp. 188–213).
55 Jeffrey Alexander, *Theoretical Logic in Sociology, Vol. IV: The Modern Reconstruction of Classical Thought: Talcott Parsons* (University of California Press, Berkeley, 1983), p. 271.
56 *Neofunctionalism*, ed. Jeffrey Alexander (Sage, London, 1985).
57 Amitai Etzioni, *The Active Society* (Free Press, New York, 1968), p. 125.
58 Giddens, *Constitution of Society*, p. 25.
59 Hans-Ulrich Wehler, *Modernisierungstheorie und Geschichte* (Vandenhoeck & Ruprecht, Göttingen, 1975), p. 11.
60 I shall not cite examples of every one of these arguments as my intention is not to write a history of the discussion but merely to provide an overview of weaknesses in differentiation theory. A useful outline of some of the objections, in particular with regard to the causes of differentiation, is to be found in Uwe Schimank, 'Der mangelnde Akteurbezug systemtheoretischer Erklärungen gesellschaftlicher Differenzierung', *Zeitschrift für Soziologie*, 14 (1985), pp. 421–34. Further objections are elucidated by Karl Otto Hondrich, 'Die andere Seite sozialer Differenzierung', in *Sinn, Kommunikation und soziale Differenzierung. Beiträge zu Luhmanns Theorie sozialer Systeme*, ed. Hans Haferkamp and Michael

Schmid (Suhrkamp, Frankfurt/Main, 1987), pp. 275–303. On earlier criticisms, see Anthony D. Smith, *The Concept of Social Change. A Critique of the Functionalist Theory of Social Change* (Routledge, London, 1973).

61 Georg Simmel, *Über soziale Differenzierung. Soziologische und psychologische Untersuchungen* (Duncker und Humblot, Leipzig, 1890).

62 Shmuel Eisenstadt, 'Social Change, Differentiation and Evolution', *American Sociological Review*, 29 (1964), pp. 375–86.

63 An analysis of fundamentalism on the basis of differentiation theory is to be found in Frank Lechner, 'Fundamentalism and Sociocultural Revitalization: On the Logic of Dedifferentiation', in *Differentiation Theory and Social Change. Comparative and Historical Perspectives*, ed. Jeffrey Alexander and Paul Colomy (Columbia University Press, New York, 1990), pp. 88–118.

64 See in particular the relatively early critique by Reinhard Bendix, 'Tradition and Modernity Reconsidered', *Comparative Studies in Social History*, 3 (1967), pp. 292–346.

65 Dietrich Rüschemeyer, 'Partial Modernization', in *Explorations in General Theory in the Social Sciences: Essays in Honor of Talcott Parsons*, ed. Jan J. Loubser et al. (Free Press, New York, 1976), pp. 756–72.

66 Smelser, *Collective Behavior*.

67 Robert Bellah, 'Religious Evolution', in Bellah, *Beyond Belief* (Harper & Row, London, 1970), pp. 20–50.

68 See in particular the foreword and conclusion to *Differentiation Theory and Social Change*, ed. Alexander and Colomy.

69 A particularly valuable contribution to the normative significance of differentiation is Michael Walzer, *Spheres of Justice. A Defense of Pluralism and Equality* (Robertson, Oxford, 1983).

70 Cf. Klaus Müller, 'Modernizing Eastern Europe: Theoretical Problems and Political Dilemmas', *European Journal of Sociology*, 33 (1992), pp. 109–50; see also the editors' introduction to *Der Zusammenbruch der DDR. Soziologische Analysen*, ed. Hans Joas and Martin Kohli (Suhrkamp, Frankfurt/Main, 1992).

71 The same qualification applies to the interesting contributions made by Schimank in 'Der mangelnde Akteurbezug' and his 'Gesellschaftliche Teilsysteme als Akteurfiktionen', *Kölner Zeitschrift für Soziologie und Sozialpsychologie*, 40 (1988), pp. 619–39. – Another important study, Helmut Willke, *Entzauberung des Staates. Überlegungen zu einer sozietalen Steuerungstheorie* (Athenäum, Königstein, 1983), inquires into the possibilities of control under conditions of differentiation, but not into the possibilities of controlling the differentiation itself.

72 I use this term in the sense it is used by Anthony Giddens and *not*, like Jürgen Habermas, with reference to Edmund Husserl, as the point at issue here is not a matter of epistemological theory but the relationship between action and social order. Cf. Jürgen Habermas, 'Vorlesungen zu einer sprachtheoretischen Grundlegung der Soziologie' (1970/1), in

Habermas, *Vorstudien und Ergänzungen zur Theorie des kommunikativen Handelns* (Suhrkamp, Frankfurt/Main, 1984), pp. 11–126, here pp. 35ff. For a critique of Habermas' view that the obsolescence of the production paradigm renders all versions of constitution theory obsolete, see chapter 2.2 of the present volume, esp. pp. 102–5.

73 See Charles Taylor's very enlightening remarks in the context of his discussion of Foucault's concept of 'strategy': Charles Taylor, 'Foucault on Freedom and Truth, in his *Philosophical Papers*, vol. 2 (Cambridge University Press, Cambridge, 1985), pp. 152–84, esp. pp. 169ff. – The classic texts on unanticipated (!) consequences of actions as an argument for functionalism are those of Robert Merton: See Merton, 'The Unanticipated Consequences of Purposive Social Action', *American Sociological Review*, 1 (1936), pp. 894–904; Merton, *Social Theory and Social Structure* (Free Press, Glencoe, Ill., 1957). – An equally classic line of argumentation in favour of methodological individualism on the basis of unintended consequences of action is that of Karl Popper, *Poverty of Historicism*, 2nd edn. (Routledge & Kegan Paul, London, 1960). In my view the conclusions to be drawn from the phenomenon of unintended consequences of actions support neither functionalism nor methodological individualism. As is well known, John Dewey developed his political philosophy, which is neither functionalism nor methodological individualism, from precisely this phenomenon of unintended consequences of actions and the feedback from those affected by those actions being relayed to the original actors: 'We take then our point of departure from the objective fact that human acts have consequences upon others, that some of these consequences are perceived, and that their perception leads to subsequent effort to control action so as to secure some consequences and avoid others.' See John Dewey, *The Public and Its Problems* (Allen & Unwin, London, 1927), p. 12.

74 Taylor, 'Foucault', p. 171.

75 See n. 57 above.

76 Cf. this spectacular gap in Jeffrey Alexander, *Twenty Lectures. Sociological Theory after 1945* (Columbia University Press, New York, 1987).

77 Still the best overview of these attempts is that provided by David Maines, 'Social Organization and Social Structure in Symbolic Interactionist Thought', *Annual Review of Sociology*, 3 (1977), pp. 235–59.

78 See esp. Giddens, *Constitution of Society*.

79 See, for example, Michael Mann, *The Sources of Social Power*, 2 vols (Cambridge University Press, Cambridge, 1986); John Hall, *Powers and Liberties. The Causes and Consequences of the Rise of the West* (Blackwell, Oxford, 1985); Randall Collins, *Conflict Sociology* (Academic Press, London, 1975); Pierre Bourdieu, *The Logic of Practice*, tr. R. Nice (Polity Press, Cambridge, 1979).

80 Cornelius Castoriadis, *The Imaginary Institution of Society*, tr. K. Blamey (Polity Press, Cambridge, 1987); Alan Touraine, *The Voice and the Eye*, tr. A. Duff (Cambridge University Press, Cambridge, 1981). These works

also bear a certain affinity to the work of Unger, the Brazilian social philosopher, who – inspired by the experience of the capitalist development in non-western cultures – has presented an attempt at an ambitiously broad 'anti-necessitarian' theory. See Roberto Mangabeira Unger, *Politics*, 3 vols (Cambridge University Press, Cambridge, 1987).

81 Here I refer, on the one hand, to Alexander's neo-functionalism and to a certain extent also, on the other, to Habermas' *Theory of Communicative Action*. On the relationship of these two thinkers to functionalism, see chapter 4.2 above.

82 Both Jeffrey Alexander and Bernhard Giesen observe that theoretical currents are at present converging in this respect. Alexander, however, comes dangerously close to depreciating most of these currents by overemphasizing the potential of a self-critical continuation of Parsonianism. See Jeffrey Alexander, 'The New Theoretical Movement', in *Handbook of Sociology*, ed. Neil Smelser (Sage, London, 1988), pp. 77–101; Bernhard Giesen, *Die Entdinglichung des Sozialen. Eine evolutionstheoretische Perspektive auf die Postmoderne* (Suhrkamp, Frankfurt/Main, 1991), esp. pp. 112–13.

83 Anthony Giddens, *A Contemporary Critique of Historical Materialism, Vol 2: The Nation-state and Violence* (Polity Press, Cambridge, 1985), see esp. pp. 310ff.

84 An outstanding critique of Giddens' proposals on this subject is John Breuilly's 'The Nation-state and Violence: A Critique of Giddens', in *Anthony Giddens. Consensus and Controversy*, ed. Jon Clark, Celia Mogdil and Sahan Mogdil (Falmer, London, 1990), pp. 271–88. See also Wolfgang Knöbl, 'Nationalstaat und Gesellschaftstheorie', *Zeitschrift für Soziologie*, 22 (1993), pp. 221–35.

85 Cornelius Castoriadis, 'Réflexions sur le "développement" et la "rationalité"', in Castoriadis, *Domaines de l'homme* (Seuil, Paris, 1986), pp. 131–74.

86 See Habermas, *Communicative Action*, vol. 1, pp. 102–42.

87 See chapter 4.2 of the present study.

88 Such attempts are at present under way, originating from the same sources as those from which some of the currents of constitution theory flow. See, for example, Samuel Bowles and Herbert Gintis, *Democracy and Capitalism. Property, Community, and the Contradictions of Modern Social Thought* (Routledge, London, 1986); Ulrich Rödel, Günter Frankenberg and Helmut Dubiel, *Die demokratische Frage* (Suhrkamp, Frankfurt/Main, 1989); Jóhann Páll Arnason, 'The Theory of Modernity and the Problematic of Democracy', *Thesis Eleven*, 26 (1990), pp. 20–45; Benjamin Barber, *Strong Democracy. Participatory Politics for a New Age* (University of California Press, Berkeley, 1984). Since much of this section of my text is confined to the level of a cursory outline, I would like to remind the reader that the purpose of this book is to present a theory of action and therefore that any discussion of macrosociology and theory of democracy here serves only to open up the perspective for further research.

89 Alain Touraine, *The Postindustrial Society*, tr. L. Mayhew (Wildwood House, London, 1975).

90 Alain Touraine, *Le retour de l'acteur* (Fayard, Paris, 1984), p. 14.

91 Alain Touraine, 'Krise und Wandel des sozialen Denkens', in *Die Moderne-Kontinuitäten und Zäsuren* (special issue of *Soziale Welt*) 1986, ed. Johannes Berger, pp. 15–39, here p. 35.

92 Karl-Werner Brand, Detlef Büsser and Dieter Rucht, *Aufbruch in eine andere Gesellschaft. Neue soziale Bewegungen in der Bundesrepublik* (Campus, Frankfurt/Main, 1986), p. 277. – Ulrich Beck, *Risk Society. Towards a New Modernity*, tr. M. Ritter (Sage, London, 1992). – Beck, *Gegengifte. Die organisierte Unverantwortlichkeit* (Suhrkamp, Frankfurt/Main, 1988). What Brand et al. cautiously formulate as an empirical question is made by Stefan Breuer to sound as though everything had already been decided – negatively. See his remarks on Beck in 'Das Ende der Sicherheit. Ulrich Beck's "Gegengifte"', *Merkur*, 43 (1989), no. 8, pp. 710–15.

93 Niklas Luhmann, *Ecological Communication*, tr. J. Bednarz (Polity Press, Cambridge, 1986), p. 121.

94 Ibid., p. 122.

95 Ibid., p. 125.

96 An excellent refutation of Luhmann's radical, and indeed increasingly radical, 'control pessimism' is formulated by Fritz Scharpf, 'Politische Steuerung und politische Institutionen', *Politische Vierteljahresschrift*, 30 (1989), no. 1, pp. 10–21.

97 Luhmann, *Ecological Communication*, p. 126.

98 Beck, *Gegengifte*, p. 162.

99 Claus Offe, 'The Utopia of the Zero-option: Modernity and Modernization as Normative Political Criteria', *Praxis International*, 7 (1987), pp. 1–24.

100 This is an idea expressed by Richard Münch in numerous works, most recently: Münch, *Dialektik der Kommunikationsgesellschaft* (Suhrkamp, Frankfurt/Main, 1991).

101 Klaus von Beyme, *Theorie der Politik im 20. Jahrhundert. Von der Moderne zur Postmoderne* (Suhrkamp, Frankfurt/Main, 1991), p. 352.

102 Zsuzsa Hegedüs, 'Social Movements and Social Change in Self-creative Society: New Civil Initiatives in the International Arena', *International Sociology*, 4 (1989), pp. 19–36.

103 A similar line is taken by Michael Walzer, 'Liberalism and the Art of Separation', *Political Theory*, 12 (1984), pp. 315–30.

104 Agnes Heller and Ferenc Feher, *The Postmodern Political Condition* (Polity Press, Cambridge, 1988), pp. 138–9.

105 Zygmunt Baumann, 'Is There a Postmodern Sociology?', *Theory, Culture & Society*, 5 (1988), pp. 217–37.

106 Robert Hughes, 'The Patron Saint of Neo-pop', *The New York Review of Books*, 36 (1989), no. 9, pp. 29–32, here p. 30.

107 Scott Lash and John Urry, *The End of Organized Capitalism* (Polity Press, Cambridge, 1987); Albert Scherr, 'Postmoderne Soziologie – Soziologie

der Postmoderne? Überlegungen zu notwendigen Differenzierungen der sozialwissenschaftlichen Diskussion', *Zeitschrift für Soziologie*, 19 (1990), pp. 3–12.

108 Max Weber, 'Roscher und Knies und die logischen Probleme der Nationalökonomie', in Weber, *Gesammelte Aufsätze zur Wissenschaftslehre* (Mohr, Tübingen, 1973), pp. 1–145, here, p. 33, fn. 2.

109 See chapter 1.5 of the present study.

110 John Dewey, 'Progress', in Dewey, *Characters and Events*, vol. 2 (Allen & Unwin, London, 1929), pp. 820–30, here, pp. 820–1.

111 For example, Peter Sloterdijk, *Eurotaoismus. Zur Kritik der politischen Kinetik* (Suhrkamp, Frankfurt/Main, 1989).

112 This seems to have been the tendency in Foucault's later development. In his books on the history of sexuality he examines, under the label of an aesthetic of existence, possibilities of a person's non-instrumental relationship to him- or herself. Cf. Michel Foucault, *The History of Sexuality*, 4 vols, tr. R. Hurley (Penguin, Harmondsworth, 1979).

113 In his critical appraisal, Terry Eagleton formulates the postmodernist critique of the concept of identity as reducing the subject to 'a dispersed, decentred network of libidinal attachments, emptied of ethical substance and psychical interiority, the ephemeral function of this or that act of consumption, media experience, sexual relationship, trend or fashion. The "unified subject" looms up in this light as more of a shibboleth or straw target, a hangover from an older liberal epoch of capitalism, before technology and consumerism scattered our bodies to the winds as so many bits and pieces of reified technique, appetite, mechanical operation or reflex of desire.' Terry Eagleton, 'Capitalism, Modernism and Postmodernism', *New Left Review*, 152 (1985), pp. 60–73, here p. 71. I fail to understand, therefore, how Koslowski can arrive at his conclusion that a return to a substantial theory of the self is a feature of postmodernism. Cf. Peter Koslowski, *Die postmoderne Kultur. Gesellschaftlich-kulturelle Konsequenzen der technischen Entwicklung* (Beck, Munich, 1987), pp. 49ff.

114 Jochen Schmidt, *Die Geschichte des Genie-Gedankens in der deutschen Literatur, Philosophie und Politik 1750–1945*, vol. 2 (Wissenschaftliche Buchgesellschaft, Darmstadt, 1985), p. 165.

115 See chapters 2.4 and 2.5 of the present study.

116 Theodor W. Adorno and Max Horkheimer, *Dialectic of Enlightenment*, tr. J. Cumming (Verso, London, 1979), p. 36.

117 For a critique of this analysis, see my essay 'An Underestimated Alternative: America and the Limits of "Critical Theory"', in *Pragmatism*, pp. 79–93.

118 Ronald Inglehart, *The Silent Revolution. Changing Values and Political Styles among Western Publics* (Princeton University Press, Princeton, 1977), and by the same author, *Culture Shift in Advanced Industrial Society* (Princeton University Press, Princeton, 1990).

119 Paul Leinberger and Bruce Tucker, *The New Individualists. The Generation*

after the Organization Man (Harper, New York, 1991); William H. Whyte, Jr., *The Organization Man* (Penguin, Harmondsworth, 1963).

120 Leinberger and Tucker, *The New Individualists*, p. 226.

121 Among the considerable volume of literature dealing with Inglehart's theory of changing values, I would like to single out Helmut Thome, *Wertewandel in der Politik? Eine Auseinandersetzung mit Ingleharts Thesen zum Postmaterialismus* (Wissenschaftlicher Autoren-Verlag, Berlin, 1985). Thome warns against seeing too direct a correlation between economic prosperity and the change in values, arguing that Inglehart 'makes no clear statement as to the relative importance of absolute level of fulfilment versus the rate of change, or of the objectively attained level of need fulfilment versus the perceived certainty of fulfilment level, nor does he comment on the possible insights to be gained by applying alternative foils of comparison: by comparing one's own situation with that of other potential reference groups, or, on the other hand, with the individuals' or groups' own past.'

122 On this point, even diagnoses normally so divergent as those of Bell and Bellah are in agreement: Daniel Bell, *The Cultural Contradictions of Capitalism*, 2nd edn (Heinemann, London, 1979); Robert Bellah et al., *Habits of the Heart. Individualism and Commitment in American Life* (University of California Press, Berkeley, 1985). Ulrich Beck, however, the writer who has done so much to promulgate the individualization theory in Germany, does not comment on the question of the relationship between anomie and autonomy.

123 Abraham Maslow, *Toward a Psychology of Being* (D. Van Nostrand Co. Inc., Princeton, NJ, 1962). Certainly since publication of Lawrence Kubie's book *Neurotic Distortions of the Creative Process* (Noonday Press, New York, 1961) the general understanding in the psychoanalytic literature has been that culturally productive activity is an *interaction* of release and control of preconscious processes of symbol formation. Owing to my lack of knowledge of theories of therapy I shall not go into the rich seam of empirical studies on this form of creativity here.

124 See Maslow, *Toward a Psychology of Being*, p. 143.

125 This point is made strongly – in opposition to Bellah and Habermas – by Charles Taylor, *Sources of the Self. The Making of the Modern Identity* (Cambridge University Press, Cambridge, 1989), p. 509.

126 On this subject, see in particular Barbara Ehrenreich, *Fear of Falling. The Inner Life of the Middle Class* (Harper, New York, 1989), pp. 196–243.

127 Thus reads the title of an excellent critique of Luhmann's moral theory: Sighard Neckel and Jürgen Wolf, 'The Fascination of Amorality: Luhmann's Systems Theory and Its Resonances Among West German Intellectuals', *Theory, Culture & Society*, 11 (1994), pp. 69–99.

128 Richard Rorty, *Contingency, Irony, Solidarity* (Cambridge University Press, Cambridge, 1989). This author, whose brand of pragmatist philosophy is informed by numerous Nietzschean and postmodernist elements, is none

the less prepared to give serious consideration to the tension between the
idea of an aestheticization of life and the prerequisites of a democractic
culture, and is at pains to proffer the following compromise solution:
'*Privatize* the Nietzschean–Sartrean–Foucauldian attempt at authenticity
and purity, in order to prevent yourself from slipping into a political
attitude which will lead you to think that there is some social goal more
important than avoiding cruelty' (ibid., p. 65).

129 Cf. Richard Shusterman, 'Postmodernist Aestheticism: A New Moral
Philosophy?', *Theory, Culture & Society*, 5 (1988), pp. 337–56.

130 Christoph Menke, 'Das Leben als Kunstwerk gestalten? Zur Dialektik der
postmodernen Ästhetisierung', *Initial*, 4 (1991), pp. 383–95.

131 This seems to me to be the purpose of Giddens' conception of 'life
politics', which complements 'emancipatory politics'. See Anthony Giddens, *Modernity and Self-identity. Self and Society in the Late Modern Age*
(Polity Press, Cambridge, 1991), pp. 209–31.

Bibliography

(Contains only those titles referred to in the text)

Adorno, Theodor W. and Horkheimer, Max, *Dialectic of Enlightenment*, tr. J. Cumming. London: Verso, 1979.

Alberoni, Francesco, *Movement and Institution*. New York: Columbia University Press, 1984.

Alexander, Jeffrey, *Theoretical Logic in Sociology, Vol. I: Positivism, Presuppositions, and Current Controversies*. Berkeley: University of California Press, 1982.

Alexander, Jeffrey, *Theoretical Logic in Sociology, Vol. II: The Antinomies of Classical Thought: Marx and Durkheim*. Berkeley: University of California Press, 1982.

Alexander, Jeffrey, *Theoretical Logic in Sociology, Vol. III: The Classical Attempt at Synthesis: Max Weber*. Berkeley: University of California Press, 1983.

Alexander, Jeffrey, *Theoretical Logic in Sociology, Vol. IV: The Modern Reconstruction of Classical Thought: Talcott Parsons*. Berkeley: University of California Press, 1983.

Alexander, Jeffrey (ed.), *Neofunctionalism*. London: Sage, 1985.

Alexander, Jeffrey, 'Rethinking Durkheim's Intellectual Development', *International Sociology*, 1 (1986), pp. 91–107 and pp. 189–201.

Alexander, Jeffrey, *Twenty Lectures. Sociological Theory after 1945*. New York: Columbia University Press, 1987.

Alexander, Jeffrey, 'The New Theoretical Movement', in Neil Smelser (ed.), *Handbook of Sociology*. London: Sage, 1988, pp. 77–101.

Alexander, Jeffrey and Colomy, Paul (eds), *Differentiation Theory and Social Change. Comparative and Historical Perspectives*. New York: Columbia University Press, 1990.

Alexander, Thomas M., *John Dewey's Theory of Art, Experience and Nature: The Horizons of Feeling*. Albany, NY: SUNY, 1987.

Alwast, Jendris, 'Die Wertung der Philosophie Nietzsches bei Tönnies', in

Lars Clausen and Franz Urban Pappi (eds), *Ankunft bei Tönnies*. Kiel: Mühlau, 1981, pp. 228–40.

Anderson, Douglas R., *Creativity and the Philosophy of Ch. S. Peirce*. Dordrecht: Nijhoff, 1987.

Arendt, Hannah, *The Human Condition*. Chicago: University of Chicago Press, 1958.

Arendt, Hannah, *On Revolution*. London: Faber, 1963.

Arnason, Jóhann Páll, *Zwischen Natur und Gesellschaft. Studien zu einer kritischen Theorie des Subjektes*. Frankfurt/Main: Europäische Verlags-Anstalt, 1976.

Arnason, Jóhann Páll, *Praxis und Interpretation*. Frankfurt/Main: Suhrkamp, 1988.

Arnason, Jóhann, Páll, 'The Theory of Modernity and the Problematic of Democracy', *Thesis Eleven*, 26 (1990), pp. 20–45.

Balandier, Georges, *Le désorde*. Paris: Fayard, 1988.

Barber, Benjamin, *Strong Democracy. Participatory Politics for a New Age*. Berkeley: University of California Press, 1984.

Bataille, Georges, *Eroticism*, tr. M. Dalwood. London: Calder, 1962.

Baumann, Zygmunt, 'Is There a Postmodern Sociology?', *Theory, Culture & Society*, 5 (1988), pp. 217–37.

Baumeister, Thomas, 'Kunst als Erfahrung', *Zeitschrift für philosophische Forschung*, 37 (1983), pp. 616–24.

Baumgarten, Eduard, *Die geistigen Grundlagen des amerikanischen Gemeinwesens*, 2 vols. Frankfurt/Main: Deutsche Verlagsanstalt, 1936/1938.

Beck, Ulrich, *Gegengifte. Die organisierte Unverantwortlichkeit*. Frankfurt/Main: Suhrkamp, 1988.

Beck, Ulrich, *Risk Society. Towards a New Modernity*, tr. M. Ritter. London: Sage, 1992.

Bell, Daniel, *The Cultural Contradictions of Capitalism*, 2nd edn. London: Heinemann, 1979.

Bellah, Robert, 'Religious Evolution', in Bellah, *Beyond Belief*. London: Harper & Row, 1970, pp. 20–50.

Bellah, Robert, Madsen, Richard, Sullivan, William, Swidler, Ann and Tipton, Steven, *Habits of the Heart. Individualism and Commitment in American Life*. Berkeley: University of California Press, 1985.

Bendix, Reinhard, 'Tradition and Modernity Reconsidered', *Comparative Studies in Social History*, 3 (1967), pp. 292–346.

Bendix, Reinhard, 'Two Sociological Traditions', in Reinhard Bendix and Günther Roth, *Scholarship and Partisanship*. Berkeley: University of California Press, 1971, pp. 282–98.

Bergson, Henri, *Creative Evolution*, tr. A. Mitchell. London: Macmillan, 1964.

Berki, R.N., 'On the Nature and Origins of Marx' Concept of Labor', *Political Theory*, 7 (1979), pp. 35–56.

Berlin, Isaish, *Vico and Herder*. London: Hogarth, 1976.

Berlin, Isaiah, 'Georges Sorel', in Berlin, *Against the Current: Essays in the History of Ideas*. Oxford: Clarendon Press, 1977, pp. 296–332.

Bernard, Michel, *Le corps*. Paris: Éditions Universitaires, 1976.

Bernstein, Richard, *Praxis and Action*. Philadelphia: University of Philadelphia Press, 1971.

Bershady, Harold, *Ideology and Social Knowledge*. Oxford: Blackwell, 1973.

Beyme, Klaus von, *Theorie der Politik im 20. Jahrhundert. Von der Moderne zur Postmoderne*. Frankfurt/Main: Suhrkamp, 1991.

Bickel, Cornelius, 'Ferdinand Tönnies' Weg in die Soziologie', in Otthein Ramstedt (ed.), *Simmel und die frühen Soziologen*. Frankfurt/Main: Suhrkamp, 1988, pp. 86–162.

Billington, James H., *Fire in the Minds of Men. Origins of the Revolutionary Faith*. London: Temple Smith, 1980.

Bloom, Allan, *The Closing of the American Mind*. New York: Simon & Schuster, 1987.

Blumer, Herbert, 'The Field of Collective Behavior', in Alfred McClung Lee (ed.), *Principles of Sociology*. New York: Barnes & Noble, 1951 (1st edn 1939), pp. 165–222.

Blumer, Herbert, 'Collective Behavior', in Joseph Gittler (ed.), *Review of Sociology*. New York: John Wiley & Sons, 1957, pp. 127–58.

Böhler, Dietrich, *Rekonstruktive Pragmatik. Von der Bewußtseinsphilosophie zur Kommunikationsreflexion: Neubegründung der praktischen Wissenschaften und Philosophie*. Frankfurt/Main: Suhrkamp, 1985.

Bollnow, Otto Friedrich, *Die Lebensphilosophie*. Berlin: Springer, 1958.

Bourdieu, Pierre, *The Outline of a Theory of Practice*. Cambridge: Cambridge University Press, 1977.

Bourdieu, Pierre, *The Logic of Practice*, tr. R. Nice. Cambridge: Polity Press, 1979.

Bowles, Samuel and Gintis, Herbert, *Democracy and Capitalism. Property, Community, and the Contradictions of Modern Social Thought*. London: Routledge, 1986.

Brand, Karl-Werner, Büsser, Detlef and Rucht, Dieter, *Aufbruch in eine andere Gesellschaft. Neue soziale Bewegungen in der Bundesrepublik*. Frankfurt/Main: Campus, 1986.

Brandenburg, Karl-Heinz, 'Kunst als Qualität der Handlung. John Deweys Grundlegung der Ästhetik'. Dissertation. Königsberg, 1942.

Brede, Karola, *Sozioanalyse psychosomatischer Störungen. Zum Verhältnis von Soziologie und psychosomatischer Medizin*. Frankfurt/Main: Athenäum, 1972.

Breuer, Stefan, 'Das Ende der Sicherheit. Ulrich Becks "Gegengifte"', *Merkur*, 43 (1989), no. 8, pp. 710–15.

Breuer, Stefan, *Max Webers Herrschaftssoziologie*. Frankfurt/Main: Campus, 1991.

Breuilly, John, 'The Nation-State and Violence: A Critique of Giddens', in Jon Clark, Celia Mogdil and Sahan Mogdil (eds), *Anthony Giddens. Consensus and Controversy*. London: Falmer, 1990, pp. 271–88.

Busch, Hans-Joachim, *Interaktion und innere Natur*. Frankfurt/Main: Campus, 1985.

Busino, Giovanni (ed.), 'Pour une philosophie militante de la démocratie.

Autonomie et autotransformation de la société', *Revue européenne des sciences sociales*, 27 (1989).

Camic, Charles, 'The Utilitarians Revisited', *American Journal of Sociology*, 85 (1979), pp. 515–50.

Camic, Charles, 'Charisma: Its Varieties, Preconditions, and Consequences', *Sociological Inquiry*, 50 (1980), pp. 5–23.

Camic, Charles, 'The Matter of Habit', *American Journal of Sociology*, 91 (1986), pp. 1039–87.

Camic, Charles, 'The Making of a Method: A Historical Reinterpretation of the Early Parsons', *American Sociological Review*, 52 (1987), pp. 421–39.

Camic, Charles, ' "Structure" after 50 Years: The Anatomy of a Charter', *American Journal of Sociology*, 95 (1989), pp. 38–107.

Camic, Charles, 'Introduction: Talcott Parsons before *The Structure of Social Action*', in Talcott Parsons, *The Early Essays*. Chicago: University of Chicago Press, 1991, pp. ix–lxix.

Castoriadis, Cornelius, 'Réflexions sur le "développement" et la "rationalité"', in Castoriadis, *Domaines de l'homme*. Paris: Seuil, 1986, pp. 131–74.

Castoriadis, Cornelius, *The Imaginary Institution of Society*, tr. K. Blamey. Cambridge: Polity Press, 1987.

Clarke, Simon, *Marx, Marginalism and Modern Sociology. From Adam Smith to Max Weber*. London: Macmillan, 1982.

Coenen, Herman, 'Leiblichkeit und Sozialität. Ein Grundproblem der phäno-menologischen Soziologie', *Philosophisches Jahrbuch*, 86 (1979), pp. 239–61.

Cohen, Gerald, 'Functional Explanation, Consequence Explanation, and Marxism', *Inquiry*, 25 (1982), pp. 27–56.

Cohen, Jean, *Class and Civil Society. The Limits of Marxian Critical Theory*. Amherst, Mass.: University of Massachusetts Press, 1982.

Collins, Randall, *Conflict Sociology*. London: Academic Press, 1975.

Conrad, Klaus, 'Das Körperschema. Eine kritische Studie und der Versuch ihrer Revision', *Zeitschrift für die gesamte Neurologie und Psychiatrie*, 147 (1933), pp. 346–69.

Cooley, Charles Horton, 'The Institutional Character of Pecuniary Valuation', *American Journal of Sociology*, 18 (1913), pp. 543–55.

Das, Robin and McCarthy, Doyle, 'The Cognitive and Emotional Significance of Play in Child Development: G. H. Mead and D. W. Winnicott', *Sociological Studies of Child Development*, 1 (1986), pp. 35–53.

Dewey, John, *How We Think*. London: Heath & Co., 1910.

Dewey, John, 'The Need for a Recovery of Philosophy', in Dewey, A.W. Moore, H.C. Brown, G.H. Mead, B.H. Bode, H.W. Stuart, J.H. Tufts and H.M. Kallen, *Creative Intelligence. Essays in the Pragmatic Attitude*. New York: Henry Holt, 1917, pp. 3–69.

Dewey, John, *Human Nature and Conduct*. London: Allen & Unwin, 1922.

Dewey, John, *The Public and Its Problems*. London: Allen & Unwin, 1927.

Dewey, John, 'Progress', in Dewey, *Characters and Events*, vol. 2. London: Allen & Unwin, 1929, pp. 820–30.

Dewey, John, 'Peirce's Theory of Quality', *Journal of Philosophy*, 32 (1935), pp. 701–8.

Dewey, John, *Theory of Valuation*. Chicago: University of Chicago Press, 1939.

Dewey, John, 'Creative Democracy: The Task Before Us', in Sidney Ratner (ed.), *The Philosopher of the Common Man. Essays in Honor of John Dewey to Celebrate His Eightieth Birthday*. New York: Greenwood Press, 1940, pp. 220–8.

Dewey, John, *Experience and Nature* (1925). London: Open Court, 1958.

Dewey, John, *Democracy and Education* (1916). New York: Macmillan, 1969.

Dewey, John, *A Common Faith* (1934). New Haven, Conn.: Yale University Press, 1980.

Dewey, John, *Art as Experience* (1934). New York: Putnam's, 1980.

Dewey, John, 'Construction and Criticism', in Dewey, *Later Works*, vol. 5 (1929/30). Carbondale, Ill.: Southern Illinois University Press, 1988, pp. 127–43.

Dillon, Martin C., 'Merleau-Ponty and the Psychogenesis of the Self', *Journal of Phenomenological Psychology*, 9 (1978), pp. 84–98.

Dilthey, Wilhelm, *Gesammelte Schriften*, vols. 5 and 6. Leipzig and Berlin: B.G. Teubner, 1924.

Dilthey, Wilhelm, *Der Aufbau der geschichtlichen Welt in den Geisteswissenschaften*. Frankfurt/Main: Suhrkamp, 1970.

Dilthey, Wilhelm, *Introduction to the Human Sciences*, tr. R. Betanzos. Hemel Hempstead: Harvester, 1989.

Dow, Thomas, 'An Analysis of Weber's Work on Charisma', *British Journal of Sociology*, 29 (1978), pp. 83–93.

Dreyfus, Hubert L., *What Computers Can't Do – The Limits of Artificial Intelligence*. New York: Harper & Row, 1979.

Dumont, Louis, *From Mandeville to Marx. The Genesis and Triumph of Economic Ideology*. Chicago: University of Chicago Press, 1977.

Durkheim, Émile, *Moral Education*. Glencoe, Ill.: Free Press, 1961.

Durkheim Émile, 'The Dualism of Human Nature and Its Social Conditions', in Robert Bellah (ed.), *Émile Durkheim on Morality and Society*. Chicago: University of Chicago Press, 1973, pp. 149–63.

Durkheim, Émile, review of Jean-Marie Guyau's, *L'irréligion de l'avenir* (1887), in Durkheim, *Textes*, vol. 2. Paris: Minuit, 1975, pp. 149–65.

Durkheim, Émile, 'La science positive de la morale en Allemagne', in his *Écrits*, vol. 1. Paris: Presses Universitaires de France, 1975, pp. 267–343; published in English as *Ethics and the Sociology of Morals*, tr. R.T. Hall. Buffalo, NY: Prometheus Books, 1993.

Durkheim, Émile, *The Elementary Form of the Religious Life*, tr. J. W. Swain. London: Allen & Unwin, 1976.

Durkheim, Émile, review of Ferdinand Tönnies' *Gemeinschaft und Gesellschaft* (1889), in Mark Traugott (ed.), *Émile Durkheim. On Institutional Analysis*. Chicago and London: University of Chicago Press, 1978. pp. 115–22.

Durkheim, Émile, 'Introduction to Morality', in Mark Traugott (ed.), *Émile*

Durkheim. On Institutional Analysis. Chicago and London: University of Chicago Press, 1978, pp. 191–202.

Durkheim, Émile, *Division of Labour in Society*, tr. W. D. Halls. London: Macmillan, 1984.

Eagle, Morris, N., *Recent Developments in Psychoanalysis.* Maidenhead: McGraw Hill, 1984.

Eagleton, Terry, 'Capitalism, Modernism and Postmodernism', *New Left Review*, 152 (1985), pp. 60–73.

Ehrenreich, Barbara, *Fear of Falling. The Inner Life of the Middle Class.* New York: Harper, 1989.

Eisenstadt, Shmuel, 'Social Change, Differentiation and Evolution', *American Sociological Review*, 29 (1964), pp. 375–86.

Eisenstadt, Shmuel, 'Charisma and Institution Building: Max Weber and Modern Sociology', in Max Weber, *Selected Papers.* Chicago: University of Chicago Press, 1968, pp. ix–lvi.

Elster, Jon, *Ulysses and the Sirens.* Cambridge: Cambridge University Press, 1979.

Elster, Jon, 'Marxism, Functionalism, and Game Theory', *Theory and Society*, 11 (1982), pp. 453–82.

Elster, Jon, 'States that are Essentially By-products', in Elster, *Sour Grapes. Studies in the Subversion of Rationality.* Cambridge: Cambridge University Press, 1983, pp. 43–108.

Elster, Jon, *Making Sense of Marx.* Cambridge: Cambridge University Press, 1985.

Engell, James, *The Creative Imagination. Enlightenment to Romanticism.* Cambridge, Mass.: Harvard University Press, 1981.

Engels, Frederick, preface to the third German edition of the 'The Eighteenth Brumaire of Louis Bonaparte', in Karl Marx and Frederick Engels, *Selected Works in One Volume.* London: Lawrence & Wishart, 1970, pp. 94–5.

Engler, Ulrich, *Kritik der Erfahrung. Die Bedeutung der ästhetischen Erfahrung in der Philosophie John Deweys.* Würzburg: Königshausen & Neumann, 1992.

Etzioni, Amitai, *The Active Society.* New York: Free Press, 1968.

Eyerman, Ron and Jamison, Andrew, *Social Movements. A Cognitive Approach.* Cambridge: Polity Press, 1991.

Fabian, Bernhard, 'Der Naturwissenschaftler als Originalgenie', in Hugo Friedrich and Fritz Schalk (eds), *Europäische Aufklärung. Festschrift für Herbert Dieckmann.* Munich: Fink, 1967, pp. 47–68.

Fechner, Rolf, '"Der Wesenwille selbst ist künstlerischer Geist". Ferdinand Tönnies' Geniebegriff und seine Bedeutung für den Übergang von der Gemeinschaft zur Gesellschaft', in Lars Clausen and Carsten Schlüter (eds), *Hundert Jahre 'Gemeinschaft und Gesellschaft'.* Opladen: Leske und Budrich, 1992, pp. 453–62.

Feuerbach, Ludwig, 'Grundsätze der Philosophie der Zukunft', in Feuerbach, *Kleine Schriften*, Karl Löwith (ed.). Frankfurt/Main: Suhrkamp, 1966, pp. 145–219.

Flam, Helena, 'Emotional Man', *International Sociology*, 5 (1990), pp. 39–56 and pp. 225–34.

Fleischmann, Eugène, 'De Weber à Nietzsche', *Archives européennes de sociologie*, 5 (1964), pp. 190–238.

Foucault, Michel, *The History of Sexuality*, 4 vols, tr. R. Hurley. Harmondsworth: Penguin, 1977 etc.

Freyer, Hans, *Theorie des gegenwärtigen Zeitalters*. Stuttgart. Deutsche Verlagsanstalt, 1956.

Garfinkel, Harold, *Studies in Ethnomethodology*. Cambridge: Polity Press, 1984.

Gehlen, Arnold, 'Vilfredo Pareto und seine "neue Wissenschaft"', in Gehlen, *Studien zur Anthropologie und Soziologie*. Neuwied: Luchterhand, 1963, pp. 149–95.

Gehlen, Arnold, 'Die Resultate Schopenhauers' (1935), in Gehlen, *Philosophische Anthropologie und Handlungslehre*, complete edition, vol. 4. Frankfurt/Main: Klostermann, 1983, pp. 25–49.

Gehlen, Arnold, *Man, His Nature and Place in the World* (1940), tr. C. McMillan and K. Pillemer, with an introduction by Karl-Siegbert Rehberg. New York: Columbia University Press, 1988.

Geulen, Dieter, *Das vergesellschaftete Subjekt. Zur Grundlegung der Sozialisationstheorie*. Frankfurt/Main: Suhrkamp, 1977.

Giddens, Anthony, 'Functionalism: Après la lutte', *Social Research*, 43 (1976), pp. 325–66.

Giddens, Anthony, *Émile Durkheim*. London: Fontana, 1978.

Giddens, Anthony, *A Contemporary Critique of Historical Materialism*. London: Macmillan, 1981.

Giddens, Anthony, *The Constitution of Society*, Cambridge: Polity Press, 1984.

Giddens, Anthony, 'Reason without Revolution? Habermas' *Theorie des kommunikativen Handelns*', in Richard Bernstein (ed.), *Habermas and Modernity*. Cambridge: Polity Press, 1985, pp. 95–121.

Giddens, Anthony, *A Contemporary Critique of Historical Materialism, vol. 2: The Nation-State and Violence*. Cambridge: Polity Press, 1985.

Giddens, Anthony, *Modernity and Self-Identity. Self and Society in the Late Modern Age*. Cambridge: Polity Press, 1991.

Giesen, Bernhard, *Die Entdinglichung des Sozialen. Eine evolutionstheoretische Perspektive auf die Postmoderne*. Frankfurt/Main: Suhrkamp, 1991.

Goffman, Erving, *The Presentation of Self in Everyday Life*. Edinburgh: Edinburgh University Press, 1956.

Gould, Mark, 'Voluntarism versus Utilitarianism: A Critique of Camic's History of Ideas', *Theory, Culture & Society*, 6 (1989), pp. 637–54.

Gramsci, Antonio, *Prison Notebooks*. London: Lawrence & Wishart, 1973.

Griewank, Karl, *Der neuzeitliche Revolutionsbegriff*. Weimar: Böhlau, 1955.

Günther, Klaus, *Der Sinn für Angemessenheit. Anwendungsdiskurse in Moral und Recht*. Frankfurt/Main: Suhrkamp, 1988.

Gurr, Ted Robert, *Why Men Rebel*. Princeton: Princeton University Press, 1970.

Habermas, Jürgen, 'Anthropologie', in Alwin Diemer and Ivo Frenzel (eds), *Philosophie*. Frankfurt/Main: Fischer, 1958, pp. 18–35.

Habermas Jürgen, 'Arbeit und Interaktion. Bemerkungen zu Hegels Jenenser Philosophie des Geistes', in Habermas, *Technik und Wissenschaft als Ideologie*. Frankfurt/Main: Suhrkamp, 1968, pp. 9–47.

Habermas, Jürgen, 'A Reply to my Critics', in John B. Thompson and David Held (eds), *Habermas. Critical Debates*. London: Routledge, 1982, pp. 219–83.

Habermas, Jürgen, 'Vorlesungen zu einer sprachtheoretischen Grundlegung der Soziologie' (1970/1), in Habermas, *Vorstudien und Ergänzungen zur Theorie des kommunikativen Handelns*. Frankfurt/Main: Suhrkamp, 1984, pp. 11–126.

Habermas, Jürgen, *Theory of Communicative Action*, 2 vols, tr. T. McCarthy. Boston: Beacon Press, 1984/1987 and Cambridge: Polity Press, 1991/1987.

Habermas, Jürgen, *The Philosophical Discourse of Modernity*, tr. F. Lawrence. Cambridge: Polity Press, 1987.

Habermas, Jürgen, *Knowledge and Human Interest*, tr. J. Shapiro. Cambridge: Polity Press, 1987.

Habermas, Jürgen. 'Motifs of Postmetaphysical Thought', in Habermas, *Postmetaphysical Thinking: Philosophical Essays*, tr. W. M. Hohengarten. Cambridge, Mass.: MIT Press, 1992, pp. 35–60 and Cambridge: Polity Press, 1992.

Habermas, Jürgen and Luhmann, Niklas, *Theorie der Gesellschaft oder Sozialtechnologie*. Frankfurt/Main: Suhrkamp, 1971.

Haga, Aanund, 'Interaktion und Intentionalität. Bemerkungen zum Versuch, die Sozialwissenschaften spiel- und entscheidungstheoretisch zu rekonstruieren', in Dietrich Böhler, Tore Nordenstam and Gunnar Skirbekk, *Die pragmatische Wende*. Frankfurt/Main: Suhrkamp, 1986, pp. 91–109.

Hall, John, *Powers and Liberties. The Causes and Consequences of the Rise of the West*. Oxford: Blackwell, 1985.

Hall, Robert T., *Émile Durkheim. Ethics and the Sociology of Morals*. London: Greenwood, 1987.

Hegedüs, Zsuzsa, 'Social Movements and Social Change in Self-Creative Society: New Civil Initiatives in the International Arena', *International Sociology*, 4 (1989), pp. 19–36.

Heidegger, Martin, *Being and Time*. Oxford: Blackwell, 1987.

Heller, Agnes, *Everyday Life*, tr. G. L. Campbell. London: Routledge, 1984; the German edition (Frankfurt: Suhrkamp, 1978) contains my introduction (pp. 7–23).

Heller, Agnes, 'Habermas and Marxism', in John B. Thompson and David Held (eds), *Habermas. Critical Debates*. London: Routledge, 1982, pp. 21–41.

Heller, Agnes, 'Paradigm of Work – Paradigm of Production', in Heller, *The Power of Shame*. London: Routledge, 1985, pp. 57–70.

Heller, Agnes and Feher, Ferenc, *The Postmodern Political Condition*. Cambridge: Polity Press, 1988.

Hennis, Wilhelm, *Max Weber: Essays in Reconstruction*, tr. K. Tribe. London: Allen & Unwin, 1988.

Herder, Johann Gottfried, 'Abhandlung über den Ursprung der Sprache' (1772), in *Werke*, vol. 2. Berlin and Weimar: Aufbau, 1982, pp. 89–200.

Herder, Johann Gottfried, 'Vom Erkennen und Empfinden der menschlichen Seele' (1774/5), in *Werke*, vol. 3. Berlin and Weimar: Aufbau, 1982, pp. 341–405.

Herder, Johann Gottfried, 'Von Kunstrichterei, Geschmack und Genie' (1800), in Herder, *Kalligone*. Weimar: Arion, 1955.

Heritage, John, 'Ethnomethodology', in Anthony Giddens and Jonathan Turner (eds), *Social Theory Today*. Cambridge: Polity Press, 1987, pp. 224–72.

Herms, Eilert, *Radical Empiricism. Studien zur Psychologie, Metaphysik und Religionstheorie William James'*. Gütersloh: Mohn, 1977.

Herms, Eilert, Epilogue to William James, *Die Vielfalt religiöser Erfahrung*. Olten: Walter, 1979, pp. 481–521.

Hinkle, Roscoe, 'Antecedents of the Action Orientation in American Sociology before 1935', *American Sociological Review*, 28 (1963), pp. 705–15.

Hirschman, Albert, *The Passions and the Interests: Political Arguments for Capitalism Before Its Triumph*. Princeton: Princeton University Press, 1977.

Hondrich, Karl Otto, 'Die andere Seite sozialer Differenzierung', in Hans Haferkamp and Michael Schmid (eds), *Sinn, Kommunikation und soziale Differenzierung. Beiträge zu Luhmanns Theorie sozialer Systeme*. Frankfurt/Main: Suhrkamp, 1987, pp. 275–303.

Honneth, Axel, 'Work and Instrumental Action: On the Normative Basis of Critical Theory', *Thesis Eleven*, 5/6 (1982), pp. 162–84.

Honneth, Axel, 'Logik der Emanzipation. Zum philosophischen Erbe des Marxismus', in Hans Leo Krämer and Claus Leggewie (eds), *Wege ins Reich der Freiheit. André Gorz zum 65. Geburtstag*. Berlin: Rotbuch, 1989, pp. 86–106.

Honneth, Axel, *The Critique of Power*, tr. K. Baynes. Cambridge, Mass.: MIT, 1991.

Honneth, Axel, *The Struggle for Recognition*, tr. J. Anderson. Cambridge: Polity Press, 1995.

Honneth, Axel and Joas, Hans, 'War Marx ein Utilitarist?', in Helmut Steiner (ed.), *Karl Marx und Friedrich Engels. Ihr Einfluß und ihre Wirksamkeit in der Geschichte und Gegenwart der soziologischen Theorie*. East Berlin: Institut für Soziologie und Sozialpolitik, 1987, pp. 148–61.

Honneth, Axel and Joas, Hans, *Social Action and Human Nature*, tr. R. Meyer. Cambridge: Cambridge University Press, 1988.

Hughes, Robert, 'The Patron Saint of Neo-pop', *The New York Review of Books* 36 (1989), no. 9, pp. 29–32.

Hugo, Victor, *Napoléon le petit*. London: Vizetelly, 1852.

Inglehart, Ronald, *The Silent Revolution. Changing Values and Political Styles among Western Publics*. Princeton: Princeton University Press, 1977.

Inglehart, Ronald, *Culture Shift in Advanced Industrial Society*. Princeton: Princeton University Press, 1990.

Iser, Wolfgang, *The Act of Reading*. Baltimore: Johns Hopkins University Press, 1978.

James, William, *The Principles of Psychology*, 2 vols. New York: Henry Holt, 1890.

James, William, *Talks to Teachers on Psychology*. London: Longman, 1899.

James, William, *Pragmatism*. New York: Longman 1922.

James, William, *The Varieties of Religious Experience*. London: Fontana, 1982.

Japp, Klaus Peter, 'Selbsterzeugung oder Fremdverschulden: Thesen zum Rationalismus in den Theorien sozialer Bewegungen', *Soziale Welt*, 35 (1984), pp. 313–29.

Jauss, Hans Robert, *Aesthetic Experience*, tr. M. Shaw. Minneapolis: University of Minnesota Press, 1982.

Joas, Hans, *George Herbert Mead: A Contemporary Re-examination of His Thought*, tr. R. Meyer. Cambridge: Polity Press, 1985.

Joas, Hans, 'Role Theories and Socialization Research', in H. J. Helle and S. N. Eisenstadt (eds), *Perspectives on Sociological Theory, Vol. 2: Micro-sociological Theory*. London: Sage, 1985, pp. 37–53.

Joas, Hans, 'A Sociological Transformation of the Philosophy of Praxis: Anthony Giddens's Theory of Structuration', *International Sociology*, 2 (1987), pp. 13–26.

Joas, Hans, 'Symbolic Interactionism', in Anthony Giddens and Jonathan Turner (eds), *Social Theory Today*. Cambridge: Polity Press, 1987, pp. 82–115.

Joas, Hans, 'The Antinomies of Neofunctionalism: A Critical Essay on Jeffrey Alexander', *Inquiry*, 31 (1988), pp. 471–94, reprinted in Joas, *Pragmatism*, pp. 188–213.

Joas, Hans, 'Institutionalization as a Creative Process', *American Journal of Sociology*, 94 (1988/9), pp. 1184–99.

Joas, Hans, 'The Creativity of Action and the Intersubjectivity of Reason – Mead's Pragmatism and Social Theory', *Transactions of the Charles Sanders Peirce Society*, 16 (1990), pp. 165–94.

Joas, Hans, 'The Unhappy Marriage of Hermeneutics and Functionalism', in Axel Honneth and Hans Joas (eds), *Communicative Action*, tr. J. Gaines and D. Jones. Cambridge: Polity Press, 1991, pp. 97–118, reprinted in Joas, *Pragmatism*, pp. 125–53.

Joas, Hans, *Pragmatism and Social Theory*, tr. J. Gaines, R. Meyer and S. Minner. Chicago: University of Chicago Press, 1993.

Joas, Hans and Kohli, Martin (eds), *Der Zusammenbruch der DDR. Soziologische Analysen*. Frankfurt/Main: Suhrkamp, 1992.

Johnson, Mark, *The Body in the Mind. The Bodily Basis of Meaning, Imagination, and Reason*. Chicago: University of Chicago Press, 1987.

Kaiser, Markus, 'Individuelle Vergesellschaftung in naturhistorischer Sicht. Ein Beitrag zur soziologischen Anthropologie'. Philosophical dissertation. Free University of Berlin, 1987.

Kaufmann, Walter, *Nietzsche. Philosopher, Psychologist – Antichrist*. Princeton: Princeton University Press, 1974.

Keller, Monika, *Kognitive Entwicklung und soziale Kompetenz. Zur Entstehung der Rollenübernahme in der Familie und ihrer Bedeutung für den Schulerfolg.* Stuttgart: Klett, 1976.

Kluchert, Gerhard, *Geschichtsschreibung und Revolution. Die historischen Schriften von Karl Marx und Friedrich Engels 1846–1852.* Stuttgart: Frommann-Holzboog, 1985.

Knöbl, Wolfgang, 'Nationalstaat und Gesellschaftstheorie', *Zeitschrift für Soziologie,* 22 (1993), pp. 221–35.

König, René, *Kritik der historisch-existenzialistischen Soziologie. Ein Beitrag zur Begründung einer objektiven Soziologie.* Munich: Piper, 1975.

König, René, 'Émile Durkheim. Der Soziologe als Moralist', in Dirk Käsler (ed.), *Klassiker des soziologischen Denkens,* vol. 1. Munich: Beck, 1976, pp. 312–64.

Korff, Hermann August, *Geist der Goethezeit,* 4 vols. Leipzig: Koehler & Armelang, 1966.

Kosík, Karel, *Dialectics of the Concrete,* tr. K. Kavanda and J. Schmidt. Dordrecht: D. Reidel, 1976.

Koslowski, Peter, *Die postmoderne Kultur. Gesellschaftlich-kulturelle Konsequenzen der technischen Entwicklung.* Munich: Beck, 1987.

Krappmann, Lothar, 'Mead und die Sozialisationsforschung', in Hans Joas (ed.), *Das Problem der Intersubjektivität.* Frankfurt/Main: Suhrkamp, 1985, pp. 156–78.

Krüger, Hans Peter, *Kritik der kommunikativen Vernunft. Kommunikationsorientierte Wissenschaftsforschung im Streit mit Sohn-Rethel, Toulmin und Habermas.* Berlin: Akademie-Verlag, 1990.

Kubie, Lawrence, *Neurotic Distortions of the Creative Process.* New York: Noonday Press, 1961.

Lacan, Jacques, *Écrits. A Selection,* tr. A. Sheridan. London: Tavistock, 1980.

Lacroix, Bernard, *Durkheim et le politique.* Paris and Montréal: Presses de l'Université de Montréal, 1981.

Lalande, André, 'Allocution', *Centenaire de la naissance de Durkheim. Annales de l'Université de Paris,* 1 (1960), pp. 20–3.

Lange, Ernst Michael, *Das Prinzip Arbeit. Drei metakritische Kapitel über Grundbegriffe, Struktur und Darstellung der 'Kritik der politischen Ökonomie' von Karl Marx.* Berlin: Ullstein, 1980.

Lash, Scott and Urry, John, *The End of Organized Capitalism.* Cambridge: Polity Press, 1987.

Lechner, Frank, 'Fundamentalism and Sociocultural Revitalization: On the Logic of Dedifferentiation', in Jeffrey Alexander and Paul Colomy (eds), *Differentiation Theory and Social Change. Comparative and Historical Perspectives.* New York: Columbia University Press, 1990, pp. 88–118.

Leinberger, Paul and Tucker, Bruce, *The New Individualists. The Generation after the Organization Man.* New York: Harper, 1991.

Lenin, Vladimir Ilyich, 'Die Entwicklung des Kapitalismus in Rußland', in Lenin, *Werke,* vol. 3. East Berlin: Dietz, 1963.

Levine, Donald, *Simmel and Parsons*. New York: Arno, 1980.

Levine, Donald, 'Simmel and Parsons Reconsidered', *American Journal of Sociology*, 96 (1991), pp. 1097–116.

Lichtblau, Klaus, 'Das "Pathos der Distanz". Präliminarien zur Nietzsche-Rezeption bei Georg Simmel', in Heinz-Jürgen Dahme and Otthein Ramstedt (eds), *Georg Simmel und die Moderne*. Frankfurt/Main: Suhrkamp, 1984, pp. 231–81.

Lockwood, David, *Solidarity and Schism: The Problem of Disorder in Durkheimian and Marxist Sociology*. Oxford: Clarendon Press, 1992.

Lorenz, Konrad, *Über tierisches und menschliches Verhalten*. Gesammelte Abhandlungen, 2 vols. Munich: Piper, 1965.

Luhmann, Niklas, 'Zweck – Herrschaft – System. Grundbegriffe und Prämissen Max Webers', in Renate Mayntz (ed.), *Bürokratische Organisation*. Cologne: Kiepenheuer & Witsch, 1968, pp. 36–55.

Luhmann, Niklas, *Zweckbegriff und Systemrationalität. Über die Funktion von Zwecken in sozialen Systemen*. Tübingen: Mohr, 1968.

Luhmann, Niklas, *Soziologische Aufklärung*, vol. 1. Opladen: Westdeutscher Verlag, 1970.

Luhmann, Niklas, *Soziale Systeme*. Frankfurt/Main: Suhrkamp, 1984.

Luhmann, Niklas, *Ecological Communication*, tr. J. Bednarz. Cambridge: Polity Press, 1986.

Luhmann, Niklas, 'Vom Zufall verwöhnt. Eine Rede über Kreativität, *Frankfurter Allgemeine Zeitung*, 10 June 1987.

Lukács, Georg, *History and Class Consciousness*, tr. R. Livingstone. London: Merlin, 1971.

Lukács, Georg, *The Young Hegel*, tr. R. Livingstone. London: Merlin, 1975.

Lukács Georg, *The Ontology of Social Being, Part 2: Marx's Basic Ontological Principles*, tr. D. Fernbach. London: Merlin, 1978.

Lukács, Georg, *The Ontology of Social Being, Part 3: Labour*, tr. D. Fernbach. London: Merlin, 1979.

Luxemburg, Rosa, 'Mass Strike, the Political Party and the Trade Unions' (1906), in Mary-Alice Waters (ed.), *Rosa Luxemburg Speaks*. New York: Pathfinder Press, 1970, pp. 153–218.

McCarthy, John D. and Zald, Mayer N., 'Resource Mobilization and Social Movements: A Partial Theory', *American Journal of Sociology*, 82 (1977), pp. 1212–41.

McCarthy, Thomas, 'Complexity and Democracy: or the Seducements of Systems Theory', in Axel Honneth and Hans Joas (eds), *Communicative Action*, tr. J. Gaines and D. Jones. Cambridge: Polity Press, 1991, pp. 119–39.

Maffesoli, Michel, *L'ombre de Dionysos – Contribution à une sociologie de l'orgie*. Paris: Méridiens/Anthropos, 1982.

Mahler, Margaret S., *The Birth of the Human Infant*. London: Hutchinson, 1975.

Maines, David, 'Social Organization and Social Structure in Symbolic Interactionist Thought', *Annual Review of Sociology*, 3 (1977), pp. 235–59.

Mann, Michael, *The Sources of Social Power*, 2 vols. Cambridge: Cambridge University Press, 1986 and 1993.

Márkus, György, 'Die Welt menschlicher Objekte. Zum Problem der Konstitution im Marxismus', in Axel Honneth and Urs Jaeggi (eds), *Arbeit, Handlung, Normativität*. Frankfurt/Main: Suhrkamp, 1980, pp. 12–136.

Marquard, Odo, 'Über einige Beziehungen zwischen Ästhetik und Therapeutik in der Philosophie des neunzehnten Jahrhunderts', in Marquard, *Schwierigkeiten mit der Geschichtsphilosophie*. Frankfurt/Main: Suhrkamp, 1973, pp. 85–106, 185–208.

Marquard, Odo, 'Geist', in Joachim Ritter (ed.), *Historisches Wörterbuch der Philosophie*, vol. 3. Basel and Stuttgart: Schwabe, 1974, columns 154–204.

Marx, Gary T. and Wood, James L., 'Strands of Theory and Research in Collective Behavior', *Annual Review of Sociology*, 1 (1975), pp. 363–428.

Marx, Karl, 'Vorwort' (1869), in Karl Marx and Friedrich Engels, *Werke*. Berlin: Dietz Verlag, 1968, pp. 559–60.

Marx, Karl, 'The Eighteenth Brumaire of Louis Bonaparte', in Marx, *Survey from Exile*, tr. B. Fowkes. Harmondsworth: Penguin, 1973, pp. 143–249.

Marx, Karl and Engels, Friedrich, 'The German Ideology', in *Marx–Engels Collected Works*, vol. 5, tr. W. Lough. London and New York: Lawrence & Wishart, 1976.

Marx, Karl, 'Economic and Philosophical Manuscripts', in Marx, *Early Writings*. Harmondsworth: Penguin, 1977, pp. 279–400.

Marx, Karl, 'Excerpts from James Mill's *Elements of Political Economy*', in Marx, *Early Writings*. Harmondsworth: Penguin, 1977, pp. 259–78.

Maslow, Abraham, *Toward a Psychology of Being*. Princeton, NJ: D. Van Nostrand Co. Inc., 1962.

Mason, John Hope, 'The Character of Creativity: Two Traditions', *History of European Ideas*, 9 (1988), pp. 697–715.

Mason, John Hope, 'Thinking about Genius in the Eighteenth Century' (unpublished manuscript, London, 1990).

Mead, George Herbert, untitled manuscript, beginning with 'The human individual has as part of his self the physical organism', University of Chicago, *Mead-Papers*, box 1, folder 4.

Mead, George Herbert, 'The Definition of the Psychical', in *Decennial Publications of the University of Chicago*, First Series, vol. 3. Chicago, 1903, pp. 77–112.

Mead, George Herbert, review of B.M. Anderson Jr., *Social Value. A Study in Economic Theory*, *Psychological Bulletin*, 8 (1911), pp. 432–6.

Mead, George Herbert, *Philosophy of the Present*. La Salle, Ill.: Open Court, 1932.

Mead, George Herbert, *Mind, Self and Society*. Chicago: University of Chicago Press, 1934.

Mead, George Herbert, *Philosophy of the Act*. Chicago: University of Chicago Press, 1938.

Mead, George Herbert, *Selected Writings*, Andrew Reck (ed.). Indianapolis: Bobbs-Merrill, 1964.

Menke, Christoph, 'Das Leben als Kunstwerk gestalten? Zur Dialektik der postmodernen Ästhetisierung', *Initial*, 4 (1991), pp. 383–95.

Merleau-Ponty, Maurice, 'Les relations avec autrui chez l'enfant', *Bulletin de psychologie*, 18 (1964), pp. 295–336.

Merleau-Ponty, Maurice, *Adventures of the Dialectic*, tr. J. Bien. Evanston, Ill.: Northwestern University Press, 1973.

Merleau-Ponty, Maurice, *Phenomenology of Perception*, tr. C. Smith. London: Routledge, 1982.

Mertens, Wolfgang, 'Psychoanalytische Theorien und Forschungsbefunde', in Klaus Hurrelmann and Dieter Ulich (eds), *Neues Handbuch der Sozialisationsforschung*. Weinheim: Beltz, 1991, pp. 77–98.

Merton, Robert, 'The Unanticipated Consequences of Purposive Social Action', *American Sociological Review*, 1 (1936), pp. 894–904.

Merton, Robert, *Social Theory and Social Structure*. Glencoe, Ill.: Free Press, 1957.

Mestrovic, Stjepan G., 'Durkheim, Schopenhauer and the Relationship between Goals and Means: Reversing the Assumptions in the Parsonian Theory of Rational Action', *Sociological Inquiry*, 58 (1988), pp. 163–81.

Mestrovic, Stjepan G., *Émile Durkheim and the Reformation of Sociology*. Totowa, NJ: Rownam & Littlefield, 1988.

Meyer-Drawe, Käte, *Leiblichkeit und Sozialität, Phänomenologische Beiträge zu einer pädagogischen Theorie der Inter-Subjektivität*. Munich: Fink, 1984.

Mills, C. Wright, 'Situated Action and Vocabularies of Motive' (1940), in Mills, *Power, Politics and People. Collected Essays*, I.L. Horowitz (ed.) London: Oxford University Press, 1967, pp. 439–52.

Mitzman, Arthur, *The Iron Cage. An Historical Reinterpretation of Max Weber*. New York: Knopf, 1969.

Mommsen, Wolfgang, 'A Notion of Universal History and Political Thought', *International Social Science Journal*, 17 (1965), pp. 27–45.

Müller, Hans-Peter, 'Durkheim's Political Sociology', in Stephen Turner (ed.), *Émile Durkheim. Sociologist and Moralist*. London: Routledge, 1993, pp. 95–110.

Müller, Klaus, 'Modernizing Eastern Europe: Theoretical Problems and Political Dilemmas', *European Journal of Sociology*, 33 (1992), pp. 109–50.

Münch, Richard, 'Teleonomie und voluntaristische Handlungstheorie. Replik auf Helmut Fehr', *Soziale Welt*, 31 (1980), pp. 499–511.

Münch, Richard, *Theory of Action*. London: Routledge & Kegan Paul, 1987.

Münch, Richard, *Understanding Modernity*. London: Routledge & Kegan Paul 1988.

Münch, Richard, *Dialektik der Kommunikationsgesellschaft*. Frankfurt/Main: Suhrkamp, 1991.

Neckel, Sighard and Wolf, Jürgen, 'The Fascination of Amorality: Luhmann's Systems Theory and Its Resonances among West German Intellectuals', *Theory, Culture & Society*, 11 (1994), pp. 69–99.

Nietzsche, Friedrich, *The Birth of Tragedy*, tr. R. Hollingdale. New York: Anchor Press, 1988.

Nietzsche, Friedrich, 'Schopenhauer als Erzieher', in Nietzsche, *Werke* I. Munich: Hanser, 1969, pp. 287–366.

Nisbet, Robert, *The Sociology of Émile Durkheim*. Englewood Cliffs, NJ: Prentice Hall, 1965.

Nolte, Paul, 'Optimist der liberalen Gesellschaft: Talcott Parsons', *Merkur*, 41 (1987), pp. 579–89.

Offe, Claus and Wiesenthal, Helmut, 'Two Logics of Collective Action: Theoretical Notes on Social Class and Organizational Form', *Political Power and Social Theory*, 1 (1980), pp. 67–115.

Offe, Claus, 'The Utopia of the Zero-option: Modernity and Modernization as Normative Political Criteria', *Praxis International*, 7 (1987), pp. 1–24.

Olson, Mancur, *The Logic of Collective Action*. Cambridge, Mass.: Harvard University Press, 1965.

Pareto, Vilfredo, *Compendium of General Sociology*. Minneapolis: University of Minnesota Press, 1980.

Paris, Rainer, *Klassenbewußtsein und Intersubjektivität. Zur handlungstheoretischen Reformulierung des Klassenbewußtseinskonzepts*. Frankfurt/Main: Campus, 1984.

Park, Robert, *The Crowd and the Public*, tr. C. Elsner. Chicago: University of Chicago Press, 1972.

Park, Robert and Burgess, Ernest, *Introduction to the Science of Sociology*. Chicago: University of Chicago Press, 1921.

Parsons, Talcott, '"Capitalism" in Recent German Literature: Sombart and Weber', *Journal of Political Economy*, 36 (1928), pp. 641–61 and 37 (1929), pp. 31–51.

Parsons, Talcott, 'The Place of Ultimate Values in Sociological Theory', *International Journal of Ethics*, 45 (1935), pp. 282–316.

Parsons, Talcott, *The Structure of Social Action*. New York: McGraw Hill, 1937.

Parsons, Talcott, *The Social System*. Glencoe, Ill.: Free Press, 1951.

Parsons, Talcott, 'Cooley and the Problem of Internalization', in Albert Reiss (ed.), *Cooley and Sociological Analysis*. Ann Arbor: University of Michigan Press, 1968, pp. 48–67.

Parsons, Talcott, *Social Structure and Personality*. London: Collier-Macmillan, 1970.

Parsons, Talcott, 'Review of Bershady', *Sociological Inquiry*, 44 (1974), pp. 215–21.

Parsons, Talcott, *The Early Essays*. Chicago: University of Chicago Press, 1991.

Parsons, Talcott and Schütz, Alfred, *The Theory of Social Action: The Correspondence of Talcott Parsons and Alfred Schütz*, R.Grathoff (ed.). Bloomington: University of Indiana Press, 1978.

Paulus, Peter, *Zur Erfahrung des eigenen Körpers*. Weinheim: Beltz, 1982.

Peirce, Charles S., *Collected Papers*, 8 vols, C. Hartshorne and P. Weiss (eds). Cambridge, Mass.: Harvard University Press, 1932–58.

Piaget, Jean, *Psychology of Intelligence*, tr. M. Piercy and D.E. Barlyne. London: Routledge & Kegan Paul, 1950.

Piaget, Jean, *Biology and Knowledge*, tr. B. Walsh. Edinburgh: Edinburgh University Press, 1971.

Piaget, Jean, *The Moral Judgement of the Child*, tr. M. Gabain. Harmondsworth: Penguin, 1977.

Plessner, Helmuth, 'Lachen und Weinen' (1941), in Plessner, *Philosophische Anthropologie*. Frankfurt/Main: Suhrkamp, 1970, pp. 11–171.

Pocock, J. G. A., *The Machiavellian Moment. Florentine Political Thought and the Atlantic Republican Tradition*. Princeton: Princeton University Press, 1975.

Pope, Whitney, 'Classic on Classic: Parsons' Interpretation of Durkheim', *American Sociological Review*, 38 (1973), pp. 399–415.

Popper, Karl, *Poverty of Historicism*, 2nd edn. London: Routledge & Kegan Paul, 1960.

Prendergast, Christopher, 'Alfred Schütz and the Austrian School of Economics', *American Journal of Sociology*, 92 (1986), pp. 1–26.

Proudhon, Pierre-Joseph, *La révolution sociale démontrée par le coup d'état du 2 décembre*. Paris: Garnier frères, 1852.

Rabehl, Bernd, *Marx und Lenin. Widersprüche einer ideologischen Konstruktion des 'Marxismus-Leninismus'*. Berlin: Verlag für das Studium der Arbeiterbewegung, 1973.

Raschke, Joachim, *Soziale Bewegungen. Ein historisch-systematischer Grundriß*. Frankfurt/Main: Campus 1985.

Reynolds, Vernon, *The Biology of Human Action*, 2nd edn. San Francisco: W. H. Freeman, 1980.

Riquelme, John Paul, 'The Eighteenth Brumaire of Karl Marx as Symbolic Action', *History and Theory*, 19 (1980), pp. 58–72.

Rochberg-Halton, Eugene, 'On the Life-Concept in Social Theory', *Comparative Social Research*, 11 (1989), pp. 319–43.

Rödel, Ulrich, Frankenberg, Günter and Dubiel, Helmut, *Die demokratische Frage*. Frankfurt/Main: Suhrkamp, 1989.

Röder, Petra, 'Von der Frühromantik zum jungen Marx. Rückwärtsgekehrte Prophetie eines qualitativen Naturbegriffs', in Gisela Dischner and Richard Faber (eds), *Romantische Utopie – Utopische Romantik*. Hildesheim: Gerstenberg, 1979, pp. 149–73.

Rorty, Richard, *Contingency, Irony, Solidarity*. Cambridge: Cambrige University Press, 1989.

Rothacker, Erich, 'Das Wesen des Schöpferischen', *Blätter für deutsche Philosophie*, 10 (1937), pp. 407–29.

Rothacker, Erich, 'Vom Geist des Erfindens', *Stahl und Eisen. Zeitschrift für das deutsche Eisenhüttenwesen*, 57 (1937), pp. 1–5.

Rucht, Dieter, 'Sociological Theory as a Theory of Social Movements? A Critique of Alain Touraine', in Rucht (ed.), *Research on Social Movements. The State of the Art in Western Europe and the USA*. Frankfurt/Main: Campus, 1991, pp. 355–84.

Rüfner, Vinzenz, 'Homo secundus Deus. Eine geistesgeschichtliche Studie zum menschlichen Schöpfertum', *Philosophisches Jahrbuch der Görres-Gesellschaft*, 63 (1955), pp. 248–91.

Rule, James B., *Theories of Civil Violence*. Berkeley: University of California Press, 1988.

Rundell, John F., *Origins of Modernity. The Origins of Modern Social Theory from Kant to Hegel to Marx*. Cambridge: Polity Press, 1987.

Rüschemeyer, Dietrich, 'Partial Modernization', in Jan J. Loubser, Rainer C. Baum, Andrew Effrat and Victor Meyer Lidz (eds), *Explorations in General Theory in the Social Sciences: Essays in Honor of Talcott Parsons*. New York: Free Press, 1976, pp. 756–72.

Saretzki, Thomas, 'Collective Action versus Functionalism? Some Remarks Concerning Hans Joas's Critique', *Praxis International*, 8 (1988), pp. 52–72.

Scharpf, Fritz, 'Politische Steuerung und politische Institutionen', *Politische Vierteljahresschrift*, 30 (1989), no. 1, pp. 10–21.

Scheler, Max, 'Versuche einer Philosophie des Lebens, Nitzsche–Dilthey–Bergson', in Scheler, *Gesammelte Werke*, vol. 3. Berne: Franke, 1955, pp. 311–39.

Scheler, Max, *The Notion of Sympathy*, tr. P. Heath. London: Routledge, 1979.

Schelsky, Helmut, *Thomas Hobbes. Eine politische Lehre* (1941). Berlin: Duncker und Humblot, 1981.

Scherr, Albert, 'Postmoderne Soziologie – Soziologie der Postmoderne? Überlegungen zu notwendigen Differenzierungen der sozialwissenschaftlichen Diskussion', *Zeitschrift für Soziologie*, 19 (1990), pp. 3–12.

Schilder, Paul, *Das Körperschema. Ein Beitrag zur Lehre vom Bewußtsein des eigenen Körpers*. Berlin: Julius Springer, 1923.

Schilder, Paul, *The Image and Appearance of the Human Body. Studies in the Constructive Energies of the Psyche*. New York: Kegan Paul & Co., 1935.

Schimank, Uwe, 'Der mangelnde Akteurbezug systemtheoretischer Erklärungen gesellschaftlicher Differenzierung', *Zeitschrift für Soziologie*, 14 (1985), pp. 421–34.

Schimank, Uwe, 'Gesellschaftliche Teilsysteme als Akteurfiktionen', *Kölner Zeitschrift für Soziologie und Sozialpsychologie*, 40 (1988), pp. 619–39.

Schluchter, Wolfgang, *Die Entwicklung des okzidentalen Rationalismus*. Tübingen: Mohr-Siebeck, 1979.

Schmid, Michael, 'Arbeitsteilung und Solidarität. Eine Untersuchung zu Émile Durkheims Theorie der sozialen Arbeitsteilung', *Kölner Zeitschrift für Soziologie und Sozialpsychologie*, 41 (1989), pp. 619–43.

Schmidt, Jochen, *Die Geschichte des Genie-Gedankens in der deutschen Literatur, Philosophie und Politik 1750–1945*, 2 vols. Darmstadt: Wissenschaftliche Buchgesellschaft, 1985.

Schnädelbach, Herbert, *Philosophy in Germany 1831–1933*, tr. E. Matthews. Cambridge: Cambridge University Press, 1984.

Schopenhauer, Arthur, *The World as Will and Representation*, tr. E. F. J. Payne. Colorado: Falcon's Wing, 1958.

Schulz, Walter, *Philosophie in der veränderten Welt*. Pfullingen: Neske, 1984.

Schütz, Alfred, *The Phenomenology of the Social World*, tr. G. Walsh and F. Lehnert. Evanston, Ill.: Northwestern University Press, 1967.

Schütz, Alfred, *Collected Papers*, 3 vols. The Hague: Nijhoff, 1971/2.

Searle, John, *Intentionality. Essays in the Philosophy of Mind*. Cambridge: Cambridge University Press, 1983.

Seel, Martin, *Die Kunst der Entzweiung. Zum Begriff der ästhetischen Rationalität*. Frankfurt/Main: Suhrkamp, 1985.

Shils, Edward, 'Charisma, Order, and Status', *American Sociological Review*, 30 (1965), pp. 199–213.

Shusterman, Richard, 'Postmodernist Aestheticism: A New Moral Philosophy?' *Theory, Culture & Society*, 5 (1988), pp. 337–56.

Sica, Alan, *Weber, Irrationality and Social Order*. Berkeley: University of California Press, 1988.

Siep, Ludwig, *Anerkennung als Prinzip der praktischen Philosophie. Untersuchungen zu Hegels Jenaer Philosophie des Geistes*. Freiburg: Alber, 1979.

Simmel, Georg, *Über soziale Differenzierung. Soziologische und psychologische Untersuchungen*. Leipzig: Duncker und Humblot, 1890.

Simmel, Georg, 'Bergson und der deutsche "Zynismus"', *Internationale Monatsschrift für Kritik, Wissenschaft und Technik*, 9 (1914), pp. 197–200.

Simmel, Georg, *Lebensanschauung. Vier metaphysische Kapitel*. Munich and Leipzig: Duncker und Humblot, 1918.

Simmel, Georg, 'The Conflict in Modern Culture' (1918), in *Georg Simmel on Individuality and Social Forms*, tr. D. Levine. Chicago: University of Chicago Press, 1971, pp. 375–93.

Simmel, Georg, *The Philosophy of Money*, tr. T. Bottomore and D. Frisby, 2nd enlarged edn. London: Routledge & Kegan Paul, 1978.

Simmel, Georg, *Schopenhauer and Nietzsche*, tr. H. Loiskandl, D. and M. Weinstein. Amherst, Mass.: University of Massachusetts Press, 1986.

Sloterdijk, Peter, *Eurotaoismus. Zur Kritik der politischen Kinetik*. Frankfurt/Main: Suhrkamp, 1989.

Smelser, Neil, *Theory of Collective Behavior*. London: Routledge & Kegan Paul, 1962.

Smith, Adam, *Theory of Moral Sentiments*. Oxford: Clarendon Press, 1976.

Smith, Anthony D., *The Concept of Social Change. A Critique of the Functionalist Theory of Social Change*. London: Routledge, 1973.

Smith, Dorothy, 'A Sociology for Women', in J. A. Sherman and E. T. Beck (eds), *The Prism of Sex. Essays in the Sociology of Knowledge*. Madison: University of Wisconsin Press, 1979, pp. 135–87.

Sorel, Georges, *Reflections on Violence*, tr. T. E. Hulme. London: Allen & Unwin, 1916.

Srubar, Ilja, *Kosmion. Die Genese der pragmatischen Lebenswelttheorie von Alfred Schütz und ihr anthropologischer Hintergrund*. Frankfurt/Main: Suhrkamp, 1988.

Stauth, Georg and Turner, Bryan, 'Nietzsche in Weber oder die Geburt des modernen Genius im professionellen Menschen', *Zeitschrift für Soziologie*, 15 (1986), pp. 81–94.

Stone, Gregory and Farberman, Harvey, 'On the Edge of Rapprochement: Was Durkheim Moving Towards the Perspective of Symbolic Interaction?', *Sociological Quarterly*, 8 (1967), pp. 149–64.

Straub, Jürgen, 'Identitätstheorie im Übergang?', *Sozialwissenschaftliche Literaturrundschau*, 23 (1991), pp. 49–71.

Suchman, Lucy, 'Representing Practice in Cognitive Science', *Human Studies*, 11 (1988), pp. 305–25.

Sztompka, Piotr, 'Social Movements: Structures in Statu Nascendi', *Revue internationale de sociologie*, 2 (1989), pp. 124–55.

Taylor, Charles, *Hegel*. Cambridge: Cambridge University Press, 1975.

Taylor, Charles, 'Action as Expression', in Cora Diamond and Jenny Teichman (eds), *Intention and Intentionality. Essays in Honour of Gertrude E. M. Anscombe*. Brighton: Harvester, 1979, pp. 73–89.

Taylor, Charles, *Philosophical Papers*, 2 vols. Cambridge: Cambridge University Press, 1985.

Taylor, Charles, *Sources of the Self. The Making of the Modern Identity*. Cambridge: Cambridge University Press, 1989.

Taylor, Charles, 'Embodied Agency', in Henry Pietersma (ed.), *Merleau-Ponty. Critical Essays*. Washington, DC: University Press of America, 1990, pp. 1–21.

Taylor, Charles, 'The Importance of Herder', in Edna and Avishai Margalit (eds), *Isaiah Berlin. A Celebration*. Chicago: University of Chicago Press, 1991, pp. 40–63.

Therborn, Göran, *Science, Class and Society. On the Formation of Sociology and Historical Materialism*. London: New Left Books, 1976.

Thomas, William I. and Znaniecki, Florian, *The Polish Peasant in Europe and America*, 2 vols. New York: Knopf, 1926.

Thome, Helmut, *Wertewandel in der Politik? Eine Auseinandersetzung mit Ingleharts Thesen zum Postmaterialismus*. Berlin: Wissenschaftlicher Autoren-Verlag, 1985.

Tiemersma, Douwe, '"Body-Image" and "Body-Schema" in the Existential Phenomenology of Merleau-Ponty', *Journal of the British Society for Phenomenology*, 13 (1982), pp. 246–55.

Tiles, J. E., *Dewey*. London: Routledge, 1988.

Tilly, Charles, Tilly, Louise and Tilly, Richard, *The Rebellious Century*. Cambridge, Mass.: Harvard University Press, 1975.

Tönnies, Ferdinand, *Der Nietzsche-Kultus. Eine Kritik*. Leipzig: Reisland, 1897.

Tönnies, Ferdinand, 'Autobiographie', in Raymund Schmidt (ed.), *Philosophie der Gegenwart in Selbstdarstellungen*, vol. 3. Leipzig, 1922, pp. 199–234.

Tönnies, Ferdinand, 'Zweck und Mittel im sozialen Leben', *Hauptprobleme der Soziologie. Erinnerungsgabe für Max Weber*, vol. 1. Munich and Leipzig: Duncker und Humblot, 1923, pp. 235–70.

Tönnies, Ferdinand, *Community and Society* (1887), tr. C. P. Loomis. New York: Harper & Row, 1957.

Touraine, Alain, *Sociologie de l'action*. Paris: Seuil, 1965.

Touraine, Alain, *The Postindustrial Society*, tr. L. Mayhew. London: Wildwood House, 1975.

Touraine, Alain, *The Voice and the Eye*, tr. A. Duff. Cambridge: Cambridge University Press, 1981.

Touraine, Alain, *Le retour de l'acteur*. Paris: Fayard, 1984.

Touraine, Alain, 'An Introduction to the Study of Social Movements', *Social Research*, 52 (1985), pp. 749–87.

Touraine, Alain, 'Krise und Wandel des sozialen Denkens', in Johannes Berger (ed.), *Die Moderne–Kontinuitäten und Zäsuren*. Special issue of *Soziale Welt* (1986), pp. 15–39.

Touraine, Alain, 'Commentary on Dieter Rucht's Critique', in Dieter Rucht (ed.), *Research on Social Movements*. Frankfurt/Main: Campus Verlag, 1991, pp. 385–91.

Trapp, Manfred, 'Utilitaristische Konzepte in der Soziologie. Eine soziologische Kritik von Homans bis zur Neuen Politischen Ökonomie', *Zeitschrift für Soziologie*, 15 (1986), pp. 324–40.

Trotsky, Leon, *The Permanent Revolution*. London: New Park, 1962.

Trotsky, Leon, *History of the Russian Revolution*, tr. M. Eastman. London: Victor Gollancz, 1934.

Tucker, Robert C., 'The Theory of Charismatic Leadership', *Daedalus*, 97 (1968), pp. 731–56.

Tugendhat, Ernst, 'Habermas on Communicative Action', in Gottfried Seebass and Raimo Tuomela (eds), *Social Action*. Dordrecht: Reidel, 1985, pp. 179–86.

Turner, Bryan, *The Body and Society. Explorations in Social Theory*. Oxford: Blackwell, 1984.

Turner, Ralph and Killian, Lewis, *Collective Behavior*. Englewood Cliffs, NJ: Prentice Hall, 1972.

Turner, Ralph H., 'The Use and Misuse of Rational Models in Collective Behavior and Social Psychology', *Archives européennes de sociologie*, 32 (1991), pp. 84–108.

Turner, Victor, *The Ritual Process*. Ithaca, NY: Cornell University Press, 1969.

Turner, Victor, *From Ritual to Theater*. New York: PAJ Publications, 1982.

Unger, Roberto Mangabeira, *Politics*, 3 vols. Cambridge: Cambridge University Press, 1987.

van de Voort, Werner, 'Die Bedeutung von Vorformen des kommunikativen Handelns für die Entwicklung der vorsprachlichen Intelligenz beim Kinde', in Anton Leist (ed.), *Ansätze zur materialistischen Sprachtheorie*. Kronberg: Scriptor, 1975, pp. 206–33.

Visalberghi, Aldo, 'Remarks on Dewey's Conception of Ends and Means', *Journal of Philosophy*, 50 (1953), pp. 737–53.

Wagner, Peter, *Sozialwissenschaften und Staat*. Frankfurt/Main: Campus, 1990.

Waldenfels, Bernhard, 'Mens sive cerebrum. Intentionalität in mentalistischer Sicht', *Philosophische Rundschau*, 31 (1984), pp. 22–52.

Waldenfels, Bernhard, *Ordnung im Zwielicht*. Frankfurt/Main: Suhrkamp, 1987.

Wallwork, Ernest, *Durkheim, Morality and Milieu*. Cambridge, Mass.: Harvard University Press, 1972.

Wallwork, Ernest, 'Durkheim's Early Sociology of Religion', *Sociological Analysis*, 46 (1985), pp. 201–18.

Walzer, Michael, *Spheres of Justice. A Defense of Pluralism and Equality*. Oxford: Robertson, 1983.

Walzer, Michael, 'Liberalism and the Art of Separation', *Political Theory*, 12 (1984), pp. 315–30.

Warner, Stephen, 'Toward a Redefinition of Action Theory: Paying the Cognitive Element Its Due', *American Journal of Sociology*, 83 (1978), pp. 1317–49.

Washida, Kiyokazu, 'Handlung, Leib und Institution – Perspektiven einer phänomenologischen Handlungstheorie', in Yoshihiro Nitta (ed.), *Japanische Beiträge zur Phänomenologie*. Freiburg: Alber, 1984, pp. 319–49.

Weber, Max, 'Basic Sociological Categories', in Weber, *Economy and Society*, tr. Günter Roth and Claus Wittich. New York: Bedminster Press, 1968.

Weber, Max, 'Die "Objektivität" sozialwissenschaftlicher und sozialpolitischer Erkenntnis', in Weber, *Gesammelte Aufsätze zur Wissenschaftslehre*. Tübingen: Mohr, 1973, pp. 146–214.

Weber, Max, 'Roscher und Knies und die logischen Probleme der National-ökonomie', in Weber, *Gesammelte Aufsätze zur Wissenschaftslehre*. Tübingen: Mohr, 1973, pp. 1–145.

Wehler, Hans-Ulrich, *Modernisierungstheorie und Geschichte*. Göttingen: Vandenhoeck & Ruprecht, 1975.

Wenzel, Harald, *Die Ordnung des Handelns. Talcott Parsons' Theorie des allgemeinen Handlungssystems*. Frankfurt/Main: Suhrkamp, 1991.

Westbrook, Robert B., *John Dewey and American Democracy*. Ithaca, NY: Cornell University Press, 1991.

Whyte, William H. Jr., *The Organization Man*. Harmondsworth: Penguin, 1963.

Wiesenthal, Helmut, 'Rational Choice. Ein Überblick über Grundlinien, Themenfelder und neuere Themenakquisition eines sozialwissenschaftlichen Paradigmas', *Zeitschrift für Soziologie*, 16 (1987), pp. 434–49.

Williams, Raymond, *The Long Revolution*. London: Chatto & Windus, 1961.

Willke, Helmut, *Entzauberung des Staates. Überlegungen zu einer sozietalen Steuerungstheorie*. Königstein: Athenäum, 1983.

Wilson, R. Jackson, *In Quest of Community. Social Philosophy in the United States 1860–1920*. New York: Wiley, 1968.

Winnicott, Donald W., *Playing and Reality*. Harmondsworth: Penguin, 1974.

Winnicott, Donald W., *The Maturational Processes and the Facilitating Environment*. London: Karnac, 1990.

Wirth, Louis, 'Review of Parsons' "The Structure of Social Action"', *American Sociological Review*, 4 (1939), pp. 399–404.

Wolf, Herman, 'Die Genielehre des jungen Herder', *Deutsche Vierteljahresschrift für Literaturwissenschaft und Geistesgeschichte*, 3 (1925), pp. 401–30.

Zander, Jürgen, 'Ferdinand Tönnies und Friedrich Nietzsche', in Lars Clausen and Franz Urban Pappi (eds), *Ankunft bei Tönnies*. Kiel: Mühlau, 1981, pp. 185–227.

Zilsel, Edgar, *Die Geniereligion. Ein kritischer Versuch über das moderne Persönlichkeitsideal mit einer historischen Begründung*. Vienna and Leipzig: Braumüller, 1918 (reprinted Frankfurt/Main: Suhrkamp, 1990).

Zilsel, Edgar, *Die Entstehung des Geniebegriffs*. Tübingen: Mohr, 1926.

Zurcher, Louis and Snow, David, 'Collective Behavior: Social Movements', in Morris Rosenberg and Ralph Turner (eds), *Social Psychology*. New York: Basic Books, 1981, pp. 447–82.

Index of Names

Adorno, Theodor W., 102, 252
Alberoni, Francesco, 286n
Alexander, Jeffrey, 13, 21, 25–6,
    44, 50, 87–8, 210, 220–2,
    229–30, 262–3n, 289n, 290n,
    291n
Alexander, Thomas, M. 276n
Alwast, Jendris, 265n
Anderson, Douglas, R. 275n
Anscombe, Gertrude, E. M.
    266n
Apel, Karl-Otto, 134, 277n
Arendt, Hannah, 114–16, 140,
    269n
Aristotle, 81, 152
Arnason, Jóhann Páll, 47, 101,
    102, 262n, 270n, 291n
Augustine, Saint, 117

Balandier, Georges, 284n
Barber, Benjamin, 291n
Bataille, Georges, 284n
Baudrillard, Jean, 245
Bauman, Zygmunt, 292n
Baumeister, Thomas, 276n
Baumgarten, Eduard, 275n,
    279n

Beck, Ulrich, 239, 241–3, 292n,
    294n
Bell, Daniel, 294n
Bellah, Robert, 63, 229, 281n,
    289n, 294n
Bendix, Reinhard, 260n, 289n
Berger, Johannes, 292n
Bergson, Henri, 51, 68, 117, 125,
    248, 274n
Berki, R. N., 269n
Berlin, Isaiah, 73, 266n, 273n
Bernard, Michel, 281n, 283n
Bernstein, Richard, 3, 288n
Bershady, Harold, 13, 31, 259n
Beyme, Klaus von, 292n
Bickel, Cornelius, 265n
Billington, James H., 273n
Bloom, Allan, 72, 266n
Blumer, Herbert, 208, 286–7n
Böhler, Dietrich, 160–1, 277n,
    284n
Bollnow, Otto Friedrich, 273n
Bonald, Louis de, 19
Bonnier, Jules, 176
Bourdieu, Pierre, 233, 290n
Bowles, Samuel, 291n
Brand, Karl-Werner, 292n

Index of Subjects

abduction, 127, 134–5
accommodation, 142
action: consequences of *see*
   consequences of action;
   quasi-dialogical nature of,
   160–1; typologies of, 39,
   145–6; *see also* collective
   action; communicative action;
   economic action; expressive
   action; goal-oriented action;
   instrumental action;
   normatively oriented action;
   production model of action;
   purposive-rational action;
   rational action; social action;
   teleological action
action theory: debates on, 3–4;
   emergence of, 7–69; Parsons',
   7–18; and systems theory,
   217–19; voluntaristic, 8,
   18–19, 66
adaptation, 138, 142
adjustment, 142
aesthetics, 73, 82, 84, 120, 139,
   258
Agil scheme, 221

alienation, 90–1, 92–5, 96–7,
   101; method of, 213–16
altruism, 22, 24, 62, 91, 203
analytical philosophy, 3, 4,
   31–2, 86, 102
anarchism, 246
animals, 77, 79, 174–5
anomie, 51, 53, 61, 241, 254
anthropological philosophy,
   90–1
anthropology, 28, 39, 46, 76,
   78–9, 86, 171–2; Gehlen's,
   172–5; *see also* expressive
   anthropology; philosophical
   anthropology
appetence behaviour, 174
art, 33, 130, 134, 141, 190–1;
   Dewey's theory of, 132,
   138–44, 153–5; Herder's
   theory of, 80
associations, 201
assumptions, tacit, 5, 41–2,
   147–8, 156–7, 163, 167, 184,
   196, 250–1
authenticity, 252
autonomy, 5, 147, 188–90, 194,
   242, 251, 254, 255

production, 71, 72–3, 85–105;
craft, 93, 103; relations of, 97
production model of action, 71,
89–102, 106, 113
progress, 48, 218; belief in, 28,
246–50, 255; economic, 51
proletariat, 94, 110, 112–13, 114
Protestantism, 19, 48
psycho-social analysis, 252,
255–8
psychoanalysis, 17, 120, 176–8,
184–5; Freudian, 171, 188–9
psychology, 2, 39, 123; of
creativity, 252; empirical, 73;
functionalist, 136; hedonistic,
15, 41; humanist, 254–5; *see
also* developmental
psychology; folk psychology;
mass psychology; social
psychology
psychosomatic medicine, 171–2
public sphere, 113
purpose, 40, 152–3, 156, 158
purposive-rational action, 16,
40, 80–1, 101, 147, 149–50

rational action, model of, 1, 2, 4,
5, 12–15, 18, 23–4, 27–30,
34–5, 43, 75, 87, 196–8;
rejection of, 146–95
rationality, 246, concept of,
146–7; and creativity, 73;
crisis of, 51–2; modernity and,
42–3; and praxis, 102–3; role
in action, 196; Weber's scale
of, 39–40
rationalization, 38, 47, 68, 102;
processes, 43, 120, 198; of the
subsystems, 243; use of term,
236
realism, analytical, 8, 13–14,
23–31, 30–1

reality, constitution of, 163–7
reality principle, 164
reason: and imagination, 85;
language and, 76–9
reconstruction, 6, 41–2, 101–2,
116, 126–44, 147, 163
reflection, 9, 15, 58, 60, 79; *see
also* self-reflection regulation
of action, 159–67
reification, 219
religion, 90, 135–7; Dewey's
theory of, 142–3, 153–6;
Durkheim's theory of, 16, 41,
49, 53, 61–4; Weber's
sociology of, 21, 45, 46, 48
religious experience, 136–7,
142–3, 191–4
Renaissance, 73, 74, 121
reproduction, symbolic and
material, 218–19
republicanism, 74
resistance, 141–2, 198, 228
resource mobilization, 203–4
responsibility, 249–50
revolution, 37, 71, 72–3, 94–5,
105–16, 114–16, 224–5, 243;
concept of, 109, 114–15;
institutionalized, 49; theory of
permanent, 108
right, Hegel's philosophy of, 89
risk society, 241–3
ritual, 16, 33, 42, 62, 64–5, 186,
192–4
role-taking, 182–3, 187–8
Romanticism, 76, 84, 91, 190,
246, 258
routine, 5, 128–9, 133, 197
rules: of action, 58, 59;
normative, 16, 104

sacred, the, 16, 44, 64–5, 192–4
sanctions, 16